The
Monfils
Conspiracy

Other Books by Denis Gullickson

Before They Were the Packers: Green Bay's Town Team Days

Vagabond Halfback: The Life and Times of Johnny Blood McNally

The
Monfils
Conspiracy

The Conviction of Six Innocent Men

DENIS GULLICKSON

JOHN GAIE

Forewords by Cal Monfils
and Mike Piaskowski

iUniverse, Inc.
New York   Bloomington

The Monfils Conspiracy
The Conviction of Six Innocent Men

iUniverse books may be ordered through booksellers or by contacting:

iUniverse
1663 Liberty Drive
Bloomington, IN 47403
www.iuniverse.com
1-800-Authors (1-800-288-4677)

Because of the dynamic nature of the Internet, any Web addresses or links contained in this book may have changed since publication and may no longer be valid. The views expressed in this work are solely those of the author and do not necessarily reflect the views of the publisher, and the publisher hereby disclaims any responsibility for them.

ISBN: 978-0-595-48473-7 (pbk)
ISBN: 978-0-595-49096-7 (dj)
ISBN: 978-0-595-60565-1 (ebk)

Library of Congress Control Number: 2009928885

Printed in the United States of America

iUniverse rev. date: 8/31/2009

Dedication

Our goal in writing this book—more than seven years in the making—has always been to expose the truth and inform the public. Our efforts have taken much time and due diligence.

With that, we dedicate these efforts to all the fine people who have worked at, and those who continue to work at, the former James River paper mill in Green Bay, Wisconsin, and to all the truly innocent individuals incarcerated in the prisons of this nation.

Under a government which imprisons any unjustly, the true place for a just man is also a prison.

—Henry David Thoreau

Contents

Foreword

My brother Tom Monfils was an ideal big brother. He may have been ten years older, but he was never too old to spend time with me. Growing up, he would take me everywhere with him and involve me in all his projects. And he always had projects, whether they were for him or someone else. He really liked to help people if he could. My brother was the type of person who liked and valued quality people, young or old. It's why he got along so well with some of the older workers at the mill.

The greatest memories my brother left me involve music. He would always let me listen to his albums and even buy some for me. Many times, I can listen to music and it reminds me of a time with Tom. I miss him very much.

To me, Tom's death is still a mystery. We all know the terrible ending, but what really happened just before that? I do not speak for the rest of my family but only me when I say, "What a terrible investigation process." And much of that was "tailor-made."

As I sat and heard the final verdicts, I still felt empty. I felt bad for Tom's wife and children and also all the families of the defendants, some of whom I knew before the trial. I am not saying that all six of these men are innocent. But I am not convinced that they are guilty of murder. As forgiving as that may sound, I also wish the worst to whoever killed him. That person should realize that jail is only temporary, but death is forever. The real killer will always be on the winning end.

I feel that the six men should get a chance to at least be heard by a new panel and, if they had no direct involvement in the murder, at least be cleared of that charge.

At the time of writing this, I have not yet read the manuscript for this book. I have had a few meetings with Denis, John, and Mike and feel they are very sincere people trying to help others, with no benefit to them but the satisfaction of seeking the truth. I think they may have performed the most detailed research on this case to date. All the items in this book reflect their investigative work and opinions.

With the amount of questionable investigating, I would not object to a review of this case on both sides of justice. Again, these are only my views and do not reflect those of my family or Tom's.

—Cal Monfils

Foreword

Dear Readers,

This is a book about the investigation and prosecution surrounding the death of one of my coworkers, Thomas J. Monfils. Written by Denis Gullickson and John Gaie, it is a true story about how a simple search for the truth by the police became a misguided agenda that destroyed the lives of six innocent men and countless families. It is about how this case became the largest miscarriage of justice in the history of the state of Wisconsin, an injustice that continues to this day. It is a case that gives great reason to be thankful Wisconsin does not employ the death penalty.

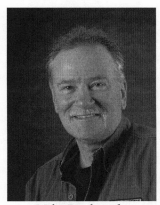

Mike Piaskowski
Dan Gair, Blind Dog Photo©

My name is Mike Piaskowski. On October 28, 1995, five coworkers and I were convicted of first-degree intentional homicide and sentenced to life in prison for Tom's death. After I was incarcerated for five and a half years, Senior Federal District Judge Myron Gordon of the Eastern District of Wisconsin overturned my conviction for lack of evidence. In his ruling Judge Gordon wrote, "[A guilty verdict] required the jury to pile speculation on top of inferences that were drawn from other inferences ... such a verdict is not rational." In February of that year, Eastern District Judge Lynn Adelman affirmed Judge Gordon's decision; and later that summer Justices Evans, Easterbrook, and Manion, from the United States Court of Appeals for the Seventh Circuit, granted my permanent unencumbered freedom. I was released from incarceration on April 3, 2001. As of this writing all five of the other defendants, convicted at the same trial under the same circumstances over twelve years ago, remain in prison for a crime that I firmly believe they did not commit, for a crime that may not have even happened.

In his ruling Judge Gordon also wrote, "The issuance of a writ of habeas corpus is a 'grave remedy' reserved for 'grave occasions' … this is such an occasion.… Because the evidence was not sufficient to support his conviction, the double jeopardy clause of the Fifth Amendment bars a retrial."

This means I cannot be reprosecuted for this crime. There is nothing preventing me from coming forward with information, good or bad. The fact of the matter is that I have done nothing but tell the truth, the whole truth, and nothing but the truth, *so help me God*, since day one. The problem was not with what I had to say. The problem was with what the investigators wanted to hear. They were the ones who refused to accept my testimony. They were the ones who refused to recognize any evidence contrary to their theory. As a result, they are the ones that just plain got it all wrong.

In today's world, with all of the advancements in forensics, crime scene investigation, and criminal profiling, I can only imagine how crazy it must sound for me to suggest that the Monfils investigation was so far off track that it convicted six innocent men. Hard to believe I'm sure—*but it is true*. If I hadn't been a part of this nightmare myself, I would not believe it either. After all, the authorities could not be *that* wrong … could they?

I do not claim to know what happened to Tom, but I positively do know and emphatically state the following: I had absolutely nothing to do with Tom's death. *I have no knowledge about Tom's death.* I never witnessed anything concerning Tom's death. And nobody has ever provided me with information about Tom's death.

I also know that the police theory of what happened that day is dead wrong. The very scenario that led to my conviction never took place at all—with me or without me. Whatever happened to Tom had to have happened to him someplace else in some other way.

I have always considered myself a pretty good citizen, willing to do my share, help the less fortunate, go the extra mile, and then some. The fact is that if I had seen anything happening to Tom I would have been one of the first to step in to break it up. If I had even heard anything I would have been the first to speak up.

In the beginning, as my world was being turned upside down, just the thought of being wrongly accused of such a heinous crime was pretty devastating. Unfortunately I was soon to learn that being wrongly convicted would be a lot worse—as it nearly became my end. Lady Justice failed me when I needed her the most. The very society that I loved and defended with honor in Vietnam had cast me aside. Never had I felt as lost and hopeless as when being led out of the courtroom in chains—a disjointed feeling of lifelessness and mental anguish that haunts me to this day. For all practical purposes, my life's journey was over. Intensified by the uncertainty of its end, I secretly wished it were. I now understand and appreciate the reason for the suicide surveillance during those first few weeks of captivity.

I learned that one of the best ways to deal with the sadness and depression of life in prison was to try to remain positive. Even in the midst of so much evil I would force myself to look for the good in people and try to remember that things could always be worse. In a strange way I was truly fortunate. Every day people fall victim to situations beyond their control—accidents, birth defects, death, disease, mental illness. By comparison, wrongful incarceration seemed minor. I had a wonderful family, supportive friends, and good health. But the thing that sustained me most in prison was the certainty that the truth was on my side. I had hope. I had a light at the end of the tunnel. Unfortunately, that alone couldn't sooth all the pain. I was on a horrible emotional roller coaster. The days were long, the nights longer. Small amounts of time, like the hours between mail call and the days between visits, seemed endless. Yet larger units of time, like a month and then a year, seemed to go by so quickly that I felt my life was evaporating away without meaning.

My release from prison seemed miraculous. It's almost unheard of to have a higher court overrule a lower court, especially without DNA evidence. I would like to take this opportunity to again say thank-you to Judge Myron Gordon; to my attorney, T. Christopher Kelly; to my family; to my friends; and to all those who believed in me. I cannot imagine where I might be today without their wisdom, courage, and faith to guide me. I have been heartened by and appreciative of all the wonderful support throughout this entire ordeal. My sincere and genuine thanks go out to all who continue to believe in the truth and in me. The flaws of the system tried to destroy my credibility and to tarnish the Piaskowski name—without success. I am happy to let the world know who I am and what I stand for. My father and my family and my friends and my supporters can all be proud!

My contributions to this book have been made with the hope that it will have a positive influence on the lives of the other innocent men, and will expose this horrible injustice for what it was and what it continues to be—the largest miscarriage of justice in Wisconsin history.

There is no doubt that, other than the death penalty, the American justice system is one of the finest in the world. Unfortunately it remains painfully obvious that on occasion the system still fails terribly. It was a dangerous self-deception for me to think it incapable of error—especially right here in the small-town community of Green Bay, Wisconsin.

—Mike Piaskowski

Preface

I first met Mike Piaskowski on Sunday, October 21, 2001, at the Gingerbread House, my cottage and writing workplace near Lakewood, Wisconsin. Along with John Gaie, my dear friend and this book's coauthor, we talked, drank some beer, and watched the Packers lose to the Minnesota Vikings. That day set the stage for over seven years worth of work on this case and this book.

Even before that meeting, I had long considered writing a book on the "Monfils case." The story had consumed northeastern Wisconsin from the time of Tom Monfils's tragic death through the sensational trial that followed three years later. Despite the murder convictions and imprisonment of six men, there remained, I felt, a gaping hole in the community—a profound sense that the matter was never really settled. A gigantic question mark hung over the citizens of Green Bay.

Those feelings were intensified at a meeting at John's house in late April 2000. At that point, Mike had been incarcerated for four and a half years. The image of a guilty man might have slipped from the daily consciousness of his loved ones, but that was not the case at this meeting. Here I saw a gathering of individuals as fervently dedicated to their cause as any prayer group. They were Mike's friends, family members, and former coworkers—outraged by his imprisonment and passionate for his release. Francine Gaie, Mike's older sister and John's ex-wife, led the meeting with an absolute and unshakeable belief in her brother's innocence.

I quickly learned that this freedom train needed more than wishful thinking to keep it running. Mike's family had already pulled together $300,000 to post his bail following his 1995 arrest. At that point,

Mike's brother Casey had mortgaged his home, and many other family members, including Mike's Grandma Nonny, had contributed their life savings. Now this group gathered at John's house was struggling with how it would cobble together yet more money to keep the whole thing going. Everyone was digging deep to help, including former coworkers like Dick Ozarowicz, who was at this meeting and who was an outspoken advocate of Mike's innocence.

By the time Mike walked out of prison, the further outpouring of support would be staggering. An additional $300,000 was needed for bail following the federal court's ruling for his release. With Mike's immediate family nearly tapped out, even more of Mike's friends, family, and coworkers came forward to fill the void with substantial sums of money.

"No way," I thought. "Family and friends willing to risk their own financial security are rare enough, but guys giving hundreds and thousands of dollars each to help free a former coworker just do not exist." However, they did in this case.

Who was this "Mike Pie" and why was his innocence such a self-evident truth to these people that they were willing to take unheard of steps to gain his freedom? Perhaps it was like Mike's friend Clyde Verhaagh said, "If you'd know the guy, you'd know he wouldn't be guilty." Still, there had to be more to it.

Actually, I did have some background as to who Mike was prior to this meeting. I had worked with his father, Fran, at Sears during my college days. Fran was one of a handful of salesmen who worked in the store's appliance department. Based purely on my respect for Fran gathered over those years, I stated that "no son of Fran Piaskowski ever killed anyone." Of course, I did not know that son yet—just that father.

Like my own parents, Fran was a member of what Tom Brokaw called the "Greatest Generation." They had shaped this nation in the years after World War II with a healthy balance of fun and hard work, of tending to their families and to their community, of teaching their children the rules and then allowing them the freedom to become themselves.

Sadly, Fran died in late 2000, his last years spent anguished by the thought that his oldest son was locked up for a crime he did not commit and haunted by his own inability to free that son or to show the world his innocence. On his deathbed, Fran said he might finally be able to help "from the other side." Within a few months of Fran's passing, Mike left the Dodge Correctional Institution—one of Wisconsin's maximum-security prisons—a free man.

I finally met Fran's son in person on that October Sunday in 2001. In a way, we had come full circle. With the same certainty as the others, I will now tell you that Mike Pie is an innocent man. I have spent over seven years working on this project with him. He is a credit to his family, to the friends that supported him, and to his father.

I consider it an honor and a rare privilege to have worked with Mike and John on this book. This is our very best attempt to lay open for our readers those gaping and unresolved holes in this case and to bring about justice—in the form of new trials or complete pardons—for the rest of these wrongfully convicted men.

—Denis Gullickson

Introduction

This book is about a conspiracy but not the one you might think. Until now, people have been led to believe that Thomas J. Monfils was murdered at the James River paper mill in Green Bay, Wisconsin at the hands of a "union conspiracy" composed of at least six of his coworkers. In fact, the "authorities" say that the conspiracy went well beyond these six men, worming its way into the souls of many of the other people who worked at the mill.

The conspiracy exposed in this book is much more ubiquitous and frightening than some story of mob mentality manifesting itself in a workplace murder. This conspiracy poses a far greater threat to each of us. It is the all-too-real conspiracy of a justice system that fails between 5 and 10 percent of the time, holding at least 100,000 wrongfully convicted people in U.S. prisons as you read this. It is a tragic conspiracy that has executed innocent people. It is a conspiracy that to date has seen over 245 of its most serious convictions overturned by DNA evidence.

The conspiracy can sometimes be accidental. All too often it is not. It begins with police ineptitude or malfeasance, and it ends—tragically for the convicted—with an appeals system that nearly always rubber-stamps the paperwork of injustice. Along the way, overly zealous prosecutors, gullible jurors, and biased judges further the conspiracy.

But our version of this dangerous conspiracy is not a tale of long ago or far away. Nor is it a report of faceless statistics. It is an intensely personal story of right here, right now, in the tidy and conservative little community of Green Bay, Wisconsin. It goes like this.

On Saturday, October 28, 1995, in a Brown County courtroom,

an innocent man was convicted of first-degree intentional homicide in Tom Monfils's death. His name is Michael Lawrence Piaskowski. Mike "Pie" had been an exemplary employee of the James River paper mill. A hard-working father and husband, he was involved in numerous community charitable organizations. He was an avid outdoorsman and a conservationist, a certified judge for several international big-game hunting organizations. He had served his country in Vietnam.

Mike was framed by the Green Bay Police Department and the Brown County district attorney's office. His wrongful conviction was the result of a series of blunders and deceptions by a host of individuals. It resulted from an arrogant disregard of proper police procedures, a prosecution driven more by guilty verdicts than by justice, an apparently pro-prosecution judge, and a jury overwhelmed by extraneous detail and hoodwinked by the state's speculation.

The single-minded goal of the investigation was to pin Monfils's death on Keith Kutska, one of Piaskowski's coworkers. Kutska had exposed an inept, unorganized, and unprofessional local police department, which gave him an audiotape of a phone call that they were told to withhold. However, Piaskowski's clear recollections thwarted the effort to get Kutska. He was with Kutska around the time Monfils disappeared, and he refused to alter that fact in order to put Kutska on the hot seat. Rather than listen to this witness of unquestionable integrity, the police proclaimed him "a party to the crime" and changed his life forever.

Ultimately, the lead detective who tampered with police reports and intimidated witnesses was forced out of the police department with a damning twenty-six-page letter that offered him resignation or termination. The action of his immediate superior in releasing the audiotape was cited as the primary reason for awarding a $2.1 million civil-suit judgment to the family of Tom Monfils.

In an unjust joint trial, Piaskowski was convicted along with Kutska and four other men who were witnesses to one another's innocence. The authorities suggested that the motivation for trying the men together was one of economy—greater savings in time and resources. The real reason seemed clear from the onset: Create confusion and "throw everything at the wall and see what sticks." Tragically, it worked. One of the jurors recently came forth to say that for the first two weeks of the five-week trial they could not distinguish one man from another.

In a nearly unprecedented habeas corpus ruling, Piaskowski was exonerated and released from prison after serving nearly six years of his life sentence. U.S. District Court Judge Myron Gordon said, "No physical evidence tied Mr. Piaskowski to the crime, no testifying witness saw him participate in it, no one confessed, there was no testimony from the petitioner or any other witness establishing that he took part in the murder or intended to."

Tom Monfils's family watched Piaskowski's release from prison with a different set of eyes than most. Tom's brother Cal told a reporter he had "no opinion" on whether Mike was guilty or innocent. "That wasn't up to me and my family," he stated, "It was up to the court system." He also expressed frustration that his family had not received closure. "I guess I thought when the case was final years ago, that was kind of the end of it, and we wouldn't hear about it," he explained. "My feeling is if any one of them [the six convicted men] is innocent, they should be out. What bothers me is they [the police and district attorney] couldn't prove it the first time. It should be over. Nobody deserves to have it continue the way it is."

Nobody does. As hard as it is to believe, the members of the Monfils family are also victims of this conspiracy. They have received *an* answer but not *the* answer to their tragedy.

Piaskowski was not the only victim as this conspiracy worked its way toward getting Kutska at all costs, however. Dale Basten, Michael Hirn, Michael Johnson, and Reynold Moore were also with Kutska around the time Monfils disappeared. They, too, were swallowed up by this conspiracy. Each of them is innocent and yet remains in prison today. This is also their story.

The families of these six men have suffered needlessly and beyond repair. Only wars and natural disasters of the greatest magnitude have the kind of devastating impact witnessed in this story. The trauma these innocent individuals have suffered at the hands of this conspiracy has been mental, emotional, spiritual, physical, and profoundly devastating.

Then there is the collateral damage of this conspiracy: countless other victims—especially James River employees and their families—

who were often forced to watch without recourse as they were accused and threatened by the police and prosecutors. These people did not go to prison. They and their loved ones were left to pick up the pieces of their lives as best they could and go on.

The story told here is not pretty. It represents one of the greatest tragedies ever perpetrated by the authorities under the guise of justice in Wisconsin history. What exactly happened to Tom Monfils that fateful day may never be known. That secret has been lost with his last breath or hidden deep in the consciousness of the actual murderer. Worst of all, any chance of determining exactly what happened to Monfils may well have slipped through the fingers of a police force and a district attorney's office hell-bent on sending *these* six men to prison.

It would have been easier to write a book that simply restates the whole sordid affair as people know it—advancing the erroneous conspiracy still further. The book we have written, however, has been tougher to put together because it presents solid evidence demolishing the case paraded out by the real conspiracy. That is okay though, because this is the one that finally tells the truth.

We began our inquiry using the files that the Green Bay Police Department generated during their nearly three-year investigation in this case. This gave us the very same starting point as the investigators. Our rationale for this strategy was basic: Our meticulous use of the police discovery would lead us in the direction their investigation should have taken them and not toward the unsubstantiated theory they ended with. Through this process, every one of their departures from the path of their own facts became obvious to us. Those flaws in logic comprise much of this book.

Meticulously combing through every police detail sheet, we proceeded in chronological order from the day Tom Monfils disappeared through the days just before the trial. In the same way, we scrutinized other key case materials. On crucial points, this was done with the assistance of forensic scientists and private investigators.

One of our primary objectives was to establish an exact timeline of the comings and goings of all the people working in the immediate area of Monfils the morning of his disappearance and death. We knew that such a timeline was critical in establishing several important facts. A detailed explanation of the development of that timeline can be found in appendix I.

Unlike the police and prosecutor, we did not assume that paper-mill workers were thugs and liars. We assumed that they told the truth, especially when confronted with a matter as serious as a coworker's death and possible murder. We believed each person's account of his or her whereabouts and activities the morning of Monfils's disappearance—that is, *until* their account conflicted with the preponderance of other accounts and known facts established by records from paper machines, telephones, computers, and the like.

We proceeded to eliminate such inconsistencies through interviews and other means of fact-checking. If such a conflict could not be eliminated, it was labeled with a red flag. In the process of eliminating such inconsistencies, we conducted more than fifty interviews with dozens of mill employees, including, of course, the six men themselves. Such inconsistencies could be as minor as where a person set down a cup of coffee or as major as what workers were present at a particular place and time.

Our interviews with the authorities were vital. District Attorney John Zakowski literally opened his conference room to us, providing us with all the materials we requested. Our attempts to speak with the chief investigators at the Green Bay Police Department were far less successful. Early on, communications officer Bill Galvin let us know that none of the lead detectives wanted to be interviewed. Galvin did invite us to contact deposed detective Randy Winkler. We tried that several times, ultimately without fruition. Finally, now-retired Police Chief Craig VanSchyndle obliged us with an interview though there was little he could offer. Our exposé of the specious police investigation can be found in chapters six through eleven.

We were intrigued by what Zakowski called the "key" in his case—the infamous Fox Den role-playing incident. To investigate this incident, we interviewed Ron and Charlotte Salnik, owners of the Fox Den tavern. We also interviewed all the principals involved in this alleged incident as well as one of the confidential informants working for detective Winkler during that time. The Fox Den incident is thoroughly explored and debunked in chapter eight.

In order to examine the impact of a joint trial on the six men, we attempted to contact all of the jurors—with little success. We interviewed the men's defense attorneys as well. We also spoke with all key prosecution witnesses who would agree to speak. Our in-depth examination of the trial can be found in chapters twelve through sixteen.

In closing, we will pass along this thought, brought forth by one family member: These were hard-working family men. Not one of them had ever been a part of something as hideous as what the authorities accused them of. These men had no experience in handling the guilt or distress that would have been gnawing at them. Yet, through three years of intense scrutiny and all the years since their conviction in 1995, not one of them has ever broken down and confided in a loved one about his role in this crime.

How is that possible? The answer, of course, is painfully obvious: These men—one and all—are innocent of harming Tom Monfils. They told the authorities everything they knew. Meanwhile, the conspiracy that convicted six innocent men remains firmly in place.

1

Tears of Unbelievable Joy

Free at last! Free at last! Thank God almighty, I'm free at last!

—From the "old Negro spiritual" quoted by Dr. Martin Luther King, Jr.

Tuesday, January 9, 2001, was just an ordinary day in the life of Francine Gaie—or so it seemed. As controller for an international company, MEGTEC Systems, she was immersed in wrapping up the financial results for 2000. And she was emotionally drained. Her dad had passed away just six months before, and her brother Mike Piaskowski remained in prison—an innocent man behind bars since 1995 for a crime he did not commit. His appeals seemed to be going nowhere. Mike had lost every appeal at the state level and was on perhaps his last attempt—a writ of habeas corpus that had been filed in the spring of 2000 with Judge Myron Gordon of the United States District Court in Milwaukee. And it too seemed to be going nowhere. There was little hope of winning this one. Writs of habeas corpus are seldom granted.

Francine had last visited Mike in prison before Christmas and honestly did not know if she had the strength to visit him there again.

She had steadfastly stood by him throughout his nine-year ordeal and had made regular and frequent visits to him since his incarceration. Now she was losing hope. At times she had almost wished he was not innocent—it would have been much less painful to see him there.

On that afternoon in January, Mike's ordeal was not on her mind—only the business of closing the books. At 2:00 p.m. her office phone rang. "This is Joe from Channel 2 News." Had she heard the news? Mike had won his appeal and was to be released! Unbelievable! She screamed in surprise and disbelief. Everyone in the office came running to see what had happened. She rushed to place a call to T. Christopher Kelly, Mike's appellate attorney. He took the call immediately. As Chris explained, he had been trying to reach her since 11:30 a.m. but had called her at home, not the office. Chris confirmed, "We could not have gotten a better decision. Mike was not simply granted a new trial—he was granted an outright release!" They both cried. They both laughed.

Next on the agenda were numerous calls to the family to announce the incredible news. Then there came the calls from all the news media wanting interviews and family reactions. As one reporter later explained, Judge Gordon's ruling was faxed to the newsroom where it laid quietly in a pile of unread faxes for some time. When it was finally read, the reaction in the newsroom was electric. Mike Piaskowski was to be released!

Within a half hour, Francine did a number of television interviews on the front lawn of MEGTEC Systems. Then she and her sister Christine rushed to bring Mike the good news. The media followed them for the ninety-mile trip to the Dodge Correctional Institution in Waupun. By the time they reached the prison, Mike already knew. He had heard from fellow inmates. Of course, it was all over the news. With a huge smile on his face, Mike teased them with "Hello strangers. I haven't seen you in a while. Did it take all this to get you here?"

Judge Gordon's decision gave the Wisconsin attorney general twenty-eight days to appeal. But what everyone did not realize then was that the journey was to be much longer. It was to be one full of suspense, elation, disappointments, hard work, stress, obstacles, and finally success. Each obstacle was met with fierce determination. Mike was innocent. Judge Gordon agreed. Mike should be freed.

In February, U.S. District Judge Lynn Adelman ruled that Mike could be released pending the state's appeal of Judge Gordon's ruling and set the bond at $25,000. But the state turned the knife again. The authorities appealed Mike's release. A stay was issued. Finally, on Monday, March 26, 2001, the United States Court of Appeals for the Seventh Circuit ruled that Mike could be released pending the state's appeal—but increased the bond to $300,000. As Mitch Henck, spokesman for Attorney General Jim Doyle, said, "We never thought bond should be increased because we feared Mr. Piaskowski would flee. We did it because we thought the weight of the crime dictated a more appropriate bond."

Francine disagreed. She felt this was no way to treat an exonerated man. Plus, the family would have a hard time raising $300,000. It looked like Mike might have to wait out his appeals in prison after all. But the family was determined to get him released. They began calling everyone who could help. Not so surprisingly, they all stepped up to the plate—Mike's friends, family, extended family, coworkers, and a sympathetic soul who had once won some money in a lottery.

On Friday, March 30, Mike's daughter Jenny Hruska, Francine, and her ex-husband John Gaie (coauthor of this book) set out for Milwaukee with checkbook in hand. They planned to post bond in Milwaukee and then head for Waupun to pick up Mike from DCI. It was exhilarating. When they arrived at the courthouse in Milwaukee, the clerk of courts informed them that bail could only be paid with a cashier's check. They brought only a personal check. It was too late to travel back home, get a cashier's check, and return to Milwaukee.

After consulting with the powers-that-be, the clerk agreed to accept a personal check, but the family would have to wait until after the weekend, when it cleared the bank before an order for Mike's release could be issued. Frustration—one more obstacle! The family's journey to Waupun was considerably more subdued than the one to Milwaukee. Mike took the news well. By all calculations it now looked like Tuesday, April 3, would be Mike's release date.

Over the next three days Francine repeatedly called her bank's automated account information for her checking account balance. Again and again and again, the balance was in excess of $300,000. No, the check had not cleared. The wait seemed an eternity.

Early on Tuesday she awoke and reached for the phone before crawling out of bed. The automated teller announced, "Your account balance is $123.67." She screamed in elation. The check had cleared!

Francine called Christine and told her, "I'm going to Waupun to get Mike." Christine wanted reassurance that Mike would be released that day because she did not want to take another day off from work for nothing. Francine insisted she was going down there, and she was not leaving without him no matter how long it would take. The family had done everything that they were asked to do. They had posted the $300,000, and the check had cleared. The court had their money, now she wanted her brother. Francine recalls, "I expected them to live up to their part of the bargain. It was time to give us Mike!"

The whole family wanted to go along to pick him up: Mike's daughter Jenny, his sister Christine, his former in-laws, and, of course, Francine. Others would be there in spirit: his dad, mom, and grandmother Nonny, all of whom had passed away. It was a sunny but chilly April morning when the small entourage set out for Waupun. When they arrived the warden informed them that he needed a signed court order before Mike could be released—more red tape. Spirits remained high as they headed to a local restaurant for lunch. It was back to the prison after lunch—but no order yet. They were told they could not wait inside the prison waiting room. All had to wait outside—even the little children. The wind had picked up. To keep warm, everyone wrapped themselves in blankets.

News reporters and photographers from all the local TV stations and newspapers began to gather. They set up their cameras just outside the glass doors where Mike would emerge. The group was bantering among themselves. Everyone waited in anticipation.

On April 3, 2001, Mike Piaskowski walked out of prison and into the fresh air of freedom. Green Bay News-Chronicle front page.

Time dragged on, and still no word from the court. A number of calls were made to Judge Adelman's clerk in Milwaukee checking on the status of the court order. What was holding everything up? First Judge Adelman was in chambers and could not be disturbed. Then he was in court. Finally they were informed that he had signed the order. It would be mailed to the prison. Mailed? That would take days! Could they fax it? Yes, they would. But time was becoming critical. The staff at both the courthouse and at the prison usually quit at 4:00 p.m. If the paperwork was not completed by then, Mike would have to spend another night in prison. Because the prison and the court were not communicating with each other, it was up to the family, especially Francine, to facilitate the paperwork. The warden agreed to stay late but mentioned something about 4:30.

Francine made another call to the clerk and learned the fax had gone to the wrong prison—the Green Bay Correctional Institute instead of the Dodge Correctional Institute! Murphy's Law! Could they fax it to DCI? Yes, but what is the fax number? Call to the warden: What's your number? Call to the clerk with the number, who then faxed the order to DCI. Finally the warden received the fax. It was official! It was 5:15 p.m. But wait—there was one last hurdle. The routine prison headcount had to be taken—another forty-five-minute delay.

Mike was included in his last prison headcount and released at 6:06 p.m., Tuesday, April 3. He walked out of DCI a free man into the arms of his family and the watchful media. There was laughter and tears of joy. Their wildest dreams had been fulfilled. Michael Piaskowski was free. They would never have to go back to DCI again!

Mike's first words to the news media were directed to the Monfils family: "Our hearts always have gone out to the Monfils family." He denied involvement in Tom's death and knowledge of who may have killed Tom. "Tom was a workplace friend of mine," Mike said. He would have done anything to prevent harm from coming to Tom. "Had I known anything, I would have been the first to step up to help Tom."

For Mike, the ride home was like floating on a cloud. He rode in Francine's car with Jenny and Christine. He made numerous cell phone calls to the other vehicles and to friends at home. He was amazed to be using a cell phone and marveled at the beauty of the brown and barren late-winter landscape. The family's first destination was the cemetery to visit those who were only able to be present in spirit—Dad, Mom, and Nonny. It was dark when they arrived. It seems—somehow— more appropriate: But why, they all wondered, had he been put through all this in the first place.

2

Justice Denied

The fewer the facts, the stronger the opinion.

—Arnold H. Glasow

At approximately 7:45 a.m. on Saturday, November 21, 1992, Tom Monfils, an employee at the James River paper mill in Green Bay, Wisconsin, disappeared without a trace from his work area. An all-out effort to find him somewhere at the mill was conducted because every sign suggested that he had never left work. His car remained parked outside the mill, and his street clothes hung in his workplace locker. The following evening, his lifeless body was found at the bottom of a tissue chest with a rope and a weight tied to his neck. At a news conference eighteen days later, the Green Bay Police Department announced that Monfils had been murdered.

The event jarred the city of Green Bay like nothing before. Sure, Green Bay had witnessed its miscellaneous murders and other crimes over the years—but they were nothing like this. The community had always considered itself a safe, secure little corner of the world—big enough to dabble in some of the amenities of larger cities yet small enough to keep that hometown charm. The Green Bay yellow pages list over seven pages of churches—the vast majority Catholic and Lutheran. The Green Bay skyline is decorated with steeples pointing heavenward.

The city had carried on a love affair with its NFL Packers for more than seventy years—a fact that caught the quaint fancy of people throughout the nation. Green Bay football fans were known to wear wedges of yellow foam on their heads in the shape of cheese just to celebrate their small-town hurrah. Thanks to the Packers's success, the city has long referred to itself as "Titletown."

Green Bay is a city of just over 100,000. It is a conservative little port town located where the Fox River flows north into the Bay of Green Bay, a part of Lake Michigan. If Lake Michigan is an upside-down mitten, then Green Bay sits at the tip of its thumb. Established in 1634, it is the oldest settlement in the Midwest—older than Chicago. Thanks to its location, the area was teeming with Native American activity well before the white settlers moved in.

Some Green Bay Statistics
- Population (2000): 102,313
- Males: 50,433
- Females: 51,880
- Land area: 43.9 square miles
- Median resident age: 33.2 years
- Median household income (2000): $38,820
- Median house value (2000): $96,400
- Races in Green Bay: 83.2 percent white non-Hispanic; 7.1 percent Hispanic; 4.1 percent American Indian; 3.7 percent; 3.2 percent Asian; 2 percent mixed races; 1.4 percent African American
- Education for population over 25 years of age: 82.6 percent high school or higher; 19.3 percent bachelor's degree or higher; 5 percent graduate or professional degree
- 5 percent unemployed
- Mean travel time to work: 17 minutes
- Marital status: 49.3 percent married; 31.3 percent never married; 11.6 percent divorced; 6.3 percent widowed; 1.4 percent separated
- Nearest city with a population over 200,000: Milwaukee, 101 miles away, population 596,974

- Industries providing employment: 21.3 percent manufacturing; 16.4 percent education, health, and social services; 13.6 percent retail
- City-data.com crime index (2002): 257 (U.S. average: 330)

Green Bay is a major Great Lakes port, and its most important export is paper. Scattered among the steeples are a handful of smokestacks puffing profit and pollution into the air 24/7. At this very moment, at the base of each of these smokestacks, men and women work to produce napkins, paper toweling, and countless rolls of toilet paper.

In 1992 the James River Corporation was an international company headquartered in Richmond, Virginia. James River owned and operated major papermaking operations in the United States and, more recently, had expanded to Europe. Back then the Green Bay mill was more than ninety years old. Now known locally as "Northern," it is located near downtown Green Bay, at the junction of the Fox and East rivers. As one of James River's expansion acquisitions back in the early 1980s, it was grouped with several other papermaking facilities in their towel and tissue division. Because the corporation has changed ownership a few times since then, the Northern mill is now known as Georgia Pacific–East, a part of Koch Industries, a privately held company.

It was against this rather ordinary backdrop that Tom Monfils had allegedly been murdered while working at the James River mill. A twenty-nine-month investigation into the matter would end in a dramatic, yet shaky conclusion on April 12, 1995, when eight of his coworkers were arrested. Six of them would be charged with conspiring to murder Monfils and two others charged with various related misdemeanors. Another worker would be summarily fired for failing to back the police theory about the crime. Hundreds of others would have their normally quiet worlds torn asunder. Yet even after the arrests, the police would continue their investigation full-throttle, pleading with the community for help in coming up with solid evidence.

The bulk of speculation among Monfils's coworkers was that he had committed suicide. Over the years, they said, he had told them bizarre stories of his Coast Guard days when he helped retrieve bodies out of the water that were attached to car bumpers, flywheels, and heavy engine parts. The workers thought that Monfils—seriously stressed out from intense pressure put on him by coworkers that morning—might have simulated one of these scenes to affect his own death.

The police saw it quite differently. As their investigation unfolded and was shared with the public, it became rather apparent that this was no ordinary "whodunit" at all. The events leading up to Monfils's disappearance and death were filled with multiple twists and turns. Later on, a close look at these details exposed a rather shocking fact, one at the very starting point of the case: The Green Bay Police Department itself had dirt on its face in regard to the circumstances that led to Monfils's death.

There emerged a tangled story of a stolen piece of electrical wire and an anonymous cassette-tape recording of a phone call made by Monfils to the police. The word was that the stolen wire and the tape had set in motion the events leading up to his death. The facts around the stolen wire were still unknown, but the tape had been obtained by one of Monfils's coworkers and held a key role in his death. It had been played over and over at the James River mill the morning of Monfils's disappearance. And how had the tape made its way into the hands of his coworker in the first place? That's where the GBPD came in. It was the police themselves who had given the tape to Monfils's coworker.

How all of these pieces fit together and led to Monfils's death is a compelling story in its own right. Add to that the whispers of a union conspiracy and cover-up, rumors of drug smuggling and large-scale employee theft, brutal retaliation, and a mutilated corpse; and you have the makings of a real thriller.

If that is the story you are looking for, however, you will be disappointed. If you are one of those people who like to suggest that you "know how those unions operate," you will be disappointed. If you are someone who likes to think that it is the good guys in uniform protecting and serving the rest of us by rounding up the bad guys, you will also be disappointed. This is a book about how all of those sensationalistic details got whipped around, ground up with uncorroborated circumstantial evidence, and half-baked into the arrest and conviction of six of Monfils's coworkers—all of whom were and are innocent. This is a story about the investigation into a mill worker's death all right, but one that proves that the mystery surrounding that death remains completely unsolved.

On April 12, 1995, after an investigation that had seen 862

excruciating days tick by, eight of Monfils's coworkers were arrested by the Green Bay Police Department and charged with playing a part in his murder. Six of the men were charged with first-degree intentional homicide—party to a crime. The other two were charged with injury to business—restraint of will, a misdemeanor. In September, a joint felony trial was held for all six men facing murder charges. On October 28, a jury brought in from another Wisconsin county found all six of the men guilty as charged. They were sentenced to life in prison. It is there that five of them still sit today—innocent men with little recourse but to file appeals through this nation's court system and pile hope upon hope that someone somewhere will realize their innocence.

In January 2001, a federal judge, Myron Gordon, ruled for the release of one of the men, Mike Piaskowski, on a writ of habeas corpus. Gordon stated in his ruling that "no reasonable jury" could have convicted Piaskowski on the flimsy evidence presented by the prosecution. Sadly the other five men, convicted by that same unreasonable jury, remain in prison today, just as innocent as Piaskowski.

This is his story, and this is their story. It is the story of a police force whose investigation was tainted from the very first moments by a bias—what we will call "blinders." Contrary to what the Green Bay authorities will tell you, this was never a story of a "union conspiracy" or "a mob of union thugs" who set out to teach a coworker a lesson, got carried away while roughing him up, and had to murder him to save their high-paying jobs. The Brown County district attorney and his crew have beat that horse to death, repeating the scenario so often that it has become accepted as the truth, at least in some circles.

But not here. When examined without blinders, the evidence clears each and every one of these men of the murder of Tom Monfils. The GBPD used every trick in their "how-to guide" to catch these innocent citizens and paint a picture of their guilt: stakeouts, phone taps, handwriting exemplars, and lie-detector tests. The police spread rumors throughout the mill to see how they would come back to them. They rummaged through garbage cans at the men's homes. They shook down their family and friends in interviews that were far more like interrogations of war criminals. When the police had not uncovered even the smallest shred of evidence against the men, they did the next best thing—they bolstered a very weak hypothesis with hearsay.

The hope of these authors is that this book will help turn the tide of justice in the men's favor. Please remember them as you read this book. On the night Monfils's body was removed from a tissue chest at the James River paper mill, they were innocent men. Throughout the three-year investigation, they cooperated with the police as innocent men. On the day they were arrested, they were innocent men. On the day they were pronounced guilty in the eyes of the law, they remained innocent men.

They are still innocent men today. They were never "The Monfils Six," as portrayed in the local media. Each had his own family, personal background, individual work ethic, and a completely independent personality. They were never members of a "union conspiracy," as described by the police and district attorney.

Not one of them had any reason to harm Tom Monfils. Not one of them had anything against him except Keith Kutska, who had been the subject of Monfils's anonymous tape-recorded phone call. It was Kutska's drive for revenge that put Monfils under pressure the morning of his disappearance. As for the other men, their most basic instincts would have told them to leave Monfils alone instead of jeopardizing their freedom, families, and jobs in order to participate in a murder. As far as Kutska went, he was far more interested in having Monfils stick around so he could regularly berate him for making the call in the first place.

On the morning of Saturday, November 21, 1992, when Monfils was last seen alive, these six men represented about as disjointed a group as you could assemble—hardly the makings of a unified mob bent on violence over an anonymous phone call. They came from four different work sites in the mill and were members of two separate unions. They were 28, 41, 43, 45, 46, and 51 years of age. Four of the six had been born and raised in the Green Bay area, having their roots planted squarely in the community. The other two had lived in the area for about a decade. Their interests varied widely, and their contacts with each other were limited to a mill retirement party or similar social occasions. In fact, two of them, Rey Moore and Mike Hirn, had never even met one another.

They were your typical Green Bay guys. All of them had families. They were sons and fathers, husbands, brothers, and uncles. All were married except Mike Hirn, who was in a steady relationship and had a child. They were not very different from the people we all know from our own workplaces: normally hard-working, sometimes quirky, basic, decent men with good intentions and their priorities in life set pretty straight. Other than Rey Moore, their contacts with the law were completely ordinary. They were working stiffs without any fancy ideas or outlandish plans. They had hitched their personal wagons to the success of their employer. They worked their jobs and enjoyed their time off with their families and friends; and then, when the time finally came, they would retire and live out their lives like the rest of us. These guys had no intention or inclination to ruin their lives or the lives of others by participating in the murder of a coworker.

Their union involvement was nothing more than routine, ranging from "never give an inch to management" to "I make the meetings when I can." Kutska and Moore were the most consistent participants in union activities. Kutska, in local 327, often lamented the lack of involvement of other workers in the union, making it a point to attend nearly every union meeting he could. He often said he would see the rest of them at the monthly meetings, when it was time to discuss wages and benefits. It seemed that was when everyone became an active union member.

Moore was in the other union, local 213, where his involvement ranged from shop steward to union officer. He had a reputation as a union guy. As a striking worker at the Nicolet paper mill in nearby De Pere, Moore had once berated a replacement worker who had taken one of the mill jobs during a labor dispute. Moore also made it known on the James River mill floor when some of those same replacement workers went to work at the James River plant a few years later.

The rest of the guys went to some meetings, especially when a new contract had to be voted on, and skipped most others dealing with more mundane issues. That was it for their union involvement.

They worked different jobs during different shifts at four different locations in the mill. They were all considered competent to very competent at their jobs. Kutska had already been a regular machine tender, the person that actually controls the paper machine, for years. Piaskowski, a back tender, or second-in-command, was considered more than competent when doing his job and when filling the top spot. Dale Basten and Mike Johnson were roving troubleshooters in the instrumentation department. Part of their duties involved finding solutions to pneumatic problems and maintaining the computers that controlled the machines. Basten was a working foreman and, as such, made as much as $70,000 a year—a big reason for him not to have helped do away with anybody. Hirn and Moore worked in ancillary positions. Moore was in an area in the mill called "the penthouse," a part of the pulp mill where he helped prepare the wood pulp used in the papermaking process. Hirn worked in the shipping department where the finished paper products were sent out of the mill.

Their characters were as dissimilar as could be. Basten was considered a bit of an eccentric but mostly labeled as a workaholic who put in lots of hours in order to maintain a healthy income. Neighbors knew him as a quirky guy who liked to drive his motorcycle and play his guitar on his front porch. His two daughters adored him.

Mike Hirn was the young guy. He kept to himself but was popular with his immediate coworkers. He loved the outdoors and just about every activity that went with it—boating, skiing, snowmobiling, or, as he said, "just spending time with Mother Nature." He enjoyed his time off work so much that once he had earned enough seniority, he transferred from the paper machines to the shipping department— taking a pay cut in the process—so he could have his weekends off. People talked about Hirn having a temper and a role in some Green Bay barroom scuffles. But these same people recounted his overt fondness for his grandmother, who had helped raise him.

Mike Johnson was known as a quiet guy, kind of a loner, who eschewed stopping at the bar with other mill workers for a couple of beers after work. Johnson said his family came first, and he involved himself in the rearing of his children. He had married a widowed Korean native, "Kim"; he doted on her and his adopted children as much as he did his own. Johnson was also known by acquaintances to be devoutly religious, another reason for him not to have played a part in harming Monfils.

Keith Kutska was described in a variety of ways—from a bully to an intelligent guy—depending on who was doing the describing. Some people called him a blowhard. One worker told a story of Kutska pulling practical jokes on him until he stood up to Kutska and told him to knock it off. The worker said he had no more trouble with him after that. Kutska's defense attorney, Royce Finne, called him "soft-spoken and intelligent." Kutska was, and remains, well read and opinionated. His hobby was astronomy, but his interests were as diverse as ancient history and presidential politics. He was no shrinking violet for sure.

He distrusted the government and mill management and sometimes went over the top when demonstrating that distrust. Still, no one could question his ability to do his job.

Rey Moore was the only one of the men with a significant police record, something he deeply regretted. He had done some time in prison as a young man for robbery. But his friends suggested that he was the proverbial shirt-off-his-back kind of guy. Former paper mill supervisor Gregg Stephens identified Moore as the guy you would go talk to if you needed a work situation straightened out to everyone's satisfaction. Moore knew, said Stephens, "how to communicate and negotiate." Moore was well known throughout the mill as one of the workers who volunteered to tap the rest of work force for contributions to the annual United Way campaign.

Most of the six men were outdoor enthusiasts, though no one as much as Mike Piaskowski. He was an avid hunter and a respected measurer and scorer for five national organizations that tracked and recorded record-setting big-game animals. Mike "Pie" was popular with other workers as well as with mill management. He brought the same competence to the job that he exhibited when recording the vital statistics of the rack on a white-tailed deer. Whether it was forming a group to study mill safety or a fishing excursion, he was seen as an organizer and a motivator. His handshake was ever ready, sincere, and good as gold when it came to delivering on a promise. Countless people have stated emphatically that had "Pie" seen something happening to Tom Monfils, he would have stepped in and stopped it immediately.

When all is said and done, these six men had only one thing in common: They freely admitted that they were in the area of the number 9 paper machine at some point on the morning of November 21, 1992, and that they listened to the tape recording of Monfils's anonymous call to police—as had twenty or thirty of their coworkers. They were not and are not killers. They did not band together as a mob of union thugs and confront Monfils. They did not work themselves into a frenzy that went too far. They did not get rid of his body "in order to save their high-paying jobs"—an expedient cliché paraded out by the district attorney.

When Brown County District Attorney John Zakowski was presented with the idea that these guys were not the kinds of characters who would commit murder, he told these authors, "It doesn't matter who you are. It's what did you did on November 21, 1992." Mark those words. It does not matter who you have struggled to be all your life. It does not matter what values you have cultivated and cherished or what good you have tried to do. And you can toss out the lessons you have learned and then taught your children. If the police think you are guilty, and a prosecutor says you are guilty, well then, by God, you must be capable of jettisoning every bit of your character in order to commit that crime—and you must be "guilty!"

Here are the other five men who were wrongfully arrested, convicted, sentenced, and incarcerated for killing Tom Monfils.

Dale Basten

Born May 11, 1941, in Green Bay

Dale is the son of Harold and Ethel Basten. He has one brother, Lee, and lived in Green Bay all his life. At the time of his arrest, he had been married to Cheryl Ann Mann for seven years. They had two daughters, Amber and Emily. Dale was married once before, in 1962. That marriage ended in divorce and produced no children. Dale's neighbors describe him as "different," though one of his former high school classmates was cautious about describing Basten as different, suggesting that one could "misinterpret that." The classmate said that Dale was "a happy-go-lucky guy." Another former high school classmate said, "He always had a good job. You could tell that by the vehicles he was driving. He was pretty much of a loner. He had a real good head on his shoulders. He caught onto things real fast." One of his neighbors said that Dale "had a temper." Another said, "He's never done anything [bad] in the neighborhood. If you needed a favor, he would be willing to help."

Dale attended Green Bay's parochial schools and went to Premontre High School for part of his junior year, when he dropped out. He started at the Northern paper mill on October 9, 1961, where he worked for thirty-five years, including the period when it transitioned into the James River mill. Dale worked in three departments: converting, 1961–1971, where his top job was as a winder man; construction pool, 1971–1975; and instrumentation, 1975–1995, where he eventually became the working foreman.

His interests included motorcycles, boating, and snowmobiling. He fished but did not hunt. Dale and his first wife won the WNFL Snowmobiling husband and wife relay. He was known in his neighborhood for playing the guitar. "I wouldn't say he was a good guitar player," said one neighbor. "He just plucked a little."

He was one of two men whose families were able to post the $300,000 bond after being arrested. He owned his home as well as a cottage. Cheryl told a reporter that Dale was a devoted husband and father who often took the family to their cottage on Edgewater Beach Road.

Dale Basten at Christmas time at the Green Bay Correctional Institution

- Defense attorneys: Avram Berk and Nila Robinson
- Parole eligibility date: October 1, 2012
- Age at that time: 71
- Dale says he had no part in the murder of Tom Monfils and will never admit to a crime he did not commit.

Michael Hirn

Born May 6, 1964, in Green Bay

Mike's parents, Garth Hirn and Trudy Marie Geurts, divorced when Mike was ten years old. Both remarried. One brother, Jeff, is deceased. He also has a half-brother on his father's side. Through his parent's divorce, he grew very close to his grandmother. Though he was never married, he does have a son.

Mike attended Dickinson Elementary School in De Pere and graduated from De Pere High School in 1982. His high school physical education teacher, Ed Stenger, still says, "Mike Hirn is a good kid."

Mike describes himself as an avid outdoorsman, even today, despite his incarceration. "I love to fish and hunt, but there are many activities I enjoy. In summer I love to be up north on the water in my boat. I love to water-ski and barefoot ski. I like to teach others how to ski. I like to swim and fish when I'm not skiing. In the fall, bow hunting is my sport of choice. The peace and tranquility of the woods is awesome. In the winter, I take my snowmobile to wherever I have to go for snow. Also, in the summer, I play league softball a couple of nights a week. I also enjoy golfing when I can find someone to go with. I was taught at an early age to respect the woods and the water."

Mike worked at part-time jobs from age fourteen on. He took care of lawns, worked in the meat department at a grocery store, and pumped gas. After high school, he was employed at his grandfather's gas station and in security. He worked from 1984 to 1987 at Broadway Chevrolet-Olds.

On August 10, 1987, he was hired at James River. Mike worked the seven-day swing shift on paper machines until he asked to be transferred to the shipping department "because you only worked a five-day swing shift, which gave me my weekends off." He worked in that department until his arrest on April 12, 1995. He was working the day he was arrested.

Mike bought a home in 1991 where he lived with his girlfriend and their son.

"I know Mike's not guilty," his grandmother, Lorraine Geurts, told a reporter. She said there was no way the family could raise Mike's [$300,000] bail. "We're just going to wait … and see what happens."

**Mike Hirn in a much happier moment,
snowmobiling along Wisconsin's Oconto River**

- Defense attorney: Gerald Boyle
- Parole eligibility date: April 1, 2010
- Age at that time: 45
- Mike says he had no part in the murder of Tom Monfils and will never admit to a crime he did not commit.

Michael Johnson

Born August 15, 1947, in South Dakota

Mike is the son of Oliver L. Johnson and Nanette J. Daily. On June 13, 1984, he married Yun Cha "Kim" Wisniewski, who was born in Korea, in a civil service at the Brown County courthouse. Mike has three daughters, a son, and nine grandchildren.

People who know Mike described him as "a deep thinker" and "very religious." Some said he was a "genuine believer in the Lord."

Neighbors described Mike and Kim as quiet people who thoroughly enjoyed the home they owned on the eastern shore of Green Bay. According to one daughter, Mike prided himself on his role as "head of the household," and he took well to the father role.

Mike Johnson and his wife, Kim, at church on Christmas

- Defense attorneys: Eric Stearn and Vance Waggoner
- Parole eligibility date: April 1, 2011
- Age at that time: 64
- Mike insists he had no part in the murder of Tom Monfils and will never admit to a crime he did not commit.

Keith Kutska

Born March 9, 1951, in Green Bay

Keith is the second oldest of four brothers and one sister. He was educated at St. Jude's Grade School in Green Bay and graduated from Green Bay East High School. Kutska's father, Norman, was an airport custodian and then a Green Bay Correctional Institution guard. His mother was Nathalie Mae Judkins. Their marriage broke up in 1967, and they split their children between their two households.

Keith married Ardis "Ardie" Balwierczak on July 31, 1971. "He was just nice," Ardie told a reporter. "He wasn't afraid to show that he liked me, and he wasn't afraid to tell me that he liked me." Their son, Clayton, was born on October 3, 1972. In 1973 they bought a house in the town of Suamico. Twelve years later, they bought a house on Wilson Road in Abrams, where they lived on the day Keith was arrested.

Keith worked on the loading dock for a produce wholesaler after graduating from high school in 1969. He began his paper mill career at the American Can Company, which later became James River. He started as a helper in the converting department and moved to the paper machines department about a year later. His first job there was as a spare hand, eventually working his way up to one of the top jobs as a machine tender on machine 6 eighteen years later. For a while he was moved back to the back tender position when that paper machine was permanently shut down. He was one move away from permanently returning to the machine tender position when he was arrested.

Keith's hobbies were eclectic, ranging from trout fishing to French cooking. He started camping with Ardie early in their marriage and began to explore astronomy. Later, Keith said, "Ardie got a horse and I got a nice telescope. As Suamico began to expand, we moved to Abrams where Ardie could keep her horse and the skies were darker for astrophotography."

Keith is a bit of an enigma. As the central figure in the Monfils case, his propensity to speak his mind on topics from politics to labor-management issues to his disdain for being reported for employee theft by a coworker was a key piece in the prosecution's case. He is well read on topics from Roman and Russian history to law.

Keith Kutska with one of his grandchildren

He is especially critical of the recent Bush administration as well as people who he believes follow rules and norms blindly. Once, when told that "thumbing his nose at everything and everybody" was his problem, he said, "That's why I'm here in prison, not because I murdered anyone."

- Defense attorney: Royce Finne
- Parole eligibility date: April 1, 2015
- Age at that time: 64
- Keith says he had no part in the murder of Tom Monfils and will never admit to a crime he did not commit.

Reynold Moore

Born December 9, 1946, in Tupelo, Mississippi

Rey is the son of a sharecropper, the fifth of eight children. He had three years of college and was a journeyman cement mason. He lived in Tupelo from 1946 to 1957. After his father's death in 1957, Rey, his mother, two brothers, and a sister moved to Milwaukee, where he lived until 1965. He then moved to De Pere, where he lived until the time of his arrest.

He was married to his wife of twenty-four years, Debra, at the time of his arrest. They have four children: Malcolm, Ivy, Kayce, and Reynold III.

Rey's hobbies included fishing, camping, and gardening. He kept bees at one point.

He received numerous awards for community service from 1963 to 1989. He was involved in politics and labor unions at an early age. At sixteen, he was the chairman of the Wisconsin Youth National Association for the Advancement of Colored People. At eighteen, he was direct action chairman for Milwaukee's senior NCAAP. In 1988, he was a delegate to the Democratic National Convention in Atlanta. In 1993, he served on the search committee to find a new director for United Way of Brown County.

Rey worked in a number of jobs in high school—at grocery stores, in a foundry, and as an apprentice cement mason. He worked at Nicolet Paper in De Pere until a strike in 1987 led to the break-up of his union. He then worked as an auto mechanic until 1989, when he started at the James River mill.

Rey has a police record that includes a 1966 felony robbery in Milwaukee, issuing worthless checks in Brown County in 1972, and selling two packets of marijuana in Brown County in 1973. He was fired from James River in March 1993 after the investigation uncovered that he had not disclosed the felony conviction on his original job application. Rey worked in the pulp mill department.

Neighbors describe him as "quiet" and "friendly." One said, "He would do anything if you ask."

Rey Moore at Dodge Correctional Institution

- Defense attorney: Robert Parent
- Parole eligibility date: April 1, 2010
- Age at that time: 64
- Rey says he had no part in the murder of Tom Monfils and will never admit to a crime he did not commit.

3

Death at the Mill

I do not fear death, for in death we seek life eternal.

—Apparent suicide note found at the James River mill

On Sunday night, November 22, 1992, Green Bay received the shock of its life. It was a whisper past ten o'clock, and the small city had just pulled down its shades for the night. Its citizens were about to doze off—bracing for another workweek—when the late-night news cut to a breaking story at one of the paper mills just a few blocks from downtown.

The reporter stood on the sidewalk along Day Street, outside the James River mill. In the background, lights from the mill guardhouse and entrance cut through the cold, dark Wisconsin night. It was a surreal scene. Details were sketchy, said the reporter. A body had been found in a pulp chest at the mill, a discovery that had come on the heels of a missing-person report filed the day before on one of the mill's workers. The worker's name was not being released, pending an autopsy and notification of the family.

Connecting the dots was a bit easier for anyone who had paid attention to the odd events unfolding over that entire weekend: The body was very likely that of Thomas J. Monfils, 35, a mill employee who had disappeared at work the previous morning. The mill had conducted an intensive search for Monfils following his disappearance but had found nothing. Equipment had been shut down, and workers had been pulled off their jobs in order to take part in the search.

Police were investigating the incident, the reporter said.

A Different World

The mill in which the body had been found was a noisy and dirty place, hellish and raw. It was a world of its own, with steel and wires and pipes located in caves and tunnels that seemed to stretch far below the earth. Its workers quickly learned to tune out the constant noise. They were required to wear hearing protection—some even wore earmuffs on top of earplugs. Although that helped a little, the chronic whir and whine of the paper machines still eroded their eardrums and their ability to concentrate. The concrete mill floor throbbed constantly. Workers felt an incessant, pounding charge that shot up through the soles of their feet and out their nerve endings.

To outsiders, the jobs at the mill were considered an easy way to the good life. But the people who punched into this world knew that it consisted of stretches of punishing boredom punctuated by stints of frustrating work in demanding conditions. The mill turned out paper twenty-four hours a day, seven days a week, every day of the year. In order to maximize the work force during a twenty-four-hour period, the mill had its employees working on rotating shifts. As a result, the same worker was coming and going at all hours. Noise, heat, hard work, monotony, constantly changing hours, fatigue—it was quite a recipe. If seven little men were cheerily singing "Hi-ho, hi-ho, it's off to work we go," no one in the plant would hear it.

This sort of pandemonium prevailed over the mill on a normal day, but *this* Sunday night was anything but normal.

In the depths of the mill, away from any news cameras, a small group of people was watching a sloppy mess of paper pulp pour from the bottom of a round, two-story pulp chest and onto the mill floor. The "tissue chest"—one of several large pulp storage tanks used in the papermaking process—looked like a barn silo with its top removed. From the chest, the slop continued to run into sewer grates and then out of the mill into a lagoon north of the mill grounds. Normally the pulp, which looked like thin oatmeal or watery cottage cheese, was fed from the chest into the various machines in the mill, where it was diluted, sprayed into a thin sheet, dried, and turned into paper. This night, the chest was being drained at the request of mill authorities as a part of the search for Tom Monfils.

Monfils had been missing since the previous day, and it seemed almost certain that he had not left the mill. Mill workers had been conducting the all-out search since the previous morning. A similar chest, immediately next to this one, had already been drained, and a third was also being emptied. These chests were being drained as a last-ditch effort—every other nook and cranny of the mill had already been searched.

When about three-fourths of its contents had been emptied, some of the workers in the search gazed over the chest's four-foot ceramic-tiled wall. What they saw was nightmarish: a body floating face down in the pulp. They notified mill security, and mill security notified the police. In turn, the police contacted Brown County Coroner Genie M. Williams. Green Bay firefighters had also arrived on the scene to assist in retrieving the corpse.

Disappearance

Green Bay police had completed a possible missing-person report around two o'clock the previous afternoon. The missing person, a mill worker, was described as a white male, six-feet tall, and 180 pounds, with brown hair, blue eyes, and a mustache. He was last seen wearing tan shorts, a white T-shirt, and a blue baseball cap. The missing man's name was entered as Monfils, Thomas J. His address was 2178 True Lane, Ashwaubenon. His date of birth was given as 4-9-57. Officer Lavonne Crummy took the report, and the case was assigned to Detective Sergeant Al Van Haute and given number 92-16653.

That afternoon Officer Crummy had met with Susan Monfils, the missing man's wife, at the James River mill. According to Crummy, Susan had spoken with mill personnel as early as 10 a.m. Actually; weekend mill supervisor Pat Ferraro had first called the Monfils's home between 9:30 and 10 a.m. and spoken with the couple's eleven-year-old daughter, Theresa. Ferraro told the girl her father was missing and asked if he had come home. Theresa left the phone for a few minutes. When she came back she told Ferraro to "call back in an hour." In what Ferraro described as a "short time," Susan called him at the mill. Ferraro asked her if her husband had shown up at home. He had not.

Ferraro told Susan that Tom was missing and that they had checked the mill and the machines "quite thoroughly looking for him." Susan told Ferraro that she was worried and that she was coming down. She asked Ferraro what had happened, and he told her of a confrontation her husband had with some of his coworkers. Susan told Ferraro that she was concerned that her husband was hiding somewhere because he was afraid he was going to be hurt.

With that, Susan and Tom's father, Ed, drove to the mill. Ed had recently retired from the mill himself. They found no satisfactory answers there and drove to the police station to file the missing-person report. The mill's own search efforts, though ongoing, had come up empty-handed. At that point, the mill also contacted the Green Bay Police Department, and Officer Crummy was dispatched to the scene.

Crummy contacted the mill's human resources director, Jack Yusko, explored the situation with him, and learned some background. Crummy wrote that Monfils had left his paper machine post "wearing tan shorts and a T-shirt." In regard to the fact that Monfils had been wearing shorts, Crummy added a parenthetical observation: "(40 degree temperature outside)." She recorded that there were "unconfirmed sightings of him [Monfils] at approx. 8:00 [a.m.] on the 3rd floor and in another area of the mill." Crummy also wrote that the Monfils family had a cottage "in Oconto Co. on White Potato Lake ... and [Monfils] could have left the mill and hitchhiked there. Oconto to be notified."

A chilly Saturday afternoon was ticking by, and things were getting fuzzier by the minute. Working between the mill and their station on Adams Street, the police were struggling for some answers. Susan Monfils told Officer Crummy that her husband was a dedicated employee, a good husband and father, a nondrinker, and a nonsmoker. Joan Monfils, Tom's mother, told Detective Sergeant Don Chic that her son had no "financial problems, marital problems, nor any other problems." Crummy concluded her report by stating that the time was

6:35 p.m. and the missing man had "not yet been located, no further details at this time."

That afternoon, Lieutenant Gordon Heraly also contacted Susan, asking if she would give the police permission to release information to the news media regarding her husband's disappearance. With that, Susan was on her way to the police station. There, she asked that information not be released "at this time," stating that she would notify police if she changed her mind.

By evening, the Oconto County Sheriff's Department had checked the Monfils's family cottage and reported back that no one was there. At the mill, Officers Heraly and Crummy interviewed a few of Monfils's coworkers. In the process, they learned of a meeting between him and three other employees prior to his disappearance, but they were "unable to take statements from the three people at this time due to the fact that the mill was short of men tonight." Many mill workers had taken time off for the opening day of Wisconsin's gun deer season, and the mill was operating with a makeshift, skeleton crew. Heraly continued, "We could only talk with one man at a time and it was only for a short period of time. James River would of [sic] had to shut the paper machine down or call other employees in to run the machine. All three employees will be at work at 7 AM until 7 PM on Sunday 11-22-92."

By 7 p.m. Saturday, many of Monfils's coworkers had headed home. However, his car remained in the parking lot, and his street clothes continued to hang eerily lifeless in his work locker.

At 9:50 p.m. Heraly was back in contact with Susan Monfils. She told Heraly that it would be okay to release the information to the news media. That was the last entry on his police detail sheet except for a simple observation: "The only way out of the mill is thru [sic] the front gate or out the rear train doors to the river. We checked the river banks with negative results."

By early Sunday morning Susan had returned to the mill. She pressed her way into the mill, past the guards. She insisted that she be allowed to search the mill herself. She made contact with mill supervisor Gregg Stephens, who served as her escort while trying to appease her. She also spoke with the president of her husband's union, Marlyn Charles. There was still no sign of her husband, and she left the mill with no answer as to his whereabouts.

At 9:50 a.m. she recontacted the police. She had, she told them, contacted credit card companies to see if any charges had been made on the couple's cards. None had. She had also driven to the cottage but had not found her husband there. She wondered aloud about an account that her husband had with the James River credit union. Because it was the weekend, she had been unable to see if any money had been withdrawn from that account, which, she said, contained about $3,000. She also told the police about her return trip to the mill and her contact with Marlyn Charles.

The search for Monfils inside the mill, which had begun Saturday morning, continued; but only the most remote and unlikely spots remained unchecked. As yet no one knew that Monfils was dead, his body anchored at the bottom of the mill's tissue chest. The lack of success intensified the search efforts as well as the frustration and speculation among the mill's employees. The police contacted the fire department and suggested they search the riverbank; Officer Crummy would accompany the fire crew. Police impounded Monfils's car as evidence, and they also reinterviewed the three coworkers with whom Monfils had met prior to his disappearance.

Discovery

On Sunday night, Susan Monfils drove to the police station to check on the progress of the investigation. She told the police that her husband had won numerous awards from James River, including a personal letter from the president of the company. She told police that her husband was well liked by fellow employees, and she named six men whom she identified as Tom's friends at work: "Lonnie Kostrova; Dennis Ruebens; Tim Swiecichowski; Woody; Carl Stencil (Tom's boss), and Bob Thut who is head supervisor."

Susan told police that she felt her husband went somewhere to think. Clearly that explanation was a way of processing her own thoughts—an effort to reassemble her world in the midst of this bedlam. Just as she was relating these details to Detective Sergeant Van Haute, Police Sergeant Robert Haglund informed Van Haute that a body had been located at the James River mill. Without verifying the victim's identity, Van Haute and Sergeant J. Kaminski relayed this information to the missing man's wife.

Van Haute recorded Susan's immediate reaction. "At first she was silent then she completely broke down. She eventually asked us to call a priest from St. Matthews. Father Tom came to the station." In the minutes before the clergyman arrived, Susan was in total anguish. After he came, she mustered the energy to ask to go to Fox Valley Hospital, a mental health facility. Sergeant Kaminski and Father Tom accompanied her there. Van Haute and Heraly then drove to 332 South Roosevelt Street, the residence of Ed and Joan Monfils and, again without official identification of the body, informed the missing man's father about what they knew. With that, Van Haute headed for the James River plant.

The scene there was grizzly. Ralph Verheyen, one of the workers who discovered the body, described the situation in a statement to Detective Sergeant Denise Servais. Verheyen told Servais he had come into work at 5 p.m. both Saturday and Sunday. On both days, he had helped search for the missing man. On Saturday he had looked down along the river as well as in his own work area.

Verheyen recalled that Tina Waack, his coworker in the stock prep department, had told him to not send any more stock to the tissue chest because it was being shut down. That had occurred about 8 p.m. Sunday. At that point Verheyen figured it would take about four hours for the chest to completely drain down. The shut-down order had come through Waack from her supervisor, Gregg Stephens. Stephens also had been involved in the search both days. He had been especially meticulous in searching, he said, because he felt Monfils was "very resourceful."

An hour and a half earlier, it had already become painfully obvious to Stephens that there was a problem with the tissue chest. The agitator blade at the bottom of the chest had been shut down and restarted at least once, but the flow of material was sluggish at best. The tissue chest had been kept running until the last possible moment for one simple reason—it was the pulp source for the majority of the paper machines. If it were shut down, nearly the entire mill would grind to a halt. But with Monfils still missing and problems with the chest itself, Stephens determined there was only one thing to do.

With the tissue chest emptying, Verheyen decided to take a walk around the area. As he was about to return to his own work area, he met Kelly Drown and Bill Watzka, who both worked on the wood-chip piles. Drown had expressed her concerns regarding the lack of progress in the search to Stephens. In fact, said Stephens, Drown had been adamant in her opinion that the mill was not doing enough to find Monfils.

Verheyen told Drown that the tissue chest was being drained so the workers could look in there. With that, Verheyen, Drown, and Watzka walked over to the chest. Verheyen was going to show them exactly what the chest looked like and where it was located. Because of its obscure location in the mill, many workers had never even seen the chest or known its whereabouts.

The three workers approached the chest area from the eastern part of the mill and then went to its northern wall. Verheyen and Drown looked over the edge. Watzka did not. It took Verheyen and Drown a moment to actually draw the scene into focus. Drown said the two of them "looked in the tank and saw something that was 'tannish' color. Then we saw the mid-section of the body and realized that was a body in the tank."

Verheyen said he noticed something in the pulp. At first, he thought it was a piece of junk but quickly realized what is was. "Then it was swirling around with the stock. It rolled over and I saw his stomach. I then realized it was the body, obviously Monfils."

Drown said that Watzka did not look into the chest himself "but knew from our reaction what was there." Verheyen called mill security guard Peggy Phillips and told her that Monfils's body was in the tissue chest.

Among the first police officers on the scene were Inspector Bruce Hamilton, Detective Sergeant Don Chic, and Detective Sergeant Servais. They were met there by two uniformed officers, Wesely and Allen, who had also been dispatched to the mill from regular patrol duty. Chic recorded arriving on the scene, after receiving a call from Phillips, "at around 9 p.m."

Once at the mill, the officers assembled near the gatehouse and were escorted to the tissue chest area by mill security. Chic went down to the lower or basement level of the chest. There he found Stephens as well as mill worker Al Kiley. Kiley was working the pump that was draining the pulp, while Stephens was operating the drain valves and overseeing the process.

Upstairs each of the officers, in turn, peered down over the chest wall and saw the body. Inspector Hamilton logged information about the chest that he had gathered shortly after arriving, describing it as "a large pulp holding tank." He also stated that there was a four-foot, nine-inch retaining wall around the tank that holds about 20,000 gallons of watered-paper pulp. Hamilton wrote that he had spoken to Robert Thut, a superintendent, and he was told that two paper machines had been shut down.

Thut also told Hamilton that the tank area "was not a work area. These are strictly holding tanks that need no work done on them or with them. The only reason anyone would have to go near them would be to check the water level to confirm the meter reading." Hamilton asked Thut where Monfils's workstation was in relation to this tank. Thut told him it was about fifty yards away, around the corner. Thut also told Hamilton that the company would make available scaled engineer drawings of the area. Hamilton himself made a drawing of the scene. He then ordered the fire department be contacted to help in recovering the body. He also had the police department's photo identification section called to the scene.

About this time, Detective Van Haute, who had finished his meeting with Susan Monfils at the police station, arrived at the mill. He was immediately taken to the tissue chest where he observed a body floating face down inside a large vat.

Coroner Genie Williams then joined the officers. Her first glimpse of the mess was from the upper level as she peered over the chest-high wall. Like the workers and the police, she could see the body about fifteen feet below. In her first notes, scratched out right there, she recorded that the body could be seen from both the north and south sides of the chest. It appeared, she wrote, as a "torso … showing the arms to the wrist and the legs to mid thigh." While much of the pulp had been drained from the vat, the body was still afloat in pulp. Williams described an area of red-brown discoloration visible around the body. Everything in the tissue chest, body and pulp, was quite still, she observed. The body was located "west of center on the south side of the tank."

Williams then went down a cramped, steep, spiral stairwell into the basement. There she joined the rest and continued to take notes of the scene and the police procedures. She saw that the pulp was being run out the bottom of the chest "via a large pump." She also observed a "boot and some body material which upon inspection appears to be skin with some underlying muscle attached has been taken from a trap surrounding the pump." The police bagged that material, she noted, "for retention."

At this point Williams returned to the upper level of the chest. Looking once more over the ceramic wall on the chest's north side, she observed an agitator at the bottom of the south wall. Measuring forty-eight inches in diameter, the agitator consisted of three blades, each twenty inches wide and three-eighths of an inch thick. Under normal conditions, it churned the pulp matter in the chest at 100 rpm. Williams noticed that the body was "to the west of this propeller but in the area of it."

Retrieving the Body

After several failed attempts to raise the body to the top of the chest with hooks and ropes, the authorities decided to use the inspection port at the lower level of the chest for its removal. The inspection port, about the size of a large manhole cover, was also on the south wall, to the east of the agitator. It was accessed from the basement.

Once the pulp was drained to a point below the port, members of the Green Bay Fire Department entered the chest and shoveled out some of the pulp, wrote Williams, "to facilitate body removal." It was then moved "from the original position of sighting to the port opening." A sheet and a disposable body bag were placed on the floor, and the firefighters proceeded to move the body through the inspection-port opening.

As the body emerged in a prone position, the firefighters had to contend with a fifty-pound iron weight attached to its neck with a homemade "jump rope." The weight was typical of those used throughout the mill for various tasks ranging from holding water hoses in place to holding doors open. The rope was about five-eighths of an inch thick, with handles made of six-inch sections of gray plastic electrical conduit on either end.

At this point, Williams continued:

> The body appears to be that of a Caucasian male. It is in an advanced state of decomposition as evidenced by odor, severe discoloration, bloating, skin slip, and some apparent purging in areas of laceration. The lower legs above the ankles are severed in an irregular manner. Both feet and lower legs are attendant. No rigor mortis is present. The pupils cannot be evaluated due to the condition of the body. Livor mortis cannot be determined. Further description of injuries will await an autopsy, which will be ordered. The body is placed into the white disposable bag at 2:25 a.m. The body is removed from the immediate area to an adjacent room where it is then placed into a heavy-duty pouch for transport. The bagged body is placed on a stretcher belonging to Metro Ambulance. The scene is departed at 2:30 a.m.

Outside the mill the full horror of this spectacle was yet to be realized. Around town, speculation had already begun after the story about Monfils's disappearance was reported on the Saturday's local evening news. The Sunday paper also ran a small piece. While he had officially been missing since about 1 p.m. the previous afternoon, positive identification would have to wait a few hours. Still, this was almost certainly the body of Tom Monfils.

All this happened just in time for the discovery to be reported on Sunday's ten o'clock news. But facts were scarce. A body was found. The investigation was continuing. That was about all casual observers knew when they went to sleep that evening.

4

Details Emerge

There is nothing to fear except the persistent refusal to find out the truth, the persistent refusal to analyze the causes of happenings.

—Dorothy Thompson

It was now very early Monday morning. If this mutilated cadaver was that of Tom Monfils, then a tiny mystery had been cleared up, but another one—of horrific proportions—was just beginning. Police were focusing on some sketchy details. A confrontation of some sort had reportedly occurred early that Saturday morning between Monfils and three of his workmates. Those involved emphasized that it was definitely not a physical confrontation but rather a tense verbal exchange. Sometime after that event, his disappearance and, apparently, his death had occurred.

At 2:40 a.m. the body in the bag was placed into an ambulance and was on its way to Memorial Crematory. By 3 a.m. the heavy-duty outer pouch was sealed with a metal seal, initialed by Coroner Genie Williams, and placed inside the crematory cooler. At that point, reported Williams, "investigators of the Green Bay Police Department are consulted for further information." Official identification of the body was pending.

By 4:00 a.m., the coroner's office was operating under reasonable certainty that the body was that of Tom Monfils. At that early hour, Williams contacted Monfils's parents to confirm for them that a body had been found at the mill and was in the coroner's custody. Shortly after noon, personnel transported the body from Malcore Funeral Home to St. Vincent Hospital, where an autopsy was performed.

At 12:32 p.m. the seal of the bag was photographed and removed. The "gross autopsy" would take the next four and a half hours. "During the course of the autopsy," Williams recorded, "the skin of the hands is removed as it is in a detached 'washer woman' condition." That skin was used to create fingerprints, and those prints, compared to records on file with the police, confirmed the body's identity. The dead man was now definitely identified as Thomas J. Monfils.

"Gross autopsy findings," wrote Williams, "in addition to the ligature previously noted, include multiple areas of trauma to the head, neck, chest, and abdomen as well as a traumatic amputation of both legs below the knee."

The death certificate would be signed out "as pending," Williams concluded. The autopsy ended about 5 p.m., and the body was released to the Lyndahl Funeral Home.

Suicide or Foul Play

That afternoon, the newspaper headline of the *Green Bay Press-Gazette* shouted, "Foul play is suspected in death." The story that followed relayed information that had come from Deputy Police Chief James Taylor in a press conference earlier that afternoon. "Coworkers found Thomas James Monfils, 35, of 2178 True Lane, Ashwaubenon, in the vat about 9:30 p.m. Sunday," the paper reported.

According to Taylor, "The vat had to be drained of wet paper pulp to allow recovery of the body which had been damaged by a large propeller at the bottom of the vat." The paper also cited Taylor as stating that "suicide and foul play" were the only likely possibilities. Since the autopsy had not been completed at that point, police could not positively identify the body, Taylor said, but "we don't have anyone else missing from there."

The *Press-Gazette* seemed to have grabbed at the idea that it was foul play rather than suicide, even though the police had offered either possibility at their press conference. The foul-play angle was bound to reach out and grab a few more readers at the boxes and newsstands.

Up to this point, the local news had consisted of the usual turkey-month mix. Suddenly, it had taken a decided turn toward human life and death. While Taylor's briefing had comprised the major story on the front page, the *Press-Gazette's* local/state pages led with a look at Tom Monfils himself. "Monfils loved to help others," its header read. Mostly the story quoted Monfils's mother, Joan, who referred to her deceased son as a "very special fellow."

The article related that Monfils had regularly visited an elderly woman, Louise La Luzerne, and had become a handyman and something like an adopted son to her. "He and his wife were my best friends," La Luzerne told a reporter, adding that she doubted any suicide theory. "He sure didn't have any reason to do this to himself," she said. "He was a happy guy."

Tom's aunt, Erma Klaus, told the paper that Monfils loved to scuba dive and had recently traveled to St. Thomas Island to pursue that interest. He had taken his family to Disney World in Florida the previous spring, she said. Monfils's mother also gave the paper the basics of his schooling at Roosevelt Elementary School and East High School. After graduating, she said, he had spent four years in the Coast Guard, where he was named Coast Guardsmen of the Year and received a congressional award. Monfils's family, reported the paper, include "his wife Susan and their children, Theresa, 11, and John, 9." Other survivors were his father, Ed; his brothers, Mark and Cal; and his sisters Lois, Yvonne, and Bobbi Jo.

That first *Press-Gazette* story was followed by more details on Tuesday, including a graphic of the pulp chest done by staff artist Joe Heller. "Monfils was alive and had a 40-pound weight tied on his neck when he was pushed or jumped into a pulp tank," the paper reported.

The other Green Bay paper, the *News-Chronicle*, strictly a morning paper, got out its first report on the Monfils story that same day. "Police still seek clues in worker's 'suspicious' death," its front page read. That report suggested that the victim "couldn't be identified by sight because the body was dismembered by the agitator." It also stated "sixteen investigators worked on the case Monday, mostly interviewing plant workers. It quoted Deputy Chief Taylor as saying James River itself had been very cooperative.

Hushed Tones

While the city buzzed with talk of Tom Monfils's death, it was mostly neighbor to neighbor or in the corner booth at the coffee shop. Nearly every conversation included the same wistful sentiment: This kind of thing just did not happen in Green Bay. Between the citizens and the police or the media, however, there was an amazing silence. According to *Press-Gazette* reporter Don Langenkamp, no one in town wanted to go on record as saying anything about the case.

Was the reticence of the citizens a cause or a symptom? The story of Tom Monfils's disappearance and death was emerging with undertones that were less than glowing toward the police. There was talk about Monfils making an anonymous call to the police a week or so before his death and the police releasing a copy of that call to one of his coworkers. In some way, went the story, the release of this tape was related to Monfils's death. Thanks to that information, there was a striking drop-off in calls to the police hotline.

On Wednesday, November 25, in a *Press-Gazette* article, Green Bay Police Chief Bob Langan emphasized "that his department almost never reveals the names of tipsters who request confidentiality." Langan was hoping that people would continue to support the efforts of the police in its investigation by calling in "information we cannot get in another way." Langan was assuring the citizens that they could trust the police not to release their names. But, he said, the callers had to tell the police that they wanted confidentiality. If they did not, Langan said the callers ran the risk of having their names released under Wisconsin's Open Records Law.

Langan's appeal did not seem to calm people's fears. A *Press-Gazette* graphic on Thursday, December 3, showed that calls to the Green Bay Area Crime Stoppers hotline had dropped dramatically the previous month. With 134 calls in the year's first ten months, 1992 had seen the greatest activity for the Crime Stoppers program since its inception. Now, just five calls had come in over five weeks's time.

Over the next several days, the papers and local television stations continued their coverage of the Monfils story but with dwindling intensity. By Friday, less than a week after Monfils's disappearance and death, the story had slipped to the local/state pages. That day's headline said it all: "No new information in Monfils mill death."

On Monday, November 30, James River authorities announced the suspensions of the three men who had allegedly "confronted" Monfils the morning of his disappearance. According to Marlyn Charles, the president of the union local to which Monfils as well as the three affected workers belonged, the suspensions were not for disciplinary reasons. "The company told us it was for their benefit," Charles said. "It was for their own safety on the job because of their mental state. They're working around big machinery and they have a lot hanging over their heads, and the last thing James River wants is for somebody to end up in a machine." Deputy Chief Taylor said that the police had not requested the suspensions.

James River had also gone to great lengths to secure the mill. According to Taylor, mill management had hired two off-duty police officers to patrol the mill's entrance from Wednesday through the weekend "to give the workers a safer feeling." Mill executive Jack Yusko said the off-duty police were there "to ensure the safety and security of our work force." The company was picking up the costs of the officers's wages, fringe benefits, and the use of squad cars and other equipment, Taylor said.

The police also determined that the rope that had been tied around Monfils's neck and attached to the weight was a jump rope. It had been used for exercise during free time, said Taylor, and it had been kept near paper machine 7 where Monfils worked.

As far as results from the autopsy went, Taylor said the police were waiting on tests performed on Monfils's body. He said that he was ruling out nothing as a cause of death, but he said that the body showed no obvious signs of gunshot or knife wounds. The exact how and why of Monfils's death was still up in the air.

On Thursday, December 3, the *News-Chronicle* ran an article titled "Police Fight Time, Rumor Mill." The investigation continues, the report went, "[a]s does the circulation of a number of rumors surrounding the case." Some of the scuttlebutt had it that Monfils's discovery of illegal activity at the mill had led to the Saturday morning confrontation with his coworkers. Taylor stated that any reports that Monfils had stumbled into a burglary ring or a drug ring were simply not true.

On the following Tuesday the *Press-Gazette* broke a five-day silence on the case with the headline "Still No Conclusions in Mill Death." Chief Taylor seemed to be ruling out suicide but still would not commit to homicide pending the results of the tests being done on tissue samples. "The young man had everything going for him—a good job, a family," Taylor said. "He was basically planning for the future."

In the early stages of their investigation police had questioned over a hundred people, most of them workers at the mill. Management had decided to continue posting off-duty police officers there during shift changes. Taylor suggested that the practice would continue at least through Friday, December 18. The State Crime Laboratory in Wausau was performing tests on the jump rope and weight using laser technology to search for fingerprints. The knot was also being examined, said Taylor, to see if Monfils could have tied it himself.

Suicide or foul play? Either way, the people of Green Bay were haunted by tragedy in their midst. Either way, the rumors continued to fly until they got some answers. So did the speculation and fear.

On Wednesday, December 9, a second tremor shook Green Bay. Tom Monfils's death was ruled a homicide, and a press conference was held to announce a full-scale murder investigation by the GBPD.

An Anonymous Phone Call and a Stolen Extension Cord

For the first few weeks of the investigation, news had appeared sporadically, but it had mostly been a reiteration of the previous facts. Now that Monfils's death had been ruled a murder, the focus had shifted to catching the party or parties responsible. In just three weeks, Green Bay had gone from a town reasonably comfortable with its answers to a community plagued with questions. A murder investigation was under way, and some unsettling things were starting to come out in the light of day.

Police were honing in on the so-called confrontation between Monfils and some of his coworkers the morning of his disappearance.

A story was taking shape of a workforce less than focused on turning out rolls of toilet paper that Saturday morning.

There was also something about the playing of that audiocassette tape—a tape that was supposedly embarrassing to Monfils himself. The tape had been played at the mill again and again during the early morning hours of November 21 for anyone who was willing to listen. And although the person on the tape never revealed his name, everyone who listened to it seemed to recognize the voice. It was Tom Monfils.

What exactly was the nature of the tape? It was a police recording of an anonymous call Monfils had made to the police at 4:45 a.m. on Tuesday, November 10. On the tape, Monfils was saying that Keith Kutska would be taking some "yellow extension cord material" from the mill without permission when he finished work that day. Monfils described it as an "employee theft" to the police phone operator taking the call.

Furthermore, Monfils was asking the police to inform plant security personnel and have them stop Kutska on his way out of the plant. Monfils said that he was not going to inform plant security himself, and he made it clear that he wanted to remain anonymous. He even told the operator that Kutska would have the cord "in a bag or wrapped around himself" and that the police should be sure to come in an unmarked car and not park anywhere "in front" of the plant where Kutska might see it. If that happened, Monfils said, "He [Kutska] would ditch [the cord]."

This was the same audiotape being played at the mill the morning of Monfils's disappearance. And who was the worker playing the tape? Well, that was … Keith Kutska. And how had he come by it? Now that was the really strange part. Kutska had gotten it from—of all people or places—the Green Bay Police Department. Somehow, under their mixed-up interpretation of Wisconsin Open Records Law, the police had handed Kutska a taped copy of the recording. On Friday, November 20, Kutska had swung by the police department after work, handed them five dollars and a cheap replacement cassette tape. In return he received an unabridged edition of Monfils's anonymous call. It was really that easy.

According to Kutska, after one listen to that tape, a picture began to take shape for him; facts replaced hunches and questions found answers.

It was inside these double doors that mill security stopped Keith Kutska and asked him to open his laundry bag. Because he refused, mill management suspended him the following day, costing him about $840 in wages.

He flashed back to Tuesday, November 10, when he had punched out at 6:34 a.m. Sure enough, as Kutska was leaving the mill gatehouse after punching his card, Gary Schmitz, one of the mill security officers, had hailed him. John Gilson, another guard, had been there too. Schmitz had asked him to stop and open the bag he was carrying. He had refused, saying there was nothing in the bag but dirty laundry, and he kept on walking, briskly now. He had been asked two more times to stop and open his bag. He had again refused. He had to hurry and get the car home to his wife, he told Schmitz.

If Kutska had stopped, Schmitz would have found a section of yellow electrical cord in his bag—about fifteen or sixteen feet of it. It was cord that belonged to the mill, and Kutska had not abided by the mill's scrap policy in securing it. Technically he was stealing. On the other hand, with a scrap pass, he could have walked out of the mill that day waving the cord in the air over his head like a lasso. Without a pass, he had to try to sneak it past the guards just as he was doing.

Although Schmitz did not discover the theft, he wrote a report on the incident. According to that report, written in the gatehouse just after the incident, Kutska had "fled" the scene, almost at a run.

The incident at the gatehouse troubled Kutska enough that he called union president Marlyn Charles that evening to tell him about the unusual hubbub as he had left work that day. Kutska told Charles that he was worried about possibly losing his job. Mill management had not contacted him yet, Kutska told Charles, but he was pretty certain something would be coming down the next day when he went to work. Charles told Kutska that he would talk to management and find out what was going on.

The next day, Wednesday, Kutska reported for work at two in the afternoon as scheduled. Just as he had expected, he found himself immediately whisked into a disciplinary review meeting in the mill office area. Charles was there as Kutska's union representative. Mill management asked Kutska about his actions the day before. Kutska fully acknowledged that he had refused to stop at the gatehouse and open his bag when asked to do so. He was then asked whether he had stolen the electrical cord. That, he flatly denied.

For failing to stop and submit to the search at the gatehouse and because the mill believed it had reasonable suspicion that he had taken the electrical cord, Kutska was issued a five-day suspension without pay, beginning that moment.

Ironically, it was in that same disciplinary meeting that Kutska learned just how this snare had engulfed him. Paul Dolson, a member of management in the mill's human resources department, told Kutska that the mill had received a call from the Green Bay police. As a result, the guards at the mill were alerted to Kutska's leaving with the contraband. Dolson told Kutska that it had all started with a call to the police from "an hourly employee" within the mill itself.

Following his suspension meeting, Kutska would later tell police, he "started putting the puzzle together." He did not think a fellow union member would make the call. He theorized that someone in management might have seen something and that the report of a call to the police was just a bluff. But he was looking for something concrete. He figured that a police report had to exist if such a call was actually made.

On their way out of the meeting Kutska ran a few ideas by Charles.

"Do you think we should try and find out who it was that did that, that made that phone call?" Kutska asked. He speculated that they could "get computer records from the mill of phone calls leaving the mill."

Charles was doubtful on that score, suggesting that the company would probably not release such information.

"Well, what if I called the police station?" Kutska wondered.

"I don't know if they would give it to you either," Charles replied.

"Well," said Kutska, "you don't know if you don't ask."

With that, Kutska left the mill for a five-day out-of-work stint, for which he would not collect a paycheck. Over that period, a few people from work contacted Kutska, he said. They wanted to know "what happened and who called the police department." From those contacts, Kutska said, he was "under the assumption then that the general people in the mill already knew that somebody called the police department about it."

The Scrap-Pass Policy

Allowing workers to take home scrap materials is really a very practical thing for manufacturing companies such as James River—it reduces landfill fees and saves valuable storage space. At the same time, it is a benefit to the workforce, giving all active employees an opportunity to obtain unwanted company property for personal use. In order to assure that there was some organization to the program, James River instituted what was called a "scrap pass."

Although scrap-pass policies and procedures have been updated and changed over the years, they have essentially remained the same. Basically any employee on a first-come, first-served basis can request anything the plant no longer has a use for or does not want to waste storage space on. It does not matter if the items are new or old, used or obsolete, whether it is parts or supplies, raw materials or finished product. All things destined to the scrap heap are fair game.

```
┌─────────────────────────────────────────────────────────────┐
│                      SCRAP PASS                               │
│  James River Corporation                 Green Bay Mill       │
│                                                               │
│  Employee: _____Clock #_____  │
│                                                               │
│  Department:                                                  │
│                                                               │
│  Description of item(s):_____  │
│                                                               │
│  Vehicle entry required: yes_____no_____Void after date:_____  │
│                                                               │
│  Authorized: _____  │
│                                                               │
│  Signature: _____Date:_____  │
│                                                               │
└─────────────────────────────────────────────────────────────┘
```

The Tale of the Tape

On Monday, November 16, Kutska's suspension was over, and he was back at work on a 3–11 p.m. shift. That first day back, he was approached by what he called "a lot" of his fellow workers, "hoards" of them he said in his first detailed police interview a week later. Many of them asked him who he thought made the call. He said he did not know. He also recalled several of them telling him, "I hope you don't think I did that."

Kutska later suggested that calling the police department about the call was not a decided course of action for him at that point. "But, when a lot of people started inquiring about it," he would state in subsequent testimony, "I went home and I thought about it and the next morning I thought, 'Well, I'll call and find out.'" In that same testimony, however, he contradicted that by suggesting, "Everybody knew Monday and Tuesday that I was going to try to pursue finding this tape." So, if Kutska was convinced by his coworkers to find out who did it, it was also clear that they had not even touched his arm in order to twist it. On the mill floor, he talked about getting an attorney to help him secure the recording.

That same morning Kutska did call the police. "I got the desk," he remembered, "and they referred me to a sergeant." That sergeant, Karen Sopata, took down what Kutska was telling her and said someone would get back to him.

Lo and behold, someone did get back to him. Sopata had passed the message along to Lieutenant Mike Mason, who actually contacted Kutska at his home in nearby Abrams. Kutska told Mason that he was trying to find out who had reported him to mill security because that person had gotten him into trouble. He also insisted to Mason that it had been a *false* allegation made against him and that he felt more than justified in pursuing the matter.

According to Mason, Kutska said that he was "very concerned that someone was out to get his job." He told Mason that he was a long-time loyal employee and felt he was now in trouble with management and was considered a possible thief. Kutska told Mason that he had already talked to mill security, who told him that the call to stop him had come into the gatehouse from the police, and that someone had contacted the police from the mill. All Kutska wanted to know, he told Mason, was who was out to get him by making false allegations.

When Kutska asked Mason if there was a police report of the call, the lieutenant said no. Kutska then asked if the police recorded incoming calls. Mason told him "yes, we do record calls but unless we know approximately what time the call came in, it would take a long time to locate it on tape." He explained to Kutska that the police department had a twenty-four-hour reel-to-reel tape and that they hung on to the tapes for sixty days.

Mason told Kutska that before he could help him further Mason would need a little more information, namely the date and time the call that reported him was made from the mill. Mason also looked up who was working in the radio room the night of November 10. He found out and advised Kutska to call back the following day, Wednesday, between 10 and 10:30 p.m. and to talk to Sergeant W. Wians. Perhaps Wians would remember the call and approximately what time it had been made.

With very little effort on his own part, just one call, Kutska was already about to strike pay dirt. It was all falling into place—at least for the short term.

The next two days, Wednesday, November 18, and Thursday, November 19, were Kutska's regular days off. On Wednesday, he called Sergeant Wians and left a message. Wians called him back about 10:30 p.m., saying he "couldn't find any conversation on the tapes, like the one he [Kutska] was talking about." That set Kutska back a little, but only because he did not know how close this thing was to falling into his lap.

In the interim, Kutska went about trying to nail down the time of the call. He spoke with the security guys at the gatehouse and a coworker, Andy Lison. From them, he was able to determine that the call had been made from the mill at about 4:30 a.m. the morning of November 10. Before lunchtime on Thursday, Kutska called Mason back and gave him the approximate time of the call.

Later that afternoon, Mason's diligence paid off, and he was back on the line to Kutska. He told Kutska that he had found the call Kutska was asking about. What he did not tell Kutska was that he had done a quick check on Kutska's record and "found it to be very minor with no arrests or entries as a suspect."

Because he was certain that Kutska would be asking for a copy of the tape and because he had concerns about releasing it, Mason had gone two steps further. First, he had spoken with Shay Gierczak, the records manager at the police station. She was also unsure. So Mason and Gierczak called assistant city attorney Judith Schmidt-Lehman and ran the release of the tape past her.

Schmidt-Lehman asked whether or not there had been "a specific promise that the caller would be kept anonymous." Even though Monfils had said that he wanted to remain anonymous and even though Mason heard the police operator say "Okay," the staggering conclusion was that no such "specific promise" had been made.

Kutska asked Mason if he could have a copy of the call, and Mason told him he could. Mason even went on to explain that he had talked to the city attorney about releasing the tape. The implication was clear: This was even kosher from a legal standpoint.

Mason had listened to the master tape and determined the call came in at 4:45 a.m. The caller was certainly fingering Kutska as a potential thief, and he was definitely describing how the police should proceed in apprehending him. The phone operator was asking why the caller was contacting the police. According to Mason's own account as he listened to the tape, the caller "stated that he wanted to be anonymous and wanted the police department to make the call." Then he heard the police phone operator say, "Okay." Mason then listened to the phone operator call the gatehouse at James River, passing the information on to the security guard there. The guard said he would take care of it; no police car was ever sent.

On Friday Kutska was scheduled to work from 7 a.m. to 3 p.m. At the mill that day, his coworkers were curious. "Everybody asked me if I could get it [the tape]," he recalled, "and I said, yeah, I could pick it up after three o'clock."

At 3 p.m., he drove the dozen or so blocks to the police station and went in to claim his prize. He asked to see Lieutenant Mason and was informed that Mason was off that day. Kutska said, "Well, he was supposed to have a tape for me to pick up." With that, according to Kutska, the female officer at the desk gave him "an envelope with a tape in it." In return he gave her five dollars and a blank replacement tape.

Kutska's seventeen-mile drive up Highway 41 to Abrams seemed to take twice as long as usual. When he finally got home, he popped the tape into his cassette player and pressed "Play." At that point, alone in his home, he readied himself for what he was about to hear. "Green Bay Police," he heard a woman's voice say.

"Ah, is this the Green Bay Police?" a male voice asked.

"Yes it is."

The wheels were spinning in Kutska's head. He knew that voice.

"Okay, I'd like to report an employee theft, which is gonna occur at James River," the voice continued.

Ah ha! The whole thing was making sense to Kutska now. It was Tom Monfils! Sure enough, Kutska had pretty much suspected him all along. He and David Webster, a coworker, had been right. They had spent some time on Monday, November 16, running down a list of employees who worked on the paper machines, and they pretty much narrowed it down to one or two people. Damn! It was Monfils after all!

"I'm sorry," the phone operator at the police station said referring to the reported theft, "which is going to occur?"

"Right," Monfils continued. "Keith Kutska, an employee that's taking stuff out of the paper mill."

Even though he was expecting it, Kutska was electrified when he actually heard Monfils say his name. "Okay," the female voice said, "it, ah, did not occur yet?"

"Not yet, no," Monfils said. "It's ... he gets off shift at, ah, 6:30, about 20 after. They work from 20 after to 20, ah ..."

Kutska was further shocked to hear Monfils actually coaching the police. Bad enough that he was calling them, but here he was practically serving as police dispatcher. A little further in the tape, Monfils was telling the cops how they should respond, what kind of car they should send, and where they should park it.

"Malicious," Kutska thought. "This is just plain malicious." He recalled that on the morning of the call, he and Monfils had met between the wet end of paper machine 9 and the dry end of paper machine 7. They were talking about the paper cores getting wet on machine 7. They had chatted, felt Kutska, "like good friends." That was just twenty minutes or so after Monfils had made the call to the police. If Monfils had a beef with him, Kutska wondered, why would he not have said something right then and there? Kutska was steaming.

Now it was a question of what to do with the tape. Kutska began to plan his next steps. For sure, Monfils was not going to get away with this. It was only about five o'clock in the evening, but the black of the late-autumn night had already slammed down hard on northeast Wisconsin. No matter, Keith Kutska's Friday night was decided and he was energized.

A Complete Transcript of Monfils's Call

Call taker:	Green Bay Police.
Monfils:	Ah, is this the Green Bay Police?
Call taker:	Yes it is.
Monfils:	Okay, I'd like to report an employee theft which is gonna occur at James River.
Call taker:	I'm sorry; which is going to occur?
Monfils:	Right. Keith Kutska, an employee that's taking stuff out of the paper mill.
Call taker:	Okay. It, ah, did not occur yet?

Monfils:	Not yet, no. It's … he gets off shift at, ah, 6:30, about 20 after. They work from 20 after to 20, ah …
Call taker:	Okay, and what is your position there?
Monfils:	Ah, just an employee. I witnessed, ah, him, you know, loading the stuff up or whatever to get ready to take it out.
Call taker:	Did you notify security?
Monfils:	Ah, no I didn't … I … what I want you to do is, you to contact them. I don't want anything to do, you know, so basically it will be anonymous and you will contact them to let 'em know it's gonna happen.
Call taker:	Okay. Who is it?
Monfils:	Keith Kutska.
Call taker:	Keith Kutska?
Monfils:	Keith Kutska.
Call taker:	Keith Kutska.
Monfils:	Right. And it's ah like it's like yellow extension cord material. It's quite expensive.
Call taker:	Okay. And what time is he getting off?
Monfils:	He gets, anywhere from 20 after 6 till probably 20 to 7.
Call taker:	Now what's the location of the building or what machine is he on or where does, what does …
Monfils:	Well, he works on a paper machine.
Call taker:	On the paper machines?
Monfils:	Right. He would know; they would know him in the gatehouse.

Call taker:	They would know him. So they would know what entrance he comes out of.
Monfils:	He can only go out the main gatehouse.
Call taker:	Okay.
Monfils:	Now if you would go to the mill, don't take a marked car and don't park it even an unmarked … anywhere in the front anywhere. Cuz I'm sure if he saw it he would ditch.
Call taker:	So you think he does this regularly?
Monfils:	Well it's been known.
Call taker:	Okay.
Monfils:	But he, ah, ah, he's known to be violent, so …
Call taker:	Do you know anything else about him?
Monfils:	Ah.
Call taker:	I mean, what do you mean by violent? Does he have weapons or does he just fight?
Monfils:	No, no, just, you know, if … he did something, if … steps … he may fly off the handle.
Call taker:	About how old is Keith Kutska?
Monfils:	Ahm, probably about 42, 40.
Call taker:	Okay. And where does he put this material, where would he have it?
Monfils:	I imagine he'll wrap it in a bag or wrapped around himself, something like this.
Call taker:	In a bag. They let you carry bags out there?
Monfils:	Or wrapped around his person, like a cord-type material.
Call taker:	I thought you said you saw him loading it up?
Monfils:	Well, unreeling it and you know, packaging it.

Call taker:	Okay.
Monfils:	Getting it out, rolling it up to take it out.
Call taker:	Okay, but you don't know how he's gonna get it out yet.
Monfils:	Well, he's gotta walk through the gatehouse.
Call taker:	Okay, so he couldn't of already gone out and put it in his car or something?
Monfils:	See, they're allowed to just check randomly.
Call taker:	Okay, but you're allowed to just check packages out?
Monfils:	Right, yeah, like a lunch box or bag with dirty clothes that could be …
Call taker:	Okay. Alright, they will know him; I don't have to get a clothing description or …
Monfils:	No, no.
Call taker:	Okay, can you just hold on for one second. This is the first time I've taken something like this. I just wanna make sure if we need anything else, okay?
Monfils:	Okay.
Call taker:	Just a second … Sir?
Monfils:	Yeah.
Call taker:	Okay, is there anything else you can think of or …
Monfils:	That would be it. Just like I say if … you, if they would want you to bring a car, don't bring a marked one and don't park in the front.
Call taker:	Okay. Where is he parked, do you know?
Monfils:	Ah, in the lot outside someplace.
Call taker:	Just in the main lot.

Monfils: Yeah.

Call taker: Okay. And this is Procter and Gamble.

Monfils: No, no. James River.

Call taker: Oh, good thing I asked you again. I …

Monfils: James River, it's on … Day Street.

Call taker: On Day Street?

Monfils: I think it's Day, runs right up to it.

Call taker: Is there a certain building number or anything?

Monfils: Ah, the main gatehouse at James River. I can give you the phone number.

Call taker: Okay, what is it?

Monfils: 433-6228

Call taker: Okay, we'll look into it.

Monfils: Thank you much.

Call taker: Thanks, bye.

A Secret Tug of War

Michelle Wichman, a GBPD communications center operator, had taken Monfils's call. Because she had contacted James River security personnel and had not dispatched police to the mill, Wichman did not write a report of the call. As a result, no record of the call was logged at the police department. Still, there was the tape itself, which would now become the object of Kutska's quest.

A look at how Kutska finally procured that tape is enlightening, but it is not comforting. The entire time he was working to secure a tape of Monfils's call, Monfils was secretly working doubly hard to keep it out of Kutska's hands.

To be sure, the police had not just turned the tape over to Kutska when he first contacted them. On the other hand, they did not exactly make it difficult for him either. His efforts to get the tape, and Monfils's simultaneous efforts to make sure he did not get it, were like two ships in the night heading toward each other on a collision course.

Sadly, the police department was no more a participant in the events than the ocean in which the Monfils and the Kutska ships navigated. It should have been the port authority, which made absolutely sure those ships never made contact. In the end, the police did their best to serve Kutska, but they did not do much at all to help Monfils.

Monfils himself was extremely uncomfortable that his phone call had been taped in the first place. He was especially concerned that Kutska would find out that there was a tape and that he would get a copy of it. If that happened, even though Monfils had not told the cops his name, Kutska was sure to recognize the voice, and Monfils was fearful of what might happen then.

Monfils's first call had been the one to report Kutska for theft. His second call, to Detective Denise Servais on Thursday, November 12, had been a relief of sorts for him. She had, Monfils felt, guaranteed him that the tape would not be released. "There's no way that it [the tape] can get out," he quoted her as saying when he made his third call to police. In fact, she had been even clearer than that, suggesting that there was no way "in hell" the tape would be released.

But things had changed since he spoke with Servais. Kutska had come back to work on Monday, November 16, after his five-day suspension, and he had been talking to his coworkers about the incident. He had been stating that since he had not stopped for the guards at the security gate and since they had not actually found any contraband on him, he had been charged and disciplined by the company without cause. Kutska was striking the pose that he had been wronged at the gatehouse and that he was now going to "fight the good fight" against an unfounded five-day suspension. That, Monfils fretted, changed everything.

On Tuesday, November 17, Kutska had made his first call to the GBPD about the possibility of getting some kind of record of who had made the anonymous call. At 10:46 that same night, Monfils placed his third call to the GBPD, desperately begging to stop the release of any information. The contrast was stark: Kutska was on a leisurely stroll, looking for the possibility of finding out who had reported him. Monfils was frantic, a starving man maybe down to his last morsel.

Again, Michelle Wichman answered the phone. There was a new urgency in Monfils's voice. He would spend the next eleven minutes trying to grab a sliver of security.

"Ah yes," he said. "I'd like to speak to somebody, the highest guy up you have."

Wichman asked him what the problem was, but Monfils would have none of that basic, introductory stuff. "Ah, I'd just like to speak to somebody," he said. "I had called earlier one time. I'd like a …"

"Alright," Wichman interrupted, "just a second."

This time, he got Lieutenant Ken LaTour. After describing the situation to LaTour as best he could, Monfils explained the new developments. Kutska had come back to work, he said, and now he was talking about getting a lawyer and getting the tape and "verifying through the voice track who did report him." Monfils suggested that Kutska was "at a point where he's hunt …" He did not finish the word, but it is absolutely clear that he was suggesting that Kutska was "hunting" for the person who had done this to him.

Lieutenant LaTour laughed. The whole situation seemed a little bit funny to him. He said he did not know "that it isn't a matter of public record."

Monfils told LaTour that he had made it clear when he called the first time that Kutska was a guy he feared. "Ah … the thing is … ahm," he said, "when it was reported you know, when I did report it, I let him know that, you know the people that were taking the information that this guy is, you know he ain't a nice guy."

LaTour muttered his acknowledgement.

"I told 'em," Monfils continued, "you know, that he was violent or whatever."

LaTour gave him another "Mmmmm mmm."

Monfils continued, "And … ah and I know, you know, I've worked with this guy for ten years and past history and everything like this and, ahm, I do fear for myself if this recording would get out. Now I don't know if there's any way that this can get out or do I have any recourse as far as to contact like a district attorney or something like this."

LaTour restated an earlier suggestion, that Monfils should call back the next day and talk to either Captain Irv Nelson or Specialist John

Lampkin in the communications section, "with all of the computers and all the tapes and stuff like that."

Monfils and LaTour continued their conversation for several more minutes. Monfils told LaTour that he was "a hundred percent positive" that Kutska had taken the electrical cord.

LaTour suggested that the James River security personnel "didn't do their job then, huh?" since they had not actually stopped Kutska at the gatehouse.

Monfils agreed. "That's right," he said, "which leaves me in a hell of a bind if he would be able to obtain copies of this."

LaTour again recommended that Monfils contact Specialist Lampkin. "Maybe he can put your fears to rest," LaTour told Monfils, "or at least give your information about, ah, what you would have to do in order to have yourself protected properly on this too, you know."

Monfils again explained his fear of Kutska. He called Kutska a "biker-type" and said, "He [Kutska] has nothing to lose in life anyway."

"Well that usually fits the character mold for those kind of people, so ...," LaTour replied.

"But that doesn't do me any good if he decides to," Monfils interjected. "You know in the middle of the night I don't show up at home. And it's very well, you know, that fits with me, and I do, and I, and no way do I think that he wouldn't do it." Monfils even suggested that Kutska had a history of bragging about taking care of matters in a physical fashion.

Monfils asked LaTour to give him his name, which LaTour did. Then LaTour asked him his name, and Monfils would only say, "Okay. It's Tom."

"Tom?" LaTour repeated.

"I'll give you my first one," Monfils said, "but, ah, like I said, nobody knows about this but me ..."

"Mmmmm," LaTour put in.

"And I really don't want anything to, you know, I hate ..." Monfils continued.

"Well it's not like I'm gonna go and call James River about ya," LaTour told him, and he laughed.

Monfils then said that he had "little faith" in the security at James

River. "It was around the plant ten times before you know, five minutes after it happened," Monfils added.

Tom Monfils made numerous calls to authorities in an attempt to keep the police from releasing a tape of his anonymous phone call. The authorities failed him. That failure eventually cost the city of Green Bay over $2 million.

LaTour assured Monfils that he knew all about the "grapevine" at such places.

Then Monfils told him for the second time in their conversation that because of this whole mess he had not gotten much sleep in the last several days.

LaTour again told him that Specialist Lampkin would be able to address his concerns the next day.

"I hate to make it sound like I don't trust you," Monfils then said. "But I'm, you know, I don't think—if you've ever been put in a position like this I'm sure you would feel the same."

LaTour compared Monfils's position to his own. "Well I've been threatened with some people trying to tell me that they're gonna kill me so many times I just tell 'em to grab a number and stand in line, now that doesn't bother me," he said.

Clearly he had missed the point: He was a cop, and Monfils, a civilian, had never before experienced this kind of situation.

That was basically the end of their conversation. When he hung up the phone, Monfils was no more certain that the tape would not end up in Kutska's hands than he had before he punched in the phone number to the police department.

The next day, Wednesday, November 18, Kutska was enjoying a day off and considering his next steps. As LaTour had suggested, Monfils called Lampkin. It was Lampkin's task to handle requests for tapes, and he assured Monfils that the tape would not be released, "because it would have to cross his desk first." That had to have assuaged Monfils's trepidation some. However, like his three predecessors, Lampkin made no written record of his conversation with Monfils. That night Kutska had been in contact with Sergeant Wians and been forced to give up attempts to get the tape, at least for the time being.

On Thursday, November 19, his second day off, Kutska phoned GBPD's Mike Mason in the morning with the approximate time of the original call. That afternoon, Mason called Kutska back to tell him that the tape was his. Besides locating the tape of the call and checking Kutska's record, he had cleared the tape's release with the department's records manager and a city attorney.

Mason had also checked the computer to see if there had been any written report relating to Monfils's original call. There were none. Nor did he find any written records of any of Monfils's subsequent calls. At that point, the records did not exist. As a result, Mason was unaware of Monfils's several pleas for anonymity to the police.

The next day, Friday, November 20, Kutska was handed the tape.

Monfils's Final Tug

It was on that same day that Monfils again contacted Specialist Lampkin. He was told in no uncertain terms that the tape would *not be released.* Lampkin even went a step further and transferred the call to Deputy Chief Taylor to ease Monfils's concerns.

This was the same Taylor who would, just a few days later, figure so prominently in the early stages of the investigation into Monfils's death.

Taylor would be doling out the information regarding the progress of the case to the media. He would be deciding which pieces of the puzzle they would get and which ones would remain a closely guarded secret because they were sensitive to the ongoing inquiry. What he would never tell them was that he himself had let the ball drop when it came to releasing the tape, the tape that was being played the morning of Monfils's disappearance.

Of course Monfils did not know that his pleas would fall on so many deaf ears. He had to believe he was making some progress of his own. Here he was, talking to the deputy chief! He told Taylor everything, especially that he was afraid of Kutska getting a hold of the tape. Taylor assured him that the tape was not going to be released. But that was as much as Taylor did. Like Wichman, Servais, LaTour, Mason, and Lampkin, he did not put anything in writing regarding his conversation with Monfils.

While talking to the deputy chief had to have calmed Monfils a bit, his efforts did not end there. He took the further step of contacting the district attorney's office. There he spoke with Assistant District Attorney Patrick Hitt, who said he was certain that there were grounds within Wisconsin's Open Records Law to prevent the tape's release. He told Monfils that he would immediately contact Deputy Chief Taylor and tell Taylor not to release it.

Hitt did just that after speaking to Monfils. Taylor told Hitt that he was familiar with the case. Hitt told Taylor that he would contact Lampkin to tell him not to release the tape, but Taylor told Hitt that he would do it. Taylor guaranteed Hitt that the tape would not be released to Kutska. The whole situation was now in Taylor's hands.

Unfortunately Taylor did next to nothing. He checked the computer to see if there had been a written report made on the November 10 call. There had not, so Taylor found none. Then, in his own words, he "just let it go." The tape was sitting on a desk in the records office, about thirty feet from him, and he just "let it go."

Under the cover of darkness, the two ships, Monfils and Kutska, continued to close. The police department was responsible for making sure the ships did not collide, and the deputy chief was asleep at the helm.

Kutska had returned to work after his suspension, playing the wronged party. He had struck a profile on the mill floor of righteous indignation. He had involved dozens of people in a guessing game of whether or not he was going to get the tape. He had made two simple phone calls, and it was all going his way. Meanwhile, without tipping his hand, Monfils was doing everything he could to cover his tracks. He was alone. He had not even told his wife about his phone calls.

By the end of that day, the tape had been let go. By about 3:30 that afternoon, it was on its way to Abrams, where Kutska would listen to it intently. From there, all of Monfils's worries would be realized.

Lost in a Fog of Guilt

From the first minute of the investigation to its last, the detectives of the Green Bay Police Department pursued this case in a heavy fog that they had not created. That fog was the result of the actions and inactions of the supervisors back at headquarters and their colleagues at the switchboard. The department displayed a lack of structure that carelessly put Tom Monfils in jeopardy. It was not the fault of the detectives in the GBPD that others in the department had failed to protect him, but a *shared sense of guilt* caused by that carelessness engulfed them like a fog—obscuring their objectivity.

The facts are plain. When Monfils learned that Kutska was working to get a copy of the tape, he desperately recontacted the Green Bay police four more times. He also called the Brown County district attorney's office. Each time, he begged that the tape not be released.

He pleaded for his safety and expressed a profound fear of Kutska. Each call, every plea, all of his fears were ignored—the dreaded tape was released. The police had now become directly involved in the course of events that led to the death of Tom Monfils—be it murder or suicide.

The detectives's ability to conduct an objective investigation was out the window from the start. That damned Kutska, a mere mill worker, had duped the department into releasing an audiotape that identified his tormentor. That sense of guilt shrouded their efforts and shaded the investigation from the start. It never went away. It was there every time the media criticized their lack of progress. It was there every time a fact challenged their theory. It was there every time a troubling witness was disregarded.

After the Monfils trial, as James Lewis was replacing the retiring chief, the local press focused on the fact that Lewis was "an outsider." Ray Barrington, of the *Green Bay News-Chronicle,* stated that Lewis would be the "first chief for Green Bay—at least in recent times—to come from outside the ranks of the department."

As he assumed command, Lewis knew he was taking over a department so entrenched in its "good old boy" ways that it might resent his leadership. "My biggest challenge," he said, "will be getting over the apprehension that the department has about an outsider. I'm going to have to build bridges and get their confidence."

Lewis also knew that systemic changes were necessary if he was going to prevent the kind of ineptitude shown in the Monfils case. "We should be trying to get more focus toward the line-level people and less toward management. I'd like to look at the promotion system and get merit built in as much as possible."

Well into Lewis's tenure, the editorial page of the *Green Bay Press-Gazette* suggested that one scant bit of comfort from the Monfils case was that the "personnel and structure are far better now at the Green Bay Police Department than six years ago when the beginnings of the Monfils case were mishandled."

Indeed, it had been a good old boys's network. Each one had been doing his own thing and documenting nothing—guided by no clear policy or direction from the old boy at the top of the network, Chief Robert Langan.

5

Papermaking 101

We don't accomplish anything in this world alone ... and whatever happens is the result of the whole tapestry of one's life and all the weavings of individual threads from one to another that creates something.

—Sandra Day O'Connor

By the 1890s, a synergy of natural resources had turned tiny Green Bay into a hub for the manufacture of paper products. By 1923, the city of 33,000 was the world's largest producer of toilet paper, turning out enough each day to wrap around the earth twice. Through world wars and economic slides, as well as stretches of tremendous national growth, Green Bay mills have been churning out paper products to the present day.

Since the beginning, the jobs at those mills have been a staple in a thriving Green Bay economy. For years one or more of "Titletown's" paper mills have ranked among the city's largest employers. The paychecks from those jobs have shored up individual families, making an entire community tick along like a fine watch. But the world inside those mills is a mystery to those who do not work there. A basic knowledge of that world—especially day-to-day operations around the paper machines—is important to this story: It underscores the innocence of these six men.

Although there have been many technological advances in papermaking since the Monfils incident, the basic process remains the same, the bond between the workers and their machines has not changed, and the reliance the workers expect from one another continues.

Crews, Machines, Turnovers, and Paper Breaks

A typical paper machine crew consists of four workers. The lead man, the "machine tender," assumes the most responsibility by overseeing the entire process. Second in command is a "back tender." His primary job is controlling the "dry end" of the paper machine. It is his responsibility to make sure that the sheet of paper product coming off the machine meets all the required specifications. The third and fourth hands are responsible for most of the hands-on work: completing the roll changes on time, taking tests, reattaching the sheets after paper breaks, changing filters, cleaning up, and other such tasks.

By working together, a good crew can complete a roll change, or "turnover," without breaking off the sheet of paper coming from a machine. Likewise, they can take care of the occasional paper break in short order. Then they can get back to the much-easier aspect of their job, simply monitoring the papermaking process. It takes a while for a crew of four individuals to meld into such a cohesive unit, but once they do so, the complex process of making paper becomes far more efficient.

The paper machines themselves are huge. Though no two "Yankee dryer" machines are identical, they have some general characteristics in common. Their job is to take wet pulp stock in one end and transform it into paper by the time it reaches the other end. Logically the incoming end is called the "wet end," and the outgoing end, where the paper is wound into large rolls, is called the "dry end." The distance between the wet and dry ends of the Yankee machines is typically about 150 feet—about half of a football field in length.

At the wet end, the pulp slurry is run into the machine from various pipes. The actual flow and the type of material being allowed into the machine determine the type of paper being made. This "recipe" of specific pulp is diluted as it enters the machine at the "head box" on the machine's wet end. Then the watery pulp is sprayed onto a continuous screen, a wire mesh about twenty feet wide. This is the point at which the sheet of paper product is first formed and most of the water removed as it runs through the screen. From there, the wet sheet flows through the felt-press section, where even more water is squeezed from the product. Then it is completely dried on the surface of a large, rotating, steam-filled pressure vessel called the "Yankee." "Doctor blades" are then used to continuously scrape the sheet off the Yankee. After being removed from the Yankee, the sheet passes between large, solid-steel calender rolls to adjust its thickness. At that point, it is split into two separate rolls and wound onto heavy cardboard cores at the machine's reel, or dry end.

There are plenty of things to monitor, especially if a machine is acting up. Even though computers control much of today's papermaking process, hands-on quality testing is ongoing for the work crew. The different pulps are checked in several ways by the pulp lab before being fed into the machines. Paper samples are cut from the parent rolls every hour and brought to the lab for testing. All characteristics of the sheet are then monitored. The sheet's basis weight, caliper, color, dust contamination, moisture content, dirt, strength, softness, absorbency, and holes are all examined. Monitoring, controlling, and adjusting all of this can be a handful on a normal day. If a machine is acting especially finicky, the crew is in for a long, hot, dusty, noisy, sweaty, and frustrating shift.

At the dry end, heavy, hollow cardboard cores are kept handy on carts. On the 7 and 9 paper machines at the James River mill, the cores were ten inches in diameter and ninety-three inches in length. It was onto these cores that the final paper product is rolled. To replenish the supply of empty cores, the third or fourth hand goes to the core-storage area and returns with a cart loaded with cores.

To begin the actual papermaking process, two of these cores are placed end-to-end on a "reel spool shaft" and, as the dry paper product emerges from the machine, it is spun onto these two cores. Once the cores are full, the workers on the machine begin a process called a "turnover." The purpose of the turnover is to take the two full cores—now called "parent rolls"—off the machine and replace them with two more empty cores without disrupting the whole sequence.

The process goes just like that: an unrefined pulp slurry coming into one end of the machine and high-quality paper product coming out the other. A good crew operates like the well-oiled offense of a professional football team. Each player knows his role and knows what to expect from his teammates even without verbal communication. Although the exact procedures vary slightly from one paper machine to the next, the turnover process on the 7 and 9 machines, at least, were nearly identical.

About ninety seconds before the parent rolls are full, a blue warning light begins flashing to alert the crew. The fourth hand then has enough time to remove the empty core's adhesive-tape covering and place the core, or "reel spool," in the "saddle" so that the turnover can begin. A yellow light follows the blue one and tells the third hand to start the reel spool spinning. After the spool has spun for about thirty seconds, a green light begins flashing. This is the third hand's signal to lower the spinning spool onto the sheet on the reel drum. In essence, this procedure cuts the sheet from the full reel and automatically begins a new pair of parent rolls on the new reel spool.

Performing a smooth turnover can induce a spirit of ennui in a crew. For the third and fourth hands, the turnover process lasts about eight to ten minutes. After that, the crew has twenty minutes or so of waiting around for the next set of rolls to grow large enough to remove from the machine. Workers have various ways of dealing with the time between turnovers: using the restroom, getting something to eat or drink from the break room, or making a phone call. Sometimes they want to get away for a few minutes to visit a friend on another machine or in another area of the mill. For those that stay in the area of the machines, the control booths, called "coops," are a good place to pass the time.

Although all four members of the machine crews are required to be on the job at all times, it is permissible for them to take turns and leave the area for short periods of time, providing the job is running properly. In order to take such a leave, a crew member has to be caught up with his duties, make sure that none of the other crew members is gone, and then let at least one of them know that he was leaving. It is imperative that only one of the crew be away from a machine at any one time.

At James River, some guys had their own peculiar diversions. Some would exercise. Others would read. Some would go for walks. Because he was often gone from the paper-machine area between turnovers, Tom Monfils was one of the guys known as a wanderer. He liked to travel to other parts of the mill and check things out.

Watches and jewelry are not allowed on the mill floor. So no matter what workers do between turnovers, they have to have an internal clock or keep an eye on the clocks throughout the mill so they know when to get back to their area. If they do not, the entire applecart is upset, and the rest of the team has to scramble to cover the absent worker's responsibilities.

There are four crew members on a paper machine for a reason. Three can handle the job, but it is tough work. There are rare times—typically an extreme emergency—when a machine has to be operated by just three workers. It happened the day of Monfils's disappearance, when one guy was pulled off of each machine in order to conduct the search. However, working short-handed is so tough that a mill typically divides the missing worker's pay between the three coworkers who are assuming his duties. It is virtually impossible for a paper machine to operate with just two workers.

When things are going well, the job is pretty manageable, but there are also snafus with machines that occur unexpectedly. The crew has to be ready for them. The most common of these is a paper break, occurring when the paper literally breaks somewhere on the machine as it dries. Such breaks are caused by many different things: bad blades, dirty felts, bad wire, weak stock, or stock that is too wet or too dry or off-specification in some other way. Paper breaks are unpredictable and cause serious headaches and backaches. Once a machine starts having paper breaks, it sometimes continues for the better part of a shift.

If all has gone well, the finished parent rolls are picked up by lift trucks and hauled either to a storage room or directly to a "winder." These rolls are ninety-two inches wide and sixty inches in diameter, and they weigh up to a ton or more. If they are acceptable, these parent rolls then give birth, on the winder, to hundreds of thousands of offspring in the form of little rolls of toilet paper, paper toweling, or napkin packets. These are then wrapped, boxed, and hauled off to store shelves. If the parent roll does not meet standards, it is placed in a storage room. From there it is chopped up, put into a repulper machine, and fed back into the system a second time.

The rooms or buildings that house these machines are huge and sometimes cramped. At the James River plant, the 7 and 9 paper machines sat next to each other, end-to-end. The fact that the dry end of paper machine 7 was about twenty feet from the wet end of paper machine 9 was a source of problems on the floor. Plastic sheeting hung all around the wet end of the 9 machine to prevent its water spray from ruining the paper and paper cores at the dry end of the 7 machine.

Inside the Coop

Noise, grime, heat, and humidity are by-products of the paper machines's operation. The steamy atmosphere around the ones at the James River mill made it possible for a worker to wear shorts and a T-shirt, even in the dead of a Wisconsin winter. Tom Monfils was one of the guys known to dress this way year-round.

Because of the extreme conditions, Monfils and his coworkers often sought refuge inside the control room, or coop, of their respective machines. Also sometimes called "booths," the coops are much more than the name implies. For the workers, they are sanctuaries in the midst of the mill chaos. The rumble of the plant does not completely disappear inside them, but if a paper machine is humming along, a crew can monitor the papermaking process from inside the coop's relative comfort.

The entrance to each coop is actually a small room of its own called an "air lock." The air lock protects the electronic equipment inside the coop from the usual mill-floor conditions. Through the use of this two-door system, most of the heat, humidity, and dust can be kept outside. All workers have to do is open the first door, enter the air lock, shut the first door behind them, and then open the second door into the actual coop.

While the coops at James River were not large—about twelve by eighteen feet—they easily served as a quiet and comfortable break room for a half-dozen workers. In the mill's typical coop, console tables inside ran along three of the walls and left a walking space in the middle about four feet wide. Several chairs were typically distributed throughout the coop—three of them always parked in front of the computer monitors sitting on the console at the coop's front. The console ran the length of the coop right beneath a window. Looking out that window, workers could watch their respective paper machines. Two computer printers sat atop the console along the back wall. Below the printers was a bookshelf.

The coops were air-conditioned, primarily to protect the computers inside them, but the workers also benefited. Typically the coops were also equipped with a microwave, a coffeemaker, and a radio. There was also a telephone for mill-related use, though it was pretty common for workers to make and take personal calls. Each paper machine had its own telephone number, so family and friends could easily reach the workers without going through a central switchboard.

Inside these coops, somewhat removed from the distresses of the mill, the workers exchanged stories about work, life, their families, and their outside interests. The four-person crew, plus a visitor or two, could easily fit into the coops while hashing over personal or official company business. If need be, an additional chair or two could be pulled in from a room at the back of the coop. This back room was slightly larger than the coop itself and housed the actual mainframe computer as well as some basic maintenance items.

Just outside, somewhere in front of each coop, was a smoking table. Smoking was not allowed inside the coops or in many other parts of the mill. If a worker wanted to catch a smoke, he had to sit at the table. The area around the smoking table was clearly delineated—a five-foot-by-five-foot area of the floor was painted red and edged in safety yellow. A worker could sit at the smoking table out of harm's way, despite being in the general vicinity of the paper machine.

There were also small, portable, two-person booths near the reel end of each of the paper machines. These were about six feet by eight feet and were separate from the main control room. They were often referred to as the "small coop" or the "fourth-hand coop" because the lowest guy on the totem pole would sometimes find himself relegated there. Two guys could easily fit inside, but three became a crowd. These coops had served as retreats for the machine tenders and back tenders before the computers had come into play and the larger coops were needed. As a result, these small coops—originally a sign of prestige—were now a sign of low seniority. The small coop for paper machine 7 sat partially recessed into the wall, just north of the main coop. Just north of it was a "bubbler," or drinking fountain. The small 9 coop sat oddly out in the aisle past the main coop, at the north end of the 9 machine.

For most of the people who worked on the paper machines, the goal was simple: learn as much about the process as you could, and work your way through the ranks until you were a machine tender making top dollar. However, it was not just a matter of learning to sit on your behind better than the rest. The machines could be fickle, and the responsibility of overseeing the machine and the crew through the papermaking process could be a heavy one, especially on some days. Every change in the product you were producing and every change in your crew increased the variables that affected product quality. If you could not control those, you certainly would not find your crew setting any production records, and that would reflect on you as a machine tender.

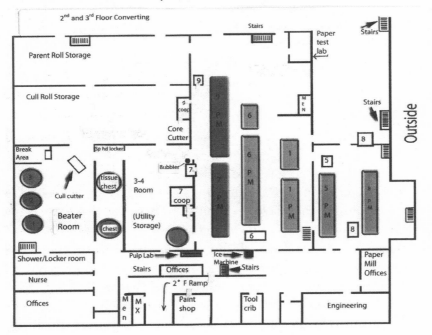

The second-floor area of the James River mill. Tom Monfils's body was found in the tissue chest near the beater room. The paper machines are to the right. (Top of diagram is north.)

6

Two Ships Colliding:
Kutska and Monfils

Kutska was just being Kutska. He didn't want Tom to suffer and die. He wanted Tom to live and suffer.

—Mike Piaskowski

After punching out at the mill on Friday, November 20, Keith Kutska drove the dozen or so blocks across downtown Green Bay to the police station. There he secured his audiotape copy of Tom Monfils's anonymous phone call. In essence the Green Bay police had handed him his gold cup.

After eagerly listening to the tape that night, Kutska could barely sleep. By very early the next morning, he was at work, tape in hand, playing it for everyone who would give it a listen. His main objective, however, was to play the tape for Monfils himself and to get an admission from Monfils that he had indeed made the anonymous call recorded on the tape.

Because both Monfils and Mike Piaskowski were working on paper machine 7 the next day, Kutska figured the logical place to play the tape for Monfils was the coop at paper machine 7. There, he would have Randy Lepak join them from his job on paper machine 8.

Kutska had the tape. Next, he would get the admission he was seeking.

Nothing to Live For

Did Tom Monfils have reason to fear Keith Kutska to the extent he did? He had described Kutska as a "biker-type" and suggested that Kutska "had nothing to live for." But what did that mean? Kutska was forty-one years old. According to his Green Bay police information sheet, his nickname was "Mex." To some, he did have the look of an overweight Mexican bandit: He had dark features and a full, droopy mustache. He stood an even six-feet tall and weighed 240 pounds. He was described as "stocky" on the police sheet. His upper left arm boasted a homemade tattoo that read "Born to Win" over a couple of dice.

As far as having "nothing to live for," that was obviously a dubious interpretation on Monfils's part. Kutska owned an old farm and thirty-six acres of land at 3079 Wilson Road in Abrams, where he lived with his wife, Ardis, and his son, Clayton. He also owned a rental house in Suamico, another small town about halfway between Abrams and Green Bay. Kutska had been born and raised in Green Bay and started working as a teen. He was a knowledgeable, avid amateur astronomer and read books on history and philosophy. He encouraged and supported his wife's interest in horses and took his wife and son camping. He liked to fish and drink beer. He was proud of his home stereo system and enjoyed listening to music, especially classic rock.

His interest in politics did set him apart from many of the other mill workers. He definitely leaned left on most issues. He had once dogged former Eighth District Republican Congressman Toby Roth down Green Bay's Walnut Street during a Labor Day parade, shouting to Roth, "Tell the people your voting record on labor, Toby. Tell them your record." It gave Kutska great pleasure that Roth disappeared from politics soon afterward.

Kutska was active in the union and often lamented the lack of attendance at union meetings. It ticked him off when members showed up in droves to vote on a new contract but left the more humdrum union business to someone else. Kutska admitted that he liked to "shake the level" at the workplace when it came to labor-management relations. Once, when posing for a performance award picture, he tried cajoling mill superintendent Bob Thut into wearing a union T-shirt for the photograph. He would also show up at open management meetings wearing a Greenpeace T-shirt, knowing full well that the paper industry and the environmental group often butted heads on pollution issues.

Kutska was not timid. But suggesting he had nothing to live for was more than a stretch and a matter of peculiar perspective. Still, Kutska was a lightning rod of workplace opinion. Descriptions of him generally ran the gamut, reflecting more on the speaker's vocabulary than on any exact assessment of Kutska. Some people merely called him a bully; others said he was an intimidator. Still others said he liked to create situations and then sit back and watch them unfold. Piaskowski said he "could see other guys calling Kutska a bully, but mostly because he liked to play mind games with people."

Whether Tom Monfils sensed it during the week of November 16 or not, Kutska suspected him of making the call. David Webster remembered that on Monday, November 16, he and Kutska had run down the list of possibilities. They had narrowed it down to two— Jerry "Buck" Herman or Monfils. "We decided it was probably Tom," Webster remembered.

According to Dennis Servais, another worker, Kutska had told him on Tuesday that he wanted to say something about seeking a copy of the tape in front of Monfils, just to gauge his reaction. But Servais also remembered that Monfils showed no reaction when Kutska mentioned this in front of Monfils.

It was odd then that Mike Hirn described a reticent Kutska the day before he got the tape. Hirn recalled that Kutska said he had ideas about who had made the call, but that he was not going to say who he thought it was. "That," Kutska told Hirn, "would be just like the person that called ... accusing people without having proof." Kutska also told Hirn that he had secured an attorney and that he was talking to someone at the police department about getting a copy of the tape.

Catch-22

On the surface it would seem that Tom Monfils and Keith Kutska represented different parts of the human spectrum. One need not look further than the audiotape itself and the circumstances surrounding it to see that. Monfils had made an anonymous call. He had gone outside the chain of command at the mill to do so. He even refused the suggestion from the police to contact mill security personnel himself.

If the scenario had played out perfectly, Monfils would have sat back and watched Kutska take the fall for his theft, including possibly losing his job. And in all likelihood Monfils might never have said a word about it to anyone. According to his wife, Susan, he had never even told her that he had made the call, although he had told her about Kutska's encounter at the gatehouse and his getting suspended from work. She recalled that he had gone on to speculate about what "kind of person would do that [make a call to report Kutska]."

The day of his disappearance, Monfils's father, Ed, told Detective Sergeant Chic that Tom had definitely crossed some lines of protocol "by calling the police about another employee that may have stolen something from the plant." Ed Monfils also stated, "Tom is the kind of person that if confronted with a situation like this morning, would possibly just take off for a period of time to cool off."

Susan Monfils also offered that same scenario early in her husband's disappearance. The morning of Sunday, November 21, she told Detective Baudhuin that Tom was the kind of person "who dislikes arguments. He would rather leave and drive around for a short period of time and return when he was settled down." She also told Baudhuin that her husband had found himself in a "Catch-22" situation. Since he had reported a fellow union member for theft, she thought he would be kicked out of the union. Then, because James River was a closed union shop, he could no longer work there.

Obviously, Monfils had not left the mill to cool off or to settle down. But immediately after his disappearance, this was the most optimistic of all possible scenarios for his family. They were holding out hope. The father's description of his son and the wife's description of her husband both seemed to confirm one idea: that facing the pressures coming to bear on him that morning, Tom would not have stayed on the job.

The following morning, Susan described her husband as "an ideal father and husband." But she also told police that she was not absolutely certain that he would not have harmed himself over the situation he was now facing. "It is possible," she told police, "because his life is the mill."

Susan also told police that she was unsure if someone would try to hurt her husband because of the tape incident. She felt, she said, that "everyone at the mill would understand Tom's motives" and that "he had friends at the mill." She still had her doubts that it was even her husband's voice on that tape. When she and her mother-in-law had first heard it the previous afternoon, she had thought that the voice did not sound like Tom's. On the other hand, Joan Monfils, Tom's mother, had been quite sure the voice was that of her son.

The police then asked Susan if her husband might have had a girlfriend and if he might be hiding out at her house. She told them that they had a solid marriage, that Tom was not having an affair.

The idea that Tom Monfils had a plethora of friends at the mill is an issue worth exploring. Gregg Stephens, the pulp mill supervisor, suggested that Monfils was "close to only a small group of people, and he only got along with a small group." Stephens said Monfils "wasn't too well liked" because he handled his job duties in a way that was not always safe or sound and that went against the tried-and-true way of doing things. Coworker Jim Boucher said it flatly. "I didn't like Tom, I'll admit that. He was very irresponsible in his work. He would screw around."

Susan had named Carl Stencil as one of Monfils's friends, but Stencil had a slightly different view. "I was a machine tender and he was a fourth hand, and I would tell Tom to do something and he would just refuse," said Stencil. "He would say things to me like 'Things are changing around here, Carl. Pretty soon you'll be the fourth hand and I'll be the machine tender.'"

Steve Moesch was a "spare hand," one of the newer employees who filled in as needed. He said he liked Monfils. They "had a lot in common," Moesch said. They both had two children, both did not drink, and both liked to work on their houses. "Monfils never had problems with anyone," Moesch stated, "and he was well liked." Moesch would fill in for Monfils on paper machine 7 following Monfils's death.

Cindy Huth, who worked in the beater room, also liked Monfils. Following his death, she was very upset, said Stephens, because she had failed to warn Monfils of the approaching storm over the tape.

The question of whether Monfils would commit suicide over the tape incident and the fallout from it is an important one, an obvious watershed. At the onset the camps split decisively one way or the other. Many workers said suicide was possible, even likely. Others—those who might have been referred to as Tom's "friends at the mill"—said, "no way!"

Jim Seidl, a back tender on paper machine 5, described Monfils as "very diabolical." He said he was sure that Monfils had taken his own life. He referred to the fact that Monfils had been in the Coast Guard and that he knew how to tie the knots on the rope that connected his neck to the weight. Seidl said that Monfils "was smart enough to know that he would have to sink to the bottom and that's why he used the weight, so he would sink and not attempt stopping the suicide."

Seidl said that he had worked with Monfils for eleven years and "knew him well." He also spoke of Monfils's mixed-up priorities, saying that Monfils's job was "first on his list," with his children probably fourth and his wife fifth. Seidl said that Monfils was a "brownnoser and would tell on his fellow workers—most all the employees knew about this."

Don Boulanger, who was working as a back tender on the 9 machine the morning of Monfils's disappearance, also felt it was suicide. Boulanger told police that following the playing of the tape that morning "Tom flipped and killed himself. Life would have been miserable if he had stayed there [at the mill]." Others, like Randy Wisniewski and Randy Lepak, thought Monfils "just cracked."

Every mill worker—whether they knew Monfils well or not—seemed to hold an opinion on the subject of whether or not he had taken his own life. The two camps seemed to split about fifty-fifty.

Born to Win

Unlike Monfils, Kutska was right there, in everyone's face—right or wrong. He was no crouching tiger. He was no mystery either. He had thumbed his nose at the mill's scrap-pass policy and he had gotten caught. At first, he told everyone that he had not taken the contraband electrical wire and had been wrongly accused. He was the victim. Some of his first thoughts following his suspension meeting were to find out just how this had happened to him. He was righteously indignant.

When he came back from his suspension, he was not contrite. According to Kutska, he was the one who had been abused. He wanted to know exactly what happened that day as he left work. He went to the police hoping to get a copy of the call. He was going to contact a lawyer and fight this thing. He sure was not going to shrink back into the wall and forget about this. Not Kutska. When you are "Born to Win," you make lemonade out of your lemons, spoiled or not.

Kutska knew that the mill scrap policy was not so sacrosanct in the first place. Plenty of guys had a raincoat, or a piece of felt, or some stainless steel nuts and bolts at home, items they had procured from the mill. Not every item had been cleared to take home under mill scrap policy, you could bet on that. Stories of mill supervisors and managers parking their cars inside the mill compound and driving out with a trunk full of surreptitiously gathered paper products were not so uncommon either. Situations like the stainless-steel electric fish-scalers being turned out by one of the maintenance departments (for workers and managers alike), using parts gratis from the mill, were another story. So if you were Kutska, you had to wonder why the whole scrap-policy thing had come down on your head alone.

But Kutska was Kutska. Many people in the same situation would just bite the bullet. They would have accepted their discipline, wiped the sweat from their brow, and shut their mouths. Sure the whole thing sucked. Most people would have told themselves, "Oh, well, live and learn." Why push the thing any further? Most people would have seen it that way. But not Keith Kutska.

His wife described him as a "very up-front person" who confronted his problems. It was one of the reasons, she said, that he could not understand someone operating behind his back. If that person had a problem with him, he should have come right to him or gone through the mill's chain of command, not gone outside the mill to the police. Well, here was a problem for Kutska: a suspension resulting in the loss of five-days's pay, and he was dead set on confronting it. The way Kutska described it, he had "a right to know just who his accuser was."

As far as his work ethic went, Kutska went by the book. If a task could be found on his job description, he would do it and do it well. If it was not, he did not break a sweat getting to it. He would tell you, straight up, that it was not his responsibility—that it was someone else's job, and he was not about to take away another person's opportunity to make a living. He was not a Boy Scout, and he did not pretend to be.

Kutska was never cited for doing a lousy job, but he also did not win any medals for his mill-floor leadership or esprit de corps either. With Kutska, it seemed, it was a case of "what you see is what you get."

But maybe Keith Kutska was not the up-front person his wife wanted to believe. On the mill floor, he had a reputation as a "manipulator," a guy who liked to start something and then step back and let it play out. Some called him calculating and bent on revenge. He was not always so brutally honest either. After all, he was telling everyone outright, or letting them believe, that he did not take anything out of the mill that day. Several mill employees recalled banter they had with Kutska where he skirted around the issue of whether or not he was actually taking something. Piaskowski recalled strongly that Kutska had led him to believe the accusations made by Monfils on the tape were false.

Supervisor Bill Czaja remembered stopping by Kutska to ask him "how he'd enjoyed his days off," referring to Kutska's suspension. He said he was "giving Keith the berries for losing time for not showing what was in his bag." Kutska let Czaja believe that he was not stealing anything, but Czaja later told police he did not actually believe that.

Czaja also recalled Kutska telling him on Friday that the extension cord incident "wasn't over yet." When Czaja asked him what he meant, Kutska said Czaja would "find out next week." Czaja would be up north deer hunting, he told Kutska, so Kutska said he would find out when he got back. Czaja said he figured Kutska was going to pull something like messing up an already overloaded work schedule by calling in sick on deer-hunting weekend. Whatever Kutska had up his sleeve, Czaja figured he would hear "what type of prank he pulled over the weekend." Czaja also stated that most people would not pull anything on Kutska because they knew he would get back at them.

Coworker Tim Swiecichowski had an interesting exchange with Kutska in the parking lot outside of the mill regarding the purloined electrical cord. "Everybody knows you took the cord," Swiecichowski told him.

"Oh yeah! How's that?" Kutska asked.

"Because otherwise you would have opened your bag," Swiecichowski said. Kutska chuckled a little and walked away.

Monfils's Motivations

So the two of them, Kutska and Monfils, seemed to be very different from one another—one operating behind the scenes and the other making scenes. But what prompted Monfils to set out to get Kutska anonymously? Were Monfils's actions really those of a dedicated employee concerned over a piece of stolen electrical cord? Did Monfils have such a straitlaced objection to another worker violating the mill scrap policy? Was Kutska that much of a menace? Maybe that machismo of Kutska's was a part of the answer. Monfils's description of him during his calls to police suggests that, so does his reference to a "past history" between the two of them.

The exact reason or reasons that Tom Monfils made his original call to police on Tuesday, November 10, 1992, will never be known. His only other words on the subject came just minutes before his disappearance when he said he had "a stake in the company" and "a future to be concerned about." Several workers have speculated that it may well have revolved around an upcoming union vote on a shift change. No one knew, or will ever know, for sure.

Monfils was known as something of a "company guy." Some of his coworkers saw this attitude as a little bit over the top, especially from a guy who sometimes neglected his bottom-of-the-totem-pole fourth hand duties while assuming the third hand or back tender job. Still, more than one person referred to Monfils's strong dedication to his employer.

In a similar vein, when it came to union involvement, Monfils was not at the front of the line. He saw himself as something of an independent operator, earning his own way through the ranks of the paper machine hierarchy. One coworker said that he felt Monfils considered the union as "more of a necessary evil."

Coworker Jim Boucher had worked with Monfils for almost four years on paper machine 7 as third and fourth hands, respectively. Boucher eventually transferred from machine 7 to the engineering department. One of the reasons, said Boucher, was that "I wanted to get away from Tom Monfils." Boucher said he had a strong negative reaction when he read in the newspaper that Monfils was a "dedicated employee."

Boucher recalled Monfils himself skirting the mill scrap policy.

Once, both of them had gathered together some mill materials to use as exercise equipment between turnovers. Boucher remembered that Monfils had snatched up "a shaft and some green gears" for weights on one of his walks around the mill. Boucher himself had scrounged some ropes from a felt roll. With some pieces of PVC pipe for handles, Boucher fashioned some jump ropes. The jump rope he made for Monfils would end up tied to Monfils's neck and the weight at the bottom of the tissue chest.

Following his death, the media would take the label of "company guy" and turn it into "martyr who died because of his dedication to his employer." Not everyone agreed with the assessment. One worker, who had spent time working on the paper machines with Monfils, said:

> Monfils was being way less than candid when he said
> the reason he made the call was because he had "a stake
> in the company and a future to be concerned about."
> Tom had a reputation for going into the maintenance
> shops at night and making up "government projects" to
> take home. That's probably the reason he had to make
> his call to the police anonymously.

Another small infraction of company policy involved the place where Monfils parked his car, particularly in winter. The parking lot closest to the front gate ran along the west side of a small Quonset hut. The parking spots along the building itself were set up with electrical outlets for the engine heaters of the company cars, not for those of employee vehicles. Still, whenever he could, Monfils parked there so that he could plug in his heater, all free of charge. Just like the company cars that were parked there, he would leave his car unlocked and his keys inside in case it had to be moved. The gatehouse was just a hundred feet away and within easy view of the guards through a TV monitor. This is where Monfils's car was parked on the cold and blustery morning of November 21, 1992.

Monfils's sense of humor was inconsistent and sometimes way over the top. Mike Piaskowski recalled a time when he bought the wrong scope for a new hunting rifle, and Monfils decided to rib him about it. From around the mill, Monfils picked up parts and rigged up an oversized replica. He called it "Pie's scope" and hung it on the wall in coop 7.

But there was also a side to Monfils's humor that was hard to explain. It probably spun out of the same spot as his Piaskowski-scope joke, but it was much darker. He would post newspaper articles of other guy's misfortunes on employee bulletin boards. If a coworker had a drunk-driving conviction, Monfils would copy the newspaper article and post it in some of the machine control rooms with added commentary.

When Steve Stein and his wife, Jean, who also worked at James River, had a premature baby, the story of the child's fortunate survival and happy homecoming was featured in the *Green Bay Press-Gazette*. Monfils took the story as it appeared and made some hurtful alterations. Following that incident, Stein suggested that Monfils "was in dire need of psychiatric help." In fact, the incident did come to the attention of mill authorities, and Monfils faced serious disciplinary action for it. It was Stein himself who stepped in, probably saving Monfils's job. Stein suggested that instead of firing Monfils, the mill should "just make sure he got some help."

A gibe toward a fellow worker over his hunting scope is one thing, a jab at a fellow worker over his premature daughter is quite another. One of the jokes was an attempt to fit in—to reach out to a coworker with some personal license earned through equanimity and friendship, to tease. The other was difficult to understand or explain on any level.

One coworker said that in general Monfils's sense of humor seemed to lack much compassion for others. Yet many of his supporters cited Monfils's frequent acts of compassion as one of the distinguishing parts of his character.

As with most other people, Monfils had his quirks, both those related to his work habits and to his personality. As with most other people, he skirted mill policies when it was to his advantage. None of these quirks were so egregious that they should have led to his death, but he also was not the Boy Scout that many made him out to be after his tragic fate. If the *Press-Gazette* was guilty of victim glorification, they were not alone. A *Milwaukee Magazine* article painted a picture of Monfils as someone with just one fault—that of being overly zealous when it came to the well-being of his family, his community, his employer, and his fellow human beings. It was unnecessary to trash Monfils following his death, but nominating him to sainthood was not a fair or balanced picture either. He was a person—just like all individuals—revered by some and criticized by others.

In the end it seems clear that Kutska and Monfils were your usual mix of character strengths and human failings, of things to be lauded and foibles needing attention. It was Steve Stein who suggested that they were actually "a lot alike." If that was the case, then Monfils's anonymous call took on some intriguing twists.

Circadian Rhythms

When the police handed Keith Kutska the tape of Tom Monfils's anonymous phone call, they handed him the key to Pandora's Box. But was this whole thing over a simple personality clash? The audiotape's contents were certainly enough to send one of the ships, Kutska, banging into the other.

In retrospect, however, there may well have been some additional underlying threads to the tension between the two. These were strains that had little to do with an anonymous phone call or a hunk of electrical cord. Maybe the call and the cord were mere catalysts that brought something else to the boiling point. Maybe Monfils had simply had it with Kutska's mill-floor antics and abuses—the past history he had described to Lieutenant LaTour. If so, with a simple phone call, the stolen cord could be used to figuratively hang Kutska. But no other workers ever pinpointed a specific incident between the two that explained Monfils's reasons for making his call.

Is it possible that the whole situation had a lot more to do with circadian rhythms? Is it possible that Kutska and Monfils were simply the opposing battery terminals between which the sparks of contention would fly?

Jim Graves, a worker at James River, felt certain that the battle between the two men was really just a clash of opinions over a work-schedule change that was looming on the horizon. For months, the mill had been engaged in an effort to upgrade the quality of the working conditions—including work hours and schedules. Some jarring changes lay ahead.

In order to keep the machines running, the mill's papermaking operation had four crews, A, B, C, and D. One crew was always off, and the other three broke the twenty-four-hour day into three eight-hour stints. The four crews then rotated through the shifts. Working these "swing" shifts, a worker could find himself getting lost in his own work schedule. In a month's rotation, a worker would find himself working every one of the three shifts.

The harmful effects of shift work on a person's natural, or "circadian," rhythms are well documented. British and U.S. studies have shown a long-term impact on the physical health of workers who slog through a life of changing work shifts, especially the increased risk of getting several forms of cancer as well as stomach problems and heart disease. Most striking, however, is the significant impairment to shift workers's mental and emotional health. These studies have shown that such workers suffer from "increased irritability and moodiness and being overly emotional, sensitive, and defensive." The negative effects were especially noticeable in workers pulling night-shift duty. Was it possible that James River employees were predisposed to a volatile situation coming to a head?

James River was certainly aware that changes had to be made. Many of the mill employees, including Mike Piaskowski, had been working on a "quality of work life" effort, a project once known as E.I. (Employee Involvement). The effort was a joint company and union program created to resolve production and work-life issues. For almost a year, Piaskowski served as the program's facilitator. One of the larger problems the group tackled was how best to run a continuous manufacturing operation without impairing the workers. The group examined every idea that was put on the table.

Piaskowski recalled his group's analysis.

> We looked at as many as fifty-two different ways of running a manufacturing operation twenty-four hours a day, three hundred and sixty-five days a year. A university had done some research on this and we reviewed their findings. They had studied all aspects of swing shift design. Everything, from what time the shifts started, to which direction the shifts rotated, to when days off were needed, to how many days in a row were necessary, and how all of this effected everyday life.
>
> What we found, based on that university study, was that, when they ranked all of the various shift

possibilities, the two "southern swing shift" rotations that we were using at James River were listed second to last and dead last. They were the absolute worst for a person's physical health, mental health, family health and the health of your marriage.

James River was considering chucking its southern swing shift and adopting a schedule of four twelve-hour days, more commonly known as "four-on, four-off." This was a life-changing proposal that became a major point of debate throughout the mill. Most of the younger workers liked the idea. Recognizing the benefit of more days off, they viewed it as an opportunity to follow more interests outside of work. Many, like Monfils, had young families at home, and they saw the change as an opportunity to spend more time with them. Some coworkers suggested that Monfils also liked the change because it would free up more of his time for work on his rental properties. Those opposed to the change tended to be older workers, like Kutska. These individuals had adjusted their lives to the present system, accepted the routine, and they were not looking for any disruptions.

The arguing back and forth over the switch occupied the workers for months. At one point Jim Graves referred to it as a "war of words." Kutska's opposition to the possible shift change struck Piaskowski as odd. "I was surprised to hear that Kutska didn't want it," Piaskowski said. "And I was lobbying hard to him whenever the conversation came up, saying, 'You're crazy, why wouldn't you want it? Your travel to and from the mill is reduced by a third. And all that travel time doesn't become work time, it becomes free time.'" More than once, Piaskowski called Kutska "goofy" for not wanting the change. "With the time you spend traveling to and from work, you'd benefit from it more than most," he told him.

Piaskowski could not say exactly why Kutska was opposed to the change. After all, Kutska had about a thirty-minute drive each way between his home in Abrams and the James River plant. "Maybe he just didn't like the twelve hours," Piaskowski would later speculate. "When you end up working your butt off because nothing goes right, twelve hours can be an awfully long day. But then again, maybe he was just set in his ways." Kutska's wife said she thought that because he had broken both his ankles in the past, twelve hours on his feet would be too much.

All the guessing aside, Kutska explained it differently. He did not like the idea of giving an inch to management. He said he could see abuses, especially if someone's relief partner could not come in and he would have to stay extra hours or an extra shift on top of the twelve hours he had just worked.

Like Piaskowski, Monfils liked the proposal, and he lobbied hard for it on the mill floor. In pushing the idea, however, he found himself juxtaposed against a "biker-type" like Kutska on the issue, and it did not put Monfils in a good spot. Monfils was not Piaskowski, who could call Kutska straight-up "goofy." He had far too little seniority—both in years and mill-floor moxie—to spar one-on-one with Kutska.

Union Charges

Much has been made of the strength of the union at the James River plant. Following the police and prosecution's line of thinking, immediately after news of the Monfils tape spread through the mill, the union was somehow strong and cohesive enough for Monfils's coworkers to form a mob, rough him up, realize their mistake, cover their tracks by getting the weight and the rope, and haul his body to a tissue chest two buildings away. And then they would remain completely close-mouthed about their actions for fifteen years and counting. Also, other workers—not directly involved in these actions—would have had to look the other way while all this was taking place. Incredibly that whole line of thought is still held by some today. The impossibility of all this is borne out in the time lines found in appendices II and III.

Actually there were two unions at the time of the incident, Local 213 and Local 327, both belonging to the UPIU (United Paperworkers International Union). Local 327 solely represented the paper-machine department employees. Local 213 covered the converting, shipping, pulp, and maintenance departments—basically the rest of the mill. As far as the actual dedication to either of these unions went for the average mill worker, the issue settled primarily along the lines of how a person felt about unions in the first place. Actual dedication to either of these unions was about as varied as their members.

To this day there are people who contend that this was a union killing, plain and simple. They further suggest that the six men who went off to prison for the crime are operating under a union code of silence. That is, of course, nonsense. That notion of a code of silence is itself an interesting thing. Would that be a voluntary code or one that was forced on the men? If it were voluntary, why would any of them remain silent any longer than he had to before it destroyed his life? If it is forced, then the long and vindictive arm of the union must be responsible.

Is it possible for a union to exert that kind of pressure on guys who are sitting in prison? Those who theorize about one-world governments and some kind of subversive, universal brotherhood of laborers would say yes. Those with a better grip on reality would laugh. In 1990 the workers running the paper machines paid about $18 a month in union dues, a sum that provided a modicum of protection in terms of wages, hours, and conditions of employment. It was hardly a relationship sealed in blood. Based on interviews with many people who still work at the mill, that union-conspiracy-to-commit-murder theory is about as ridiculous as it gets.

At the time union leadership consisted of a local president, vice president, secretary, and treasurer. Local 213 had shop stewards who mitigated mill-floor gripes, while local 327 did not. Certainly different union presidents approached the job differently. Mike Piaskowski saw Marlyn Charles as a "50/50 guy"—a president who was fifty percent pro-union and fifty percent pro-company. That was, said Piaskowski, a departure from his predecessor, Francis "Butch" Belleau, who was much more pro-union.

The question of union strength aside, on the evening of Friday, November 20, 1992, Keith Kutska had the audiotape of Tom Monfils's call to the police, which had been handed to him by the GBPD. There was something in the air that was far more immediate and dangerous than a debate over shift changes or union brotherhood. Kutska felt he had been wronged to the tune of $800, and he was going to get his revenge, not by hurting someone but by hitting him or her where it hurt—in the pocketbook. That was an eye-for-an-eye. He wanted to press union charges and see where it took him and his now-known adversary, Monfils. The union could try to fine Monfils, maybe even blackball him. There was even a possibility that Monfils would lose his union card and therefore his job.

Kutska's Plan

With these thoughts racing through his head that Friday evening, Kutska needed a mobile means of playing the tape at the mill the next morning. At the very least, he was going to have to bring it for Marlyn Charles. He tried a portable cassette player that belonged to his son, Clayton, but he could not get it to work.

At that point, Kutska called his friend Brian Kellner, who also worked at James River. Kellner lived right down the road, on the other side of the little town of Abrams. He and his wife, Verna, were friends with Kutska and his wife. Kutska asked Kellner if he had a small cassette player. Kellner did. So Kutska jumped into his pickup truck and went over to Kellner's house. Here was an opportunity to finally share his prize with someone else. With his two friends, he popped the tape into Kellner's cassette player and hit "Play" once more.

Verna did not know the guys from the mill that well, so she was unsure of just whose voice it was. She agreed that it could be "Tommy" Monfils. Brian debated with Kutska a little about just whose voice it was. Finally, he agreed that it was Monfils's.

Soon afterward Kutska left for home with the cassette player. Once home Kutska set out to contact Marlyn Charles. He had his culprit. Now it was time to hold Monfils accountable, thought Kutska, and his first move was to enlist the union's help. He called Charles and played the tape for him without telling him whose voice he thought it was. When asked, Charles suggested the voice was that of Monfils. Kutska concurred.

Kutska said he wanted to "file union charges" against Monfils. That is exactly how he put it. Based on his conversation with Charles, Kutska planned to get an admission from Monfils at work the next day. Kutska said he would play the tape for Monfils in front of some of the other guys. Charles agreed with him, suggesting that it would be best if Kutska had two or three witnesses if Monfils admitted that he had made the call.

Kutska also called his buddy Jim Melville, another mill worker. Melville had been on vacation since late October, primarily to hunt for white-tailed deer. He returned home that night and had a phone message to call Kutska. He did. Kutska filled him in on the anonymous call and his suspension for not opening his laundry bag. Then he played the tape for Melville. Kutska asked Melville "whose voice it was." Melville was sure that it was Monfils's.

Then Kutska was on the phone to Piaskowski and Randy Lepak, who were nearing the end of their shifts at James River. Kutska contacted them in their coops—Lepak by paper machine 8 and Piaskowski by paper machine 7. Kutska knew they were both scheduled to work the next day, and he knew both of them well enough to ask them to be his two witnesses. Ironically both had been on vacation during the previous week when Kutska and Monfils had been in contact with the police about the release of the tape. Neither was aware of Monfils's telephone call to police until they returned to work. Both had heard rumors about Kutska's suspension. Over the phone Kutska played the tape for each of them, first to Lepak and then to Piaskowski.

Lepak said that "within three words" he knew the voice on the tape was that of Monfils. He was so certain that he told Kutska to "turn it off."

Kutska then played the tape for Piaskowski and asked him if he would "serve as a witness when he surprised Monfils with the tape" the next day. "Okay," Piaskowski told him, "but don't expect me to lie for you."

"Good," Kutska said. "That's exactly what I want."

Piaskowski hung up the phone and discussed the situation with coworker Dennis Servais, who was also in the 7 coop. Piaskowski told him that Kutska was looking for "two or three witnesses" when he played the tape for Monfils. Kutska already had Lepak lined up; Piaskowski thought that Servais would be the third witness since he would also be working on the 7 machine the next day.

It was all so convenient for Kutska. Even getting the tape had been a cakewalk. He was set as machine tender, lead man, on the 9 machine, while Piaskowski would be machine tender on the 7 unit. As third hand, Monfils would be working with Piaskowski, Servais, and Pete Delvoe. All Lepak had to do was stroll over from his job as back tender on machine 8.

Kutska's reasons for picking Piaskowski were pretty obvious to those that know "Pie." Besides the fact that he was working with Monfils, he was known as a levelheaded guy. He was also respected as an arbiter and a decision-maker. At the mill "Pie" was one of those guys who went beyond the routine and looked at the bigger picture. Through the years, along with being a fill-in foreman for a while, he was a constant and dependable volunteer for safety, production, and activity committees.

In fact it was a stroke of luck for Kutska that "Pie-oot-ski," as Kutska called him, would even be at the mill that Saturday morning. It was, after all, opening morning of the gun-deer season. By the time Kutska had contacted him at work the night before, most avid hunters like Piaskowski were well entrenched in their hunting camps up north, counting the hours until daybreak. But Piaskowski and his wife were having some difficulties, and he decided to volunteer to work, allowing some other worker time off to go hunting the next day. It would put more money in the family's bank account and keep him around home when he would normally have been off at deer camp.

Kutska's reasons for getting Lepak's help were probably a little more nefarious. Lepak and Kutska were pretty close—close enough to refer to one another as "friend." Each year around Memorial Day, they went on a fishing vacation. More important, Lepak—known as "Wimpy" on the mill floor—was also a big, burly guy. He stood over six feet tall and weighed three hundred pounds. His presence while Kutska played the tape for Monfils the next morning would certainly be helpful, even if he did not say much. Lepak would fill up a vital part of the physical space, shading Monfils's horizon while Kutska played the tape. There was even some word that the union itself had cautioned Lepak about using his size to "intimidate" other workers around issues like the upcoming vote on twelve-hour workdays.

Looking at it from the vantage point of a union arbitration hearing some nine months later, Lepak felt that he was being used by Kutska in his role as a witness that day. He was there for his size and his reputation as an intimidator. That was not, however, obvious to him at the time. Of course, that was Kutska's normal modus operandi—using someone to his own end. At the time Lepak felt he was "acting only as a witness for the union rules." Kutska was focused on that, on the action the union could take. There was, says Piaskowski, "no discussion of any kind about ever laying a hand on Tom."

A Talk with Tom

At home on Friday night, Kutska gained a bit of experience in playing the tape for his coworkers over the phone and gauging their reactions. He had a couple of goals related to the tape for Saturday morning. First, he wanted to present it as evidence for union purposes on an official level. Second, he wanted to use it as a statement of what he saw as Monfils's character. In pursuing union charges, he would have to get Monfils's admission that he had made the call to police, that it was his voice on the recording. In embarrassing Monfils, Kutska could exercise all the drama he wanted as he put the tape player down in front of the guys, created an air of mystery, and started the tape spinning.

Kutska had the tape. He had lined up his witnesses. He had an approximate time, and he had a basic plan for how it would unfold. He had been cautioned by Marlyn Charles the night before and again that morning not to shake Monfils down. If he were going to press union charges against Monfils, he would have to keep his cool and get a simple admission from Monfils that the voice on the tape was really his. The stage was set.

In his first in-depth interview with police following the discovery of Monfils's body, Kutska delineated his activities that morning. While much of what he told the police in that statement consisted of outright lies, half-truths, and omitted details, some parts of his statement can be relied upon for their veracity.

Kutska told police that once he "had the tape on Friday," he "couldn't sleep." By 4:35 the next morning, he was at the mill. He had gotten up at 4 a.m. and driven the twenty-one and a half miles from Abrams to the mill. Once there, he changed clothes and went to the 9 paper machine where he was to serve as machine tender.

Even though Kutska was set to work a 7 a.m. to 7 p.m. shift, it was fairly common practice at the mill for workers to relieve their partners about a half-hour early. On this particular morning, however, Kutska's partner, Jerry Puyleart, had plans to make it to the woods for the opening of deer-hunting season. Ostensibly, that is why Kutska reported for work much earlier than normal. For sure there was something else up his sleeve, a hidden agenda, the need to play the tape early and often for everyone who would listen. The suspense—created the previous week around whether he would actually procure the recording—simply heightened the drama. Naturally it also increased the size and intensity of his audience.

Also, by coming into work this early, he was able to play the tape for guys on the graveyard shift. On a normal day Kutska would have missed the opportunity to play the tape for many of them. But by the time the night crew punched out this particular morning, at least a dozen of them had heard the tape firsthand.

After arriving at paper machine 9, Kutska talked to Puyleart about the product to be run that day and the status of the machine. Puyleart told him that there had been "a problem with the weight of the paper." The sensor was not relaying information to the computer properly, so Kutska might have to run the machine manually. As a result, samples of the paper would have to be taken at each turnover and tested by the lab until the problem was solved.

Once he understood the situation with machine 9, Kutska went to the area of machine 8 to speak with Marlyn Charles. He had the tape with him. Kutska went to see him, he said, to ask Charles "what to do about the tape." This visit was also about parading his spoils to some of the others on the night shift.

Using another tape recorder in the 8 coop, Kutska made a copy of the tape for Charles. There were now two copies of the tape to be played for workers on the mill floor. Kutska remembered Jim Frisque, Charlie Hagerty, and Bob Brier being in the 8 coop at that point. Frisque was Kutska's union vice president, and Brier, who actually worked on machine 5, was treasurer. They all heard the tape at that point. Kutska then left the 8 coop and went back to his machine with the original tape in hand.

Back there Kutska met up with Don Boulanger, who was working as his back tender that day. Kutska told Boulanger that he needed a little favor. He was going to play the tape for Monfils, he said, and he needed someone to let him know when Monfils was inside the 7 coop after the 7 a.m. turnover. Although reluctant, Boulanger agreed to do it. He said he would either wave his hand or scratch his head as a sign.

Kutska then made another trip back to the 8 coop. He was checking in with Charles and with Lepak, who had just started his shift. At that point Charles gave Kutska an admonition: "Don't agitate or threaten him, just talk nice." Lepak remembered understanding that they would get in trouble if they threatened or harassed Monfils.

By the time Lepak and Piaskowski punched in at 6:07 and 6:10 a.m. respectively, Kutska had already created quite a stir with his tape and its double. Piaskowski remembered seeing Monfils coming in just behind him. Monfils's punch card read 6:11.

At 7:05 Lepak went to coop 9. Mike Johnson, an instrumentation mechanic, was inside. He had come to the coop because the 9 machine was still getting an erratic reading on its stock flow. Such a problem was not uncommon, but this particular morning it was difficult to determine whether the faulty read was a computer problem or a mechanical failure. With Lepak now present, Kutska played his tape once more so Johnson could hear it.

Lepak recalled Kutska's mood in general, saying he "was not hot or irate, only pissed." Both he and Kutska understood their advice from Charles—no threats and no intimidation, just a nice calm talk.

Now it was time to play the tape for the guy who had assumed the starring role on the voice track. Kutska and Lepak headed out of the 9 coop and stood for an instant just inside the doorway. Kutska was looking for Boulanger's signal. It was slow in coming.

There had been a paper break on the 7 machine, and the crew— Piaskowski, Monfils, and Pete Delvoe, who was fourth hand—had been pressed into service to address it. Usually this would be a task performed by Monfils, Delvoe, and Servais. Servais, however, was in the basement, the machine's lower level, doing his appointed rounds. So Piaskowski jumped into the fray in his place.

Boulanger was waiting for the 7 crew to get their machine back up to speed. Finally they did— Piaskowski and Monfils were now both inside the coop. Delvoe had gone to the 9 smoking table. When Boulanger gave his signal, Kutska and Lepak headed south toward the 7 coop. Kutska let Lepak enter first. That way, he would not spook Monfils by walking into the coop with a tape player in his hand.

Monfils was seated in the very first chair by the computers, nearest to the door, reading a newspaper. He had his knees propped up on the counter and the newspaper resting in his lap. He was facing slightly into the coop with his back toward the door.

Piaskowski had been seated well inside the 7 coop, two chairs past

Monfils. He had gotten to his feet and was just about to leave to do his rounds when Lepak entered. Lepak held out his hand in front of him, signaling for Piaskowski to stop. Piaskowski was surprised that Kutska was there so soon, but he knew what was up and took his seat again.

Lepak grabbed a chair along the back wall, alongside the door that went into the coop's back room. "Hey Pie," Lepak said as he sat down, "how's the divorce going? Gabe wants me to tell you that he's praying for you." Larry "Gabe" Goeben, another paper machine worker, was a religious guy who would sometimes offer a prayer of petition for his coworkers. It was just small talk on Lepak's part—a way to pass time until Kutska got inside the coop.

In an instant, Kutska entered. He took up a position next to the air-lock door.

Monfils seemed to pay no attention to the goings-on—even though Al DeBauche, one of the night-shift guys who had heard the tape, had warned Monfils that Kutska had the audiotape. It is possible that Monfils figured DeBauche was simply regurgitating scuttlebutt about Kutska wanting to get the tape—either that or DeBauche was out-and-out mistaken. After all, Monfils had been assured the previous afternoon by an assistant district attorney and the deputy chief of police that the tape was not going anywhere.

"Hey, Pie-oot-ski," Kutska said, "you'll never guess the name of this tune!" With that, Kutska put the tape player on the counter near Monfils and punched the Play button.

And play the tape did. In the middle of a noisy mill, the coop was suddenly as quiet as a snow-covered Wisconsin forest on a moonlit night. Quiet except for the sounds emanating from the cassette player.

There it was—Tom Monfils's voice, loud, and clear, and unmistakable. It was about 7:13. While the tape was playing, Lepak recalled the expression on Monfils's face as "indescribable, I'd never seen anything like it." Piaskowski remembers that "Tom looked dumbfounded." Despite DeBauche's warning, Monfils was completely shocked to be hearing the tape.

It was all very real now. Yes, Monfils knew he had contacted the police from work on November 10 to report Kutska for stealing, and he knew the call had been taped. He knew that Kutska had been working hard to get a copy of it.

But Monfils also knew that he had contacted the Green Bay Police Department five times after that. Both Patrick Hitt from the district attorney's office and Deputy Chief Jim Taylor from the GBPD had assured him the previous afternoon that the tape would not be released. Monfils must have thought, "There is no way they would give Kutska the tape after telling me they would not." But the fact that a copy of that tape was playing right here, right now, brought the whole thing into a terrible reality for Monfils. His world collapsed. It was no wonder he was dumbfounded—the authorities had lied to him. He was devastated.

"Why'd you do this to me?" Kutska asked Monfils. "That's your voice," Kutska said. "Why'd you do this to me?"

A few seconds ticked by.

"I expect an answer," Kutska said.

Another few seconds passed. By this time, Monfils had turned slightly to face Kutska.

"Well, what'd you gonna do, just sit there and stare at me all day?" Kutska asked.

"Yeah," Monfils spoke for the first time.

"Do you deny that it's you?" Kutska asked.

"No," Monfils replied.

"Do you admit that it's you?" Kutska was looking for the admission he had been seeking all along.

"What?" Monfils was buying himself some time to consider the vast expanse of his situation.

"Do you admit that it's you on the tape?" Kutska repeated.

"Yeah," Monfils said.

"What did I ever do to you to deserve this?" Kutska asked. "What'd you want to do this to me for? I've never done anything to you."

Monfils remained silent for a few seconds more and then said, "I have a stake in the company and a future to be concerned about."

Kutska could not bite into an innocuous explanation like that—he was not really open to any kind of an explanation, especially from Monfils.

"This is just malicious," Kutska said. "You made the call at ten minutes to five and at ten minutes after five, you and I were standing by number 9's head box, talking about cores on number 7 like good friends. If you had a problem and didn't like what I was doing you could have said something to [me, rather] than … [making the call]."

With that, Kutska was out the door of the coop, tape recorder in hand. He closed the door behind him, self-righteously indignant again. He was a kid leaving the principal's office after shifting the blame to another culprit and, in the process, taking himself off the hook. By securing the tape, playing it to his coworkers, and now getting Monfils's admission to making the call, Kutska told these authors he had "put Tom on Front Street."

Lepak and Piaskowski were still in the coop with Monfils, and they had their own dismay to express. "I can't fucking believe you would do that, Tom," Piaskowski told him. "We're friends. We're family here. We don't do those kinds of things to each other." With that, Piaskowski left the coop.

"You coulda cost Kutska his job," Lepak spit the words at him. "What a chicken-shit thing to do. You're just lucky it wasn't me, or I'd a fuckin' killed you." Then Lepak left.

The entire encounter had taken less than two minutes. In the 7 coop Monfils sat in exactly the position he had been in when the session began. He had turned his head back to its original position, the whole event spinning through his mind. Kutska *had* gotten the tape after all. All the promises Monfils had heard from the police about the tape not being released had faded into thin air. His workday had barely begun, and he was facing a paper mill's worth of grief for what he had done.

Outside the 7 coop, the rest of the mill workforce was engaged, some in making paper and some in discussing Monfils's admission to making the call. At some point he would have to make his way back out there. Another turnover was rapidly approaching, and as third hand he would have a lion's share of responsibility for getting the job done.

A little before 7:30, the turnover lights came on. A short while later, at 7:34, the turnover had been completed and logged. Monfils recorded the appropriate information on the end of the parent rolls that he and Pete Delvoe had just taken off the 7 machine.

About four minutes later, at about 7:38, lab technician Connie Jones saw a visibly shaken Monfils as she made her way toward the 9 coop. He was sitting on a stool near the weigh-sheet table by machine

7's dry end, where he had marked the rolls. He appeared to be "mentally processing," said Jones.

Once inside the 9 coop, Jones heard the tape and wondered aloud who the guy was who had made the call. Through the window of the coop, Kutska pointed Monfils out to her and some other workers. Jones was surprised to see that the man being pointed out was the same distressed guy she had just seen at the 7 weigh-sheet table.

This glimpse of Monfils, from an angle out the 9 coop window, was the last time anyone saw him anywhere near the paper machines. As Jones left the 9 coop heading back to her lab, she purposely looked for him but could not see him anywhere in the area.

By 7:45 it was obvious that Monfils had left the work area. For his three coworkers on the 7 machine, another turnover was looming. At about 7:56, Piaskowski contacted foreman Pat Ferarro, asking him if he knew where Monfils was since he was not at his workstation. The turnover was completed without him.

By 8:15, the search for Tom Monfils had started. By 8:45, that search was in full swing.

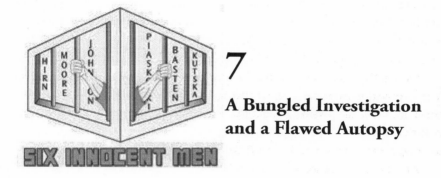

7

A Bungled Investigation
and a Flawed Autopsy

*I was there—the bubbler area was
never a crime scene. No such thing
ever took place. Whatever happened
to Tom had to have happened to him
someplace else.*

—Mike Piaskowski

Tom Monfils had vanished from his work area without much of a trace.
The ensuing all-out search would turn up some very odd things—all
of which suggested that he had not left the James River mill. His street
clothes hung in his workplace locker. His car remained parked just as
he had left it that morning, with the keys still in the ignition.

By Sunday evening, coworkers had found Monfils's body—
anchored at the bottom of the tissue chest by his own jump rope and a
forty-eight-pound weight. His body had been partially mutilated by an
agitator blade at the bottom of that chest. The police investigation—
begun as a "possible missing person report" the day before—was
now an investigation into that missing person's mysterious death. An

exacting search for the truth of what had happened to Monfils was in order. In fact, it was a rightful demand—an expectation of justice for the Monfils's family and for the Green Bay community.

But that is where things went terribly wrong. What happened next was not an unbiased, straightforward investigation into Monfils's death. Instead the fog of humiliation surrounding the Green Bay Police Department caused it to continually veer off the straightest path between Monfils's death and the answers surrounding that death. The police did not let the crime scene evidence and the evidence they would gather over their two-and-one-half-year investigation guide them to the truth. Instead they embarked on a narrow mission with Keith Kutska fixed firmly in their sights. In the process, the truth of what actually happened to Monfils would be lost.

The criminal justice annals are filled with examples of the police blindly pursuing a premature theory rather than testing the validity of that theory through investigation. It is why, nationally, over 125 innocent men on death row have been set free thanks to DNA analysis or other irrefutable evidence. In each of these cases, the police got it wrong—often by focusing their efforts on "getting their man." In each one, a district attorney then took that police work and prosecuted that person. Then a jury convicted that person, and at least one judge—and most likely several—upheld that conviction. Literally thousands of other felony cases have also been overturned for similar injustices after the authorities ventured in the wrong direction and never looked back.

The Monfils case is hardly the first or the last one in which an innocent person, while protesting their innocence, was sent to prison. However, given that there were six innocent people all protesting their innocence, this case reeks with incredulity.

The prosecutor, judge, and jury will get their share of scrutiny later in these pages. But the conviction of six innocent men began with a police investigation that was plodding and sluggish from the start. None of the initial facts came back to support the original police theory—that Keith Kutska had orchestrated and had been involved in the murder of Tom Monfils.

It would take some thirty-four months to construct a case against Kutska, because the preponderance of the evidence pointed away from his guilt, not toward it. In the process—from their questionable crime scene work to their overplayed melodrama during the men's arrests—certain members of the Green Bay police force would became major players in this injustice.

A Botched Crime Scene

Studies have shown that when the cause of death is presumed to be obvious—such as accident or suicide—some law enforcement officials have a tendency to remove the body right away in order to wrap up the case. In doing so, they jeopardize the opportunity for authorities to revisit the crime at some future date.

When it comes to investigating crime scenes, Anne Wingate, Ph.D., knows state-of-the-art police procedure. Wingate spent time as an officer attached to the Major Crime Scene Unit in Albany, Georgia, and as the head of the Identification and Crime Scene Unit in Plano, Texas. In her book *Scene of the Crime: A Writer's Guide to Crime-Scene Investigation,* Wingate suggests that there are twelve rules for investigators to follow when they arrive at the scene of a crime. One might call them the Twelve Commandments of Good Crime Scene Investigation. They are:

Rule # 1:   Don't touch anything.

Rule # 2:   Don't touch anything.

Rule # 3:   Don't touch anything.

Rule # 4:   Don't touch anything.

Rule # 5:   Don't touch anything.

Rule # 6:   Write everything down.

Rule # 7:   Write everything down.

Rule # 8:   Write everything down.

Rule # 9:   Write everything down.

Rule # 10:   Write everything down.

Rule # 11:   Isolate the witnesses.

Rule # 12:   Define the scene.

Obviously Wingate believes that the first "ten rules" are so important, so basic, and so fundamental that she repeats them—to near comic effect. But they speak seriously to the extreme caution that must govern every movement made by investigators at a crime scene. They sound ridiculous until one has actually considered the importance of following them. Let us apply Wingate's rules and speculate about what would be going through the mind of a crime scene investigator applying them.

Do not assume a thing. Let the evidence lead you. Do not, under any circumstances, let your foregone conclusions or your preconceived notions enter into your investigation. Let your natural skills of observation and your crime scene investigation training govern your every move. Even if you think you know what happened, do not go racing from the scene to a courtroom. Nothing is ever that obvious or clean. If you want to solve this crime, if you want to get the person or persons who did this, if you want to give justice to the victim and the community, then you had better do your absolute and unbiased best to determine the who, what, when, where, how, and why of the crime.

Before you begin to interact with the crime scene in any fashion, proceed with open eyes and an open mind. Do not affect one piece of evidence in any fashion. Observe all things carefully. Let your training guide you without emotionality. Then, when you think you have observed everything, look again, and again. Do not, in your eagerness to solve the crime, do anything that might harm your ability to prove the crime. Do not, in any way, impair your own ability to reconstruct the crime scene or to preserve vital evidence that you will need in making your case and prosecuting those who are responsible for the crime.

The proper treatment of a crime scene is such a crucial part of police work that it has its own title, "Crime Scene Protection." An expert on protecting a crime scene is D. H. Garrison, Jr., a crime scene technician with the Forensic Services Unit of the Grand Rapids, Michigan, Police Department. In an article in the *FBI Law Enforcement*

Bulletin, he asserts, "Ask crime scene technicians, to name the biggest problem that they encounter on the job and you will consistently hear the same response—crime scene contamination by curious officers, detectives, and supervisors."

Garrison writes that "widespread trampling of crime scenes can prove very damaging to investigations. Often, it results in several of the more sensitive forensic techniques—such as trace analysis, blood spatter interpretation, and DNA comparison—not being used to their fullest potential." For instance, Garrison cites the futility of crime scene technicians "collecting hair or fiber samples after a roomful of officers have shed all over the scene." He also states that "crime scenes often yield forensic evidence that leads to the apprehension of dangerous criminals. Perhaps just as often, though, potentially valuable evidence is destroyed or rendered useless by careless behavior at the crime scene."

One of Garrison's strongest concerns is that police departments establish strict, clear, written procedures governing "crimes scene protection and preservation" for their investigators. He also states that the example of senior detectives and supervisors is imperative in setting a tone within a police department for crime scene protocol. This is a role, he says, that "cannot be overstressed." Tragically the Green Bay Police Department had neither in place.

Why is all of this information about crime scene protection so important to Monfils's disappearance and death? Because anyone who values police science would be dismayed by the work of the Green Bay police at the James River mill the night of November 22, 1992. Thanks to the official police videotape of the event and the observations of mill workers present that evening, we can observe numerous violations of sound police protocol.

The workers present will not soon forget the experience. However, human memory, while helpful, can also be faulty and tainted. The mistakes made by the GBPD, documented on the very videotape they produced at the scene, though, are not likely to be misinterpreted. The police not only tainted the course of the rest of their investigation, they also made it virtually impossible for an unbiased investigation to get at the truth today. In essence, by their sloppiness that night, they ruined key evidence.

The first thing the videotape reveals is the appalling condition of

Monfils's body and the equally important idea that any person should have been subjected to a death as grizzly as this one. The scenes that show Monfils's body in the tissue chest and its subsequent removal are horrific. By the time it was sighted, his body had been submerged in watery paper pulp for about thirty-six hours. As it was removed, it was painfully clear that the body had been decimated by the agitator blades at the bottom of the chest.

Because of their strategic importance, however, the sloppy procedures of the Green Bay police at the crime scene are nearly as appalling. Thanks to their own video, the following failures are there for all to see.

- *Failure to assure the integrity of the crime scene.* Police jackets were thrown on, covered up, and disturbed areas with potentially important evidence within the crime scene. One mill worker said he was "shocked" to see a "bunch of cops leaning on the edge of the tissue chest, looking down at Monfils's body." This was, said the worker, "immediately after" the police had arrived on the scene. "I couldn't believe it," he said. "They were totally messing up the top edge of that tissue chest. What if there was evidence there? If so, they sure as heck were destroying it." The videotape confirms this worker's observation.

- *Failure to properly secure the crime scene and isolate witnesses.* Mill workers were used to initially secure the scene while the officers waited for detectives to arrive. One mill worker remembered being asked to close the doors to the crime scene area by a member of mill management because a crowd of onlookers had gathered just outside the open doorway leading to the tissue chest. Another worker remembered how nonchalant the cops seemed to be about what happened. "[The police] didn't ask us any questions; they were too busy watching everything, too." The videotape shows these same things.

- *Failure to use caution in the investigation.* The worst example of this was probably the futile attempts of the police to hoist Monfils's body out of the chest with a gaff hook tied to a rope—all the while doing some damage and risking more substantial damage to his corpse and the surrounding evidence. The videotape captures this travesty as well.

- *Failure to ascertain the exact circumstances regarding the body or to gather important evidence from the crime scene.* Given that Monfils had disappeared about 7:45 a.m. the previous day, his body could have been submerged for as long as thirty-six hours before it was finally removed from the tissue chest. Obviously the environment—the tissue chest and its contents—in which the body had spent more than a day and a half, contained vital information. The videotape does not show one investigator in the tissue chest conducting any kind of examination. The police records include no information from such an examination.

The police had failed to instantly secure the area or immediately isolate and interview potential witnesses. They had carelessly thrown their jackets around. They had disturbed the edge of the tissue chest without first checking for evidence. They had failed to examine and document the area around the body before attempting to move it. Believe it or not, curious mill workers—potential suspects—were asked to stand guard at the various entrances. No yellow police tape cordoned off the area until much later that evening.

The most egregious example of substandard investigative work that night was likely the useless attempts of the police to pull Monfils's body up and out of the chest with a gaff hook tied to a rope—a distance of nearly twenty feet. They had not even climbed down into the chest to ascertain the basic circumstances surrounding the victim before they began yanking on the body from above. Had they done a little investigating, they would have noticed the weight and rope tied around the neck and realized they would never be able to retrieve the body that way.

They had not even taken the time to consider using the large maintenance/emergency access port to retrieve the body. This was the door they ended up using, but only after their futile attempts to hook the body from above failed and they were forced to try something else. At one point during their gaffing attempts, the videotaping suddenly stopped. When it resumed, it shows that an emergency ladder had been dropped into the chest, but it was not used by the detectives to climb down into the chest and investigate the crime scene up close. Instead a second gaff hook had been placed into the waistband of Monfils's shorts because the first gaff hook had begun to straighten out from their ill-advised pulling.

Remember, this was the police video—not a video produced by someone who was trying to embarrass them. They were documenting their own work at the crime scene for the entire world to see. And what the entire world could see was some very careless crime scene work.

At no point did any member of the investigating unit climb down into the chest to take a sample of the watery pulp mixture. Nowhere does a record exist of the temperature or the chemical makeup of the contents of the tissue chest. This would have been important information in analyzing the condition of Tom Monfils's body. All the police did was watch the pulp as it spilled out of the vat and into the sewer.

At no point did anyone climb down into the chest to ascertain the relationship of the body to the agitator. This would have helped determine just how much damage its blades had done during the thirty-six hours the body was in the tank. Nowhere does a record exist of the exact measurements of the body in relation to the agitator blade that had clearly caused many of its injuries.

The police did not even remove the agitator for comparison testing—much less keep it for evidence. Their sole investigation into the extent of injuries caused by those blades consisted of pressing a piece of Styrofoam packing material (see photo, page 107) onto the edge of one of the blades—taking what would amount to a very inaccurate and partial impression of that edge. Monfils had sustained a major blow to the back of his head. Dependable impressions of the edges of all three of the blades would have gone a long way to resolve the very real possibility that the injury to the back of his head had been caused by an agitator blade. The Green Bay Police Department gathered none of this information. Instead they speculated about the existence of some mysterious or hypothetical weapon.

One has to wonder, "Where's that agitator today?" Surely it was eventually retrieved by the police at the order of the district attorney because of its key role in determining injury-comparison information. Certainly it is preserved in the GBPD evidence room—a significant piece of the forensics record.

No. That agitator was never removed. It is still down there at the bottom of that same pulp chest, its blades churning pulp slurry, possibly to this very day. Right there, at the very epicenter of this investigation, it continues to rotate at that very same 100 rpm— eerily symbolizing the many nagging questions in this unsolved case. Apparently the investigators at the crime scene that night were not adherents to "Locard's principle" either. That principle—highly valued by good investigators and forensics scientists—says, "Every contact leaves a trace."

When the Green Bay Police Department finished with their crime scene investigation, there was no going back. They failed to ascertain many important pieces of evidence, and they permanently damaged others. They failed to treat the crime scene with the care it demanded, and they failed to retain at least one key piece of evidence.

Did they do this because they walked into the crime scene with the idea that they knew what happened and how it happened? Mostly likely they did. More important to this case today, however, is the fact that their handling of the crime scene makes it impossible to go back and retrieve or revisit vital evidence that could point a finger in the right direction.

The agitator at the bottom of the tissue chest. Monfils's body was removed through the port on the left. The weight had settled into the sump, lower right.

This travesty of good investigative procedure does not end there. Failures at the crime scene quickly unfolded into failures at the autopsy. These initial failures upon failures, coupled with a "shared sense of guilt" concerning the release of the anonymous audiotape, created a mindset that shaped the entire investigation. The Green Bay authorities—charged with investigating Monfils's death and uncovering the truth of what happened to him—failed at their most important mission. All of this shoddy crime scene work can be explained by one thing: The police on the scene that night had their minds made up. Retrieving Monfils's body was a mere formality.

Steve Stein was one of the mill workers present in the tissue chest area during most of the police crime scene work that night. Here are his observations: "I think the cops thought Tom had killed himself. They didn't do any investigating. I mean, I kept expecting them to take a measurement or dust for some fingerprints, you know, investigate the scene. It was more like, 'the guy killed himself; let's just get him out of there.'"

Stein's observations seem to be borne out when one views the slapdash proceeding on the police videotape. Stein is not a forensics expert—which makes his observations all the more significant. He was looking with wide-open eyes for some display of the professionalism you would expect from a modern police force. Stein does not recall being impressed any moment that night with the idea that the police were there to conduct a meticulous and objective investigation of a crime scene where a murder may have taken place. The only way he could explain their nonchalant attitude was that he thought the police had already reached the conclusion that Monfils committed suicide. Other workers on hand that night have echoed Stein's observations of shabby police work.

Where Is the Yellow Tape?

We have all seen it—the yellow tape that the police string up to clearly mark a crime scene. But you will not see any such tape when you watch the body-recovery video in this case. The Green Bay Police Department failed to cordon off the crime scene with yellow tape to define and protect it during the crucial first stages of the investigation. Numerous mill workers have commented on how freely they were able to come and go as the police worked to extricate Monfils's body from the tissue chest.

The missing yellow tape not only tells us that the police investigation was sloppy, it also supports the notion that it was biased from the get-go against Keith Kutska. The yellow tape should have been strung immediately around the area of the tissue chest where the body was found. From that clearly defined center, the investigation would have moved cautiously outward.

Sadly the yellow tape was not put up until much later that night—well after the crime scene had been severely compromised and the body had been removed from the mill. By then the investigation had already centered on Kutska. In an interview with District Attorney John Zakowski and Assistant District Attorney Larry Lasee, Lasee unwittingly revealed the preliminary bias in this case when he stated that the yellow tape—had it been run even when it should have been—would have run from the area around the tissue chest toward the area of paper machines 7 and 9 (about two hundred feet away). Then, he said, it would have shot back to the chest. It was a bizarre, oblong, and circuitous route through doorways and around machinery—a route that ensnared only Kutska and the others who were with him or near him.

There was no arguing with the idea that the police seemed to be operating with a foregone conclusion that night. It is discernable on their official videotape. Otherwise how would one explain their slipshod treatment of the crime scene and their other failures as documented on the tape?

"Way to Go, Kutska!"

Steve Stein was right in thinking that because the cops thought they already knew how Monfils had died; they did not have to conduct a real investigation. He was merely wrong in thinking that their foregone conclusion was that Monfils had killed himself. The police were already looking in an entirely different direction—toward Keith Kutska.

Along with violations of good forensics by the police, the videotape reveals a remark that proves the police had Kutska in their sights from the start. Even on the edited version given to each defendant, the remark can be heard. As the police cameraman narrates his way toward the tissue chest containing the lifeless body, we hear, "The approximate time is 11 p.m. Specialist Byrnes, Specialist Lange, along with Deputy Chief Taylor, Detective Sergeant Hamilton, and Detective Sergeant Servais. We're at James River looking at a vat. Mr. Monfils is located in the bottom of this vat."

A moment of silence follows. All that can be heard is the noisy machinery of the mill. Suddenly, we hear someone say, "He's in there—face down."

A brief second later, another voice says, "Way to go, Kutska!"

What was that? "Way to go, Kutska!?"

The full meaning of this terrible scene had not yet been realized. Monfils's body had not even been retrieved from the tissue chest. An autopsy had not yet been performed. Witnesses had not yet been interviewed. Physical evidence had not yet been gathered. In fact, the crime scene had not even been properly secured. Still, a voice can be heard to lay responsibility for the death directly at the doorstep of Keith Kutska.

"Way to go, Kutska!" The seeds of a witch hunt had been sown. Without a single shred of hard evidence, the police had already tipped their hand as to whom they would pursue in their investigation. While this was the first instance of tunnel vision constricting the police investigation, it would hardly be the last. Steve Stein could not have been more correct in assuming that members of the GBPD were operating with their minds already made up.

Kutska had to have done this. At least, it seemed pretty obvious to the person making the "Way to go, Kutska!" comment. One has to wonder just who jumped to that conclusion. Who made the logical mistake of *post hoc, ergo propter hoc* (after this, therefore because of this)?

One also has to know that Deputy Chief Taylor's rather red face was present at the James River mill that night. Combine Taylor's presence with the idea asserted by several GBPD investigators that they knew within twenty-four hours who had done this and why—and you have all the makings of a possible witch hunt on your hands.

The District Attorney Weighs In

These authors asked Brown County District Attorney John Zakowski, the lead prosecutor in the trial of the six men in 1995, if he had seen the crime scene videotape. He said he had. He was then asked if he was concerned about the procedure followed by the GBPD. His response was that he was "far more alarmed by the condition of Tom's body." One can empathize with that sentiment. What one cannot understand is how concern for the body would preempt concern for the police procedures. Those procedures were the absolute, first, and single-most important step toward getting true justice for the victim's family.

Late in the summer of 1994, as the investigation dragged on into its second year, Zakowski expressed some concerns about not having enough evidence to bring the case to trial. Clearly he was not completely satisfied with the case the GBPD tried to hand him at that time. But in regard to how the police proceeded at the crime scene, he let his emotional response toward the victim overrule his need for the absolute best in police work.

Any compassionate person understands Zakowski's reaction regarding the condition of Monfils's body. Tom was a victim and he did not deserve the fate that befell him. However, any thinking person can see that in his response to these authors, Zakowski evaded the question about the quality of the GBPD's work at the crime scene. Those interested in truth and justice understand that the ultimate honor one can pay a victim of foul play is to use the absolute best in forensic science and investigative techniques to determine the facts.

The Conspiracy Net

The Green Bay Police Department's investigation into the death of Tom Monfils would continue for 841 days. Begun with "Way to go, Kutska," it became a steamroller, slowly and methodically inching toward a certain target—apparently willing to plow over or pulverize any fact that got between the police and their theory that Kutska was responsible for Monfils's death.

In that stretch of time, the GBPD would try every trick in the book to get even a whiff of credible evidence. In the process they would drop their net on five other men who could not get out of the way of the get-Kutska machine. The police centered their investigation on Kutska, and Kutska could not be extracted from the rest of the men he was working with the morning of Monfils's disappearance. The police investigation would reach outward—not from the crime scene of the tissue chest—but from Kutska himself.

His alibi witnesses—Dale Basten, Mike Hirn, Mike Johnson, Rey Moore, and Mike Piaskowski—were to be thrown into the fire as a part of a union conspiracy. Though to a lesser extent, so too were the rest of the work crews on the 7 and 9 paper machines—Don Boulanger, Dave Daniels, Pete Delvoe, Jon Mineau, and Dennis Servais. The police suspect list would also include Randy Lepak and Marlyn Charles.

The fine line separating a suspect from a witness depended entirely on whether the police felt a person was cooperating with their theory or running counter to it. If a worker could not get out of the way of the steamroller, he would be crushed along with Kutska, no matter what. Over those 841 days, the police engaged in numerous futile attempts to come up with evidence that these men had something—anything—to do with Monfils's death:

1. Interviewed and reinterviewed all these men multiple times.

2. Placed pen registers on their telephones in order to track incoming and outgoing phone calls.

3. Collected and went through the men's garbage.

4. Confiscated tools and personal items belonging to the men.

5. Tailed the men around town, both conspicuously and inconspicuously.

6. Interviewed and reinterviewed the men's coworkers, families, friends, and neighbors.

7. Found a confidential informant who would surreptitiously tape Keith Kutska while prodding him to talk about the case.

8. Took handwriting samples from the men.

9. Administered lie detector tests.

10. Floated rumors about the men through the mill.

11. Threatened coworkers with the loss of their jobs if they did not cooperate with the police investigation.

When it was all said and done, not one of these investigative techniques took even a single step toward proving the guilt of Kutska or the other men. In fact, with this many dry holes in their case, it was looking like the police would never get their man. It was beginning to look as though all of these attempts to prove the men's guilt were turning out instead to prove their innocence. The steamroller was sputtering to a slow and embarrassing stop. That is until, in the nick of time, lead detective Randy Winkler produced a long shot, the Fox Den Bar story; more on that later.

But the question has to be asked: Why was the GBPD hell-bent to get Kutska and the other men if the facts were showing that they were not involved in Monfils's death? The answer is simple: He had gotten the tape from the police and embarrassed them in the process. Now Monfils, who had been betrayed by the police, was dead. The hunt for Kutska was easy to figure out, even if he was innocent. But what about the rest of the men?

Projections

In psychology, when people attribute their own feelings, beliefs, and attitudes to others, they are engaging in what is called "projection." It happened in this case—much to the detriment of six innocent men. The French have a saying for it, "A man doesn't look behind the bedroom door unless he has hidden there himself." Here were some of the more-prevalent projections driving this investigation:

Projection 1: A union conspiracy
The police contend that an incredible union conspiracy explains the fact that none of the six defendants "turned" or "rolled over" on the others. Not one of the men cut a deal with the police to save himself and his family from the horrors of a life sentence in prison.

For two and a half years, the police tried to solve this case by begging for a confession from any one of these defendants—a confession that would implicate the others and verify their assumption that Keith Kutska was guilty of the murder. The police repeated the overused and antiquated cliché "the first one on the bus gets the best seat" ad nauseum. The six defendants, as well as many of their coworkers whose jobs and livelihoods were threatened by the police, heard this promise over and over again. In fact, it became far more of a threat than a promise. Irrationally the police claimed the total failure of their threatening promise clearly proved the existence of a union conspiracy of lies and silence. Of course, it did no such thing. It proved that people were telling the truth.

Ironically there is probably no tighter union bond than the police brotherhood itself. It is so strong that it has a name, "the blue wall of silence." As of this writing, the authors have been unsuccessful in their efforts to interview any member of the GBPD about the Monfils investigation. This excludes retired chief Craig VanSchyndle who played a marginal role in the case as a detective.

There is a special bond among police officers. When a Wisconsin police officer is killed, hundreds of fellow officers from all over the state and beyond show up to pay homage to their fallen comrade. It is precisely this kind of brotherhood loyalty that has been projected upon these mill workers—simply because they belonged to a union.

Projection 2: They acted to protect their high-paying jobs

"The defendants took Tom Monfils's life to protect their high-paying jobs." This is the motive for murder repeatedly put forth by District Attorney Zakowski. While he has stated that the men made as much as $100,000 per year, their actual wages ranged between $38,557 and $75,620.

However, Zakowski also had a highly desirable and very powerful position—a job that happened to be under fire by the local newspaper. An election was coming up. His prestige and reputation in the community as well as his own $78,872 salary were on the line.

Projection 3: They are invested in their stories

When asked why—after all these years—not one of the men has come forth from prison to change his story, Zakowski replied, "They are too invested in their stories." His point was that the five men sitting in prison would not come forward now because they would find it too embarrassing to do so. That is just hooey. Each man is growing older by the day.

However, what is not hooey is that District Attorney Zakowski is very much invested in *his* story. For Zakowski to come forward now and admit his mistakes could be career suicide. And that would certainly embarrass him.

Another Catch-22

Far from being too invested in their stories, it would be far more to the advantage of the remaining incarcerated men to abandon their protests of innocence. In 2010 the first of them will be eligible for parole. If these men do not acknowledge guilt and convince the parole board of their genuine remorse, they could well remain in prison for the rest of their lives. Each and every one of them has told these authors that he would choose to die in prison rather than to admit to a crime that he did not commit. That does not sound like being too invested in a lie. It does sounds like being very much invested in their innocence.

Then there is Mike Piaskowski. He has been exonerated. He has his freedom back. He can never be tried again for this crime. Why has he fought for more than seven years on behalf of the innocence of the other five men? Why has he not just slipped back into society, grateful for his freedom and willing to leave it go at that? Mike has no vested interest in any false story. At this point, he could only have a vested interest in the truth.

Forensics and the Scientific Method

In forensic science a theory must be consistent with all of the facts and inconsistent with none. If, after testing it, you discover that your original theory does not fit the facts, then you must modify your starting assumptions to fit the facts. You may *never* modify the facts to fit your theory.

If you are a member of a police department charged with solving a crime and you do some preliminary investigating, you can arrive at what you think may have happened. That assumption is your starting theory. To the GBPD, the starting assumption was immediate and obvious. It went something like this:

- Without giving it much thought and after being told not to, we trusted Keith Kutska so much that we gave him a taped copy of an anonymous phone call made to us by a coworker, Tom Monfils. On that tape the caller reported that Kutska was about to walk out of the James River paper mill with a fifteen-foot piece of electrical wire that he did not have permission to take. When he contacted us, Kutska told us that the call was all

115

a lie—that he did not actually take anything from the mill. So we handed the tape to him.

- Once he had gotten the tape, Kutska knew who had made the call. He was angry with Monfils and played the tape for him at work, hoping for Monfils to publicly admit to making the call. Shortly afterward, Monfils disappeared from his work area. The following night he was found dead—his body at the bottom of a pulp chest at the mill with a weight and rope around his neck.

- Therefore Keith Kutska killed Tom Monfils.

In the scientific method you make observations and objectively record the data. For the police, the process is called an investigation. The real test of the police theory—that Kutska did it—requires that all the facts fit the theory.

Had the police conducted their investigation scientifically, they would have clearly marked their crime scene with yellow tape and moved their investigation outward in concentric circles from there until it enveloped one or more suspects. It was fair enough to keep Kutska in mind, knowing that the yellow tape would include him eventually. Even then, however, the police would have had to establish a connection between Kutska and the crime scene in order to prove their initial assumptions.

Had the police run their yellow tape as they should have and had they followed it as it ran outward from the pulp chest, the first workers they would have encountered were David Wiener and Charles Bowers. Wiener and Bowers worked in a secluded part of the mill, often alone. Each would have been worth a serious look as the police tested their theory; and if there was absolutely no connection between Wiener and Bowers and the crime scene, the investigators would have moved on to the next worker or workers as they expanded their circle. Eventually, they would have put their focus on Kutska and would have plenty of tough questions to ask him.

The police did not do it that way. Instead they mentally ran that yellow tape from the pulp chest to any area where Kutska had been that morning. They completely ruled out any other person who might have warranted a good look. Because of this, the investigation fell flat on its face—at least in supporting the police department's starting theory. They did everything they could think of to prove that they were right all along. Still, every time they tested their theory, the facts said that it was wrong—that Kutska and the other guys just were not guilty. The investigation was mired in the wrong direction, and it was going nowhere fast.

The police were not, however, anxious to accept what looked to them like failure. After all, if Kutska was not responsible, then the police themselves were suddenly a lot more responsible. If Monfils had taken his own life or if someone completely outside their theory had killed him, then the foolish release of that cassette tape by the police took on some pretty serious overtones.

Was It a Witch Hunt for Kutska?

Five innocent men sit in Wisconsin prisons today, the direct result of the investigation by the Green Bay Police Department. Early on, the *Green Bay Press-Gazette* called for an independent investigator in the Monfils case. The GBPD, it felt, was in over its head. More important, they had a bias—something the newspaper did not point out. That bias became clear the very second one of the investigators at the crime scene blurted out, "Way to go, Kutska!"

When, against the advice of the district attorney's office, Deputy Chief Jim Taylor allowed the tape of Monfils's call to be given to Kutska, Taylor and the GBPD became legally responsible for Monfils's welfare. With Monfils dead, one can only wonder what kind of investigation that same police department, under Taylor's direction, would be moved to conduct.

However, the injustice continued. In the wake of a blown crime scene and a flawed early investigation came a dubious autopsy—performed under the watchful eye of the Green Bay Police Department. It was more of the same.

Police Set the Stage

Shortly after noon on Monday, November 23, 1992, the body of Tom Monfils was transported from Green Bay's Malcore Funeral Home to St. Vincent Hospital where a medical-legal autopsy was performed.

The prospector was Dr. Helen C. Young, with Janice Fox assisting her. Also present were Green Bay Police Department detectives. At 12:32 p.m., the seal of the bag was photographed and removed. The "gross autopsy" would take the next four and one-half hours.

Outside St. Vincent, the streets of Green Bay were buzzing with gossip. Most Mondays, the talk would have been over the Packers game the day before. The Packers had beaten their archrival Chicago Bears, and Green Bay was rejoicing. A young, new quarterback was turning some heads, though he was hurting. Brett Favre had sustained a first-degree separated left shoulder when Philadelphia Eagles's defensive end Reggie White had slammed him into the Milwaukee County Stadium turf the previous Sunday. Still, Favre had recovered in time to beat the Bears and added to a seven-game starting streak in the process.

If not the Packers, citizens of northeast Wisconsin had a lot of other things to discuss. William Jefferson Clinton had just been elected president. The Wisconsin gun-deer season was in full swing. Decorations were being hung in anticipation of the approaching Thanksgiving and Christmas holidays; and to the day, twenty-nine years had slipped by since JFK's assassination.

Now, with this Monfils thing going on, tongues were wagging all across the city. A blue-collar town had been set on its ear by Monfils's death. Nearly everyone knew somebody who worked at one of the city's paper mills. And what they knew was that a death at the mill was shocking, but the whisper of a possible murder was unbelievable.

The Monfils case would occupy Green Bay headlines every day for the next week. Every whisper in the case turned into a lead story. Then, without any new significant details, a second week passed without a word. On Tuesday, December 8, the *Press-Gazette* broke a five-day silence on the case with the headline "Still No Conclusions in Mill Death." In the piece, Deputy Chief Jim Taylor seemed to be ruling out Monfils taking his own life. Still, Taylor would not commit to suicide or homicide, pending the results of the tests being done on tissue samples.

The following day, Green Bay got news it did not want. Seventeen days after the discovery of his body, Monfils's death certificate was amended as follows:

CAUSE OF DEATH:
- A. Asphyxiation
- B. Aspiration/ligature strangulation
RULING:
- Homicide

Murder? Yes, according to Coroner Genie William's official ruling, Monfils had been the victim of foul play.

"Monfils Was Murdered" was the headline on the *Press-Gazette's* lead story that evening. "Asphyxiation due to or as an occurrence [sic] of aspiration/ligature strangulation" was how the *Green Bay News-Chronicle* said it in its main story the following day entitled "Monfils Murdered." The GBPD was now directing all its efforts toward solving a homicide case, reported both papers.

Sitting side-by-side at the December 9 press conference were Deputy Chief Taylor and Coroner Williams. Taylor told reporters that the homicide ruling completed a portion of the puzzle in the case, which he described as "unusual, intricate, involved, and bizarre."

When asked about possible suspects, Taylor replied, "At this point everybody's a suspect and nobody's a suspect." Taylor said that the autopsy did determine whether one or multiple individuals were involved, though he would not say which way that determination was leading police. He declined to say whether the crime lab tests had unearthed any fingerprints on the rope or weight. He said there was no timetable for making arrests.

Taylor also told reporters that the homicide ruling confirmed his "gut feeling" all along that Monfils had been murdered. When asked about the tape of Monfils's phone call to police, Taylor referred reporters to city attorney Tim Kelley's office. Taylor was not about to get into all that messy tape business.

Reporters could not get a copy of the tape, Kelley told them, because it was now part of an ongoing investigation.

Coroner Williams told reporters that the murder determination was solely based on the physical evidence she examined and that it did not rely on the results from the State Crime Lab or interviews that the police had conducted. Though she would not spell out exactly how, Williams also stated that the dynamics of the pulp chest—agitator speed, how it was filled and emptied, and its contents—all contributed to her ruling of a homicide. The day before, she had met for three hours with James River engineers to learn about the chest, she said.

Neither Taylor nor Williams would tell reporters exactly how Monfils had died or whether or not he was already dead before he ended up in the pulp chest.

They both seemed to be in concert on one other point. The week before, Taylor had said that pulp in Monfils's air passages indicated that he was alive when he went into the pulp chest, but Williams had said she could not draw that conclusion without test results. Now, at this press conference, they swept the issue under the rug, and both refused to comment on their earlier difference of opinion.

It had all fallen into place for the GBPD. They were now full bore into a homicide investigation centered on the man who had done them wrong. It was not that Kutska had pried Monfils's audiotape from their tightly clenched fists or slipped it out of the police station while they were not looking. He had just used their incompetence against them.

Taylor himself had been told not to allow the tape to leave the station, but he had failed to prevent its transfer to Kutska. Two nights later, as head of the detective division, he was at the James River mill supervising the crime scene when Monfils's body was removed. It could easily be called a huge conflict of interest. The blue wall of silence had begun to envelop the deputy chief that evening as it put its protective arms around him. The spotlight would now silently illuminate Keith Kutska.

Specific Problems with the Autopsy

There are serious questions about the validity of the autopsy performed on Tom Monfils that Monday afternoon. Like many other aspects of this case, the autopsy speaks volumes about the police agenda, both in its limited scope and starting direction. One glaring issue is the exclusion of a psychological autopsy to examine Monfils's mental state in the days and weeks leading up to his death, particularly the morning of his death.

While the procedural aspects of Helen Young's medical-legal autopsy were basically sound, the extent of those procedures was hardly all encompassing. The faulty procedures represented the worst fear of

Dr. Henry Lee, the world-renowned forensic scientist—that of human behavior affecting the purity of forensic science. The driving need of the GBPD to downplay its part in the release of the audiotape eclipsed the need for forensic science to divine the truth.

Here are some serious, inherent flaws in the scope of the autopsy performed on Monfils.

Basic, important autopsy steps were omitted.
- Head injuries were not shaved or cleaned for proper examination, identification, and documentation.
- Fingernail clippings and/or scrapings were not taken for trace evidence and DNA laboratory analysis.
- Hair samples at depressed-skull injury sites were not taken for microscopic hair damage analysis.
- Deep-bruise defensive-injury tests were not done.

Comparison tests to identity possible causes were not done.
- The edge of the pulp chest agitator blade was never compared to the depressed skull injury.
- The Stanley knife blade, steel-toe work boots, and broken glasses found floating in the vat were not compared to any of the multiple cuts or bruises.

Three major injuries were not fully accounted for.
- The cause and effect of the broken jaw as being the primary debilitating injury was ignored.
- The explanation of the contrecoup brain injury contradicts testimony given.
- The cause and result of a large laceration in the ventricle wall of the heart remains unexplained.

Samples were not taken, and additional tests were not ordered.
- To determine pre-mortem versus post-mortem trauma of the lower abdominal area.
- To determine the age of the contrecoup brain injury.
- To find and identify other possible trace evidence.
- To corroborate and substantiate other autopsy findings.

There are serious crime scene concerns related to the autopsy.
- Dr. Young did not visit the crime scene.
- The crime scene was not secured adequately or long enough.
- The pulp-agitator blade was never taken as evidence.
- Quality impressions of the agitator blade were never taken.

There are basic ethical questions related to the autopsy.
- Why the difficult-to-impossible-to-determine trauma was firmly identified as a pre-mortem injury?
- Why that same improperly identified trauma was then allowed to be misrepresented as though it could have only occurred prior to the body's entry into the tissue chest?

In spite of these flaws, six innocent men were arrested, tried, convicted, and sent to prison for the practical remainder of their lives.

In his book *Famous Crimes Revisited: From Sacco-Vanzetti to O. J. Simpson,* Dr. Lee refers to "science and human behavior" as "two spheres that are not always compatible." In the book, Lee is "transported back and forth in time at will" while observing seven of the most famous crimes of the twentieth century from crime scene investigation to verdict. Lee suggests that the "march of forensic history" in the seven cases had brought the scientific and human spheres "closer together." However, he expresses continuing concern that "the most recent cases," although "informed by science (e.g., DNA)," were "still determined by fallible human beings who interpret and define and have the potential to manipulate the data."

The Monfils case could well have qualified as the eighth case examined by Dr. Lee. It was marked by all the shoddy procedural practices he had warned against: unsound and/or unethical practices, such as not securing the crime scene; faulty identification, collection, and mishandling of evidence; staging of the crime scene; planting, suppression of, and tampering with evidence; perjury; falsification of and/or destruction of records and; breach of autopsy protocol.

Coincidentally the O. J. Simpson case, reviewed by Lee in his book, was the contemporary of the Monfils case. Its verdict was rendered right in the middle of the Monfils trial. However, the difference between the two cases, in terms of science, is stark. The Simpson trial was characterized by an abundance of forensic science, particularly blood evidence. For its amazing lack of scientific evidence, the Monfils case was a throwback to the Dark Ages.

The Absence of a Psychological Autopsy

There are also legitimate concerns over the amazing lack of a psychological autopsy in this case. This is not to say definitively that Tom Monfils took his own life. However, given many of the extraneous circumstances surrounding his death, this was a course of action that should have been taken—if for no other reason than to rule it out. Again it is a step that an investigative body would normally have taken, one that a police department with a partial responsibility for what happened to Monfils did not take.

In her book *The Criminal Mind,* Katherine Ramsland, Ph.D., writes:

> A medical autopsy determines cause and means of death by examining the body. In cases where the manner of death is unexplained, such as someone hit by a car, and it's not clear whether it was a suicide, a homicide, natural, or accidental, a psychological autopsy may assist the coroner or medical examiner in clearing up the mystery. The idea is to discover the state of mind of the victim preceding death. The results may be used to settle criminal cases, estate issues, malpractice suits, or insurance claims. The database generally consists of the following:
> - An examination of the death scene (similar to the examination of a crime scene).
> - A study of all documentation pertaining to the death, such as witness statements and police reports.
> - Interviews with family members and associates.
> - Medical autopsy reports.
> - History of taking medication.
> - Reports about conflicted relationships or other stressors.
> - Unusual recent behavior.

- All relevant documents pertaining to the individual's life history, like school or employment records, letters, and diaries.
- Changes in wills or life insurance policies.

One cannot say with any certainty that Monfils took his own life. One cannot say with any certainty that he did not. What one can say with absolute certainty is that the Green Bay police never seriously looked in that important direction.

Likewise they failed to gather evidence at the crime scene that might have shown that Monfils had committed suicide. The simple fact is that not one of the injuries to his body is inconsistent with the remote possibility that he put himself into the tissue chest.

Unbiased Autopsy Nearly Impossible

Why had so many vital tests been omitted in Dr. Young's autopsy? Why was there no psychological autopsy? Why were Dr. Lee's worst fears of human behavior influencing science so apparent in this case? The answer may be simple: A less than objective GBPD could easily have been motivated to influence the scope of the autopsy itself.

Police involvement in an autopsy can vary from jurisdiction to jurisdiction. However, in a closely knit small town like Green Bay, the influence of the police on the overall autopsy process can be strong. According to Green Bay forensics expert Robin Williams, the Green Bay police are almost certain to impose themselves and their will on the work of the coroner or medical examiner. While they may not "insist on a certain finding," said Williams, they will "almost always give their strong input into the process and the findings."

At the time of the Monfils autopsy, the problems inherent in the small-town networking between the Green Bay police and the pathologist were exacerbated by Brown County's use of an antiquated system that utilized an elected coroner rather than an appointed medical examiner. Under such an arrangement—where a coroner is interested in retaining his or her position by being reelected—it is uncommon for a coroner to take an assertive position in any case. That is particularly true if that position runs counter to the rest of the county's power structure, especially the police with whom the coroner so often works.

Brown County's coroner at the time, Genie Williams, may have been well intentioned, but it is equally clear she was under the thumb of the police department. That can certainly be gleaned from the December 9, 1992, press conference where she appeared with GBPD Deputy Chief James Taylor to announce that Monfils's death was a murder.

Having the coroner under the strong influence of the police department is a serious problem in any case. In the Monfils case it was disastrous. The impact on Williams's crime scene investigation and on Dr. Young's ensuing autopsy cannot be overlooked. There are at least four areas in which this influence seems to have affected the autopsy's findings—helping to smooth the way between the police theory and the case as it was presented by the state at trial.

First, the autopsy seems to have completely ignored the idea that any of the injuries or trauma suffered by Monfils could have been created during what is known as the peri-mortem period. This is the period of time between the moment at which a person's respiration stops and the time the heart physically stops beating—known to be as long as fifteen minutes or more.

Second, in spite of the advanced state of decomposition of Monfils's body, the autopsy claims to have been able to differentiate and accurately identify all of the trauma and injuries to the body without hesitation.

Third, having ignored the peri-mortem period, the conclusion was then drawn that all of the pre-mortem injuries happened before Monfils entered the tissue chest, suggesting that the pulp agitator only caused post-mortem trauma.

Finally, the sheer number of what were then labeled as pre-mortem injuries was used to perpetuate the theory of an attack on Monfils by multiple individuals—a piece of the state's theory that seems to have convinced the jury that a mob of angry coworkers pummeled Monfils before putting him into the tissue chest. Using this series of questionable autopsy findings—made under the heavy influence of police investigators—the prosecution insisted to the jury that one person could not possibly have caused all the damage to Monfils's body.

With this autopsy and these conclusions as a starting point and with a strong fixation on Keith Kutska, it is easy to see how the entire investigation headed down the wrong track. Call it a chicken-or-egg question, but the autopsy rulings put blocks under and supported the framework for a very questionable theory: one that involved a confrontation between Monfils and his coworkers and that would still take an incredible two years to construct.

A bungled crime scene investigation and a flawed autopsy were hardly the beginnings of an investigation headed toward the truth of Monfils's fate. From these spurious beginnings, the police would launch their investigation—solely focused on Kutska and the others. Pointed in the wrong direction and unwilling to veer from that course, the GBPD would trudge along for well over two years. At several points their investigation would grind to a near-standstill. At others they would be challenged with far more proof of the men's innocence than their guilt. The police would need some kind of miracle if they were ever going to prove their theory. And when that miracle finally came, it would prove to be the most convenient kind imaginable but totally uncorroborated.

8

The Big Roundup and the Fox Den Myth

The great enemy of the truth is very often not the lie—deliberate, contrived and dishonest—but the myth—persistent, persuasive and unrealistic.

—John F. Kennedy

The front-page headline of the Wednesday, April 12, 1995, *Green Bay Press-Gazette* jarred the people of northeast Wisconsin awake: "Eight Arrested In Monfils Slaying."

Over twenty-eight months had passed since Tom Monfils's bizarre death inside the James River paper mill. Thanks to a stalled police investigation, many in the community had put the story on the back burner.

This was a special edition of the paper, hot off the presses in time for the evening commute. The early edition had led with a story on the future of one of the city's Fox River bridges. Green Bay was experiencing one more slow news day—until this turn of events in the Monfils case. Now every newspaper box was an open floodgate, and the citizens's thoughts raced back to the most recognized crime story in the city's history.

Monfils. The name itself guaranteed a spike in newspaper sales. The *Press-Gazette* had beaten the drum early and often since November 21, 1992. This late edition was jam-packed with articles on the case and the men arrested. On page four, the pictures of eight men were displayed under the headline "Details of Criminal Complaints." The men— Randy Lepak, Michael Piaskowski, Dale Basten, Michael Johnson, Michael Hirn, Rey Moore, Keith Kutska, and Marlyn Charles—were inside a half-page box with arrows pointing at each of them. Smaller boxes explained, "How police view the roles of the eight defendants."

Given the hubbub, a casual observer might have thought the Green Bay Police Department had broken up the mafia.

Police and Press Rejoice

The reporting of the *Press-Gazette* on the Monfils case had always been a little quirky. At one point, it had bullied the police for their lack of progress and had argued for an outside investigator, suggesting that the GBPD had botched the case and was incapable of conducting a decent investigation. Now that arrests had been made, it was a small-town cheerleader writing in the school paper about the great guys on the football team. Lepak and Charles had only been charged with misdemeanors, but—in what *Press-Gazette* reporter Don Langenkamp called "the big roundup"—they too had been skillfully tracked down, handcuffed, and hauled in.

Green Bay detectives were enjoying their moment of glory, and the paper was offering that angle as well. The cops had taken off their SWAT gear and gathered at a tavern just up on Adams Street from the police station. In a piece entitled "After the Bust, Cops Celebrate Triumph," Langenkamp toned down their celebratory beer drinking and high-fiving. Instead, he pointed to the "deep lines of fatigue in their faces" and their "silent thanks that no one got hurt."

That seemed a little bit over the top. These sleuths had not rounded up a bunch of "they're-not-taking-me-alive" desperadoes. These were the same guys whose pictures had been splashed across the *Press-Gazette* pages a year and a half earlier, on the first anniversary of Monfils's death. Yet not one of them had "gone on the lam," as such reporting might have put it. Quite to the contrary, each man had gone about his daily routine, his whereabouts as predictable as the time of day. Not one of the men expected to be arrested that Wednesday or any other day. Each one had laid claim to his innocence and lived accordingly.

When Police Chief Bob Langan was about to leave the bar, wrote Langenkamp, he told the local media that he could leave office "a winner" because arrests had been made in the case. Langan was departing not only for the night but also, in a sense, for his career, with his retirement just a few weeks away. "Helluva a job, you guys," he said to his detectives.

"Helluva chief," one of his detectives said as Langan left.

It was, after all, a glorious moment. They had just spent 841 days and hundreds of thousands of taxpayer dollars rounding up the same guys they had targeted on the day of Monfils's disappearance. And the rock-solid evidence they had to show for their effort? In total, that was one shaky, repressed-memory, finger-pointing flashback and some drunken, hearsay-driven barroom banter.

"Bar Talk Sparks Arrests"

The next day, the top story read, "Bar Talk Sparks Arrests." Seizing the previous day's excitement, Langenkamp and reporter Paul Srubas hyped the "Big Roundup" with snappy stuff like "a forty-five-minute drama in which five workers were led out of the mill in handcuffs and other locations" and "the arrests came off without a hitch."

Chief Langan reiterated the cunning of his police force by explaining that his men "knew where these people would be, what they'd be driving." Then Langan said something that would have produced a bittersweet laugh from anyone with a still-cautious eye. "There's a certain amount of intelligence," he said, "that goes into making eight arrests in forty-five minutes." In the blink of that same eye, well over 10,000 fruitless police man-hours had been shaved to forty-five minutes!

It was good stuff all right, though really overstated. Not one of the eight men had bolted from the police. No one had to be pepper-sprayed into submission. No one had tried to hide. There were no high-speed chases down Interstate 43. No gunplay. No hostage taking. Nothing! Hell, most of these slippery bandits had reported for work at the James

River mill that day! Even Keith Kutska, the "notorious ringleader," had been taken without incident while working at a local greenhouse.

This was Green Bay, Wisconsin—home of the Packers—and home of eight blue-collar guys who knew they were the targets of a far too narrowly focused small-town police investigation. They also knew they were being arrested for a crime they had not committed. They did not like being arrested, but they figured they could at least put their faith in a system that would help them prove their innocence once and for all.

Finally there is something the police and district attorney who gave the go-ahead for these arrests have not owned up to: Given their levels of cooperation to that point, every one of these guys would have driven to the police station and turned himself in, had the word come down to do so. The SWAT-team drama was completely unnecessary, unless you were looking to pump up the fantasy that these were "thugs" who were part of a "violent union conspiracy."

The real meat in this "bar talk" article, however, appeared just a small paragraph later, in a slight statement that might have gone unnoticed. In it, Brown County District Attorney John Zakowski said, the "one development that helped break the case" had come the summer before. The criminal complaint described this "development" as an event—a real occurrence on a particular day—when Keith Kutska was said to have conducted "a barroom demonstration of the confrontation leading to Monfils's death by having his friends playact the different roles."

Welcome to the Fox Den

Most local people know of this development as "the Fox Den Incident," named for the crossroads tavern twenty miles north of Green Bay in Morgan, Wisconsin, where it allegedly took place. Others, with less-certain knowledge of the case, point to it as that time when "one of the guys was drinking at a bar and finally told his buddies what happened to Monfils that day at the paper mill." But it really does not matter what a person calls it or how one remembers it. Just like the confrontation that it is supposed to have demonstrated—the one that is supposed to have led to Monfils's death—it never happened.

John Zakowski is a decent district attorney. Some might describe him as a bit of a zealot—certain of his sense of right and wrong and his duty to protect the citizens of Brown County by upholding the laws. A safe community needs that. John Zakowski is not, however, infallible.

When Zakowski referred to this barroom role-playing as a "development," it had to be a case of dramatic irony. He could not have known just how much of a development it really was—cut from whole cloth by Green Bay Police Detective Randy Winkler in order to make the case.

Now, after years of having the Fox Den myth breathe air, it is time to tell the world that the Fox Den role-play incident never happened—that it could not have happened. It is time to show how and why it evolved. It is, after all, John Zakowski's "key," and without that key there is nothing left to his case.

The so-called Fox Den incident was said to have occurred over the 1994 Fourth of July weekend, about a year and a half after Tom Monfils's death. As many people understand it—misled by the authorities and newspaper accounts—the incident involved Keith Kutska's demonstration of what happened to Monfils at the James River mill the morning he disappeared. At that bar on that day, brazened by a snootful of beer, Kutska is supposed to have laid out the big secret that he and the other guys and countless other mill workers had managed to keep to themselves for over eighteen months. From there, some exemplary police work brought the incident out in the light of day. That is the official version. Do not believe it. It is not the truth.

Like all good stories, the Fox Den myth finds its footing in reality. Kutska and others were at the Fox Den bar on the Fourth of July weekend in 1994. With Kutska that afternoon and evening were his wife, "Ardie," and his friends Brian and Verna Kellner. Manning the bar were owners Ron and Charlotte Salnik. Like Kutska, Brian Kellner worked at the mill. Ardie and Verna were friends, with gardening and horses as common passions. The Kutskas lived on the east side of Abrams, near the Pine Acres Golf Course. The Kellners lived on a hobby farm, just minutes down the same road, on the other side of town.

The four of them sat at the far end of the bar, away from the door. It was Kutska in the farthest stool, then Brian, then Verna, then Ardie, closest to the middle of the bar. At some point, a stranger came and picked up some package goods and—as best anyone can remember it—that was it for anyone else in the place.

All of that is true—it happened. It is the alleged role-playing and subsequent demonstration of what supposedly happened to Monfils that *did not* happen. Five months later, in late November, Zakowski's key development would come to life in a hearsay scenario coaxed from Brian Kellner and written into a statement by a determined detective, Randy Winkler. Under a barrage of threats, Kellner would sign off on the Fox Den playacting scenario, saying in essence that it occurred. Today—well away from Winkler's threats—he will tell you it was straight fiction.

According to the tale, Kutska is alleged to have gotten them all up from their barstools and ushered them to an area on the barroom floor near a standing cooler. There he is said to have moved them around, putting his hands on their shoulders and telling each of them which of his coworkers they would represent. Supposedly he was describing a confrontation that had occurred at a bubbler, or drinking fountain, tucked around a corner from paper machine 7.

Represented at this alleged confrontation were all of the guys netted in the "big roundup," save for Lepak and Charles. Another mill worker, Jon Mineau, was also said to have been present at the bubbler at the time—though he was not a part of the big roundup and never charged with Monfils's murder. Mineau has repeatedly insisted to the authorities and to these authors that he was neither present at any such confrontation nor had he ever witnessed any such confrontation. Mineau, Lepak, and Charles were fired from the paper mill one day before the trial in this case began. Those firings sent a loud and clear message to other workers who were set to testify—that a perceived lack of cooperation on their part could also cost them their livelihoods.

According to the Fox Den story, Kutska assigned Brian Kellner the role of Tom Monfils and himself the role of Mike Hirn. Brian said Verna was Dale Basten and Ardie was Rey Moore, while Verna's version had herself as Moore and Ardie as Basten. These were slight inconsistencies. They could have been attributable to faulty memory, a fair amount of drinking, or the fact that the incident never occurred. As a result, details like "who was who?" were never going to jibe.

There were other problems with the Fox Den story. Char Salnik told these authors that the Kutska-Kellner party of four was "so drunk they had a hard time getting to the bathroom, let alone all getting up for that playacting thing."

Even crazier was the idea that Char herself was supposed to have been a part of the role-playing, coming out from behind the bar to join the others. The problem was that Char's broken ankle—a recent injury—had made it tough for her to get around at all. It had kept her from working most of that summer. Strange too was the fact that neither Brian nor Verna mentioned Char's ankle when Winkler pressured them into supporting his fabrication in November. Char said she would have had to hobble out to the barroom floor on her crutches and in her plaster cast for the role-play. Yet none of that ever made its way into any of the statements or detail sheets concerning the incident.

That broken ankle was a telltale sign of a falsehood—the sort of glitch that every teenager has had to deal with when caught peddling a dubious story. But Detective Winkler seemed to neglect this detail—even after he interviewed Char and she told him about it later that summer. It was not the only detail to be ignored, but it turns out to be a pretty good-sized one in retrospect.

Let us skip over that broken ankle for now, as if it were nothing more than, well, a broken ankle. Through some role-playing out on the barroom floor, Kutska is alleged to have named names and put coworkers in certain positions as they surrounded Monfils and began taunting him at the bubbler. The story went that they had supposedly cornered him while he was getting a drink.

There was Monfils, already under a great deal of stress that morning because of his anonymous call to the police. Now his angry coworkers had him in the most vulnerable position imaginable—bent over and getting a drink of water—while they approached him from behind. As he spun around to face this mythical mob, a copy of the cassette tape bearing his call was said to have been shaken in his face; and one of his coworkers was said to have pushed him on the shoulder.

At that point, things get fuzzy—very fuzzy. That is because, first and foremost, *in reality* the role-playing and the bubbler confrontation on which it was supposedly based never happened. They get fuzzy, too, because even if you believe the role-playing happened, there is another major problem. According to the hearsay of Brian Kellner in his November statement to Detective Winkler, Kutska *left the scene* before the alleged bubbler confrontation occurred to tend to a problem on his paper machine.

So even if you accept the role-playing as gospel, Kutska could not have seen anything of the fictional bubbler confrontation after he left the area. The barroom role-playing would have stopped right there. Beyond that, Winkler—through Brian Kellner—could do no more than speculate and guess. Yet in the minds of the authorities, the imaginary film of the Fox Den playacting kept right on rolling past the point when Kutska returned to his machine. From there, it could only be a fantastic voyage. Nonetheless, Zakowski would present the "rest of the story" to a trusting jury at the men's 1995 trial as though he had factual evidence.

The Fox Den bar—twenty miles north of Green Bay

To say the Kellners and the Kutskas never talked about the case that day would be ridiculous. They may well have talked about it because it was a very serious life-changing event for the Kutska family. Kutska had already lost his job of twenty-plus years. He was being investigated for murder. The legal bills were decimating the family savings. They were working hard to sell their rental house. Neighbors were gossiping. Even though he was innocent, it was still possible that he would be going to prison—leaving his family alone and destitute. They talked about it quite a bit, said Kutska, but definitely not in the way that the police and the DA want everyone to believe.

And finally, in all of their police interviews and at trial, Char and Ron Salnik vehemently denied that any kind of role-play about Monfils's death ever took place in their bar.

The Bubbler Did It

For Zakowski, the Fox Den development was like manna falling from the heavens into the hands of a starving man. It gave legs to a bubbler confrontation, and that bubbler confrontation gave legs to everything else. Perhaps Zakowski never heard the old adage "If it sounds too good to be true, it probably is." Otherwise how could he have glossed over so many glaring wrinkles in the story? He told these authors that a part of a district attorney's job is to seriously consider the evidence brought to him by the police and to seriously consider the police themselves in the process. If he had truly done that, he would have rejected Winkler's Fox Den story as almost completely unreliable.

According to the "official" theory, Tom Monfils had been confronted twice on the morning of his disappearance: once in coop 7, when Kutska played the tape for him, and once again at the bubbler. This second confrontation can only be called speculation since it exists in one place and one place only—the hearsay of Brian Kellner. Try as they might, the police never located an eyewitness or any physical evidence of a bubbler altercation at all. Not one of the six men—even with promises from the police of total or partial immunity—has ever said yes to the bubbler story. No one has ever claimed to have seen a confrontation of any kind or even an aggregation of people anywhere near the bubbler that morning. The bubbler confrontation completely lacks corroboration.

The first so-called confrontation was never in doubt—though calling it a confrontation is questionable. Mike Piaskowski refers to it as the "Tom talk," underscoring the idea that for him at least it was far more a stern discussion than a confrontation. For Kutska, however, it was a confrontation—albeit not a physical one. Whatever you call it, this first encounter occurred in the control room of paper machine 7 between Kutska and Monfils, with Piaskowski and Randy Lepak present. Dennis Servais also caught the tail end of that encounter. It lasted barely three minutes, ending about 7:17 that morning.

The statements of Kutska, Lepak, Piaskowski, and Servais all are in agreement regarding this encounter: Kutska played the tape and asked Monfils if that was his voice.

There was no quick answer, and Kutska asked Monfils if he was denying that it was his voice. Monfils acknowledged that it was. Kutska expressed his anger and left coop 7. A few seconds later, Piaskowski and Lepak voiced their opinions of his anonymous call to Monfils as they exited. A couple of expletives were tossed Monfils's way by Lepak and Piaskowski, but there was no physical threat. No one laid a finger on him. According to Servais, Monfils had not even moved from his original position as Lepak and Piaskowski left the control room.

For the cops and the district attorney, this first "confrontation" was far too innocuous. In an effort to make something more of it, they speculated that Monfils never admitted to Kutska that he had made the call, prompting the need for the second confrontation. In independent interviews immediately following Monfils's disappearance, however, Lepak, Kutska, and Piaskowski all said the same thing—that Monfils had acknowledged making the call. Servais also told the investigators that, even though he was not there in the beginning and had not heard Monfils say it, he could still tell that Monfils had admitted making the call. It was well documented that Monfils had gone about his normal job responsibilities following the discussion.

The bottom line for the authorities was that the Tom-talk did not amount to much unless they could string it together with something more menacing. Enter the bubbler confrontation. It was just what the doctor ordered, but how would the police prove it had happened? The GBPD had been rummaging around for something like the Fox Den incident for their entire investigation. They had to have something in order to explain how Monfils got from his workstation after the 7:34 turnover and into the tissue chest where his body was found. It was a big hole in their case. The investigators had worked every angle they could think of to prove their theory—yet they had not unearthed one shred of evidence pointing to the men's guilt in harming Tom. No mention of a second confrontation of any type had ever come up.

The bubbler itself had shown up early in the investigation but strictly as a point of reference. How it became the center of this investigation is interesting, though it hardly suggests great police work. In all of the discovery material on this case released to the defendants, there are exactly seventeen references to the bubbler made by eight different mill workers. The first of these was made on November 22, 1992—just hours after Monfils's body was found. The last was made on June 28, 1993—twenty-two months before the arrests in the case.

No eyewitnesses and no forensic evidence supported the idea that the bubbler (center of photo) was the center of a confrontation the morning of Monfils's disappearance.

Not one of these seventeen references describes any kind of confrontation between Monfils and a group of his coworkers. Only two of these statements—those of Kelly Drown and David Webster— place Monfils at or near the bubbler in any fashion. Neither Drown's nor Webster's statements place a group of other people at the bubbler with Monfils. The other references are all statements by various workers saying they were at the bubbler themselves or they saw other workers coming or going through the area around the bubbler.

Neither Drown nor Webster was working the morning of Monfils's disappearance. According to Zakowski, however, it was Drown's statement that caught the initial fancy of the authorities. Zakowski told these authors that Drown's statement "corroborated the bubbler confrontation." The fact of the matter is that it does not. Drown was a relatively new employee who worked the chip pile—well outside the mill itself. She labeled her own account of Monfils at the bubbler as *hearsay*. Webster, who worked on the repulpers in the paper mill department, referred to his mention of the bubbler as a *rumor*. Drown said she heard a story that Monfils was last seen "after saying he was going to get a drink." She also said she had heard that Monfils was seen on the stairs to the third-floor converting department later that morning. This also turned out to be false. Webster said that he had "heard a *rumor* that Mike Hirn and Tom Monfils got into a pushing match at the water bubbler"—again completely incorrect.

Piaskowski and Kutska both recall being asked by the police about the various bubblers in the mill as early as Monday, November 23—just two days after Monfils's disappearance and the day after his body was discovered. Drown had given her statement about twelve hours earlier. Just a half a day into their investigation, the police were already focused on the idea that Kutska was responsible for Monfils's death and that the bubbler had something to do with it.

At trial, in his rebuttal on the last day, Assistant District Attorney Larry Lasee said the whole bubbler thing had actually originated with defendant Michael Johnson. "The bubbler theory really comes from Mr. Johnson," said Lasee. "Mr. Johnson says, 'I think Dale Basten said the last place anybody saw him [Monfils] was by the bubbler.'" Even the DA's office was unsure as to how or why the bubbler had risen to such a place of prominence in the case.

As made-to-order fiction, a confrontation like the one at the bubbler had every necessary dramatic element. It included a large group of men whipped into a frenzy and feeding off one another's outrage—making them capable of anything. It had the guys in this group motivated by the tape that Kutska had snuck out from under the noses of the police—making the police worthy of sympathy themselves. It centered on a lone victim. It left the alleged killers some wiggle room since, says Zakowski, they only meant to intimidate Monfils, not to kill him. Remember that each of the men was invited by the authorities to agree that the bubbler confrontation took place. Each of them had an opportunity—with a promise of immunity—to say that he had been a part of such a confrontation but that he had only been a bystander. Not one of them did.

At this point in the apocryphal bubbler story, even the district attorney has to admit that he was guessing. Realizing that Monfils had been seriously hurt and that this thing had gotten way out of hand, Zakowski *speculates* that every single man at the bubbler thought of just one thing: the pieces of silver they made working at the paper mill. They would lose their high-paying jobs if they were found out. And so, says the DA, they all tacitly made a plan and decided to get rid of Monfils's still-alive body to cover their tracks. These six men, from four different parts of the mill and two separate unions, with widely disparate ages and backgrounds and personalities, all of a sudden became of one mind. Without saying a word, without any kind of sit-down, parley, discussion, or game plan, says the district attorney and his crew, they proceeded to get rid of Monfils's body to save their jobs.

In a 2003 interview these authors challenged Zakowski on this theory. His idea of things did not leave room for one or more of these guys to stop the allegedly unfolding events and say, "Hey, this is going too far. Knock it off" or even "I'm out of here." It did not leave space for one of them to honor his upbringing, his sense of fair play, or his empathy for another human being to do the right thing. It did not even leave open the possibility that one of them might have decided to save his job in a far safer way—by reporting the whole mess to the authorities. Zakowski did not really answer that challenge. Instead, according to Zakowski and Lasee, paper mill workers were indeed "capable of *this* [authors's emphasis]."

In less than three minutes—went the theory—they all left coop 9, went to the bubbler, hurt Monfils, disposed of him, cleaned up the scene, bound themselves together in a lifelong pact of union-controlled silence, returned to their jobs, and worked the rest of their day without so much as a case of the jitters. Then, without any ongoing contact, they worked in concert to mislead the police through a two-and-a-half-year investigation. And over sixteen years later and counting—to a man, each one of them is still honoring that collective and individual unification of silence.

When asked why the men would continue to protect one another when a simple word might open the prison doors, Zakowski suggests that they have "got so much invested in this lie and have mislead their friends and families for so long, [that they cannot tell the truth now]." That just does not make any sense at all. Is Zakowski saying that these men would much rather sit in prison for the rest of their lives—covering up for guys they barely knew—than spend a gorgeous day on a lake, as free men, fishing with their children and grandchildren? You be the judge.

> Three may keep a secret, if two of them are dead.
> —Benjamin Franklin

Even by their own theory, the police have at least four people—Dennis Servais, Pete Delvoe, Don Boulanger, and Jon Mineau—who would have seen a bubbler confrontation had one occurred. Delvoe, Boulanger, and Mineau have all stated emphatically to these authors that they never saw any such confrontation and would have, had one happened. Servais never reported any kind of bubbler confrontation to the police in any statement he gave. While the cops worked hard to ruin Mineau's credibility and to drag him into their big roundup, they failed to do so. And the honesty of Boulanger, Delvoe, and Servais has always been unimpeachable—even though they have all had aspersions cast their way by the authorities in order to explain why they have never endorsed the bubbler story.

Meanwhile, Back at the Bar

Let us return briefly to the Fox Den role-playing incident. The state's version of it contained inherent problems: Kutska saying he did not see what had happened at the bubbler after a certain point, Char Salnik's broken ankle, who was who in the role-play, the bar owners's contention that the role-play never happened. Those things would have raised questions about the whole story and sent impartial investigators or a cautious district attorney scrambling back to square one—but not here. The DA was hungry for a development, and the police were anxious to oblige him.

A few other points should be added here, these from Kutska himself. Over numerous interviews, he was pressed on the possibility that a role-play had occurred. He was asked if he was too inebriated to remember it or if he had simply forgotten it. He was asked if he had, perhaps, shown Brian Kellner what happened at the bubbler in some other fashion than the role-play. He was also asked if he remembered talking about the case at all that day at the Fox Den. Here is a brief summary of Kutska's responses to questions about that day, straight from his present residence at the Columbia Correctional Institution in Portage, Wisconsin:

> Did we talk about the case that day? I don't remember—probably. The chances are good; I talked about the case all the time. If you want to know what I was talking about that particular day, look in the newspaper. Whatever was in there the week before is probably what I was talking about that day. But whatever it was, I would have been saying Tom killed himself.
>
> You see I didn't have a copy of the autopsy until later that summer [a fact borne out in a GBPD detail sheet dated 07/17/94]. And, until I had a copy of the autopsy, I believed it was suicide. [This statement has been supported in numerous interviews with dozens of coworkers as well as with Royce Finne, Kutska's trial attorney.] It was the autopsy that convinced me that Tom had been murdered.
>
> That Fourth of July, I still thought Tom had killed himself. So, I would have been talking suicide, not a bubbler confrontation. Besides, there was no bubbler confrontation. I didn't even know about the so-called bubbler confrontation until after I was arrested and read it in the [criminal] complaint. How could I have talked about a bubbler confrontation that didn't exist?
>
> Was I drunk that day? I wasn't falling down, but I wouldn't have passed a Breathalyzer test either, that's for sure.

According to Mike Piaskowski, Kutska's primary focus on suicide was based on a nagging sense of guilt. From the beginning, Kutska could not shake the thought that his efforts to shame Monfils that morning had driven him to take his own life.

When it is all said and done, there simply are no clear proponents for the Fox Den role-playing incident. It is no more than unsupported hearsay developed to prop up a theory.

The Fox Den's importance to the authorities cannot be overestimated. That is clear from listening to them. Zakowski told these authors it was the *key* to his case. It was such a key, in fact, that he was willing to overlook its hearsay nature and its shaky details and herald it as *the* most important element in persuading the jury of the guilt of these men.

The Press Puts Forth the Police Theory

So why and how did the Fox Den myth grow from an inspiration in the mind of Detective Randy Winkler into the winner of six guilty verdicts for conspiracy to commit first-degree intentional homicide and being party to a crime?

To answer that question, one has to take a step back. The first anniversary of Monfils's death had rolled around with very little to show for the police investigation. Despite Inspector Dick Keon telling the media early on that the police knew "who did it and how it was done," a year later they were no closer to an arrest than they had been on the day Monfils's body was found.

The *Green Bay Press-Gazette* sold plenty of papers covering the Monfils case. Pictured is a billboard in downtown Green Bay put up by the Monfils family.

The first anniversary of his death, November 21, 1993, fell on a Sunday, and the honchos at the *Press-Gazette* did not miss the opportunity to sell some papers. The newspaper splashed this front-page headline right under its masthead: "One Year Later, the Search Continues for the Killer of Tom Monfils."

Monfils's name was well over twice as large as the lead. Next to it was a picture of him at a slight angle. Under that was a large photograph of his grieving parents, Ed and Joan. They were pictured putting a flower into their son's crypt. Tacked at the bottom of the article was the picture of a note from his widow, Susan.

"All the police need to make an arrest," Chief Langan said in an article further down the page, "is an eyewitness, someone who had direct knowledge of the crime, or the cooperation of one of the lesser involved participants." Langan added that the police were "close and getting closer all the time."

Now there was mouthful. Exactly 365 days had ticked by, and the police were still dead set on the theory they had formulated in the earliest hours of the investigation. They had conducted hundreds of hours of interviews and interrogations. They had generated a file-cabinet-drawer's worth of paperwork. Still they had no hard evidence supporting their theory.

To most people it would have been time to get a new theory or at least take a long, hard look at the old one. If cutting and hammering the damn puzzle pieces into place was not working, maybe it was time to rethink whether the pieces were supposed to fit in the first place. Maybe it was time to put away the scissors and hammer and take a brand new approach. Maybe it was time to take to heart the evidence that was pointing them in an alternate direction.

The *Press-Gazette* also brought its readers up to speed on the reward for "information leading to an arrest and conviction in the case." Donors, including business leaders, were continuing to contribute money to the Thomas Monfils Fund. Those monies were to be combined with the $25,000 already on the table thanks to the two union locals and the James River Corporation. An anonymous donor was cited as saying, "the Monfils case is causing a division in Green Bay. I'd like to see that end and some healing begin. By contributing to the fund, I feel I'm helping to promote that healing." *Press-Gazette* publisher Bill Nusbaum said that Green Bay was not "the kind of community that tolerates murder."

The newspaper also promised "3 pages inside" offering updates on the case as well as some drawings by staff artist Joe Heller that would show "what may have happened."

All in all, the front-page headline could have easily read, "Police Still Have No Proof in a Case They Say They Had Solved a Year Ago." Sure there was pressure to get this thing solved. Green Bay was feeling uncomfortable. After all, it did not tolerate murder—as though some towns did. "Titletown" was nervous that the Monfils case had gone unresolved for as long as it had.

Some hope had come early in the summer when Police Chief Bob Langan said on Green Bay talk radio that arrests were imminent. But the shine had come off that promise when the *Press-Gazette* checked Langan's proclamation with District Attorney Zakowski, who was a lot less certain than Langan about how things were proceeding. Zakowski said that he had some evidence, but did he have enough? He knew his office would only have one shot, he said, and he wanted to be sure that he proceeded to trial with a case that would result in convictions. That seemed to suggest that Langan was blowing hot air about how close any arrests really were. Those arrests that were so imminent in June had not materialized. Instead here was Langan, in the newspaper five months later, once again pleading for information.

Inside the newspaper that November Sunday, *Press-Gazette* writer Tony Walter pounded out a familiar theme with an article titled "Workers at Plant Wish Nightmare Would End." Several workers interviewed said things were pretty normal at the mill and that they did not think they were working with a murderer; they felt Monfils had actually committed suicide. However, Walter's article featured quotes from workers who expressed anxiety. One worker said, "People are tired of the news [media] insinuating that everybody knows [what happened]. Nobody really does know. You go bowling or play volleyball now and people say, 'You know what happened.' We'd all appreciate it if somebody would come forward."

Just below and to the right of this piece was a real eye-catcher—more like an eye-opener. It was an article about the pending civil suit that Monfils's widow had filed the previous May. Bruce Bachhuber,

Susan Monfils's Green Bay attorney, was claiming in the suit that Tom Monfils's coworkers had attacked and beaten him and thrown him into a paper vat where he died. The article named names and ran pictures of each of these civil-suit defendants. Ironically they were the very same workers the police were focusing on—Keith Kutska, Mike Piaskowski, Mike Johnson, Dale Basten, Mike Hirn, Randy Lepak, and Rey Moore. Conspicuously absent was union president Marlyn Charles, who would be added to the civil suit about two weeks later.

The details of Bachhuber's civil suit seemed to mirror the police theory. It featured the same guys and the same speculations about their roles in Monfils's death. No surprise there, really. As it turned out, Bachhuber had been a red-carpet guest at the police station as he began his research for the civil suit. He had enjoyed hours of perusing the police work on the case. The detectives working the case had even visited his office—as many as a dozen times—keeping him updated as their investigation proceeded. No attorney ever had it so good.

For the police and the DA, a civil suit was another handy tool in what had become a game of brinkmanship with these men. Eventually guilty men would break, went their thinking. But just like the lie detector tests and handwriting samples and garbage pickups and phone taps and stakeouts before it, the civil suit and its depositions would neither shake one man off the rock-solid platform of his innocence nor prove his guilt.

All things considered, the Joe Heller drawings inside were astonishingly accurate as depictions of the police theory. Presented as possible scenarios, they took the basic facts of Monfils's whereabouts between 7:10 and 7:37 a.m. and set them in motion within the layout of the mill. There were also some cartoonlike panels depicting various other workers in the area. These drawings were amazingly accurate renditions of the police theory for one simple reason: Heller told one of these authors that he did all of the drawings at the direction of the reporters covering the case. One of those reporters, Paul Srubas, told these authors that the police had doled out the information for the drawings to the reporters.

In the third panel of Heller's drawings the bait was set. The panel presented a litany of possibilities for explaining Monfils's disappearance while trying to relate what might have been going through his mind at the time. It presented five possibilities, suggesting that Monfils might have:

- confronted Kutska or Hirn;
- gone to the locker room to call the police about the release of the tape;
- gone to the drinking fountain;
- returned to his control room;
- left in an opposite direction

So there it was—a subtle suggestion from the police—"gone to the drinking fountain"— a place for something to have happened. This seemingly harmless hint looked a lot like a wide-open receiver, waving his arms wildly in the end zone, waiting for someone to toss the football. The *Press Gazette* had snapped the ball. Now who would toss the miracle pass?

9

Winkler Emerges

*There are no whole truths: all truths are
half-truths. It is trying to treat them as
whole truths that play the devil.*

—Alfred North Whitehead

For the Green Bay Police Department 1993 ended on a disappointing note. Despite all the oomph immediately following Tom Monfils's death, the yearlong investigation had trickled down to nearly nothing. Even on the heels of the one-year anniversary splash in the *Press-Gazette*, nothing new had surfaced. A mere three pages of paperwork were generated by the entire department in December. Heading into 1994, the case was looking like it would disappear into the "unsolved" pile. Either that or a major break in the case—something akin to a miracle—would have to occur.

Detective Sergeant Randy Winkler became the lead investigator on the Monfils case in January 1994. Ken Brodhagen and Al Van Haute were assigned to the case part-time, ready if developments should occur. Winkler basically operated that entire year on his own.

In terms of producing any *real* evidence as to what had happened to

Monfils, 1994 was another barren wasteland. By the end of November, the police were more desperate than ever for even a whiff of proof to support their theory. What they did have pointed to the *innocence*, not to the *guilt*, of their suspects. More handwriting samples, more interviews with James River mill workers, and another file cabinet drawer of paperwork had not produced a break in the case. (The Fox Den incident—alleged to have occurred in July—had yet to be developed.)

The year also saw the involvement in the case of the Federal Bureau of Investigation and the United States Justice Department. It was Mike Hirn who had actually contacted the FBI through his attorney. The FBI and the Justice Department did some preliminary work on the case and then walked away; giving Hirn a "heads-up" to make sure he got himself a good lawyer. Mike Piaskowski remembered a surprise visit to his home by FBI and Justice Department agents early one Saturday morning. "From their reactions," said Piaskowski, "it sure seemed like they didn't think we were guilty of anything, just up against some incompetence that might end up costing me dearly. Unfortunately, they were right."

Handwriting Analysis

In 1994 a desperate GBPD expanded its efforts to nail Keith Kutska and the others with an ever-burgeoning bag of tricks. In one of their many futile attempts to get to the bottom of things, the GBPD collected handwriting exemplars from many of Monfils's coworkers. The effort was one more example of strange police work—not so much in why it was done as in what was done with the results.

The whole thing started when mill workers Steve Stein and Paul Wittlinger discovered some handwriting in a Green Bay area phone book housed in the small coop of paper machine 7. Written on the cover was "p.152," with a box drawn around it. Page 152 contained the Monfils name, which was underlined. The listing for "Thos & Susan Monfils" was circled. Written down the center margin were the words "I DO NOT FEAR DEATH, FOR IN DEATH WE SEEK LIFE ETERNAL." The scribbling was viewed as some kind of suicide note—until it turned out not to be in Monfils's handwriting.

The police thinking was that this fake suicide note—meant to throw the police off—would likely lead to the killer or killers. Not bad thinking really. But after all the handwriting exemplars were examined, the person indicated as the note's likely author was not one of the men named in the civil suit or brought in during the big roundup. The sample with the greatest likelihood of belonging to the note's author was that of mill worker David Wiener. Ironically Wiener had previously offered himself as a star witness against Dale Basten and Mike Johnson. Once Wiener was named as the most likely author of the note, the police dropped the whole issue. It was not the only time that Wiener would show up on the radar screen as another possible suspect; it was not the only time the authorities would turn off their radar when the blip was something outside their theory.

Confidential Informants

In April 1994, Randy Winkler found himself a pair of "CIs," confidential informants, named Dodie and Scott VerStrate. Dodie had contacted Winkler following a chance encounter with Kutska while Kutska was working as a day laborer with Scott. The VerStrates agreed that they would pretend to be Kutska's friends while scrounging up information for the cops at every opportunity. It got to the point, said Ardie Kutska, where she and Keith would hide in their own home, or turn the stereo way up, or pretend to be on their way out the door, just to avoid Dodie and Scott's visits.

It was not that the Kutska's suspected that the VerStrates's friendship was based on a clandestine microphone strapped beneath Dodie's bosom; they just could not understand why Scott and Dodie were hanging around all the time. The VerStrates were much younger than the Kutskas, and the two couples did not have much in common. Besides, Ardie told these authors, all the VerStrates seemed to want to do was talk about the Monfils case, and all she and Keith could tell them was what was in the papers or what they heard via the grapevine.

But the VerStrates' role in the Monfils case deserves to be examined. It illustrates much of what was questionable in the investigation. The bottom line is that despite plying the Kutskas for information on a dozen or more occasions, Dodie and Scott VerStrate delivered nothing of value to the investigation, yet they were handed a huge chunk of the reward money. Their testimony appeared to be substantial enough for the state to parade it out at the preliminary hearing to bind the six men over for trial, but in reality it was so shaky that it could not be used and was not used at the actual trial itself.

Dodie VerStrate herself was a bit of an anomaly in the nearby Abrams community where she suddenly appeared one day. Few people knew for sure where she came from, who she was, or where she went. The list of individuals with accounts of Dodie's questionable character and moneymaking scams is considerable. And Scott had clouds over his head as well.

In John Zakowski's conference room one day, these authors, pointing to the collection of cassette recordings made by the VerStrates, said, "There's no Fox Den role-play on any of these tapes." "No," said the district attorney, "there's not much there at all."

If anything, their taped conversations unwittingly gave Kutska a favorable sounding board, even though he did not know he was being taped. One of the VerStrate tapes even had him saying that he hoped the cops did find something, because then they would find that Monfils had killed himself. Then, said Kutska, he was off the hook. And even if the cops found out that Monfils was murdered, Kutska continued, he would still be off the hook because he had not killed him.

The funny thing about the VerStrates is that—for all their undercover work, especially around the time the Fox Den role-playing was supposed to have gone down—they never reported Kutska talking about any bubbler confrontation, or about any role-playing. Odd, since they were very familiar with the Fox Den itself, having recorded at least three of their clandestine tapes at the tavern.

The summer of 1994 was racing along, and the VerStrates were turning out to be another dead end in the police investigation. A somewhat desperate Dodie met with Winkler on both July 14 and July 17. She knew that her value to Winkler—and the gravy train that might come with it—was slipping away. On each occasion, she gave Winkler a rundown of Kutska's latest rants.

Kutska was talking about getting fired for holding unauthorized union meetings when he played the tape at work.

Kutska told the FBI that he did not have the stolen extension cord anymore, because he had tossed it out—but if they gave him five bucks he would "go buy one for them."

Kutska was going to hide all his money to avoid paying anything in the civil suit.

Kutska was saying that the Monfils investigation was the most expensive investigation in the history of Green Bay.

Kutska was saying that the Green Bay city attorney was in as much trouble as he was.

Kutska was saying that he *had* played the tape for Monfils, but how was he supposed to know that Tom would end up dead?

Kutska told Dodie all that and more, but he had not uttered one word about any kind of physical confrontation—let alone a confrontation at the bubbler. That was significant, given Dodie's constant pumping of Kutska for information on the case. Also significant was the fact that Kutska had confided in her enough to tell her that he was going to protect his assets from the civil suit by hiding them from the authorities. Equally significant is Dodie's apparent need to please that one finds in every statement she gave to Winkler. After all, time was ticking, and all she had produced was a case for Kutska's innocence.

Dodie and Scott had been on Winkler's dole for four months, and the anxious detective had to be second-guessing their worth. They were under increasing pressure to produce, and still they had not given Winkler any account of Kutska talking about a bubbler confrontation or anything even approaching it.

Kutska Hits a Raw Nerve

The VerStrates had not been able to present Winkler with an account of an altercation between Monfils and his coworkers. They were, however, able to keep him up to speed on Kutska's activities at the time. And what Kutska was up to seems to have angered and inspired Winkler enough to keep his mind focused on getting Kutska.

The night of July 17 Dodie contacted Winkler with some urgency in her voice. She did not know that Kutska had seen Winkler down at the police station that same afternoon. Kutska had brought a letter from his attorney, Royce Finne, authorizing Kutska to pick up copies "of the statements that were to be released for the civil suit."

Because there was an extensive amount of copying to be done, Kutska had to wait until 4:30 p.m. After he paid for the copies and was about to leave, he began looking through the paperwork. He then asked Winkler, "Where's the autopsy report?" Winkler told him he "wasn't getting a copy." Kutska said that he thought he was "supposed to get one," and he left without it.

Randy Winkler looked like a detective with a lot of questions in this early photo taken at the blend hopper that served paper machine 9.

While he did not have the report, Kutska did have every other piece of evidence that had been assembled for the civil trial. He drove home and poured through it. It was about an hour later that Dodie called the Kutska house. Kutska had read enough of the paperwork to see that there was nothing of substance pointing his way and he told her so.

Dodie contacted Winkler at about 9 p.m., saying that she had talked to Kutska at about 5:45, and Kutska "made it sound like he was packing up to leave." Winkler was definitely interested, but it was what she told him next that may have given the detective his fill of Kutska and made him redouble his efforts in Kutska's direction.

Dodie told Winkler that Kutska had gone through the materials he had gotten at the police station, and he had called the police "dumb fucks" in describing their investigation. Dodie told Winkler that whenever Kutska used that word she "knew Keith was talking about the police." Kutska had also told Dodie that he was getting on with his life because the cops did not have enough to arrest him. He was taking a job in Tomah, Wisconsin, and moving away. He told Dodie that the cops "didn't have shit [on him]." Dodie also told Winkler that later that evening she had called back to the Kutskas and talked to Ardie. She said she "could hear Keith in the background. Keith sounded drunk and was telling Ardie to get off the phone and get packing."

Winkler's shaky grip on objectivity must have been severely challenged by the insult. He was not the dumb one. He had somebody taping Kutska's conversations and reporting his every move, and Kutska did not even know it. Indeed! If there was a *dumb fuck* around, it was Kutska. This very same guy had stopped at the police station that afternoon wanting a copy of the autopsy report. Did he get one? No, he did not, and he had been told he was not getting one. Who won that game? Guess who "didn't have shit" then! On top of that, Kutska was hitting the road and getting on with his life. Winkler had to be thinking that it would be a cold day in hell before that happened.

Dodie VerStrate would contact Winkler once more before she faded into the obscurity afforded unproductive and potentially troublesome CIs. She called him about 9 a.m. on September 6. This time, according to Winkler's detail sheet, she had received an anonymous phone call telling her, "Your [sic] fucking with a case that's not meant to be fucked with, and your [sic] going down." Dodie said she thought it was her father-in-law, Richard, on whom she had a restraining order. She had called the caller "Richard," but the caller had said he did not know any Richard. "I'm talking about the Monfils case," said the caller. "We're closer than you think and don't think you'll make it to court."

Later that same day Dodie paged Winkler, and he called her back. She said Kutska had driven by her house and was driving by again while she was on the phone with Winkler. She recorded the times and directions and made a big deal out of Kutska going by "real slow."

The inference from Dodie's contacts that day was clear. She was being harassed because of her involvement in the case. That night, when Winkler went out to their house, Dodie and Scott expressed concern about having any further contact with Kutska. Winkler told them that phone contact would be okay, but not to go over to Kutska's house any more "for their own safety." It was crazy talk but great police drama. For Dodie, the harassment was essential. Her importance in this case was passing her by—unless she could revitalize her role by coming up with something dramatic like reporting some imminent danger she was facing.

Who made the anonymous call? Better yet, was there actually such a call? Nothing ever turned up to answer either question. However, since he was innocent, Kutska certainly had not made that call. Besides, he did not know that the VerStrate's were working undercover for Winkler, nor did the other five men. As far as Kutska's drives past the VerStrate's house went, Kutska had a rental property in the town of Suamico that he was intending to sell. He was working on it that day. The house the VerStrates were renting was on his way there. In the back of Kutska's pickup were tools and building materials. No matter. Hyping a possible anonymous phone call and Kutska's driving by was about the only way Dodie was going to maintain her importance in the case and the resulting compensation.

Did Taxpayers Fund a Useless Payoff?

What eventually happened to the VerStrates is definitely worth examining. By the time these authors were able to contact Scott for an interview he and Dodie had separated—with plenty of animosity, according to Scott. Scott was back living with his father in Abrams with plans to move out of Wisconsin for a job the next day.

After the trial, following Winkler's instructions, said Scott, he and Dodie were formally married and shunted off to central Wisconsin in a made-to-order witness protection program under the alias Valentino. In the process, Scott ended up assuming legal custody for Dodie's two children by a previous marriage. After the two of them split up, much to his dismay, Scott had to pay child support for her children. According to Scott, Dodie would have it no other way.

Sometime after the Monfils trial, said Scott, Winkler handed them $27,000 in the presence of a City of Oconto police officer as a "reward for their efforts." When Scott asked Winkler where the rest of the reward money was, Scott said that Winkler told him, "That's all you're getting." Dodie and Scott also received a special citizen's award. They were then supposed to disappear from sight and keep a low profile, Scott said, "according to Winkler, for our own safety."

Since the VerStrates were of little to no help in the investigation and they were never used at the trial, some questions have to be asked:

- Why did they receive the reward money and a citizenship award?
- Why did they have to go into some kind of a witness protection program?
- Who paid for the witness protection program?
- Where did the rest of the reward money go?
- Who made the phone call to intimidate the VerStates, if there ever was such a call?
- What exactly did Dodie mean when she stated during an anonymous appearance on Green Bay television a few months later that what she knew "would bring the Green Bay police department to its knees"?
- Was the reward money paid to the VerStrates hush money?
- Was that witness protection program a way to get them out of the area?

The Reward Fund Runaround

It took well over a year for these authors to get information on the dispensation of the reward-fund money collected in the Monfils case. When that information finally surfaced, it came from one of the sources we had first posed questions to—the Green Bay Police Department. And when that information finally came, some nagging, unanswered questions still remained. The full story of the authors's attempts to procure the information casts serious doubts about how forthcoming the GBPD is or will ever be when it comes to any information on this case. Here is a short version of what happened.

The *Green Bay Press-Gazette* was reported to have collected the original reward monies, which totaled over $60,000. We contacted them first. By return letter Bill Nusbaum, *Press-Gazette* publisher at the time, said that the GBPD had dispersed the monies.

We then approached the GBPD with a Wisconsin Public Records Law request for information on the dispersal of the monies. The GBPD referred the request to the city attorney's office. After several letters between us and the city attorney's office, we were referred back to the *Press-Gazette* and to Crime Stoppers—both private entities under absolutely no obligation to release information under the public-records law.

Time was ticking. We had already been to the newspaper, so we thought we would take a whack at Crime Stoppers, knowing full well that keeping information under wraps was the name of their game. To our surprise, Crime Stoppers did get back to us. What their representative told us was that the organization never had anything to do with the collection or dispensation of the Monfils reward monies.

It seemed that somebody was not giving it to us straight. We went back to the city attorney's office. The next thing we knew, the GBPD was back in touch. They *could* get us some of the information we had wanted a year earlier after all—if we were still interested. Well, by golly, of course we were still interested. It was why we had written all those previous letters.

The GBPD finally sent us redacted copies of paperwork showing two payouts of some of the reward monies—one for $5,000 and one for $27,000. It was information the police could have and should have provided by law a year earlier, and it accounts for only half the reward fund.

We could spend another year looking for the rest of the story about the ultimate dispensation of the entire reward-fund monies—but it is already pretty clear how that would go. The reluctance of some of the authorities to cooperate and their propensity for keeping secrets are quite disturbing. When a case is built entirely on hearsay, the recipient of a reward payoff becomes critical information!

Still Nothing

In September 1994, Sergeant Randy Winkler traveled to Pulcifer Mechanics in the tiny town of Pulcifer, Wisconsin. It was about a half-hour drive from Kutska's home in Abrams, about an hour's drive from Green Bay. Kutska had been employed there for about three months in 1993 after being fired from the paper mill. It had been nearly a year and a half, however, since he had worked there. Winkler asked the other employees of Pulcifer Mechanics what Kutska had said about the case to them.

It was a wasted trip; he came away with nothing. But the picture was clear. Still focused on his earliest assumptions about Kutska and the other men, Winkler was desperate for information to support his hypothesis. Despite this and other foraging, October gave Winkler and the rest of the GBPD more of nothing.

On October 7, in support of getting David Wiener's handwriting exemplar, Winkler outlined his case in a court order. His report was skimpy: a recounting of the case chronology, a cursory look at the various participants, and a reference to the so-called suicide note in the phone book and the circumstances surrounding its discovery. There was absolutely no mention of any role-playing at the Fox Den, even though Keith Kutska was mentioned by name more than twenty times over seven pages.

November rolled around, and much was made of Mike Piaskowski's efforts to obtain information on how the computers recorded paper breaks on the machines at the mill. Apparently no deep thought was given to why he wanted the information. Like Mike Johnson at another point, Piaskowski was trying to clear his name. He was even hoping to shed some light on the case for the investigators.

Dale Basten had also been busy this whole time, running his own oddball investigation. In part it was because Winkler had asked Basten to do just that. Some people around the mill were actually sick of having Basten ask them questions about what they knew of Monfils's disappearance and death. A few of them reported him to mill management as a serious pest. Through a misunderstanding between Basten and Connie Jones, Jones had even taken out a restraining order on him. The authorities were only too happy to comply—it painted Basten in a bad light.

Early November saw another twist in the case. Brown County Judge Richard Greenwood ordered a status conference for January 27, 1995—thereby delaying the start of the civil trial by at least three weeks. He ruled that prosecution and defense lawyers could no longer question witnesses before that date. That meant that the defense attorneys for the men named in the civil suit were prevented from questioning the "three [main] police investigators" about the Monfils murder. The defense attorneys were wondering just how they could conduct a vigorous defense with their hands tied behind their backs. They were especially interested in the ongoing interaction between police investigators and Bruce Bachhuber, Susan Monfils's attorney. That interaction, it would turn out, was substantial.

For the state, it seemed to be a case of wanting things both ways. DA Zakowski could use the greater latitude that the civil trial would have in going after the men. Some of that information might prove valuable in his upcoming murder trial. But he did not seem to like the idea of sharing his information with the defense. Now the conflict between his two desires had slowed the process for a couple of months. The pressure was on. Two trials were looming on the horizon, and Zakowski still seemed uncomfortable with the evidence the investigators had.

The second anniversary of Monfils's death passed on Monday, November 21. The *Press-Gazette* had run its update of the Monfils story in its Sunday edition instead. The articles were mostly reissues of what the public already knew, but it was the editorial that got downright offensive. "Gang Also Murdered Tom Monfils," it pontificated. The article quoted a Green Bay police officer, Greg Urban, who defined a gang as "three or more people who use common marks, signals, or clothes; choose an area and regard it as turf; and include crime as their way of life." Robert Woessner, the *Press-Gazette* opinion-page editor, was proffering the idea that the workers being looked at for Monfils's death were no different than a youthful street gang.

"Youth gangs are a menace," he wrote. "But adults who go home to their families after work can be members of gangs every bit as deadly and ruthless as any footloose band roaming the streets late at night." In closing, Woessner suggested that the community "band together to confront gangs, to help police dissolve them so all of us are safer." His last words referred to the men under investigation in the Monfils case as "callous adults." Problem was, they had not even been arrested. Problem was, they had not even been charged, tried, or convicted. When they are finally exonerated, Woessner will owe them an apology. Hopefully it will be just as emphatic and just as heartfelt as his presumptuous smear. Even then, it will never undo its own damage.

The Miracle Toss

A little over a week later Winkler reinterviewed Brian Kellner, who had first been interviewed in the earliest months of the investigation. Kellner met with Winkler at the police station twice—after work on Tuesday evening, November 29, and again on the following morning. During the two sessions Kellner supposedly related the Fox Den playacting story to Winkler. "Supposedly" is the operative word because it is tough to say just how clearly this role-play emerges from Kellner's eight-hour-plus interviews. From those two sessions Winkler generated a nine-page police detail sheet on the first day and an eleven-page detail sheet on the second. He also produced a twelve-page statement for Kellner, which Kellner signed.

To fully appreciate the development of the Fox Den incident—as well as how it grew from out of the Kellner interview—it is important to examine Winkler's activities at the time. It was from Winkler's work those last two days in November and the first few weeks into December that the Fox Den role-play was born. The miraculous evolution of the incident must also be measured against the abject lack of progress in the investigation that spring, summer, and early autumn. There was not much going on in the case when Winkler reunited with Kellner. Then, within a matter of three weeks, things really began to heat up.

If the Fox Den role-playing story is to be believed, then there are other aspects of it that would seem to undermine that belief. Kellner had not come forward to relate Kutska's playacting before this time, and neither had Kellner's wife, Verna, nor had bar owners Ron and Charlotte Salnik. All of them knew the case remained unresolved. All of them had expressed sympathy for Monfils and his family on several occasions. The Kellners both had previous police contact during the Monfils investigation. As small-business owners and citizens, Ron and Char had no allegiance to Keith Kutska, an infrequent customer at their tavern. They all understood the importance of any kind of information that might help the police in solving the case—especially something as earthshaking as the alleged role-play. Yet not one of the four went to the police. If all of this is to be believed, at least four law-abiding citizens went about their lives for almost five months, thinking nothing of what Kutska was supposed to have described to them at the bar that day. That is, until Brian and then Verna Kellner "remembered" the event!

All of this puts a tremendous focus on Randy Winkler, the detective who helped Brian and Verna "recall" the incident. How did Winkler pull off the miracle that would break this case wide-open, giving the district attorney his key? How had Winkler—a small-town boy from little Gillett, Wisconsin—arrived at such a lofty position? How was it that Winkler single-handedly finally broke the thing wide open with his amazing touchdown toss when no one else seemed able to do it?

Professional Integrity

To answer these questions, we should take a closer look at Winkler and his level of professional integrity. Three years after delivering his miraculous game-winning break in the case, in 1997 Winkler would be jettisoned from the ranks of the GBPD, then under the leadership of a new chief, James Lewis. Soon after taking office, Chief Lewis handed Winkler a twenty-six-page letter, telling him to resign or be fired. Any person with a critical eye could see what had happened at that point. Winkler had made the Monfils case all right. But after an internal review, he proved to be a soiled police officer—the good old boy who would have to take the fall for the rest of the network. He was not only expendable. He *had* to go.

Winkler, it seems, had always brought a little too much to the job. It is easy to glean this by comparing the detail sheets of Winkler with those of his partner, Ken Brodhagen, on any given interview. Brodhagen's sheets are typically clean and factual; they are straightforward and easy to follow. Winkler's are slanted and peppered with loaded comments on a person's mental or emotional state. His reports are notoriously selective in the details presented and in the fashion they are reported. They often emphasize negative information by repeating it.

The VerStrates's undercover audiocassette recordings from 1994 were another example of Winkler's questionable ways. The VerStrates did nothing to further the case. What Winkler got out of the VerStrate recordings, however, was a significant amount of power—a way to threaten mill workers and tell them lies to see what they would do. Once he had the direct link to Kutska through the VerStrates, something changed. Winkler would flex his power from that point forward, whenever he was trying to intimidate someone into a certain version of the truth. He would point to those tapes—useless as they were in actual content—to bully every person he interviewed from November 29 through December 17, 1994. With Brian Kellner and then with Verna Kellner, the gambit would work exceptionally well.

Around this time Winkler appears to have stopped doing good police work. Now he was doing *his* work. In an apparent attempt to add a mystique to his persona, he had taken to wearing a trench coat and a fedora. The case was his, and he was single-handedly controlling its direction. Nearly every detail sheet and statement generated during this period is his—despite the fact that Brodhagen and Al Van Haute still had some involvement. It was Winkler who took charge of breathing new life into the investigation.

People close to him suggest that the Monfils case consumed Winkler. There are those, including one of Winkler's high school teachers and one of his high school friends, who say the case "ruined Randy." They say that his obsession destroyed him mentally and emotionally. However, the question then has to be proffered: If Winkler did his very best to get at the truth—without ever resorting to improper tactics or tainted evidence—then why would the case have ruined him at all? Even in the face of the serious flaws and doubts in this case, Winkler might have continued to work in law enforcement. He might have continued to bask in the knowledge that his handiwork produced the key that led to six convictions in one of the highest-profile cases in Wisconsin history. Instead he was forced to resign or be fired from the department he was so determined to impress. As more than one person with some inside knowledge has asked these authors, "What does that tell you?"

Winkler's self-absorption and the resulting license to do as he saw fit in this investigation seem obvious in his interviews during the three weeks in question. His interrogations of Brian and Verna Kellner, Jon Mineau, Don Boulanger, Jim Melville, and others were much more strident and one-sided than even *his* previous efforts.

10

Winkler's Slick Tricks

If a man is offered a fact which goes against his instincts, he will scrutinize it closely, and unless the evidence is overwhelming, he will refuse to believe it. If, on the other hand, he is offered something, which affords a reason for acting in accordance to his instincts, he will accept it even on the slightest evidence. The origin of myths is explained in this way.

—Bertrand Russell

Randy Winkler had always embellished his detail sheets with fishy, interpretive glimpses into the psyche and emotional state of the person he was interviewing. But his interviews starting in late-November 1992 betray a whole new level in his penchant to psychoanalyze. Winkler's detail sheets from this period show him continually jumping between fact and speculation in an apparent game of luring the person he was interviewing into divulging something he could use. Winkler would employ all of these shenanigans on Brian Kellner.

The purpose for meeting with Kellner on November 29 was to ascertain what Kutska might have told Kellner in recent months. Winkler should have exercised caution in putting too much weight on any one thing that Kellner said. Instead, there appears to be a plan in the works—Winkler darting between things that were widely known and the details that he was feeding to—and then hearing from—Kellner.

In the grand scheme of things, Kellner was hardly a valuable interview. He had been deer hunting the day of Tom Monfils's disappearance, and his knowledge of what happened that day was no better than the hearsay and speculations of countless other mill workers. Because Kellner lived near Kutska and socialized with him on occasion outside of work, several mill workers told these authors that they thought it was Kellner who was wearing a wire when Winkler told them he had someone taping Kutska's conversations. Still it was Kellner's association with Kutska that gave undue weight to the things Kellner might say or what he might be led to say. This was especially true in light of the investigation's lack of success leading up to Kellner's interview. He was something of a last-ditch effort.

Kellner also had a widespread reputation as an embellisher. Ardie Kutska described him to these authors as a "there guy." If you had been someplace, he had been there too. Former mill supervisor Greg Stephens described him as a "oner." If you had one, he had one too—most often bigger or more expensive than yours. Several coworkers have suggested that Kellner's stories usually had a "lack of familiarity with the truth." Winkler had a tendency to bounce things off the people he was interviewing—looking for one who might give back something more than he was given or one who might prove overly pliant in the process. Kellner turned out to be his man.

Kellner's tendency to reshape the truth and his proximity to Kutska were only two factors making him clay in Winkler's hands. He also brought to the table some serious vulnerability that Winkler was happy to exploit. By this time, the Kellners had split up, and Verna was living with someone else. Kellner was dealing with child-custody and money issues, besides those of his failed relationship with Verna. Kellner's nerves were especially raw when he showed up for his interview on

November 29. He told Winkler at the very start that he "was having a lot of personal problems."

According to Winkler's detail sheet, Winkler told Kellner that he "knew Keith Kutska has been spending a lot of time at his [Brian's] house, and that he [Brian] talked with Keith about what happened to Monfils." That was Winkler's official, written version. According to Kellner, however, Winkler told him straight out as their interview began that the police had proof that Verna and Keith Kutska were having an affair. Winkler told him, said Kellner, that if he did not cooperate, the police might have to expose that affair at trial. Either way, Kellner was made suspicious of his estranged wife and his friend. On top of that, he was also at risk of having his embarrassment hung out for the entire world to see. The interview might be an opportunity for Kellner to get some payback from Kutska if there had been anything going on behind his back. It was all so very clever.

Winkler then told Kellner that he was "trying to save him from having to go to the John Doe [hearing], and to do that he had to remember what Keith Kutska told him." Winkler went on to explain "that the judge may not believe him [Kellner] about not remembering and could charge him with contempt if he [Winkler] could prove he was lying." Given this threat—along with the threats of losing his children and his job and the threat of exposing his wife's alleged affair in pubic—the interview had now, for all intents and purposes, turned into an interrogation.

From that point on Kellner recited for Winkler everything Kutska and others had told him about the case. Kellner divulged information in no particular order, a scattergun approach that gave Winkler the opportunity he needed to latch onto the most convenient details. The alleged phone book suicide note and handwriting exemplars were relatively recent discussion items. Kellner started there. Next he relayed what he had heard about the advice of union president Marlyn Charles to Kutska regarding the stolen extension cord and the playing of the tape for Monfils.

Kellner then began talking about what he had heard concerning the morning of Monfils's disappearance. At this point Winkler's detail sheet seems to get purposely vague. Twice, Winkler records that Kellner told him that Kutska "knew something was going to happen" as he played the tape in the 9 coop "because those guys were getting all bent out of shape about what was being said." Between the lines it seems obvious: Winkler feels as though he is on the verge of something. At this point Winkler infers Kutska has guilty knowledge of Monfils's death. He writes, "Brian Kellner said that Keith Kutska just wanted Monfils to get so harassed and intimidated that he would quit his job at James River, but didn't want Monfils to get killed."

Most of what Kellner gave Winkler in the interview was undependable, and much of it was just plain inaccurate. For example, because Kellner was not present the morning of Monfils's disappearance, he could only relay things he had heard from others. That is called *hearsay*. Kellner's information is also a mess when it comes to dates and times in regard to particular information. Kellner—at least according to Winkler's detail sheets—has Kutska describing Monfils's injuries, including a lump on the back of his head. Winkler writes that Kutska mentioned this to Kellner "between the 18th and 31st" of May. The fact is, that incident could have only happened late that August, *after* Kutska had gotten a copy of the autopsy report that described that lump.

Winkler's Tuesday session with Kellner, which consumed nearly three hours, was drawing to a close. It was Kellner's son's birthday, and he wanted to take his kids to a movie. He asked Winkler if he could go home. Winkler acquiesced and recorded that Kellner left at 6:30 p.m. There had been absolutely no mention of the role-playing at the Fox Den.

By 7:45 the next morning, November 30, Kellner was back at the police station. In his usual modus operandi, Winkler marked the date and time and then recorded what he had offered Kellner to drink and what he had requested. It gave his detail sheets an air of factuality. As they began, Winkler renewed his efforts to generate something substantial. The break between the two interviews had actually given him time to plan his next moves. He started with a little deceit, which he fully acknowledged in his detail sheet:

> I had spoken with Brian on 11-29-94 and told him about some tape recordings [from Dodie VerStrate] I had with Kutska talking about what happened with

Monfils. I insinuated that Brian and his wife, Verna L. Kellner (01-04-61), were on the tape recordings of Keith Kutska talking about the Monfils case. It appeared Brian believed that I had all the information he gave me on tape.

When questioning Brian I brought up things that Keith had told Scott R. VerStrate (06-14-61) and Dodie M. VerStrate (11-07-71) and things that were on the tape when Keith Kutska talked to them. I quoted Keith Kutska several times during the interview, and Brian agreed that those things were said, along with others. Brian did say several times that the things I said he didn't hear. I told him that those things could have been said to other people and not him, and I might have them wrong. I also told Brian that I was not going to tell him everything that was said so that he wouldn't know how much we had. I explained that there were times when Keith Kutska was talking about the murder that are not on tape, or we couldn't hear him. I explained that we needed his help to get those things.

Winkler had Kellner believing that this was all on tape—some tapes of Kutska talking with other workers and some tapes of Kutska talking with Kellner himself. Essentially Winkler was telling Kellner, "I've got all of this already and I'm just double-checking it with you." What he was really doing was creating something absolutely brand-new and unsupported in any way.

Winkler reminded Kellner that he was trying to do him a big favor—to "save him from having to go to the John Doe Hearing and be questioned by the District Attorney and Judge Naze." According to Winkler, Kellner said he "didn't want to be ordered into court for this and was willing to tell me [Winkler] everything now."

They were just getting started. In effect Kellner was ready to sign off on any words—his or those placed before him. He had walked through Winkler's door and was now wandering around inside a vast, unknown room. Once there, Kellner became the dupe as Winkler fashioned the Fox Den role-play incident.

Kellner's interviews for these two days do not center plainly on the Fox Den bar or any specific incident there. Rather the role-play story emerges from the ashes of a myriad of topics as tangible as the fake suicide note in the phone book and as vague as Kutska's constant rambling about the case. Kellner remembers Kutska talking about the case all the time, at several different locations: his house, Kutska's house, at work, the Fox Den—wherever.

Winkler must have liked Kellner's mention of the Fox Den. Winkler had written in one detail sheet that he "had a CI [VerStrate] go to that bar and tape record conversations with Keith Kutska on several occasions." One of the VerStrate tapes included a conversation with Char Salnik talking with Kutska about the Monfils case. Kutska was getting loud, the detail sheet noted, and Char had asked him to tone it down.

Because there is no chronological pattern to Kellner's description, a patchwork account began to unfold of the events of the morning of Monfils's disappearance. Kellner eventually offers up a bubbler confrontation, but it emerges from a jumble of at least seven diverse elements—each having nothing to do with any bubbler or any such confrontation:

- The "Tom talk," which the police liked to refer to as a "first confrontation."

- A description of the comings and goings in the 9 coop as various mill workers listened to the tape and discussed what kind of official action the union might take against Monfils for making his call.

- Mike Hirn approaching Monfils while Monfils was in the process of taking the rolls off the dry end of his paper machine. Hirn asked Monfils, whom he considered "a friend," why he would "do something like this [make the anonymous call]?" Hirn's challenge to Monfils had been at Kutska's behest, contributing to its darker nature.

- Kutska telling Rey Moore in coop 9 that he should "harass Monfils because Monfils is white and Moore is black, and Monfils couldn't say a thing about Moore harassing him because they would say Monfils was just being prejudiced."

- Rey Moore making a karate chop into the palm of his hand, saying "Now you've got him [Monfils] by the balls."
- Dale Basten pantomiming to Winkler at one point in the investigation how the person who harmed Monfils was probably shaking the tape in Monfils's face.
- The various references to the bubbler made since the earliest days of the investigation.

Kellner Signs Off

At two points in his twelve-page statement—between pages four and seven and again between pages nine and eleven—Kellner basically signed off on the events at the Fox Den. By signing his statement, he was in essence saying they occurred. But he did not write the statement. Detective Winkler did that. According to procedure, however, Winkler had given Kellner the opportunity to correct that statement. By making a few superficial changes and then signing his name to the last page, Kellner formally agreed to everything that was contained therein. Kellner did not have the temerity to fight over details. Kellner had Winkler's various threats firmly in mind, just as Winkler had intended. Kellner told these authors he was not going to argue with Winkler over a bunch of aimless gossip and some drunken speculation at a bar.

Brian Kellner (left) receiving an award for the catching the largest walleye at the James River fishing contest and banquet

In those five-odd pages, however, the Fox Den role-playing incident found its birth. It began with Kellner's vague idea of Hirn and Moore harassing Monfils. That was based on two real events. Hirn actually had a few words with Monfils at the dry end of the 7 paper machine. Later Kutska had urged Moore to "give him [Monfils] some shit"—though Monfils had already disappeared by then. Those things had happened.

Winkler's scene at the bubbler then gathered steam with the addition of a bunch of workers in the 9 coop listening to the Kutska tape. That had also happened: guys had gathered in coop 9. At his house one day, Kutska had even drawn out for Kellner where each man was standing inside the coop when listening to the tape.

Kellner's statement then relayed how a large group of workers had left the coop to confront Monfils. That never happened! Yes, guys had left coop 9 after hearing the tape but not all at the same time and definitely not for the purpose of confronting Monfils. The fact that the men had not left en masse to confront him was not going to get in the way. Not now. Not when Winkler had Kellner in free fall.

Kellner was now liberally transposing the various accounts of the morning's activities that he had heard over the span of two years, and he was melding them into one. Winkler was helping him produce a surrealistic hybrid masterpiece—one to which Kellner would blindly attach his name, suggesting that he was in fact the author. *He was not.*

Interspersing other details from throughout Kellner's two sessions, the statement Winkler eventually wrote for Kellner to sign set about constructing a bubbler confrontation and a role-play. Kellner related how Kutska had once theorized about a wrench that may have been used to strike Monfils in the back of the head. That now found itself patched into the story, as did the weight and rope found around Monfils's neck.

According to Kellner's statement, Kutska had himself "just sitting back at the time and watching what was going on while all the rest of the guys were giving Monfils shit." Essentially that was also true—a detail from several other points in the morning now spliced into Kellner's statement. Kutska had sat back, rather smugly, watching the other guys pursue his cause. He had encouraged both Hirn and Moore to give Monfils "some shit" about his anonymous call to police. Those and several other actual events found themselves merged into one—now taking place as though they were a part of a bubbler confrontation.

Kellner's recollections were delivered in a stream-of-consciousness fashion and not presented as a vivid account of an actual event. They were a part of everything Kellner could think of to give Winkler in order to save himself from realizing Winkler's many threats.

Kellner followed his mention of the Fox Den by saying that Kutska had begun to open up about the case "around the end of March [1994]." But what Kellner attributed to happening in the early spring had actually occurred in midsummer—at least according to Dodie VerStrate's reports to Winkler and Winkler's own July 17 detail sheet. Kellner's statement put it this way:

> Keith was in pretty good spirits and said things were finally coming to an end, and he was going to get on with his life. Keith was talking about getting a job at a new mill. Keith said from what he read, he was cleared as being a chief suspect in the murder. Keith said he knew he was still a suspect, but he wasn't the one that did it. Keith said that he had read all the stuff and found out the cops didn't have anything to go on.

Those were the *exact things* that Dodie VerStrate had reported to Winkler as happening in the middle of *July*. Now, at the end of November, Kellner was assigning them to *March*. Kellner's statement was saying that Kutska had "read all the stuff and found out the cops didn't have anything to go on." But it was not until July 17 that Winkler himself had handed those reading materials to Kutska.

Finally, Kutska is quoted as labeling the thing a "murder" though he had never done that for anyone until *after* getting his hands on the autopsy report in August.

Hearsay by Sketch

During the two-day interrogation, Winkler also elicited from Kellner three drawings, which were presented at trial (see figures 1–3). They were supposed to be replicas of drawings Kutska had made for Kellner on some napkins at the Fox Den bar depicting the configuration of the men in coop 9 and at the bubbler confrontation. They were neither. In reality they were misrepresentations of Kutska's renderings of a series of illustrations by *Press-Gazette* staff artist Joe Heller which are discussed in chapter 8. Kutska had seen the drawings a year earlier in the November 21, 1993, edition of the newspaper. Kutska had scratched out these drawings for Kellner on a coffee table in his living room.

While Winkler used Kellner's drawings to add substance to a bubbler confrontation, Kellner's own statement to Winkler about where they had come from is very different. It is a telltale detail that was missed or ignored during the investigation. Winkler quotes Kellner:

> When Keith drew me the drawing we were at his house, and he used the one that was in the copy that he had out of the *Press-Gazette*. I have redrawn what Keith had showed me today. Keith showed me where Servais was sitting, and where Delvoe was sitting and were [sic] everyone was at the different times.

There are plenty of other problems with the alleged bubbler confrontation as it grew out of Kellner's story. According to Kellner, Pete Delvoe, Don Boulanger, Jon Mineau, and Dennis Servais were all supposed to have been there at the bubbler and were to have seen what happened. To this day, all four of them deny having ever seen any such thing.

Kellner's interview on that Wednesday morning closes as haphazardly as it began. There is a second-hand account of the "Tom talk," some mention of the role of union president Marlyn Charles and some loose ends about when and where the tape was played. There is also further discussion of Kutska's threat of suicide, which Kellner had first mentioned the previous evening.

Winkler wrapped up his detail sheet by noting that Kellner had been given every opportunity to correct his statement before he signed it. Winkler then tossed out a subtle twist. He told Kellner that Kellner could "tell Keith Kutska about the [VerStrate] tapes and the statement if he wanted to," but Winkler preferred that he did not. Winkler told Kellner that Kutska would "get to know the statement after he was arrested" and that he, Winkler, would not tell him about it until then.

At this point, Winkler worked to ingratiate himself even more with

Kellner by talking about the alleged relationship between Kutska and Verna. Lending a sympathetic ear, he asked Kellner if Verna and Kutska "had any sort of romantic relationship," and Kellner said he did not think so. Winkler then asked him if he had talked with any of the others about the case. Kellner mentioned Piaskowski and Lepak by name but said both men did not talk about it. Winkler's detail sheet ended with the words "Brian left the station at approximately 12:15 p.m."

To this day, Kellner does not quite understand what he did or how this happened to him. He left the police station that day not even realizing the full impact of his actions. He had helped Winkler put together something the authorities had been desperate for since day one. He could never have known that he had been manipulated to create an obscure confession to murder. Rereading his statement only affirms its rather nebulous nature.

Today, Kellner will tell you definitely that he was used by Winkler. He will also tell you that the version of ramblings regarding the Fox Den role-play—as put into his statement—never happened. That scenario was, in fact, developed by Detective Winkler. Kellner has emphasized in post-trial affidavits and again to these authors that he and Kutska had indulged in a lot of speculating at the Fox Den bar that day about what might have happened to Monfils.

These authors challenged him. He had, after all, signed off on the role-play just as it was presented at trial. "Then why did you sign that statement?" he was asked. He replied, "I don't know. I just wanted to get out of there."

At first that sounded so very weak. However, according to experts in wrongful convictions, it is a common misconception that some sort of a statement must be signed before a person will be allowed to leave a police interrogation. Randy Winkler tossed the miracle pass, and Brian Kellner had unwittingly caught the ball.

Figure 1 Kellner's drawing of the Tom-talk

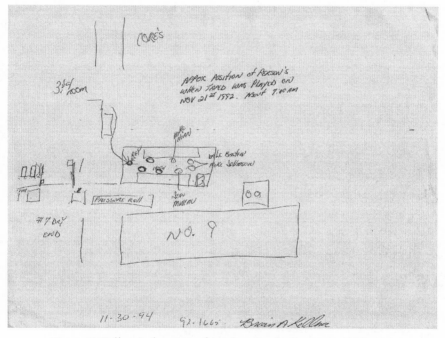

Figure 2 Kellner's drawing of workers in the 9 coop at 7:00 a.m.

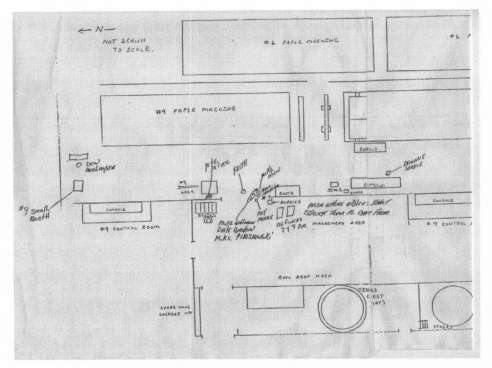

Figure 3 Kellner's drawing of the alleged bubbler confrontation

Kellner's sketches *illustrate* his completely erroneous perceptions of what he had been hearing from Kutska and others. Based on hearsay, they are essentially unreliable and worthless:

- In his rendition of the "Tom-talk," his placement of the participants is completely wrong.
- Kellner's drawing of the workers in the 9 coop is also wrong. Four of these workers, Rey Moore, Dale Basten, Mike Johnson, and Mike Hirn, were in totally different areas at 7:00 a.m. Moreover, this group was never together in the 9 coop at the same time.
- Kellner's sketch of an alleged bubbler confrontation is contrary to fact as well. When Dennis Servais was at the 7 smoking table, Monfils and Pete Delvoe were working the 7:34 a.m. turnover on paper machine 7.

Supporting a House of Cards

Randy Winkler had to sit at the station that afternoon completely satisfied. District Attorney Zakowski could no longer talk of a lack of evidence. Not now. On the surface, at least, it was all there—even drawn out on paper by Brian Kellner. Best of all, it hung the very men on whom the police had always set their sights. There was a big roundup coming in the not-too-distant future.

Still it was a house of cards—essentially constructed out of thin air. Winkler would have to get to work immediately, adding more cards to keep it standing. One might call his work over the next two weeks inspired. He had gotten an account of some role-playing concerning a bubbler confrontation. He would use that as a springboard from which to proceed. Over the next three days his work would be of strategic importance.

On Thursday, December 1, Winkler conducted his next interview. Curiously it was not an interview with Verna Kellner or Ron Salnik or Charlotte Salnik that would corroborate the Fox Den role-playing and indirectly the bubbler incident. Talking with any of them would have indicated an effort by Winkler to check the veracity of Kellner's hearsay account of a bubbler confrontation before Winkler ran with it. Instead he approached mill worker Jon Mineau, ostensibly because Mineau had been named as a part of the bubbler confrontation in Kellner's interviews.

Winkler began by telling Mineau that the police had "developed some new information and wanted him to verify what [the police] were told." Mineau said he would try, but he had already given a statement. He added that he still felt Monfils had killed himself.

Winkler told Mineau that he had been named as a part of the bubbler confrontation but that the police did not think that he played anything more than the role of a bystander. Mineau said he "didn't recall any of that happening." Winkler then proceeded to work Mineau over in every way he could to get him to support the bubbler story—giving Mineau, in the process, plenty of room to exonerate himself as a lesser player. Winkler showed Mineau where his name had been written on Kellner's drawing of the people in coop 9.

Faced with the drawing, Mineau did his best to cooperate. He suggested that he, Dave Daniels, and Don Boulanger get together to see if they could "come up with who was in the coop at the time." Mineau even volunteered to be hypnotized to help bring out anything he might not remember.

In closing, Winkler suggestively added in his detail sheet: "Jon never told us during our interview that what we told him was wrong ... he never said he wasn't there, just didn't recall it happening that way." Mineau was trying his best not to rankle the detective by arguing with him. He knew—as did every other worker—that the mill managers had given them a directive to "cooperate with the police investigation." For many workers, the directive created a no-man's-land between telling what they knew to be the truth and what the police wanted to hear. This was especially true for guys with a little less gumption to disagree with the authorities, such as Kellner and Mineau.

Winkler also asked Mineau for some drawings, but Mineau hesitated at the idea, wondering just what situation from the morning of November 21 Winkler wanted him to draw. Finally Mineau produced two sketches for Winkler. Both were depictions of where guys were sitting inside coop 9. Neither of them matched Kellner's drawings.

Winkler also asked Mineau to keep their conversation under his hat. Mineau would fail to do that, and he would end up regretting it just a few days later. It had been a trick on Winkler's part anyway.

On December 2, at about 9 a.m., Winkler finally met with Verna Kellner. Winkler began by telling her that he "knew she had talked with Keith Kutska and Keith [had] *told her everything about the murder of Tom Monfils* [authors's emphasis]." According to Winkler, Verna "had a very shocked look on her face and said, 'yes he did.'" Winkler then told her that he was "trying to save her from having to go to the John Doe, and wanted to know if she wanted to talk [to Winkler] … or did she want to go to the John Doe." Verna was very clear that she would much rather talk to Winkler than "have to go to court." Winkler was back at it. He told Verna he had "been doing some things, and [had] been up around Abrams for the past ten months." He added that he "knew all about" her and Kutska. He was working the romantic involvement angle.

Then Winkler flashed his audiotape ploy again. "I have some tapes of Keith Kutska talking about Monfils," he told her. He added that he "didn't want to have to play them in court because of what was on them." He insinuated that Verna did not want them played in court either. She agreed. Winkler was at least halfway home.

The tape trick had worked on Verna too. She knew that Kutska's conversations were being monitored, knowledge of which she had acquired in a roundabout way. Jim Seidl, another mill worker, had actually pulled Kutska outside of his house in his robe one day and told him that his house was bugged. Verna and Ardie Kutska had examined the light fixture in the Kutska's kitchen when they realized that a conversation they had about marijuana might have been overheard or recorded. This incident was in the back of Verna's mind as Winkler mentioned the tapes that morning.

Winkler was proud of his clandestine recordings. He stated in his detail sheet that he even "left the interview room and got several of the recorded conversations with Keith Kutska and our CI, and some recording equipment." He brought the stuff back into the room and plopped it on the table in front of Verna. He then told her that he had the dates that they recorded Kutska and transcripts of what was said. Winkler told her that he "was not going to play [any] of the tapes to her, or show the transcripts" because he "wanted her to tell [him] what she remembered."

If either of the Kellners had asked to hear the tapes in their entirety, they would have discovered that they themselves were not on those tapes, and neither was any mention of any Fourth of July role-playing or marijuana discussions. Had Brian or Verna asked to hear those tapes, they might have been far less compelled to fall in line with the role-playing scenario that Winkler let them believe he had on tape. Of course Winkler knew they were not likely to ask for the tapes to be played. He had boxed both of them into a corner, leading them to think that the tapes contained damning things for the two of them as well.

Verna signed a statement for Winkler that was just a reiteration of things Winkler had heard before from the VerStrates and from Brian. Verna did recall Kutska coming over to the Kellner's house the day he had gotten the autopsy report. They went out and sat on the front lawn because Verna's kids were home and she did not want them to hear what was in the report. Kutska told Verna that—now that he had seen the autopsy—he "knew Monfils was murdered." He showed the report to her and told her that according to the autopsy, "Monfils was kicked in the testicles, and hit in the head."

Verna's words are mostly muddled hearsay. She did not work at the mill. She did not know the layout of the mill or most of the people Winkler was talking about. She could only relate her impressions of all the different things she had heard from others. The only reason she could remember the names from all the gossip she had heard was because Winkler had them written on a piece of paper and placed it in front of her.

In spite of this, however, she did not confirm a bubbler confrontation. Instead she said:

> Keith told us the names of the guys that were involved and said how they had plan[n]ed to trap Tommy by the *booth or bubbler* [authors's emphasis], so that he couldn't take off or deny that he made the phone call. Keith said he played the tape for everybody in the booth. Keith said after they heard the guys all went out and surrounded Monfils so he couldn't take off. Keith said he stood back and watched as Mike Piaskowski, Mike Hirn, Dale Basten, Rey Moore, [Verna underlined

these names in her statement and wrote "I think" over Piaskowski's name] and I think he said there were more of them there, but I don't recall the names, yelled and intimidated Monfils. Keith said they were all trying to get Tommy to get [sic] walk off the job and quit. Keith said after they confronted Monfils they all went back to their jobs, and Monfils was reported missing right after that.

Verna's account of the Fox Den events that were supposed to have explained what happened at a bubbler confrontation was far less specific than Brian's. It is also very different. In fact it ends with the men going back to work after giving Monfils a hard time. These differences in the Kellners's stories do not matter when applied to a phantom event. But they do matter when it comes to establishing whether or not an elaborate role-playing incident had occurred. Here the details are essential. The fact that they are not anywhere near the same only emphasizes a lack of confirmation for the Fox Den role-playing.

New Life for a Dead-End Case

With Brian and Verna Kellner as his foils, Winkler had created the Fox Den role-play myth. The police now felt they really had something—despite the question marks that should have been there. Over the next few weeks, Ken Brodhagen and Al Van Haute would be put back into active duty on the case. The three of them were busy again. Finally the case had taken on new life. District Attorney Zakowski's criticism of "not enough evidence" from that summer did not seem to sting quite so much.

On December 3, 1994, Brodhagen and Detective Sergeant M. McKeough interviewed mill worker Tom Hendricks. They told him that they "knew he had been spending time with Keith Kutska, and that he had been present when Keith Kutska had discussed the events around the death of Thomas Monfils with him and others." Hendricks told the officers that he had gone fishing with Kutska a couple of years before, but he did not recall much. One thing he did remember, said Hendricks, was that Kutska thought Monfils had killed himself—until much later when the autopsy report convinced him otherwise. When asked which of the men he thought might be involved, Hendricks wondered about Dale Basten, but only because of rumors at the mill. None of the police contact with Hendricks verified Kellner's Fox Den story or confirmed any kind of a bubbler confrontation.

On December 6, Winkler and Brodhagen interviewed Connie Jones. Jones's previous statements were reviewed, with the intention of having her confirm a second confrontation between Monfils and his coworkers at the bubbler. If anything she blew more holes in the possibility, telling the detectives that she had plainly seen Mike Piaskowski—not in the 9 coop with the rest of the men—but firmly ensconced in the control room of the 7 paper machine where he belonged.

The next day Winkler met with Dave Daniels, who had worked on the 9 machine along with Kutska, Boulanger, and Mineau the day of Monfils's disappearance. The police interest in Daniels centered on his conversations with Mineau. They were looking hard at Mineau as a member of a bubbler confrontation—albeit one with lesser involvement, one who might roll on his "fellow conspirators." Mineau would not roll on the others. He could not. He had never observed a bubbler incident.

There was a big deal made out of whether Mineau or Daniels had gotten ice from the ice machine that morning. The idea was that if Mineau had not actually gotten the ice as he said he did, it then meant he had some unexplained time away from his work area or that he had lied to the police. It was another molehill magnified into a mountain. Basically Daniels and Boulanger had spent their downtime that morning in the small 9 coop because the main coop was crowded with people coming and going to listen to the tape. Daniels told the police that Mineau had talked to him on three occasions, telling him that the cops had a confession by Kutska on tape and that Kutska had involved Mineau in that confession. It was Winkler who had fed this counterfeit information to Mineau in the first place.

On December 8, Brodhagen and Winkler dropped in on Mineau again. They wanted a handwriting sample from him. Mineau invited the two cops into his house and filled out the exemplar at his kitchen table. As he was getting the sample, Winkler decided to give Mineau a little shot. "I hear you think it was Brian Kellner who wore the wire," said Winkler. Then Winkler recorded what he perceived as Mineau's reaction: "Jon hung his head and his face turned red, and he said that he just couldn't keep his mouth shut, he had to tell someone." If Winkler had thought it over, he would have concluded at that point that Mineau was the last guy to be a part of any conspiracy. Mineau could not keep a secret. He had not even been able to stay quiet about his first interview with the police when they told him not to tell anyone.

Winkler also pressed Mineau on the ice issue again. Mineau was unclear about how much ice he had gotten or in what kind of a container he had gotten it. Winkler mistakenly figured Mineau was hiding something. At that point Winkler told Mineau that the police "knew he is at least a witness and if he wasn't going to tell us what he saw then he was going to be against us, and a suspect." After that comment, it was pretty clear to Mineau that he needed a lawyer. He secured one as quickly as he could.

A few days later, Brodhagen and Winkler were back at the Fox Den. They wanted Ron and Char Salnik to acknowledge that some kind of role-playing had occurred in their place. The Salniks could not truthfully acknowledge it and told Winkler so. They had never seen anything like that because nothing like that had happened. As the detectives were leaving, Ron told them again that he could not remember anything other than what he had already told them, and that they could threaten him all they wanted and he was not going to admit to something he did not know.

Winkler responded by telling Ron that he had not been issued a threat. Winkler said that "it was a fact that he [Ron] may be called for the John Doe hearing and questioned there by the judge. [And] if the judge thinks he lied, or is obstructing in any way he could find him in contempt." If that was not a threat, Ron told these authors, it sure sounded like one to him.

Brodhagen went a step further, telling Char that she herself had been "recorded while Keith Kutska was giving a demonstration in the bar, about where he was while others went up and confronted Tom Monfils." Never mind that such a recording did not exist. He added that "there were other people present that he put in place to demonstrate." Firmly but politely Char told Brodhagen that "she didn't remember anything like that."

There was absolutely no reason for the Salniks to cover up a role-play, had one happened. They hardly knew Kutska at all. He was nothing more to them than an occasional customer. What reasons would they have had for pretending that a role-play had not happened in their bar if one had? They had no allegiance to Kutska or to any of the other men, whom they had never met. They had never worked at James River and never belonged to a union. They certainly were not going be a part of a conspiracy to cover up a murder.

Sadly both Ron and Char have passed away—with doubts hanging over their heads, thanks to the Green Bay authorities. Before they passed on, however, both of them emphatically told these authors two things: They had no reason to lie to the police and—as small-business owners and good citizens—they would have immediately reported a role-play if one had occurred in their bar. It is time to restore their good name and put away the doubts about the Salniks.

Mineau had now become the police's latest whipping boy. Over the next few days, Winkler and Brodhagen interviewed mill workers Ardie Schalk, Dale Verheyden, and Randy Wisniewski. The detectives were working hard to rope Mineau into their bubbler-confrontation theory. Nothing useful came of these efforts. They did hear repeatedly about Mineau's failure to keep the secret they themselves had fed him about Kutska confessing on tape. The idea that Kutska had admitted to the murder on tape was, of course, a twofold lie: There was no such tape, and Kutska had never confessed—under any circumstances—to killing Monfils. The fact that the police were hearing about Mineau's loose lips from other mill workers further undermined the GBPD's union-code-of-silence theory.

Christmas was a week away, and the police had wrapped a wonderful present for themselves and for District Attorney Zakowski—one that had topped their wish list for two years. By stage-managing Brian Kellner's misinformation, they had produced a hearsay role-playing scenario and, through that role-playing, a bubbler confrontation. They would spend the next five months working and reworking the men they thought were present at that bubbler. In the process they would generate even more paperwork. If a case was to be judged on paperwork alone, they were really making progress.

In truth 1994 was a paltry year for the GBPD in terms of evidence. It did, however, produce what Zakowski would call the break in the case—his key. Sure it was feeble and weak, but it was so very late in the game now. After all this time, they surely did not want to pull the plug and start all over again. Zakowski would cobble Kellner's hearsay together with David Wiener's drunken, repressed-memory flashback of Dale Basten and Mike Johnson in the tissue chest area (see chapter 17) as the cornerstones of his case. Four months and twelve days into 1995, the same men who had been under the microscope from day one would be rounded up in a SWAT-team action.

11

A String of
Unproven Theories

*A theory must be consistent with all
the facts and inconsistent with none.*

—Major tenet of the scientific method

Thanks to Detective Sergeant Randy Winkler, the police had hit pay dirt. Caving in to a barrage of Winkler's threats, Brian Kellner poured out everything he ever heard about the disappearance and death of Tom Monfils—especially as it related to Keith Kutska.

Winkler took that jumble and turned it into what looked like an admission by Kutska. Kellner signed off on the notion that Kutska had actually demonstrated what happened to Monfils. District Attorney John Zakowski would run with that idea, warts and all, from there.

"Way to Go, Kutska!" and the Bubbler Confrontation

The Fox Den role-play hearsay transformed the "Way-to-Go-Kutska Theory" into the "Bubbler-Confrontation Theory," looping in all of the police suspects in the process. It was a custom-ordered, brand-spanking-new drama featuring every bell and whistle on the police and district attorney's wish list.

In the criminal complaints released the day of the big roundup, the district attorney laid out what he saw as the collective and individual roles of each of the six men. The complaints set out a theory based on Kutska as the perceived "ringleader." He had—went the story—enticed various coworkers into confronting Monfils. At some point the starting theory had to expand from Kutska's solitary gripe with Monfils to a crusade taken up by a group of Kutska's coworkers. Otherwise these same men were all witnesses to Kutska's innocence.

At about 7:35 a.m. on November 21, a group of seven of his coworkers is said to have cornered Monfils at a bubbler in their work area. At the district attorney's office, these authors were told that the group had worked itself into a frenzy listening to Kutska's tape and was operating with a mob mentality. One worker is said to have stood with his face only inches from Monfils's face. Another is said to have shaken the tape in his face. All of them are alleged to have been yelling at Monfils. Someone else is said to have hit him in the back of the head, possibly with a wrench. Kutska is said to have stood back and watched it all unfold. Two workers are said to have hauled Monfils's still-alive body to the furnace room, and a third is said to have gotten the weight and rope that was attached to his neck. At that point, Monfils's body is alleged to have been dumped into the chest. With specific names attached to some of these specific actions—though not all—criminal complaints were issued.

The exact details of this scenario are the stuff of paperback fiction. The reasons why were plainly illustrated at trial by Assistant DA Larry Lasee. There were neither witnesses nor physical evidence, said Lasee. What the prosecution did have in abundance, however, were "gaps." Any missing details would have come from two very undependable sources: Brian Kellner's haphazard interviews of late November 1994 and David Wiener's repressed-memory flashback of late May 1993. Those shaky details, however, would find their way into the criminal complaints.

Though it laid out specific actions by the six men, the scenario set out in the criminal complaints was never supported by an exact timeline of these actions (let alone evidence). The best account the police could assemble was a set of twelve brief summaries—written "snapshots" if you will—covering the men's actions at five-minute intervals between 7:00 and 8:00 a.m. This method left a lot of room for creative speculation. These scenarios—assembled in the first days of the investigation—never included a confrontation between Monfils and his coworkers. Such a confrontation would have to be plugged into the vacuum of one of the five-minute gaps—exactly where Winkler put it.

The Bubbler Confrontation and a Conspiracy of Silence

Rather than yield to the commonsense odds against their Way-to-Go-Kutska and Bubbler-Confrontation theories, the police and district attorney forged ahead. In the process, they refused to see these men as individuals who had each tried their very best to cooperate from the get-go. Yet no one could supply a whisper of support for the fictitious bubbler confrontation. Instead the police and DA explained away their weak circumstantial case by attaching a Union-Conspiracy-of-Silence Theory to their other two theories. They suggested that the men in their big roundup had all hung together like radical terrorists hell-bent on a suicide mission.

> "And yet, ladies and gentlemen, none of these defendants have ever pointed the finger at one of their—at one of the others with any concrete incriminating evidence."
>
> —District Attorney John Zakowski, from trial transcript, day 27

Zakowski was not exactly lying to the jury when he said the men had never provided the authorities with "any concrete incriminating evidence." They had not. They could not; they had no knowledge of any incriminating facts that would help the police.

The fact is that these men repeatedly tried to help the police. Contrary to what the authorities will say, the men even pointed fingers at each other in an effort to help resolve this crime. Add to that the fact that the police investigation never turned up even a hint of a nefarious contact between the men—before or since Monfils's death—and you have a union conspiracy that never existed.

Information debunking the existence of a conspiracy was in the possession of the authorities all along. Consider the following accusations made by the men against one another, garnered from detail sheets and statements taken by the Green Bay Police Department itself. Also note that at trial DA Zakowski piggybacked the cops's union-conspiracy myth with the bubbler myth.

- Mike Hirn intimated that Rey Moore might be guilty because Moore seemed very nervous when the supervisor of converting, E. Galindo, went to shake his hand as she asked Moore if he knew anything about Monfils's disappearance. (GBPD detail sheet, 12/17/92)

- Hirn told the police a guy with the nickname of "Swivel Hips" had information about the case. Hirn said, "Find 'Swivel Hips' and you'll know who killed Monfils." Amusingly it turned out that "Swivel Hips" was actually Mike Hirn himself! Hirn was unaware that coworker Jim Smith and his friend Dixie privately referred to Hirn by that name. (GBPD detail sheet, 12/19/93)

- Dale Basten told Detective Denise Servais that he heard that Hirn and Monfils did not get along very well. (GBPD detail sheet, 12/02/92)

- Basten referred to Moore as a "nigger." (GBPD detail sheet, 12/04/92)

- Basten told Winkler that Moore repeatedly called Monfils a "bastard." (GBPD detail sheet, 12/08/92)

- Basten told Winkler that he thought Hirn pushed Monfils into the "vat." (GBPD detail sheet, 12/08/92)

- Basten offered to be hypnotized if it would help the police. (GBPD detail sheet, 05/28/93)

- Basten told Winkler that Hirn hated Monfils. (GBPD detail sheet, 12/08/92)

- Moore believed that Kutska had set him up. (GBPD detail sheet, 12/14/92)

- Mike Piaskowski relayed a rumor he had heard about Michael Johnson and the rope to Sergeant Van Haute. (GBPD detail sheet, 01-18-93)

- Basten suspected Hirn was the guy that killed Monfils. (GBPD detail sheet, 01/19/93)

- Basten said Kutska knew what happened to Monfils. (GBPD detail sheet, 01/19/93)

- Basten told Winkler and Van Haute that Steve Klarkowski quoted Hirn as saying that he [Hirn] had shoved Monfils. (GBPD detail sheet, 02-25-93)

- Basten again speculated that Hirn was the guy that killed Monfils. (GBPD detail sheet, 05/28/93)

- Randy Lepak said that Moore, Hirn, and Basten had been rumored as the ones responsible for Monfils's death. (John Doe hearing, 03/15/93)

- Piaskowski named Moore, Hirn, and Basten as possible suspects. (John Doe hearing, 03/15/93)

- Hirn said that Piaskowski, Johnson, Basten, and Kutska probably killed Monfils. (FBI Report 1/28/94)

- Hirn incriminated Piaskowski at trial. (trial transcript, 10/20/95)

- Hirn asked Winkler to install a recorder on his phone to record any calls from the others. (GBPD detail sheet, 01/29/94)

- Hirn offered to wear a wire to trap Basten. (GBPD detail sheet, 01/29/94)

- Hirn told Winkler that Mike Laundrie said that Johnson asked him at a union meeting, "What if it was three guys trying to scare Monfils and he slipped into the vat?" (GBPD detail sheet, 01/29/94)

- Hirn told Winkler that Piaskowski, Johnson, and Basten probably killed Monfils. (GBPD detail sheet, 01/29/94)

- Hirn said Piaskowski was cold and told the police he would kill again if he had to. (GBPD detail sheet, 01/29/94)

- Hirn stated that it was his belief that if Monfils came to foul play, it occurred behind coop 7 and that it most likely involved Piaskowski, Johnson, Kutska, and Basten. (FBI report, 1/28/94)

- Kutska speculated (by elimination) that only Basten or Johnson might have killed Monfils. (John Doe hearing, 4/12/95)

Clearly these men did point fingers—on at least twenty-five occasions—but they were innocent and could not offer concrete evidence. They were only speculating in their vain efforts to be helpful and to clear their own names. That Union-Conspiracy-of-Silence Theory can be put to rest along with other unsupported assumptions.

Stringing the Theories Together

Their starting theory—the Way-to-Go-Kutska Theory—did not get the police and the DA to the crime scene. In order to traverse that distance—both physically and hypothetically—they had to develop at least two more theories. It was the Way-to-Go-Kutska Theory twisted into the Bubbler-Confrontation Theory and propped up by the Union-Conspiracy-of-Silence Theory—each hypothetical and unproven. Every link in this chain fails to be consistent with all the known facts time and time again.

It was this very sequence of theories that the prosecution would sell to the jury. It remains the basis of their case today. Still it is a string of assumptions—singly and together full of gaping holes. It is why a federal judge would later brand the state's case as simply "inference stacking."

SIX INNOCENT MEN

12

More Slick Tricks

Oh what a tangled web we weave,
when first we practice to deceive.

—Sir Walter Scott

No single member of the Green Bay Police Department shaped the Monfils investigation more than former Detective Sergeant Randy Winkler. Of the 2,111 pages of paperwork generated during the police department's 841-day investigation of the case, Winkler wrote 1,164, or 55 percent, of them.

Over the twelve months of 1994—while in sole command of the case—Winkler generated 752 pages of detail. In that same crucial time period, all the other detectives in the department produced a mere 71

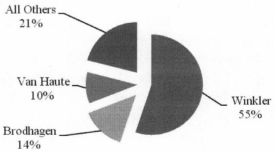

Breakdown, by percentage, of detail sheets written by GBPD detectives in the Monfils investigation

193

pages. In other words—during the time when DA John Zakowski finally got his key piece of evidence—Winkler exerted more than ten times the influence on the case than did the rest of the GBPD combined. It would turn out that some of Winkler's 1994 paperwork contained doctored detail sheets from the first days of the investigation almost two years earlier.

Why does it matter which one of the many possible detectives available to Police Chief Bob Langan was placed in sole charge of the case? Because what turned out to be the biggest death-investigation case in the history of Green Bay was now hinging on the very professionalism and character of one cop—the one left in charge.

When it came to all of the detectives working the Monfils case, the big three had always been Al Van Haute, Ken Brodhagen, and Winkler. But the roles of Van Haute and Brodhagen paled in comparison to Winkler's. During the entire investigation, Van Haute wrote just 10 percent of the detail sheets, while Brodhagen, Winkler's frequent partner, produced only about 14 percent.

Van Haute was assigned the case on the afternoon of Saturday, November 21, when it was still thought to involve a missing person. For unknown reasons Van Haute did not continue leading the investigation after Winkler was brought in. Several sources have told these authors that Van Haute was the fairest, most logical, and deepest thinker in the group. These same sources suggested that—had Van Haute been in charge—this case would have most likely seen a different result.

Brodhagen was known to be tough as nails and perhaps a bit extreme as far as internal police procedures went. The combination of these things caused him problems later in his career. However, Brodhagen's work on the Monfils case, as evidenced through his interviews and detail sheets, walked a clear and thorough line—especially when it came to recording the facts.

If Van Haute was methodical and Brodhagen was thorough, then Winkler was more like the show-off diving from a ledge into unknown waters. His superior abilities would carry him; the end would justify the means. To a person, the vast majority of the people interviewed for this book expressed dislike for Winkler and his tactics. They felt he was aggressive and accusatory. "It was like he knew everything and you knew nothing," says Mike Piaskowski. "He was more interested in you telling him what he wanted to hear than what you had to say."

The bottom line is that this case was not handled very well at all, and Winkler deserves the lion's share of blame for that. The detective work—especially Winkler's—warranted a lot more scrutiny than it got by the higher-ups at the police department and by the district attorney. Now it is time to put the police procedures in the Monfils case under the microscope.

Here is a look at some of the slick and not-so-slick tricks and some of the unanswered questions of this case left hanging in the air as a result.

Bait and Switch—Winkler versus Stein

One trick Winkler tried was the old bait-and-switch routine on mill worker Steve Stein. After interviewing him on January 29, 1994, at the police station, Winkler showed up at Stein's home while Stein was in his garage. Winkler asked him to sign a statement, asserting that Stein had failed to sign it the previous day at the police station. Three times Stein insisted that he had signed it.

Winkler said," No, you didn't. I'm in a hurry. Just sign it." He pulled a pen out of his pocket and handed it and the statement to Stein.

Just as Stein took the pen to sign his name—mostly in an effort to get Winkler off his back—Stein's wife entered the garage. "Don't sign that," she said. "Come into the house. You have to read it first."

As Stein read the document, he found himself repeating over and over, "I didn't say this" and "I didn't say that." The whole document had been altered to incriminate Mike Piaskowski.

Stein eventually ripped up the phony statement and sent Winkler packing. As it turned out, Stein had signed his original statement at the GBPD the day before, just as he had thought. It was eventually provided to the defense in the discovery files.

"For once my wife was right," says Steve with a knowing chuckle. "She saved my ass. I would have lost my job and likely gone to prison as part of a conspiracy if I had signed it and then tried to deny that it was true."

Browbeaten into Submission—Winkler versus Kellner

Unfortunately, in November 1994 Brian Kellner caved in to Detective Winkler when he was put in the same spot Stein had faced that day in his garage. Fatigued and confused by eight hours of being lied to, threatened, berated, and browbeaten, Kellner caved in, foolishly signing Winkler's account of a bubbler confrontation. Kellner figured it would be okay to accept what the cops claimed they already knew from their "secret tapes."

A bewildered but trusting and pliable Brian Kellner signed the statement Winkler had written out for him. In the days to come, Kellner would deeply regret his rash judgment. Kellner told these authors that he had tried to correct his statement on "numerous occasions" but that no one was paying attention to him anymore—not even at the district attorney's office. The die was cast. Kellner wanted to set the record straight with the truth, but it was too late now. The authorities had what they wanted, and Kellner had already signed on the dotted line. Now the cops could include the possibility of prison on their list of threats to Kellner.

Finally, well after the trial, in October 1996 and away from a domineering detective, Kellner wrote the following notarized deposition for the court of appeals. It puts the Fox Den role-play in the proper perspective:

State of Wisconsin, County of Brown

1. I am the Brian Kellner that testified at the Monfils murder trial. My date of birth is May 18, 1956.
2. At the time that Randy Winkler took a statement from me on 11-30-94, I had been interrogated for about 8 hours. During this time, Randy Winkler had threatened me with loss of my job, losing my children, and being put in jail. He told me that I was lying and that I could be treated as a hostile witness and subjected to a long and unpleasant time at a John Doe hearing. In addition to the above, Sergeant Winkler also told me that my ex-wife (Verna), who was at the time my live in companion, was having an affair with Keith Kutska. Sergeant Winkler stated that the police department had proof of this affair and that they would be bringing this out in court.

3. Many of the things that Sergeant Winkler put into my statement were his claims, not mine. At first, I challenged Sergeant Winkler when he wrote that Keith Kutska told me things that Keith Kutska had never in fact told me. Sergeant Winkler kept saying that it was "close enough" and that there was nothing in this statement that they (Green Bay Police Department) did not already know and have proof on. Sergeant Winkler said that I would be in trouble if I denied these things that the police already knew.

4. The truth is that Keith Kutska never said many of the things that are in the statement. I first heard these things from Sergeant Winkler, who told me that these "facts" came from a statement that Keith Kutska had given them (Green Bay Police Department) just days before.

5. The fact is that while Keith Kutska speculated on many things about the Monfils murder. He never told me that he knew about or saw what happened to Tom Monfils. All that Keith Kutska told me was about playing the tape for Tom Monfils early in the morning in the number seven coop. Aside from that, Keith Kutska was speculating on different things that might have happened, and was not telling me that he knew what had really happened. The list of different theories that Keith Kutska talked about was similar to the list of different theories that people around the mill had been talking about for a long time.

6. When Randy Winkler wrote down the statements as if Keith Kutska had actually told me what happened, I told him this was not the truth. Randy Winkler refused to change the statement and refused to write that Keith Kutska had only talked about a whole lot of different theories. Randy Winkler also put in many details, including names and certain locations that Keith Kutska never mentioned.

7. I signed the statement even though I did not feel that it was the right thing to do. Even Sergeant Winkler's assurances [did] not make it feel right. I signed it because I was afraid of Randy Winkler's threats and because I wanted to get it over with and go home and be alone to digest what had happened and why.

The references to Verna's affair with Keith Kutska made me
want to end this all the more.

8. About a week before the Tom Monfils murder trial I was
brought into Randy Winkler's office. Randy Winkler was upset
that I was trying to correct my statement to him. At this time
Randy Winkler told me that if I tried to change my statement
in any way I would be looking at losing my job, jail time for
perjury, and being declared a hostile witness.

9. Sergeant Winkler brought me into the D.A. office, where I met
with John Zakowski and Bill Griesbach. At this time, I told
the D.A. and his assistant that there were many parts of the
statement that Keith Kutska never said, but that Randy Winkler
put in. I was told that during the trial that these discrepancies
would be brought up and clarified.

10. I was never given the opportunity to straighten out the record
and tell the truth at the trial. Had it not been for Sergeant
Winkler's threats I would have demanded that these details be
part of the trial and the truth about what Keith Kutska really
told me would have come out.

11. I am making this statement now because it is time for the truth
to be told. I am not being harassed or threatened by anyone
to do this, unlike when Randy Winkler wrote a statement for
me and when the matter was brought to trial when Sergeant
Winkler was threatening me. It has been a long time but now
more than ever the truth must be brought out.

(Notarized signature) *Brian Kellner 10/07/96*

What most people do not know is that when individuals are
interviewed or interrogated by the police—at least in the city of
Green Bay—they do not actually write their own statement. The
investigator writes it for them, using a combination of their words and
the investigator's words, their thoughts and the investigator's thoughts.
When finished, the person being questioned is given a chance to read
the statement, correct any errors, and then vouch for its accuracy
by signing the statement in front of the investigator or some other
officer. On its face, this procedure sounds upfront, fair, and efficient.
Unfortunately it is not quite that.

First, a less-than-scrupulous investigator can tilt the words to his or her own benefit while approximating enough of the person's story to avoid raising a red flag. The skilled interrogator also knows how to create an atmosphere—be it comfortable or stressful—in order to keep the interviewee off guard.

Second, an inexperienced person is generally under the impression that he or she has very little time to amend the statement and usually hurries through it. If the signer misses anything the detective wrote that is inaccurate, incorrect, misleading, vague, or has a double meaning, it is the signer's tough luck. The words chosen by the investigator for that statement will now become legal and binding.

Detectives are taught that the use of a lie is a valid interrogation technique. It is—when used ethically. But when a lie is knowingly used to extract false statements, it is not only unethical, it is just plain wrong.

When Sergeant Winkler wrote out the statement for Kellner, he put him between a rock and a very hard place with his threats and deceptions. These included legal and economic threats as well as assaults on Kellner's manhood. In that statement, there were many things that Kellner knew to be true. Also included were things that Winkler told Kellner the police knew to be true. Kellner accepted those. After all, Winkler told him that the GBPD had it all on tape. From somewhere in the confusion emerged a pieced-together storybook tale of a role-play incident at the Fox Den.

Doctored Details

Some sleuthing by these authors turned up a rather flagrant and embarrassing truth—Randy Winkler had doctored multiple detail sheets in this case. A good look at that doctoring has exposed Winkler's crooked effort to make the outcome of the investigation fit the police theory, no matter what the facts.

By 1994 Randy Winkler had taken to wearing a trench coat and a fedora. This photo came from a roll of surveillance pictures.

Before March 1993, all of the Green Bay Police Department detail sheets, including Detective Winkler's, were typed out on an official preprinted form, GBPD D-11 (90). Sometime around April or May 1993, about four months into the Monfils investigation, Winkler began to produce his detail sheets in a clearly different format, apparently on his own computer. His efforts to simulate the layout of the official GBPD detail sheets are obvious, although he never came up with an exact match.

Winkler's initial efforts were crude and incomplete, with type frequently misaligned. A variety of continually revised and improved versions of his format appeared over the next two years. By identifying these subtle changes, one can prepare a timetable of sorts that reveals when a large number of Winkler's detail sheets were actually written—as opposed to the date Winkler put on them.

By matching the format of a Winkler detail sheet to the format of a GBPD detail sheet with an indisputable date—based on its content—one can approximate when each of Winkler's reports was actually written. The eye-opening results illustrate the magnitude of Winkler's revisions. Indeed, some of his most damning reports—with very early dates—were produced with formats that had evolved nearly two years later, some as late as late 1994.

In appendix V, eight different report formats have been reproduced. Format 1 is the GBPD form, used by the department's detectives from November 1992 to December 1994. Format 2 is the computerized GBPD form, which first appeared in December 1994. An examination of the police reports in this case has revealed the following:

- Format 1 was used by all the detectives, but was not used by Winkler after May 1993.
- Format 2 was used by all the detectives except Winkler.
- Formats 3–8 were used only by Winkler.

On January 8, 1994, Winkler had become the only detective working on the case. It was in this stretch of time—when he was "home alone"—that these authors believe Winkler first got creative by revisiting the case materials gathered to that point, especially detail sheets from the first days of the investigation.

The authors became aware of the possibility of this form of evidence tampering while reading detail sheets in the Dale Basten file. Two of the detail sheets have exactly the same date, 12/04/92, and both were produced by Winkler. One is nine-pages long, the other seven pages. The seven-page detail sheet has a somewhat smaller type font. Carefully examining the documents side-by-side, the authors noted that the first six pages of the shorter report closely match those of the longer one. Suddenly, the longer report spins off with a damning page-and-a-half insertion that is not in the seven-page version.

The shorter document is written on the original form GBPD D-11 (90). The longer report—with an extra page and a half of negative information—is written in a distinctly different format. It is a format that matches Winkler's computer work during his "creative period" almost two years later. Due to oversight, the altered version and the unaltered version both ended up in the hands of the defense attorneys in the discovery materials. At trial, Winkler was forced to admit that he had created the predated document almost two years later in October 1994 using what the authors have designated as format 7.

This admission confirmed the suspicion of these authors that Winkler altered detail sheets, and it validates our method of dating suspicious documents.

A detail sheet is a detective's written report of an interview. It can contain hearsay and the subjective opinions of the detective. There are many examples of detail sheets produced by Winkler (and only Winkler) using his evolving formats of 1994 and 1995 but predated to the early months of the investigation in 1992 and 1993. Several of his changes and additions within those detail sheets are documented in these pages.

Bullying and Threats of Job Loss—Winkler versus Melville

In Winkler's December 8, 1994, interview/interrogation of Jim Melville, the detective again demonstrated his penchant for deception and intimidation. Melville was a friend and a coworker of Keith Kutska. Winkler started by lying to Melville, trying to trick him by referring to some "tape recordings" that he claimed to have in his possession. The tapes were the rather innocuous undercover recordings made of Kutska by Dodie and Scott VerStrate. Winkler, however, purported the tapes to contain everything from Kutska's confession to embarrassing revelations about the interviewee. It was a foil that had worked with Brian and Verna Kellner just a week earlier. It had also made a huge impression on mill worker Jon Mineau, who then spread the word at the mill that the police had a tape of Kutska confessing to the murder.

Winkler told Melville that the police knew that Melville knew "what happened to Tom Monfils because it was Kutska who told him." Melville seemed to buy Winkler's lie about the tapes, but he was unfazed. Melville simply pointed out to Winkler, "If you listened to the tapes you know that Kutska was just speculating to what happened to Tom." Melville explained to Winkler that until Kutska obtained the autopsy report, Kutska had adamantly believed that Monfils's death was a suicide. After that, Melville said, Kutska accepted the death as murder because he thought Monfils's injuries must have been caused by something other than the agitator blade. Kutska also concluded, said Melville, that someone must have thumped Monfils in the head. Again Melville reiterated to Winkler that anything he and Kutska had talked about was pure speculation.

Melville then told Winkler, "Through the process of elimination and reading the depositions [Kutska] came up with the idea of what might have happened." Winkler demanded to hear the details. If Kutska's speculations to Melville were similar to the speculations reported by Kellner, then Winkler could characterize them as corroboration of the statement he had rigged for Kellner—the one with the bubbler confrontation in it. Melville, however, would not reiterate what he saw as mere speculation.

In his report Winkler reverted to his subjective "observations"— intending to discredit Melville. "I asked Melville to tell me what Kutska had said about that, and Melville obviously was avoiding answering the question. Melville was very nervous during the entire interview. I noticed some involuntary movement in the mussels [sic] in his face and could also see his pulse rate in the veins in his neck." Winkler then wrote, "I stopped asking questions of Melville at that time because it was obvious he was not going to answer them."

After taking a handwriting sample from Melville, Winkler went after him again. Still, Melville refused to deal in speculation. Winkler told him, "We have been told by James River that anyone who refuses to give information, or is arrested for obstructing, will be terminated by them." Melville said he knew that. He said that he agreed that anyone who does that "should be fired." Melville was certain that he did not fit into that category.

For a third time, Winkler asked Melville if Kutska had told him anything about what happened with Monfils. Once more, Melville stated that Kutska never told him anything about murder. Winkler then told Melville that it was obvious he was not going to cooperate and that he could go. Melville insisted to Winkler that he was cooperating. Melville was again told to go and was escorted out the front door. Winkler's detail sheet describing the interaction with Melville is dated December 14, 1994, one week after the actual interview.

Without exception, all the mill workers who were interrogated by the police and mill security were threatened with the loss of their job and possible arrest if they failed to cooperate or if they lied. All the workers tried their best to satisfy the police. Most—including the six defendants—went so far as to speculate when asked to do so. Of the hundred or so workers who were interviewed, interrogated, sweated, and squeezed over the course of two and a half years, not one was able to confirm the theory of a bubbler confrontation. Given the threats from mill management, it seems certain that most mill workers would have never hesitated to "protect their high-paying jobs" (the district attorney's words) by reporting the bubbler incident, had it actually happened.

Spreading Lies—Winkler versus Kiley

Al Kiley, another James River employee, was so disturbed by Winkler's tactics that he produced a document, denouncing his treatment by the police.

> This is my statement about what I know and what is being done to me to make me testify in the criminal case about Tom Monfils death.
>
> I am writing this because Detective Randy Winkler has been rude and disrespectful to me. Other Green Bay Police officers have also been rude and disrespectful to me in this investigation [as well].
>
> Tom Monfils was missing at work November 21, 1992. I was not working the morning he was missing. I was working when he was found on the November 22, 1992 at 10:00 p.m. Tom Monfils's body was found in the tissue chest. Detective Don Chic asked me to help him drain the tank. The tank is in a very confined area. The tank is in my area at the mill. I know how to operate the tank. It is necessary to know how to operate the tank. If you turn the wrong air valve open, about 40,000 gallons of pulp would spill out all over.
>
> As Detective Don Chic and I drained the tank, the discharges kept plugging up. We had to close one discharge and open the other discharge so we could clean out the plugged discharge. My foreman, Detective Don Chic, and I drained the tank. We worked in pulp

about 12-14 inches deep. The drain to the sewers kept plugging up. The drains plugging made it difficult to drain the tank. It was unpleasant in the tank. There were body parts and flesh floating in the pulp we were standing in. The Detective Don Chic picked up body parts and put the body parts in plastic bags. He photographed the body parts. When the tank pulp level was lowered enough to open the entry hatch, I got out of the tank. The tank smelled bad. I went home around 4:00 a.m.

Shortly after the investigation started, my superintendent, Bob Thut, came to me and said that a very reliable source had told him that I was drinking liquor on the job. It wasn't true. The superintendent, Bob Thut, said that he was considering having me fired for drinking on the job and he wanted to hear my side of the story. I asked who told him I was drinking on the job. Bob Thut said he was not allowed to tell me who said I was drinking on the job. I asked Bob Thut what the person who said I was drinking on the job smelled, liquor or beer? Bob Thut said liquor. I told Bob Thut I don't drink liquor, just beer. I told Bob Thut to verify with the person who said I was drinking on the job that he smelled liquor on my breath. Bob Thut told me he would get back to me. Bob Thut told me he couldn't believe I would be drinking liquor on the job, because he knows me too well. Bob Thut said even if it was true, things would be all right because of all the stress I was under. Finding the body parts and working in the area under fire caused the stress. Bob Thut said I could get help. I said that I was having a hard time. I said I was not drinking on the job. I begged him to tell me who was saying this about me because I could not afford to lose my job. Bob Thut said just hang in there and they would get back to me.

Two days later, Jim Melville came to me and asked if I was okay. I said why do you ask? Jim Melville told me that Detective Randy Winkler stated that I was hitting the sauce very heavy. I said that is the Son of Bitch who tried to frame me. It was not true. I don't know why Detective Randy Winkler would lie about me drinking. I went to Bob Thut and told Bob Thut that I knew it was Detective Randy Winkler who for some reason wanted to cause me trouble and lied about me drinking. I told Bob Thut that Detective Randy Winkler pulled his car up by me in the mill parking lot. Detective Randy Winkler opened his window on the passenger side. Detective Randy Winkler asked me something, which I can't remember. Detective Randy Winkler [then] asked me if I wanted a ride to my car. I said no. I told Bob Thut, that before I leave work I always clean up and brush my teeth. The day that Detective Randy Winkler offered me the ride, Cindy Heath gave me some peppermint candy she was sharing. I had two pieces of peppermint candy that day. Detective Randy Winkler must have thought that he smelled Peppermint Schnapps. The so-called liquor he smelled on my breath was peppermint candy.

Based on that peppermint candy, Detective Randy Winkler had started the nasty rumor that I was drinking on the job, that I was addicted to alcohol and in the words he used to Jim Melville, that I was "really hitting the sauce." That made me so angry that it is hard to put into words. Detective Randy Winkler almost cost me my job. He went to my coworkers; he went to my boss. I called Bob Thut. I asked that he call Detective Randy Winkler and verify that it was the smell of peppermint that started Detective Randy Winkler on the nasty rumor that he went to my boss about. I asked Bob Thut, to ask Detective Randy Winkler if Detective Randy Winkler thought I was drinking, why did Detective Randy Winkler let me drive home if I was intoxicated.

The next day Bob Thut called me. Bob Thut told me that now everything was cleared up. I told Bob Thut that I was very angry with Detective Randy Winkler. Five days later Detective Randy Winkler came to my house. Detective Randy Winkler said he was very sorry he told Bob Thut, my supervisor, that I was drinking on the job. Detective Randy Winkler said he was very sorry that he told Jim Melville that I was hitting the sauce real hard when all he had was the smell of peppermints on my breath. I told Detective Randy Winkler that if Jim Melville had not told me it was he that squealed, I would have lost my job thanks to the Detective Randy Winkler of the Green Bay Police Department.

The mill is doing its own investigation. They have a detective Frank Pinto. Detective Frank Pinto is working in the mill. Detective Frank Pinto is a thug. Detective Frank Pinto threatens all the employees. If the employees do not cooperate to convict the people charged in the criminal case, they will be fired. When employees give statements, the arrogant Detective Frank Pinto calls them liars and that he will find out the truth. There are twenty people that are liars, says Detective Frank Pinto and he will find them out. The atmosphere at work is threatening all time.

Jack Yusko, head of personnel, said that when the Monfils trial starts, the people getting subpoenas might not get paid for lost work time. Jack Yusko said that the mill would consider paying lost wages to those employees who cooperate with the police in convicting the people charged. The mill will not pay those employees who don't cooperate with the police to convict the people charged. Employees are regularly threatened to be fired by the mill if they don't cooperate with the police in convicting the people charged.

The police made my work partner, Tom Hendricks, come to the downtown police station. They questioned Tom. When Tom told what he knew, the police said he was a liar. Tom said he was telling the truth. It didn't matter what Tom said, the police said he wasn't telling the truth. It didn't matter what Tom said, the police treated him as if he was a criminal. Tom called Detective Randy Winkler a horse's ass after Detective Randy Winkler repeatedly said Tom was lying.

Detective Randy Winkler said that he would get Tom fired if he did not tell what Detective Randy Winkler wanted to hear. Detective Randy Winkler said to Tom that there is a list of twenty people, who are not telling Detective Randy Winkler the truth. Detective Randy Winkler said that he had recommended to the plant, that six of the twenty people Detective Randy Winkler thought was lying be fired. Detective Randy Winkler inferred that Tom was one of the six the police department had recommended be fired for lack of cooperation. Tom thought he was one of the six Detective Randy Winkler was describing because whatever Tom says, Detective Randy Winkler says is a lie and he does not believe Tom.

The managers at the mill and the police tell the employees to be honest and to cooperate with the police and with Detective Frank Pinto. When employees do cooperate, Detective Randy Winkler accuses us of lying. The police and the managers intimidate people by saying they are liars and threatening their jobs. The police treat innocent people like criminals.

If I don't cooperate to help convict the people charged, I will lose my job. The mill says we have to cooperate if we want to keep our jobs. The police have threatened me that if I don't cooperate they will make me sit in that trial for a month. If I won't cooperate to convict the guys, the mill says I won't get paid which I can't afford.

(Signed) Al Kiley

It is clear to anyone who studies Randy Winkler's work—just as it was so painfully clear to the mill workers he grilled—that he seldom conducted interviews, erring always toward interrogations. Steve Stein and Kiley were not the only workers who vehemently complained to the authors about Winkler's way of doing things. Add to that list Pete Delvoe and Don Boulanger, as well as Connie Jones, Tom Hendricks, Jim Melville, Randy Lepak, and the six wrongfully convicted men.

Winkler's Tainted Testimony

On day 16 and day 17 of the Monfils trial, Winkler took the witness stand and discussed his wily interrogation tricks and techniques as though he was proud of the deceptions. He also explained his view of the difference between an interview, which he said was "like a friendly chat," and an interrogation, which he said more or less challenged an "uncooperative" person who was being questioned. "As time went on," Winkler testified, "it was *very apparent* [authors's emphasis] that people were withholding information for either fear or involvement or whatever—and eventually I did become aggressive towards people to gain information."

During his testimony, Winkler was questioned about *four* separate instances where his work on the Monfils case involved false, fraudulent, or manufactured evidence.

Tainted Testimony: A Falsified Police Report

The *first* piece in Winkler's questionable trial testimony concerns his reconstructed detail sheet of the December 4, 1992, interrogation of Dale Basten. That report was the key that opened the door for these authors to examine a number of Winkler's restructured documents.

For this interrogation, as for others, Winkler wrote both an original report and a doctored report. The shorter detail sheet used format 1. The second detail sheet is almost identical to the original except that it is almost two full pages longer. It was produced by Winkler in October 1994 using format 7. In the revision, the following damning scenario was inserted into the original document:

> I talked to Dale for some time after that, and told Dale that I felt he wasn't telling me the entire truth about what happened. I told Dale that he knew Monfils was murdered and that he was either involved in it or he saw what happened.

> I continued to talk with Dale and explained that his story didn't match up with what I knew happened. I told Dale that I knew he was involved and I wanted him to tell me what happened. I reached over and touched Dale and I told Dale that I knew he was involved in Monfils death, and that I knew he didn't mean to kill Monfils. At this point Dale bent forward and hung his head down and began to cry. I said to Dale, "You didn't mean to kill Monfils, did you?" Dale said, "No. I only went up there to help Johnson. Everybody picks on Johnson and I'm the only friend he has." Dale was still crying and I said to Dale, "You didn't mean to kill Monfils, it's just something that happened. You didn't want Monfils to die, did you?" Dale said, "No," and continued to cry. I told Dale to tell me what happened. At this point Dale regained his composure and sat up in the chair and said, "Nothing, I'm not involved."

> I told Dale that I knew that wasn't true, and wanted to talk to him some more. Dale asked about the time he was at the station and asked if he was going to get paid for it. I told him I didn't know but I thought so. I asked Dale if he wanted to go and he said he did. I asked Dale if he would be willing to talk to me on 12/05/92 and he said he would.

When asked under oath about this misstep, the experienced Winkler claimed his omission of the most incriminating part of this interview with Basten was just a "serious mistake" on his part.

Assistant DA William Griesbach did his best to gloss over Winkler's "carelessness" by airing this dirty laundry in court before the defense attorneys could get at it. Winkler played his part well. He calmly admitted to predating the second detail sheet, suggesting that he "probably should have filed a supplement" instead of misrepresenting the enhanced original.

Since our collection of Winkler material contains numerous examples of predated detail sheets other than this one, it is not unreasonable to suspect that Winkler simply goofed this time, failing to pull the original from the files.

Tainted Testimony: A Falsified Conversation

The *second* falsification concerns purported statements by defendant Rey Moore. Winkler claimed Moore described two phone calls made by Keith Kutska at 7:20 a.m. the day of Monfils's disappearance. It is clear, however, that Moore was *not* present when the calls were made. In a detail sheet dated December 16, 1992, Winkler writes:

> I asked Rey about the phone call to Marlyn Charles, and Rey said he heard Keith talking to Marlyn when they were in the No. 9 coop. Rey stated Keith told Marlyn that Monfils admitted it was him [Monfils] on the tape. Rey said he told Marlyn that they walked into the coop and played the tape to Monfils. Rey stated that Keith told Marlyn that Monfils was reading the newspaper when he walked in and asked Piaskowski to name that tune. Keith told Marlyn that Monfils dropped the paper and left. Rey stated that Keith told Marlyn that he asked Monfils if he made the call and Monfils said yes, before he got up and left the coop. I asked Rey to tell me again what Keith told Marlyn and Rey stated Keith said he went into the 7 coop with Wimpy, set the tape down, and told Piaskowski to listen to this new music, or name that tune, and started to play the tape.

Rey said Keith said that he asked Monfils if that was his voice on the tape, and Monfils said it was and got up and left. I asked Rey who left and Rey said Kutska told Marlyn, Monfils left the coop.

Rey stated it was after the phone call to Marlyn that he asked Kutska to point Monfils out to him. Rey stated that Kutska pointed out a guy over by paper machine 7 where the rolls of paper come off. Rey said he was looking at the guy and Kutska told him that wasn't Monfils. Rey said that was when they decided to look for Monfils. Rey stated he left with Kutska and the two of them walked down to coop 7 looking for Monfils. I asked Rey if he was sure Hirn didn't come along with them and he said he was sure.

While dated just twenty-four days after Monfils's death in 1992, the report was actually written using Winkler's October 1994 format—the same format he admitted using in the revision of Basten's detail sheet. While Kutska did make the two calls—one to Marlyn Charles and the other to his wife, Ardie—Moore was not there to hear them. The telephone company logged the calls at 7:21 and 7:24 a.m.

Moore has always maintained that he never described these calls to Winkler, because he never witnessed Kutska making any calls. The fact that he was not there for the calls is verified by those who were present when they were made. Winkler's incriminating description of this event is a clear fraud. He made it up. Moore could not and did not describe these calls as Winkler's police report claims.

At one point, nine days after Monfils's death, Moore did estimate for Winkler that he may have come to the 9 coop at about 7:20. However, Moore continued that he was not sure of the exact time—he said that he "could be off by fifteen minutes or *more*." He explained to Winkler that after hearing the news about the tape of Monfils's call from lab technician Connie Jones, he went directly to coop 9 to hear it. Jones had seen Moore in the aisle as she returned from coop 9 to her job in the pulp lab. Less than a minute later, Moore was in coop 9. In subsequent statements—after rethinking his first estimate of the time—Moore made clear that it was actually around 7:40 and not about 7:20 that he first arrived. Again, all of this is verified by others who were present.

Winkler's deception in changing Moore's arrival to 7:20 had a twofold effect. It created an extra twenty minutes of time for a second confrontation with Monfils at the bubbler, a scenario that fit in nicely with the police theory. Winkler's adjustment also erased Jones's straightforward observations showing that Kutska and the others had no opportunity to harm Monfils.

Buried in Winkler's trial testimony is an admission that Moore's arrival at the area was not at 7:20. Upon cross-examination by Moore's attorney, Robert Parent, Winkler agreed that Moore could have been wrong about his times in his first statement and that all references to a 7:34 turnover could be corrected to the 7:58 turnover "to make it right." Sadly no defense attorney confronted Winkler with this major contradiction—one that unintentionally documents his fraudulent creation.

Moore's actual time in coop 9 is verifiable from the events that he stated he had observed while he was there. Those events are also corroborated by the observations of other witnesses as well as by the computers that log all or part of the activities described. Some examples are:

- Mike Piaskowski recalled first seeing Moore when Moore entered coop 9 after the 7:34 turnover on paper machine 7 was completed. This was just a minute or two after Piaskowski saw Jones as she returned to the pulp lab from coop 9.
- Dennis Servais stated that he first saw Moore when Moore entered coop 7 with Kutska between 7:45 and 7:50.
- Piaskowski recalled seeing Moore in coop 7 when Servais and Pete Delvoe did the 7:58 turnover.
- Servais noted that Moore left coop 7 shortly after Piaskowski called his supervisor at around 7:55 to report Monfils was off the job.
- Delvoe stated that the first time he noticed Moore was in the aisle by the south end of paper machine 7 after the 7:58 turnover.
- Jones said that Moore briefly stopped at the pulp lab on his way back to his job at about 8:00. She also noted this was about 20

minutes after she first saw him and sent him to the 9 coop to hear the tape.

These are the only times people saw Moore in the area of paper machines 7 and 9. The times range from as early as 7:45 to as late as 8:00. Absolutely nobody ever reported seeing Moore before 7:45. Clearly this is well after 7:20 and well after Kutska had made the two phone calls in coop 9.

Winkler's narrative in his December 16, 1992, detail sheet suddenly jumps from the estimated 7:20 time frame in paragraph one to 7:45 in paragraph two, when Kutska and Moore left coop 9 and went to coop 7. During Winkler's twenty-five-minute leap in time, Monfils was plainly visible in his work area as he completed the 7:34 turnover. If Moore had been there earlier, as Winkler wrote, Monfils would have surely been pointed out to him, and Moore would not have been asking questions at 7:50 in order to determine who Monfils was.

On cross-examination, Winkler boldly tried to defend his adjustments to the detail sheets by claiming that most of the information about the two telephone calls was unknown to him before December 16, 1992. However, since it is now clear that this seventeen-page detail sheet was likely revised in late 1994, it is obvious that Winkler did have all the particulars he needed to rewrite the report.

Winkler and Detective Mike Van Roy interviewed Moore back on November 29, 1992. They both wrote detail sheets on this interview; the telephone calls are *never mentioned* in either of their reports. The next day Moore signed a statement that was handwritten by Winkler. Once again, no phone calls were mentioned. In Van Roy's report, Moore indicated that he had been at the paper machines for only ten to fifteen minutes. This is entirely consistent with the description of the events by Moore, Jones, and all other relevant eyewitnesses.

Over the course of 1993 and 1994, Winkler repeatedly signed over a dozen documents, which he then had notarized by John Zakowski and others. The documents were sworn affidavits requesting various court orders giving Winkler permission to conduct certain activities in his investigation into Monfils's death. Ten of the thirteen sworn affidavits from Winkler stated that Moore had arrived at the smoking table near coop 9 at either 7:34 or 7:40. None of Winkler's affidavits have Moore arriving at 7:20.

Finally, in the December 16, 1992, detail sheet Winkler consistently used the correct spelling of Moore's first name, "Rey." Moore's first name is Reynold, not Raymond. Yet, on December 9—one week before the December 16th documents were supposed to have been written—Winkler produced a detail sheet in which he repeatedly referred to Moore as "Ray." Six months later Winkler produced another detail sheet, dated June 25, 1993. On that date, he was still using "Ray" to refer to Moore. On the questionable December 16, 1992, detail sheet, however—written in Winkler's improved 1994 format—one finds the correct spelling. This is just another little detail putting a dark cloud over the trial testimony of Winkler.

Winkler's testimony and paperwork on this entire matter are not supported in any way. Indeed they are contradicted by known facts and by Winkler himself. Because his testimony may point to conscious perjury, this question has been documented with all the available facts that support such a conclusion.

Tainted Testimony: Pressure on Rey Moore

The *third* example of Winkler's questionable testimony involves his aggressive interrogation of Rey Moore that occurred on April 12, 1995, immediately following his arrest.

Moore was so distressed over this turn of events that he failed to ask for his lawyer. In fact, his attorney, William Apple, was actually at the police station at that very moment, asking to see his client. However, the police refused to let Apple see his client on the technical grounds that no request to see an attorney had been specifically made by Moore.

At trial, Winkler testified that he was trying to get Moore to confess his involvement in the crime and that Moore knew what happened to Monfils. Moore told Winkler that he did not do anything and he did not know anything. Winkler then lied to Moore, telling him that the five white workers all had pointed the finger at him and that they were calling him "boy" and "niger" [sic].

Moore was a black man with a police record from his youth, and he was living in a community of 100,000 white people. Winkler was painting a picture for him that showed these five white guys setting him up. Even though he knew he was innocent, Moore felt he did not stand a chance. He became emotionally distraught and told Winkler he was willing to take the blame for everything. He told Winkler to just write out a statement and he would sign it. At first, Winkler claims he told Moore that could not be done. When Moore again said that he did not do anything, Winkler recognized the stalemate and proceeded to write out a statement for Moore to sign.

Winkler testified, "I wrote down on a piece of paper *what I thought* [authors's emphasis] his involvement was and handed it to him." When Moore finished reading it and insisted that Winkler's words were not true, Winkler dropped the matter.

On cross-examination by Attorney Parent, Winkler admitted that he wrote this statement for Moore to sign. Winkler then described what he thought had happened:

> Rey Moore went out by Tom. He was with others and they were all yelling at him and Tom took a swing and someone swung back. Tom got beaten up by the other guys that were there and they thought he was dead. Some of the other guys threw Tom's body in the vat to hide it from being found.

Winkler then admitted that—consistent with proper procedure— he would have put these infamous words at the bottom of the page [for Moore to sign]: "I have read this [number] page statement and I find it to be true to the best of my knowledge and have signed it of my own free will." In the end, Moore did not sign Winkler's statement. He could not. No matter how much duress he was under, Rey knew it was not true.

Winkler revealed his bias when he testified that as early as December 9, 1992—less than three weeks after Monfils's death—he had already decided that Moore was guilty. For over two years, Winkler had been telling Moore that he *knew* Moore was guilty and that he was going to prove it no matter how long it took.

It Was Not Just the Monfils Case

As a licensed counselor, Lynn Adrian has worked with many young people over the years. Her aim is to protect teen offenders from the hard realities of the adult criminal system whenever fitting. In one such case, she was confronted with what she saw as the unscrupulous actions of a Green Bay detective:

I was counseling at a nonprofit in the early-mid 1990s. I was asked to evaluate an adolescent who had been picked up in connection with a gang-related drive-by shooting on Green Bay's Chicago Street. I met with the youth and evaluated him in respect to an upcoming hearing, questioning his appropriateness as an adult.

He was tried as an adult. After being grilled on the stand for two hours by the prosecuting district attorney, I met again with the youth. The adolescent was upset about the hearing.

He indicated that before the hearing, he had been interviewed by a detective. The adolescent told me that the detective had misrepresented what the adolescent told him in a written report that the adolescent then signed.

I asked, "Why did you sign the document if it was false?"

The adolescent said that the detective told him, "Who do you think they're going to believe, a detective of ten years or a [expletive] juvenile?"

I looked at the detective's name on the copy of the police report the adolescent held in his shackled hands—"Randy Winkler."

—Lynn Adrian

Tainted Testimony: The 7:03 Paper Break

The *fourth* piece of Winkler's false testimony was an assertion in the presence of the jury that a paper break occurred at 7:18 a.m. on paper machine 7. That was not true, and Winkler knew it. The exact time of this paper break could not be documented. The only record available—a computer printout—indicated that a 2.6-minute paper break occurred sometime between 6:49 and 7:15. The computer printed out this information at 7:18.

Mike Piaskowski distinctly recalls that this paper break took place during the 7:03 turnover. He remembers thinking that Monfils's inexperience as a third hand had likely caused the paper to break and that it was going to be a long twelve-hour shift if Monfils did not get his act together. Dennis Servais, the back tender on paper machine 7, verified the 7:03 time of the paper break in a statement dated December 2, 1992. Randy Lepak testified at trial that he observed a paper break on machine 7 during the 7:03 turnover.

Piaskowski learned that the investigators were claiming the paper break had occurred much later than the 7:03 turnover and that they felt he was not telling them the truth about it. Piaskowski then contacted Rob Miller for help. Miller, an outside consultant, had created and installed several programs on the computers, including the Measurex program that recorded the "lost production time" attributed to paper breaks.

With the blessing of Dean Roork, Miller's James River supervisor, Miller looked into the issue to see if he could determine exactly when the paper break had happened. Although Miller was unable to pinpoint that information, he did write up a statement and provided computer printouts, explaining why the paper break could not have happened at the time the investigators were claiming. He then sent the information packet to Piaskowski via the intramill mail system.

Miller's unsealed packet got to the paper mill office where it would normally have been distributed to Piaskowski out on the floor. Instead, paper mill secretary Linda Vincent noticed that it was addressed to "Mike Pie" and turned it over to management. Winkler was notified. After picking up the packet at human resources manager Jack Yusko's house, Winkler wrote out a detail sheet documenting the transfer of this information to the GBPD. He also documented the contents:

> "It contained several computer printouts, and also a hand written letter from Robert J. Miller. The letter explained how to read out [sic] the computer print outs that were enclosed in the letter. The computer print outs [sic] were for paper breaks on the #7 paper

machine for November 21, 1992, (the day of Thomas Monfils's murder), and for October 31, 1994."

The police had all of the information regarding the 2.6-minute paper break; they had to know full well the truth concerning that break. Two years later, in discovery, Piaskowski finally received his mail. It contained the following note from Miller:

Mike,

I copied (the) a break on Oct 31 and the corresponding printout from the Mx printer.

As you can see, the break occurred at 11:57 Mx time and lasted 37.3 minutes. It was then *reported* at 2:25 p.m. Mx time. 2:25 Mx Time was 1:57 computer system time.

The conclusions we can draw from this pertaining to Nov 21, 1992, (reference page 2 of the printout included) are:

At 7:18 a.m., a break was *reported* that lasted 2.6 minutes. It also shows that the break happened between 6:49 and (about) 7:15 a.m. Mx Time. I estimate computer system time to be ± 10 min. Mx time.

Any other questions call me at home at 339-**** & leave message.

Rob Miller

The authorities knew the paper break could not have been pinpointed to 7:18. That, however, did not stop Winkler. He reinterviewed Connie Jones, who admitted to these authors that at the time she did not know a paper break from a garage sale. At the eleventh hour—one week before trial—Jones finally agreed with Winkler that she had not seen a turnover as she had previously thought. So she testified to the only other choice Winkler had given her—that she had seen Monfils working on a paper break, one that Winkler had helped her to recall happening at about 7:18.

In truth, Jones had seen neither a turnover nor a paper break. She had merely observed Monfils cleaning up after the 7:34 turnover. Jones had been persuaded to change her mind to support a 7:18 paper break that the state knew could not be verified. Furthermore, had she actually seen a paper break, Jones would have likely seen Piaskowski and/or Servais jumping in to assist the third and fourth hands in putting the paper sheet on a new core or back on an emerging paper roll. That is what they would do. A paper break is an emergency. The crew must respond at once to fix the problem. Jones did not observe this kind of activity.

> "We know that there was a paper break at 7:15 because Exhibit 23 has a printout that said that there was a 2.6 minute paper break that ended at 7:17 [sic]. So logically, if you go backwards, between 7:14 and 7:15 there was a paper break on machine No. 7. That's important"
>
> —DA John Zakowski's closing arguments to the jury, trial day 27

Rob Miller's explanation completely contradicts Zakowski's bold assertion. Dennis Servais, Randy Lepak, and Mike Piaskowski all associate this paper break with the 7:03 turnover on paper machine 7. Sadly, Rob Miller was not called to testify at trial, and Winkler's false testimony was not challenged.

A Shameful Deception—the Vagabond Paper Break

Rob Miller's note to Mike Piaskowski made one thing crystal clear to anyone who valued an expert's opinion: It was impossible to use the Measurex, one of two computer systems that controlled paper machine operations and recorded data, to show the exact time when a particular paper break had occurred. The authorities knew this, yet they ignored the fact to prop up their theory of a bubbler confrontation. That theory was riddled with holes, but they clung to it like a life raft, frantically patching every leak. Then, in order to position the 2.6-minute paper break where they wanted it, the state called paper mill supervisor Tony Barko to the stand instead of Rob Miller. There Barko gave a "professional"—but absolutely inaccurate—opinion to the jury.

Barko was one of a handful of James River machine managers responsible for the overall production and safety operations of specific paper machines. A chemical engineer by trade, Barko was assigned to both the 7 and the 9 paper machines. While he never physically participated in any of the day-to-day activities and procedures on the floor, Barko testified to being "familiar with" the hands-on operation of both machines.

Without knowing how his testimony was going to be misrepresented, Barko tried to explain the Measurex information from the computer printout as he saw it. To Barko, it sure did not seem like rocket science—most anyone could read it. If column A said such and such, it had to mean such and such, plain and simple. And wrong.

Barko's knowledge and experience were limited in regard to many parts of the hands-on operation of a paper machine. How to interpret Miller's printouts was just one of them. To Barko's credit, he did not claim to know everything. If asked about something during his testimony with which he was completely unfamiliar, he responded accordingly. Many of his answers during cross-examination were point blank: "I do not know the answer to that," or "I'm not schooled in the Measurex," or "I do not know."

Nonetheless, during the direct examination, Barko's answers seemed authoritative and convincing—thanks mostly to Assistant DA Griesbach's skillful line of questioning:

Q. Now, if you look at Exhibit 23, are you able to determine whether there was a paper break on machine No. 7 between that 7:00 turnover and the following turnover?

A. Yes, There was a break at approximately 7:17, page 10.

Q. 7:17. And how were you able to determine that sir?

A. There is a column labeled "break time." That indicates the length of the break.

Q. And the role [sic] labeled 7:17:30, that number is 1.4, indicating that the last break that occurred, it lasted 1.4 minutes.

A. At 7:17:40, that number has changed to 2.6 minutes. Indicating that there had been another break, and that lasted 2.6 minutes.

Q. Now, can you tell from Exhibit 23—you said the change in the break number or the break time is from 1.4 to 2.6 at 7:17; is that correct?

A. 7:17:40—yes.

Q. Can you tell when that break started?

A. The computer received that information sometime between 7:17:30 and 7:17:40. It started at least 2.6 minutes before that time. Also taking into account any delay in that transmission from the Measurex to the PC.

Q. So what you're saying is that when the computer inputs the new break time, the break is then over. Is that correct?

A. Correct.

Q. So, you go back from that time to find when the break began?

A. Correct

Q. So, am I correct then that the break appears to have occurred sometime prior to 7:15?

A. Yes.

Q. And of course, this is based upon the computer clock, not the Measurex clock or perhaps not a wall clock, which could be different?

A. Correct. Correct.

Barko's interpretation of these documents was wrong, and the state should have and could have known it. Rob Miller—the very person who created the Measurex data collection program—was available to explain exactly how to read the printouts and to make clear exactly what could and could not be determined from those printouts. Miller was never called to the stand—by the state or by the defense.

Miller was the ultimate expert, yet the state never even interviewed him. It is hard to understand why the authorities did not go to the very person most able to answer any questions. Of course, considering the state's mindset, there are two reasons why it may *not* be hard to explain the oversight. First, Miller's explanation ran contrary to their theory. Second, because Miller had forwarded the information to suspect Piaskowski, Miller was possibly seen as part of the union conspiracy—casting a veil of suspicion over any information from him. It would not be the first time that uncomfortable facts expanded the union conspiracy to include persons well outside the six wrongfully convicted men. Piaskowski had requested this information to clear his good name by going after the truth; the authorities seemed to be going after Piaskowski in spite of the truth.

Griesbach's questioning of Barko continued:

Q. So, you had a turnover at around 7:00, a turnover around 7:30, and a break at about 7:15, based on the computer clock; is that right?

A. Yes.

Q. Are we able, by looking at this document, to determine when other breaks and other turnovers occurred in the same manner, simply by looking for the reel number or turnovers and the break time for breaks?

A. Yes.

In the eyes and ears of the jury, Barko appeared to be a professional. Here was the machine manager from paper machine 7 telling them exactly how it was. He had to know all the intricate details. Barko was, after all, the person in charge, and it was his area of responsibility. The jury accepted Barko's every word. From that moment on, the infamous "vagabond paper break" was incorrectly—but firmly—established as having occurred at 7:15.

"Now We Gotchya!"

In early 1994, Mike Johnson was called in to take a polygraph test. He was perfectly willing to do it because he was innocent. Yet he was nervous because he was being accused of murder, and his entire life hung in the balance. Still, he believed that the police were looking to find the guilty and exonerate the innocent.

The lie detector test began with the usual questions, meant to establish a baseline. "Is your name ...?" "Do you live at ...?" Then the question, "Did you have anything to do with the murder of Tom Monfils?" Johnson was as sure of the answer as he was of the name of his wife and children. He was about to state an emphatic no.

Just as the question was asked, however, there came a sudden and repeated pounding on the window of the interview room and someone shouting, "Now we gotchya! Now we gotchya!"

Johnson turned around to see Randy Winkler at the window making the racket! Johnson was immediately rebuked by the person administering the test and told to face forward. Through his antics, Winkler had created a spike on Johnson's lie detector test at the very point where he was asked the question about his involvement in Monfils's death.

When Mike Piaskowski took his lie detector test, he also experienced an incident that could have caused a false reading. Just before beginning the second phase of the test, Piaskowski was told by Detective Bruce Hamilton to relax. The next series of questions, said Hamilton, were just meant to establish a baseline—they would not be asking any incriminating questions at this point. Piaskowski nodded his head in acknowledgement.

To Piaskowski's shock, the very first question had to do with his possible involvement in Monfils's death. Confused and wondering if he had misunderstood something, Piaskowski turned around in bewilderment. That is when he saw Winkler in the control room with Hamilton. Piaskowski said, "Winkler was smiling like a Cheshire cat." It was a situation that could have caused the needles on the chart to jump and spike Piaskowski's readings exactly at that point where the question was asked concerning his possible involvement in Monfils's death.

Despite these and other shenanigans, none of the six men ever flunked a lie detector test.

Another Ruse—Phonebook II

There were two mysterious telephone book writings discovered during the early stages of the police investigation. One was the purported "suicide note" that was written on an inside page of the 7 paper machine phone book. The other was a series of rambling notes that were written on the back cover of a completely different phone book.

The suicide note—covered elsewhere in this book—remains a mystery. It was found in Monfils's work area, and forensic analysis shows that Monfils did not write it. Since the actual message itself is not suicide-specific, one cannot say for certain if it was intended as a suicide note. Its importance, however, is not so much who wrote the note as why it was written. An expert identified mill worker David Wiener as the most likely "who"—something Wiener has denied. The "why" remains a complete mystery.

The second of these phone book writings was no mystery at all—except for the sinister spin Randy Winkler put on them. It was one more case of Winkler making much out of nothing to his advantage. On November 25, 1992—just three days after Monfils's body was found—eighteen-year-old Clyde Weber was recovering from a broken leg in St. Vincent Hospital. As a good citizen, Weber called the GBPD about conversations that he had recently overheard concerning the Monfils death.

What he had overheard was a conversation between his girlfriend's mother, Patricia Meyers, and Meyers's good friend Deborah Verheyen. Verheyen was telling Meyers about the tough time her husband, Ralph, was having emotionally. Ralph was one of the workers who had found Monfils's body at the mill.

About three hours after Weber's call to the GBPD, Officers Haglund and McKeough arrived at the hospital to talk with him. They did not take a statement from Weber, but told him to write down anything else he might hear; they would pick up the notes from him later.

Weber had a subsequent phone conversation with Meyers, writing down the piecemeal information from their talk on the back of the hospital phone book. For her part, Meyers was simply reiterating the info she had gotten from Deborah Verheyen. At 11:15 that night, the same officers returned, taking the phone book with Weber's notes as evidence.

On July 11, 1994—almost nineteen months later—Winkler misrepresented these phone book ramblings in a signed and notarized affidavit to Judge Peter J. Naze in order to obtain court orders. In his affidavit, Winkler stated that the Weber phone book was important to the investigation because it "came from the area of #9 Paper Machine at James River Paper Mill"—a complete distortion of the facts. Thanks to this apparent misrepresentation, Winkler was authorized to extract a second series of handwriting and fingerprint samples from the mill workers he was targeting.

Exactly how many other times the state bent the rules or used shady tactics like this to gain the upper hand on unsuspecting citizens in this case is unknown. However, one obvious question is, in our search for truth and justice, is it fair to those who are innocent until proven guilty to exploit the system like this? Another crucial question is, when the police resort to deceitful maneuvers, how important is the truth? When the end justifies the means, corruption is only a step away.

We have already learned that it is understood to be "okay" for an investigator to mislead a witness in order to get at the truth, but why would he need to deceive a judge?

Winkler Is Gone

Winkler had fallen on hard times since he had supposedly cracked the Monfils case in 1994. By late 1995, he was the talk of the town.

Not surprisingly to anyone familiar with his investigative techniques, in early 1997 he received a twenty-six-page letter from Police Chief James Lewis. The letter suspended Winkler from active duty and demanded that he resign or face being fired. Winkler was upset about this and made a big stink, demanding reinstatement and back pay.

By late 1997 Winkler gave in. He retired on "duty disability" due to "post-traumatic stress disorder and severe depression." Much of this trauma seems to have been brought on by his work in the Monfils case.

Meanwhile, Winkler was not getting much sympathy from city officials. He accused Mayor Paul Jadin and Chief Lewis of preventing him from obtaining sick-leave pay and other compensation, not allowing him to take a promotional exam, and telling him to stay out of city buildings. Not much honor in that—not for the guy who had allegedly solved the biggest murder case in the history of the city.

> "Let's see. Randy Winkler makes—and I do mean 'makes'—the biggest case in Green Bay history and instead of becoming police chief, he's fired. What does that tell you?"
>
> —former member of the Brown County Police and Fire Commission Citizens Advisory Board

In 1999 Winkler testified on behalf of former Green Bay police officer John Maloney, who was on trial for murdering his wife, Sandy. Prosecutors accused Winkler of appearing at the trial only because he had an axe to grind with the police department. It was plain: Winkler had become persona non grata since his work on the Monfils case.

In September 1999 Winkler asked to appear before the city's personnel committee. He wanted the committee to consider getting an outside investigator to "look into the actions of the Green Bay Police Department and other city officials." Unfortunately for him, such a meeting would never occur. Likely political maneuvering would see to that.

This seems to be a rather curious way to treat the hero of the Monfils case. Most would expect him to have been honored and promoted—not cast aside.

Most often, "resign or be terminated" letters are brief—a terse sentence or two. A twenty-six-page letter seems like it would contain an ocean of details outlining Winkler's job performance—some of them possibly addressing his ability to conduct a fair and impartial criminal investigation. These authors requested a copy of that letter but were denied. We can only suppose what intriguing details are hidden therein.

Slick but Not Slick Enough

It was an interesting exchange, the late-summer day these authors dropped in to visit former Detective Randy Winkler at his home in rural Gillett, Wisconsin. Winkler was not expecting us. He was aware, however, that we had been on the phone and in the area asking about him with former friends and teachers at Gillett High School. We were curious—wondering what had happened to the man since his sudden, mysterious fall from grace and his infamous departure from the GBPD.

"I hear you've been asking questions about me," Winkler said after we had introduced ourselves. We said that we indeed had been. We asked if he had time to talk to us that day. He told us that he was preparing to leave on a motorcycle trip and did not really have time. He assured us that he would get in touch when he returned. We never heard from him again—despite further efforts on our part to make contact.

Before we left, we told Winkler that we were working with Mike Piaskowski on our book. "You'd better be careful," he said, "Pie is slicker than the rest [of the six men]."

Frankly, we were miffed. You can gather up a thousand descriptions of Mike Pie, and you will get everything from "nice guy" to "someone who'd do anything for you," but you would never hear the word "slick."

However, when one thinks of the word "slick," Winkler's name does come to mind. He made the case that led to the convictions of six innocent men for the murder of Tom Monfils. That much is certain. Without someone poking the pile, he would probably have kept the feather in his fedora. His trench coat, however, definitely was mussed up when he was forced out of the ranks of the GBPD.

Visions of Grandeur and Wealth

For those who might wonder, "Why would Winkler want to do these things? What was in it for him?" the answer might be summed up in two simple words—"wishful thinking."

A quick look back into one telling incident in Winkler's history might just speak volumes. It occurred right in the middle of the Monfils investigation when Winkler and his partner, Ken Brodhagen, enjoyed one of Andy Warhol's "15 minutes of fame" episodes. It arrived thanks to a case they had helped resolve in 1991. Nearly overnight, they became nationally known sleuths—Green Bay's own hometown heroes. They were the envy of their comrades all across the country, celebrities thanks to their much-acclaimed detective prowess. It was enough to make the head swim with self-importance, not to mention the monetary implications.

Here is the story: On August 8, 1981, a forty-eight-year-old Green Bay housewife, Yvonne Rickman, disappeared while on a shopping trip with her husband to Appleton, Wisconsin. According to her husband, Ron, the two of them had been arguing on the drive and decided to shop separately. Ron finished shopping first and waited for his wife at the car until the end of the day. Yvonne never returned and was never seen or heard from again.

Although Ron was a suspect from the very beginning, no evidence was found and no charges were ever filed—at least not until ten years later, when Detectives Brodhagen and Winkler got involved in the investigation.

Ron Rickman had a checkered past and had spent some time in the state mental hospital. He had been found "not guilty by reason of mental disease or defect" in the death of two loggers in 1962. When he was released from the hospital in 1972, he moved to Green Bay where he got married, raised a family, and was considered a productive law-abiding taxpayer.

Nine years after his wife disappeared, in 1990, Ron was arrested for illegally possessing a hunting shotgun and sentenced to jail time. While in jail an informant by the name of Jimmie Cline told the GBPD that Rickman had talked to him about his wife's death. "He said he felt the same thing about his wife at that time (of her disappearance) as he felt toward those loggers he killed," Cline told authorities.

In 1991, with that as the main evidence against him, Rickman was convicted and sentenced to a life in prison. Never wavering from his claims to innocence, he died alone in his prison cell in February 2002 and is sadly missed by his daughter, Kristina, and his friends. He was 65 years old.

If one does not think the Rickman case and the taste of glory it gave Winkler had anything to do with the Monfils case, there is a pretty good indication of a very strong connection in Winkler's mind. Mike Piaskowski recalls that "several times Winkler spit at me that it took him 'over ten years to get Rickman' and that he 'was going to get me—no matter how long it took.' When I told him that I didn't know what he was talking about, he started ranting and raving even more. I didn't know anything about that case until after I met Ron Rickman in prison."

Coincidentally, a rather notable connection quietly emerges here. In both the Monfils case and the Rickman case, Winkler's success relied heavily upon vague statements, hearsay evidence, and less-than-reliable jailhouse informants to make up for a lack of factual proof.

But Winkler's visions of grandeur and wealth—stoked by his pivotal role in the Monfils investigation—might have had their true origins in another aspect of the Rickman case. In 1994 the Kaufman Company, along with Tri-Star Productions, made a movie about the case entitled *The Disappearance of Vonnie*. The two now-famous detectives—Winkler and Brodhagen—were jetted off to the movie set in Vancouver, British Columbia, to serve as the film's advisors, while representing the very proud city of Green Bay at the same time. They were on top of their own little world.

How had two small-town cops ascended to such heights? With Brodhagen in the lead and Winkler and DA John Zakowski in supporting roles, they had obtained Rickman's conviction and a life sentence for first-degree intentional homicide ten years after his wife's disappearance.

They accomplished all of this without even having proof that a murder had taken place. As *Green Bay Press-Gazette* reporter Paul Srubas put it, "The moviemaker, as well as journalists and investigators from across the nation, marveled that local investigators and prosecutors successfully convicted a man of murder while having neither a body, murder weapon, nor a trace of violence as evidence."

The answer to the question of why—given the opportunity—Winkler might rework evidence, fiddle with documents, fib to a judge, and shade testimony in the Monfils case might be obvious. Perhaps he was hoping to replicate his past glory, this time around with himself as the lead detective, the big cheese of the investigation. Then, when they made a movie out of *this* case, he would not be portrayed as a second fiddle to anyone—not to the DA, not to the police chief, and especially not to his partner, Ken Brodhagen. Winkler had an ego; it expanded rapidly inside his trench coat and fedora.

Where Were the Devil's Advocates?

Much of this book focuses on the questionable activities of Randy Winkler—and rightfully so. It was Winkler who fabricated the miraculous breakthrough that opened the door for the police and district attorney. Winkler assumed control of the case in January 1994, and by year's end he had patched together a case that held up in front of a naïve and hasty jury. He eventually paid for his tactics by being rooted out of his police career. Nowadays he is a convenient straw man for a police department trying to put its own embarrassing work in this case behind it.

But Winkler did not operate in a vacuum. His work was supported by his peers and endorsed by his higher-ups. What about the rest of the GBPD and the crew in the district attorney's office? For that matter, what about the rest of the Green Bay and Brown County community? Where were the devil's advocates, ready to ask pointed questions? Where were the skeptics, willing to take a good look at Winkler's house of cards? Where were we, the citizens and our critical minds, when we were needed most?

13

Conjecture Camouflaged as Evidence

This, however, like so much else in this case, is conjecture camouflaged as evidence.

—Judge Terence Evans, U.S. Seventh Circuit Court of Appeals

Detective Sergeant Randy Winkler made his case and sold it to his superiors at the police station and to the district attorney's office. They were too pleased with the results of Winkler's work to seriously question his means. He handed them a house of cards, and they proceeded to glue the thing together—making it look like a rock-solid proposition.

On April 12, 1995, the men were arrested in a surrealistic melodrama. The families of Mike Piaskowski and Dale Basten managed to secure their $300,000 bail, and both were able to return home to await trial. Mike Hirn, Mike Johnson, Keith Kutska, and Rey Moore, however, remained incarcerated from the day of their arrests through that entire spring and summer.

On Tuesday, September 26, their joint trial began. It would end on Saturday, October 28, with six guilty verdicts. At that point, all the men would hear the prison doors lock tightly behind them for the rest of their lives. Other than Piaskowski, they have remained incarcerated every single moment since then. Based on a federal court ruling, Piaskowski would once again breathe the fresh air of freedom on April 3, 2001, as a completely exonerated man.

The prosecution of the trial by Brown County District Attorney John Zakowski and his assistants, William Griesbach and Larry Lasee, was zealous to an extreme. A ramrod judge, James T. Bayorgeon, oversaw the proceedings. The men's defense attorneys were nearly overwhelmed by the peculiar constraints placed upon them.

After five weeks, an out-of-town jury was hoodwinked by the complicated events and the state's string of theories. It was an intricate case to begin with; the fact that all six men ended up being tried together only compounded its complexity. The union-conspiracy-of-silence theory in particular seemed to explain the many weaknesses in the prosecution's case. In 2007 one Monfils juror finally shed some light on the case for these authors. Reflecting on the confusion of *all* joint trials, the juror said, "It is too much to process and too easy to just make the same decision for [all] of the defendants."

The U.S. justice system is a fair one. At its core is the concept of *reasonable doubt*—the idea that no matter how compelling one's gut instincts are about a person's guilt, if the evidence does not support that guilt, the accused must be acquitted. The Monfils murder trial was rife with reasonable doubt. Some of it, the jury was kept from knowing. Other parts of it were dressed up as facts. Some of it just plain eluded the twelve jurors and their alternates.

In ruling on Piaskowski's behalf, however, the Seventh Circuit Court of Appeals saw right through the prosecution's theories and their ruse at trial. Presented here is a look at some of the state's insidious tricks in a case that a federal judge later branded as "conjecture camouflaged as evidence" and "inference stacking."

Passing Judgment on Union Mill Workers

According to John Zakowski and Larry Lasee, there are current and past employees at the former James River mill who are still keeping secrets about what happened to Tom Monfils. In 2003 Lasee and Zakowski told these authors that paper mill workers are capable of committing murder in the fashion that befell Monfils. When pressed on this issue—the idea that the average mill worker, the bread-and-butter citizen of northeast Wisconsin, is capable of something like this—they suggested it would be best for us to "ask someone over there [at the mill]."

They cast current papermakers like Pete Delvoe as people who knew—and *still know*—more than they were willing to share with the authorities. By extension, retired workers such as Don Boulanger also should be considered as knowing more than they have shared to date. The list grows from there. After all, Delvoe and Boulanger, as well as Jon Mineau, Dave Daniels, and Dennis Servais, were in the area of the number 7 and 9 paper machines the morning of Monfils's disappearance. Yet not one of them has ever come forward with an account of anything even remotely supporting the authorities's bubbler confrontation, not even after all these years. There is not—nor has there ever been—an eyewitness to anyone harming Monfils.

When Zakowski was presented with Delvoe's statement to these authors that had a bubbler confrontation occurred he would have seen it because he was sitting at a nearby smoking table, Zakowski did not hesitate to respond. He said that Delvoe was probably "not the only one" who knew more than he had told the authorities. It seemed painfully clear: In the minds of a couple of Brown County's key protectors, average mill workers are capable of murder. They are also capable of conspiring to cover up murder. For those of us in the real world, the state's judgment falls miserably to the floor along with their case.

Codependency Produces Injustice

Anyone who has watched the television show *Law and Order* has heard the familiar tagline "In the criminal justice system, the people are represented by two separate—yet equally important groups—the police who investigate crime and the district attorneys who prosecute the offenders."

That is exactly how it is supposed to work: two separate-but-equal parts of our criminal justice system working apart—yet in unison—to protect citizens. These are two very distinct avenues for getting at the truth: a two-pronged arbiter of justice working doggedly to prove a guilty person's guilt and an innocent person's innocence.

Unfortunately, this "two heads are better than one" idea of justice can get very muddled. First, the police do arrest, and prosecutors do convict, innocent people as well as the offenders. The statistics of overturned wrongful convictions are growing by the day. Second, in smaller jurisdictions like Brown County, the police are the district attorney's investigators, sometimes drawing together these two arms of justice closer than intended. In counties with larger populations, a district attorney has his or her own investigating division. In such an arrangement, the police theory of a crime can be verified or rejected independently.

But what about a situation where the police are looking to convince a DA of a certain person's guilt? "Way to go, Kutska!," uttered at the crime scene, had already shown the obvious direction of the Green Bay Police Department's investigation. DA Zakowski told these authors that was not a problem here. He said that a critical part of his job is always keeping a cautious eye on the police and the evidence they produce.

Zakowski also said that he was never generally dissatisfied with the work of the GBPD on the Monfils case. Nor could he think of an instance where he had sent them back for more substantial evidence. That may have been true; however, in the summer of 1994 Zakowski did publicly express concerns about the evidence the police had provided him to that point.

But could Zakowski be expected to keep an eye on the police *and himself*? What about a situation where a district attorney—say, John Zakowski—was looking to wrap up a lingering high-profile case, and a police department—say, the GBPD—was looking to get off the hot seat where it put itself thanks to a truly stupid blunder? Is there any way then that Zakowski might have overlooked the failings of the GBPD in a marriage of convenience, in a case of codependency?

Zakowski was under mounting public pressure to give Green Bay answers in the Monfils case. Besides, this would likely be the biggest case of his career. The police had been working hard to hang responsibility for Monfils's death on Keith Kutska all along. They wanted him prosecuted. Besides, they might enjoy a little bit of fame themselves. The DA and the cops needed one another.

Zakowski said he "didn't know if there were regular meetings" between his office and the investigators. "Certainly in a case of that magnitude," he said, "we met early on to get acquainted with the mill and as other information would come in; we'd meet at the office. They'd come here or we'd go there—Brodhagen and Van Haute and then Winkler."

With those last three words, Zakowski was clearly implying that Winkler was a fly in the ointment of his case. He told these authors:

> Winkler became an issue during the course of the investigation in the trial. There was scuttlebutt in terms of Winkler's methods. Whether Winkler was putting words in people's mouths, but the significance of the Fox Den Bar was that was testimony that came from Kellner himself and that was apart from really anything from the police department.

> They interviewed him and gave that information, and then [Assistant District Attorney] Bill Griesbach interviewed him, and he gave the same information and then, quite frankly, he testified to the same information at trial.

> So, I mean there's been a thinking that somehow the police tainted the investigation, but the jury heard that was an issue that was put forth before them. They had six attorneys that were always raising that issue with all these witnesses that testified.

> So, that in the end, what was significant was the testimony that came out at trial, subject to all of the cross-examination from I believe to be some really able defense attorneys.

> I mean there was a lot of good talent in that courtroom. Finne is one of the better defense attorneys. Tim

Pedretti is a former prosecutor. Nila Robinson and Avram Berk have a good reputation. Of course, Gerry Boyle needs no introduction. Bob Parent I thought did a good job. He's on hard times right now, but at the time, I thought—with Moore, I felt he did a good job. Stearn was a good—of course, he's got problems now, too, but he was a good trial attorney. He had a lot of major cases. And Vance Waggoner didn't do a lot of criminal work, but he did a good job too.

Zakowski was able to get past these authors's questions concerning Winkler because the defense attorneys had cross-examined Winkler, and they had "talent" and did "a good job." Also, to Zakowski's way of thinking, there was no way that Winkler could have been putting words in Brian Kellner's mouth either, because Kellner repeated that stuff to Assistant DA Griesbach and then repeated it in court.

How is that for two separate-but-equal parts of the justice system? How is that for a district attorney willing and able to scrutinize the police and their evidence? Had Zakowski earnestly retraced Winkler's tracks as he threw together the Fox Den role-play, Zakowski would have quickly seen that role-play for the sham it was. Instead, a DA hungry to close a prestigious case bought it all. Then Winkler—for all of his high jinks and his ultimate dismissal from the police force—was vindicated when Zakowski got his guilty verdicts.

What does all this mean? It means that the lines between "two separate yet equally important groups" got very blurred in a case of codependency. It means that real justice was swept under the rug.

Winkler came up with dubious evidence, which Zakowski eagerly used at trial. Zakowski still has his job, but Winkler was sent out on the street to look for a new life. Today the marriage is over. The codependency, however, remains firmly intact.

> "Repetition does not transform a lie into a truth."
> —Franklin D. Roosevelt

Guilty People Cop a Plea

The statistics are overwhelming. When faced with irrefutable evidence or the certainty of conviction, the vast majority of guilty people will admit their guilt and cut the very best deal they can. In fact, about 75 percent of criminal cases end in a plea bargain.

Innocent people do not often readily cut a deal. Instead, they hang onto their very last shred of hope, believing that the truth will be recognized and they will be exonerated. Rarely do they plea bargain to a reduced sentence and then only very reluctantly in the face of insurmountable odds. They carry their belief in their innocence and in the system into a trial where they believe a jury of their peers will finally see the truth.

The six men convicted of first-degree intentional homicide—party to a crime in the Monfils case—did what innocent people do. They lived their lives, staying true to their normal routines. From the beginning, they cooperated with the police. They even rode their naive belief in the U.S. justice system into a joint trial. They hired local attorneys recommended by family and friends. To a man, they were certain they would be found not guilty. They knew they were innocent, and they had no knowledge of what had happened.

Not one of these men ever considered copping a plea, despite the numerous offers of the police and district attorney to do so. Not one of the six. Why? It is so damn hard to convince innocent people to plead guilty to any crime—even a lesser crime—that they did not commit. Innocent people just do not go ahead and throw their lives away for no reason. Guilty people look for the best deal they can get.

Plan B—Frivolous Misdemeanor Charges Added

If Randy Winkler was guilty of smoke-and-mirrors tactics, then John Zakowski and his scheme team were guilty of some trickery as well. Apparently, there were some misgivings by the authorities on whether they would be able to get guilty verdicts on the homicide charge with such flimsy evidence. So they added a misdemeanor charge to some of the arrest warrants. It was either spiteful irritation or a backup plan.

The misdemeanor charge—"injury to business, restraint of will"— apparently derived from that point in the 7 coop when Keith Kutska played the tape for Monfils, with Randy Lepak and Mike Piaskowski present. The extra charge seemed to be tacked on by the state as an insurance policy. That way, if they failed to get anyone on the felony charge, they could save face by at least getting a conviction on Kutska for *something*.

The state scheduled the misdemeanor trial to begin just two weeks before the felony trial. Kutska's attorney, Royce Finne, and Piaskowski's attorney, Timothy Pedretti, were at a loss. The attorneys tried reasoning with the state, citing how unfair it was to have added the second charge. They begged to have it dropped so they could concentrate on the felony charges. Zakowski balked. His edict? The misdemeanor charge would stay.

The defense attorneys then appealed to Judge N. Patrick Crooks to have the lesser charge rescheduled and tried after the felony trial. That way, they could focus on the more serious charge first. Crooks denied the motion. They asked Judge Crooks to have the two charges combined to limit the negative effect it was having. That, too, was denied.

Kutska and Piaskowski were already behind the eight ball as far as focusing on the felony charge that could cost them their freedom for life. Their defense attorneys had already spent precious time and money on the misdemeanor charge and were destined to spend more. It was totally unfair. The state had deep pockets and endless time; the defendants did not.

In the end—after more time and money had been drained from both defendants's meager supplies—the charges were reduced to forfeiture. Both Piaskowski and Kutska were, in essence, *forced* to plead no contest, just so they and their attorneys could focus on the serious charges.

A Joint Trial—First Step to Injustice

Make no mistake about it. Without the joint trial of Dale Basten, Mike Hirn, Mike Johnson, Keith Kutska, Rey Moore, and Mike Piaskowski, you would not be holding this book in your hands right now. Without the joint trial, six men would not have been convicted of murdering Tom Monfils, and five of them would not remain behind bars today. Trying all six defendants together in a single trial doomed each man's ability to forge an independent defense. Any person unfortunate enough to be enmeshed in a joint trial would believe it to be dishonest, unethical, and unconstitutional.

The defense attorneys recognized the unfair burden a joint trial would have on a client. They filed several pretrial motions demanding separate trials. Citing tax-dollar savings and the emotional advantage for the Monfils's family, trial judge Bayorgeon denied all the defense motions.

When DA Zakowski was granted his request for a joint trial, he hit prosecutorial pay dirt. He could now use the fictional Fox Den role-playing against all of the men. The raw, speculative nature of Zakowski's plum should have caused a reasonable group of jurors to toss the role-play testimony right out the upstairs window of their jury room. They did not do that.

In a joint trial, Brian Kellner's testimony against Kutska could also be applied against the other five men. The fact that Zakowski pushed for a joint trial at all speaks to his desperation and his lack of substantial evidence against each of the men individually. An astute, unbiased district attorney would have known full well that a conspiracy—had the men formed one, as he alleged—would have crumbled in the face of the arrests, five hot summer months in the Brown County jail, a trial, and the reality of being sentenced to a life in prison.

In fact, Zakowski did know that. He had seen it happen many times before, and he would see it again and again. Still, when it came to the Monfils case, he insisted that he could not crack the airtight conspiracy of the six men without a joint trial. Here is a recent account exposing Zakowski's inherent contradiction.

Irony, Hypocrisy, or Absurdity—You Decide

Two stories caught the attention of viewers of Green Bay's Channel 26 News the night of November 15, 2005. On the surface, they were both big local stories. What was not so obvious, however, was the paradoxical link between the two—at least as they crossed the desk of District Attorney Zakowski.

First was a story of a kidnapping, rape, and attempted-murder trial in which Gregorio Morales turned against his accomplice Juan Nieto. Morales tearfully admitted to raping the victim but pointed the finger squarely at Nieto when it came to setting the woman on fire and leaving her to die. Morales was doing everything he could to "get the best seat on the bus" by cooperating with authorities while rolling over on his former friend. It was a perfect example of two guys bound together in the same crime and one of them finding the quickest way to freedom by ratting out his buddy.

The second story was an update of the Monfils case with an on-camera interview of Rey Moore. Moore professed his innocence and disavowed being any part of a "union conspiracy" to kill Tom Monfils. But it was the clip of John Zakowski in the story that raised the question of irony, hypocrisy, or just plain dim-wittedness. Zakowski merely trotted out his old lines about all six of the Monfils defendants being guilty along with more "blah, blah, blah." Was Zakowski incapable of connecting his own dots?

After all, it was his office that dealt with both these cases. In the first, he had *two* guys with far more impetus for keeping a secret and a far better chance of doing so (since there were only two of them) than ever existed for the *six* men in the Monfils case. Still, Zakowski hung onto his old saw of "the union conspiracy of silence." Did it not occur to him that what he had in the Morales-Nieto story was absolute proof of just how ludicrous his "conspiracy of silence" theory in the Monfils case was? Apparently not!

By the way, Morales and Nieto were tried separately!

In yet another case of irony, two brothers David and Robert Bintz were tried separately for the murder of Green Bay bartender Sandra Lison in 1987. It took thirteen years to solve that case, but the paradox was not lost on the Green Bay community. Each Bintz brother had his own day in court in May and July of 2000, respectively—less than five years after the joint Monfils trial. By the way, representing the state at the prosecution table in both Bintz trials were DA Zakowski and Assistant DA Larry Lasee.

The State's Hidden Agenda

Brian Kellner's trial testimony was 100 percent hearsay. It was not testimony about what Kellner knew firsthand, but about what Kutska had allegedly told him. Although there are exceptions to the hearsay rule, hearsay testimony is seldom allowed at trial. The reason is as simple as the lesson we all learn the first time we play the childhood game of "telephone," in which a secret is whispered consecutively from one person to another. As the secret is passed on, it often gets distorted. There are two reasons for this. First, some people accidentally mix up the information and cannot keep the facts straight. Second, some people *purposely* distort the information before passing it along.

Although the game is fun, to these six innocent men who were the subject of hearsay testimony in a courtroom, it was not a game—and it certainly was not fun. How do you set a distortion straight after the facts have been lost in the interpretation, passed down the line through several faceless parties?

Kellner's testimony can even be broken into two parts: single hearsay and double hearsay. While single hearsay might have some very remote value in some instances, double hearsay is more worthless than the distorted information given at the end of the telephone game.

In his single-hearsay testimony, Kellner related what *he thought* Kutska had said *about Kutska himself*—what he, Kutska, said or did at a given time. This was a case of "he said, she said." That is information that would have come straight from Kutska's mouth—not Kellner's. But Kellner's double-hearsay testimony had him relating what *he thought* Kutska had said *about what other people*—Basten, Hirn, Johnson, Moore, and Piaskowski—had said or done. This was more like "he said that she said that they said."

At the end of the day, how reliable was *any* of this? If single hearsay is so unreliable that it is never permitted at trial without special exception, double hearsay should never be allowed. Somehow, using the exception-to-hearsay-rule argument that Kutska made the statements against his own interests—which in reality he did not—the state persuaded Judge Bayorgeon to allow Kellner's testimony at trial against Kutska.

With that accomplished, the next item on the prosecutor's agenda was to convince the court to have one trial for all six defendants. The prosecution claimed it was cheaper for the taxpayers and less traumatic for the victim's family to have one trial as opposed to six separate ones.

The defense argued passionately against a joint trial by claiming the rights guaranteed in a silly old document—the U.S. Constitution. Apparently Judge Bayorgeon decided that economic and emotional points outweighed the constitutional rights of the six accused men. There would be one trial, one jury, and six defendants.

Now here is where the state's real agenda—the hidden one—kicked in. By allowing the Kellner testimony to be used against Kutska in a joint trial—even though using it against the others in separate trials would not have been permitted—the jury automatically heard the tainted evidence. Despite Judge Bayorgeon's admonition to the jury that not all of the testimony pertained to all of the defendants, the inapplicable hearsay was still heard by the jury. Everyone knows that it is impossible to un-ring a bell. It was like stopping the telephone game in the middle and saying, "If you heard something about a million dollars whispered in your ear, forget it."

The state's clever agenda to slip the Kellner double-hearsay testimony into the joint trial was successful. Without it, a key card would have been missing from the very base of their house of cards.

What Kellner Wants to Tell the World

Brian Kellner was never a willing participant in the development of this creation, but he proved malleable enough to be Winkler's foil. Kellner told these authors that he tried to set the record straight with the authorities "on at least fifty occasions." He said that at least one of those occasions took place at the district attorney's office. The authorities, he said, would have none of it. Finally, it is time for Kellner to have his day in the sun and the chance to tell the world what he wants it to know. It is the same thing he has told these authors point-blank: The Fox Den role-playing never happened; it was Randy Winkler's invention.

14

Illusionary Testimony

Imagination is the one weapon in the war against reality.

—Jules de Gaultier

As U.S. citizens, we have the right to expect that a person called to testify against us at a legal proceeding will be knowledgeable about the subject and have something significant to contribute. That person should not be one more cup in the prosecution's shell game, making the truth next to impossible to find. Unfortunately, this is not always the case. Sometimes—in an attempt to lend credibility to an issue— "inexpert" witnesses are called under the guise that their answers will be credible and important. It is a kind of illusionary testimony meant to paint a subtle picture in the mind of the jury even though the facts of the case do not support that picture.

This happened several times during the Monfils trial, and there is no small doubt that it contributed to the jury finding the six men guilty. It is a legal tactic, of course. However, if the state's case was anything more than "conjecture camouflaged as evidence," why did the state not allow the facts to stand on their own without resorting to yet another underhanded method for "proving" their theory?

Tony Barko's misinformed and misleading testimony concerning the timing of a crucial paper break (covered in a previous chapter) was only the beginning. There are more examples of the state's inexpert testimony at work.

No shred of evidence was ever found to prove that a confrontation had actually taken place at the bubbler area between the number 7 and 9 paper machines. No eyewitness ever corroborated this purported mayhem. No physical evidence was ever found, not even a microscopic DNA particle. The state knocked itself out looking for a trace of something—anything.

Even without such evidence, however, the state still theorized that Keith Kutska had cleaned up the area around the bubbler with a high-pressure water hose and thus washed away all of the DNA evidence. DNA experts can weigh in here on the foolishness of such an assertion. Yet lacking any evidence of such a cleanup—or any reliable eyewitness to such a cleanup—Zakowski planted in the mind of the jury the impression of Kutska doing just that. How? Zakowski called Jeffrey Herman to the stand.

Herman was a repulper/baler operator in the second-floor converting department. He had never worked in the paper-mill department. He had never worked on a paper machine. He had zero experience and zero knowledge of the specific tasks associated with working on a paper machine. The two small pieces of equipment he operated were in the converting department, just northeast of paper machine 9. At best, Herman had only seen paper-mill workers performing their daily routines from a distance.

There was absolutely no logical or legal reason for the state to call Herman to the stand to answer any of the state's questions on proper paper-machine procedure, especially cleanup. However, Herman had casually mentioned in an early police interview that he had seen Kutska "spraying the floor" a time or two in the past—a normal part of Kutska's duties as machine operator. On that basis alone, Herman was presented by the state as an "expert" witness on such procedures.

On the stand, Zakowski quizzed Herman about paper-machine work habits and equipment and the cleanup responsibilities of a paper-machine operator. It was all so clever—designed to create an image of Kutska scurrying around with his high-pressure hose scouring away the evidence of a bloody crime scene. The fact was that Herman had told the police he had seen Kutska doing this cleanup at the dry end of paper machine 9. This was in a completely different area—more than a hundred feet away from the bubbler. That little "tidbit" never emerged in Zakowski's questioning of Herman.

By using Herman to create the illusion of a crime-scene cleanup, the state took care of one of the biggest elephants it had lurking under the rug—the abject lack of evidence of a bubbler confrontation. Herman's inexpert testimony created an excuse to explain why the police had come up empty-handed in their search for physical evidence around the bubbler. It also set cement around their theory that there actually had been a bubbler confrontation when there had not.

"And this is a minor point, ladies and gentlemen, but again it tells you that when you hear: 'where was the evidence'; 'why wasn't there any physical evidence of a beating.' Well, remember, didn't Herman say he [Kutska] was out there with a hose?"

—John Zakowski to the jury in closing arguments, trial day 27

More Illusionary Testimony

Early on the morning of Monfils's death, the product coming off the 9 paper machine was being discarded because the weight of the paper was fluctuating in and out of specification. As machine operator, Kutska put the machine's computer into manual to help stabilize production and begin making acceptable paper. Then he had one of his crew members call in an emergency work order to the instrumentation shop. The instrumentation guys normally assist in troubleshooting problems with the machine and then getting the computer back on line.

The state speculated that Kutska purposely created the problem with the paper machine as a ruse to get instrumentation technicians

Dale Basten and Mike Johnson to the paper-mill area so they could help harass Monfils. Never mind that Jerry Puyleart, the night-shift machine tender that Kutska relieved that morning, also had the problem. In fact, Puyleart had told Kutska about the problem and had suggested that Kutska take care of it right away.

As a way of impeaching the testimony of Basten, Johnson, and Kutska in this regard, the state put Dave Daniels on the stand. On the day of Monfils's disappearance, Daniels had been working as fourth hand on the 9 machine—the lowest position on a four-man papermaking crew. Daniels was an entry-level employee with limited experience. He had never worked in any position above third hand and had never received any training in any of the positions above that.

Yet Daniels was put on the stand as though he was an expert. He was asked questions about what a machine operator like Kutska should have done about the stock-flow problem and what instrumentation mechanics like Basten and Johnson should have done to address it. Daniels was even pressed for his opinion on how long it should have taken to find and fix the problem.

Daniels's relative inexperience was set above that of Basten, the instrumentation shop's long-time working foreman, and that of Johnson, a trained and experienced instrumentation mechanic. Daniels's testimony regarding the duties of a machine operator—a position three solid rungs up the work ladder from his own—was set above that of Kutska *or any other* experienced machine operator at the mill. Together Basten, Johnson, and Kutska brought over seventy years of paper-machine operating experience to the stand. Daniels had just a limited experience as a fourth hand.

Putting Daniels on the stand for this information was akin to calling on a hospital janitor to explain which surgical procedures a doctor and his staff should have used on a patient. Sure, he might have even seen parts of various operations from a distance, but he was hardly the person who should be testifying in a court of law.

The state's hidden agenda here? It was to brand the defendants as chronic liars. And it seemed to work. Following the trial, the few jurors who talked to reporters suggested that it was the "unreliable" testimony of the men themselves that convinced the jury of their guilt.

A savvy jury would have realized that someone who had worked solely in another department was not an expert on paper-machine procedures. Perceptive jurors would have also known that a fourth hand could not provide the best insight into how a paper-machine problem should be solved. Still, guys like Barko, Herman, and Daniels knew far more than the jurors did about such things, and the DA's crew was more than happy to leave the jurors with the impression that they had heard from experts.

In a third example of highly questionable tactics, the state tried to brand Mike Piaskowski as a liar with hearsay testimony. This effort was even more convoluted than the others. During his direct examination of state witness Rob Gerbensky, Assistant DA Griesbach asked Gerbensky about a conversation that had occurred over two years earlier. The conversation, from May or June 1993, was between Gerbensky and another worker. The other worker had told Gerbensky about something a third worker thought he heard Piaskowski say eight months before the conversation with Gerbensky. It was triple-hearsay testimony, with the passage of much time making it even less reliable.

Griesbach tried not once, but twice, to work this obviously worthless testimony into the prosecution's case against Piaskowski. The first try was in the direct examination of mill worker Steve Stein, who had been the first link in the Gerbensky hearsay. At that point, Nila Robinson, defense attorney for Dale Basten, shouted her objection. Any information from such a circuitous route was surely worthless. Besides, this was going well past the hearsay leeway allowed the state in making a case. Still, Griesbach vigorously defended his right to ask the question under the exception-to-hearsay-rule.

Here is the direct examination of Steve Stein by Griesbach (trial day 14, page 125, and line 23):

Griesbach	Do you recall a conversation with one Robert Gerbensky concerning whether or not Mr. Piaskowski had talked with Keith Kutska?
Robinson	Objection, based on hearsay.
The Court	He's just asked if he recalled the conversation. If he asked what was said, then it might be a valid objection. Objection overruled.

Griesbach	My question was whether or not you said something to Mr. Gerbensky about your conversation with Mr. Piaskowski concerning whether or not he talked to Keith Kutska following the playing of the tape in # 7?
Stein	I'm not sure I understand what you mean.
Griesbach	I'm going to move on.

That did not end it for Griesbach, however. He was hell-bent on trying to make Piaskowski look like a liar. Just two witnesses later—this time with Rob Gerbensky himself on the stand—the assistant DA was at it again:

Griesbach	Now, at some point did you explain what you had seen to Steve Stein?
R. Gerbensky	Not. On that day, I didn't; no.
Griesbach	When was that?
R. Gerbensky	That was maybe a half a year to eight months later.
Griesbach	Much later?
R. Gerbensky	Yes.
Griesbach	At that point did you explain what you had seen to Steve Stein?
R. Gerbensky	Yes, I did.
Griesbach	And did he indicate any surprise at what you told him?
R. Gerbensky	He was really surprised. He said Mike told him …

At this point, Mike Johnson's attorney, Eric Stearn, objected.

Griesbach	Your honor, there's an objection. I did ask Mr. Stein these questions, your Honor. I believe this is an inconsistent statement. Mr. Stein was asked about this conversation. This witness was given a prior inconsistent statement by Mr. Stein.

The Court	What he said is still hearsay. There's no reason for it to come in. So, insofar as what Mr. Stein said, that's excluded.
Griesbach	Pardon, your honor?
The Court	Insofar as what, if anything, Mr. Stein may have said, that is hearsay. We're now talking impeaching on a collateral matter. It's not coming in, so the objection to that portion of the answer is sustained. Ask your next question Mr. Griesbach!

In a small way it was fortunate that Griesbach was directed to move on. Otherwise, the implication that Piaskowski had lied would have been hanging out in the middle of that courtroom like underwear on a wash line. The jury that convicted the defendants "on their own testimony" would have embraced the "liar image" in their deliberations even faster than they did.

The hearsay testimony of Brian Kellner, covered earlier, was more of the same. Asking Kellner—who was not even working on the day Monfils disappeared—to account for the goings-on that morning was beyond the pale. Even more deplorable, however, was threatening Kellner with the loss of his children, his job, and the possibility of being thrown into jail if he did not deliver the damning testimony the state wanted. All of this was going on, according to Kellner, while he was trying at every turn to avoid lying in court.

So what is the upshot of these and the other instances of dubious testimony presented in this trial? As far as the impact on the jury goes, it is hard to say. The Monfils jury is tight-lipped regarding its deliberations. It did not respond to the questions of these authors. Only recently has a small crack in that door opened through some contact with one of the jurors.

There is little doubt, however, that this jury was incapable of sifting through the extraneous noise to get at the essential truths. Even after Mike Piaskowski was released from prison, juror Kathy Hoffman told a reporter that she still believed that he got the weight and the rope that were found around Monfils's neck. Her belief is based on nothing more than John Zakowski's rampant speculation in his closing argument— speculation completely unsupported by any evidence of any kind.

In fact the weight found around his neck may have actually come from a locker in the furnace room next to the tissue chest. Five days after the discovery of Monfils's body, mill worker Rick Doemel told investigators that he had previously observed such a weight in an old metal cabinet next to the tissue chest. He also told them that it was gone following Monfils's death. However, the police did not followup on Doemel's observation. Mill workers were not questioned about the fate of that missing weight. The cabinet was not dusted for fingerprints or checked for other evidence.

The use of illusionary testimony and raw speculation as principal tactics in presenting its case speaks directly to the relative weakness of the state's case. It also indicates that the state was well aware of that weakness.

Still More Illusionary Testimony

Although it was not offered by the state as an expert opinion, another example of the prosecution's misleading testimony comes from the words of their witness James Maciejewski. At the time, Maciejewski was working in the James River pulp-mill department and assigned to the yard crew.

On the stand for just a few minutes, Maciejewski testified to overhearing defendants Dale Basten and Michael Johnson talking to each other in the mill's locker room sometime in early December 1992. Maciejewski testified that he could not actually hear what the two were talking about, but he did manage to hear Johnson assert in a loud voice that he was not going to change his story for anyone. To an overly zealous prosecution, the implication seemed clear—Basten was trying to get Johnson to alter what he was telling the police to avoid suspicion.

Here is Maciejewski's testimony regarding the incident (trial day 14, page 32, line 14):

Q. Can you explain what happened that day?

A. That day I was in the locker room. I was sitting by my locker and I seen Mike Johnson and Dale Basten by Dale's locker. They were in conversation. I couldn't hear what they were saying. Then, Mike Johnson, he said in a louder voice that I could hear, he says: "I don't care. I'm not changing it. I told my story. I'm sticking to it. I'm not changing it for no one."

Q. What were you doing at the time?

A. At that time I was doing one of two things. I was either writing in my book the job I was doing that day, or flossing my teeth. I really don't recall totally.

Q. You said it was Basten you could hear talk prior to Mr. Johnson's statement?

A. Well, I could tell they were in conversation. I couldn't really hear what they were saying.

At first glance, this seems pretty damning—Basten and Johnson engaged in heated discussion over Johnson needing to rework all or part of his "story." As it turns out, it was not that at all. Taken out of context, Johnson's words sound incriminating; but plugged into the reality of the situation, they actually underscore his honesty and integrity.

Here are the facts surrounding the conversation. Detective Randy Winkler himself was the subject of Basten and Johnson's conversation. Johnson was explaining to Basten that Winkler had recently grilled him and was trying to get him to alter what he had told the police in an earlier statement. While using the same tone of voice he had used with Winkler, he emphatically told Basten exactly what he had told Winkler—that he was not about to change his words. What Johnson was telling Basten was really very simple: He was not going to doctor his story for anyone, especially for a cop who wanted to twist his account of the morning of November 21 to fit the police theory.

Had anyone bothered to check out the circumstances surrounding this conversation, they would have quickly recognized how innocuous this hearsay was. No one ever did. As a result, the jury bought the idea that Johnson had inadvertently blurted out an incriminating statement. In reality, Johnson had given them crystal-clear proof that he would never lie about what he did and did not know. Still, the jury cannot be blamed for this one; they were given only one way to view it.

At trial, the prosecution presented Winkler's house of cards as though it were a complete work of art—unquestionable in its symmetry and totality.

It was, nonetheless, a feeble pile of junk that would not stand on its own without the glue provided by DA John Zakowski and his crew.

At the center of the fragile monstrosity there were six cards representing the six men charged. For the sake of brevity, let us take one of those cards at random. We will pull it from the pile for a good look, knowing that the same could be done for each man, sending Winkler's entire creation fluttering to the floor. All right, the card is that of Rey Moore—as good a card as any.

The state's case against Moore had four major parts: eyewitness identification, jailhouse testimony, hearsay testimony, and police testimony. The next four sections will examine the gaping holes of reasonable doubt that each part of the state's case against Moore is riddled with.

Faulty Eyewitness Identification

Mill worker Charles Bowers stated that on the morning of Monfils's disappearance he had seen a very dark, well-built, athletic, six-feet-tall, 190-pound black man with no facial hair walk through the area of the beaters and head north toward the converting department. In a statement to police on December 11, 1992, Bowers estimated that he had observed the man around 7:30 a.m.

When asked about Bowers's observation, Rey Moore, the only African American of the six accused men, denied that he was anywhere near the beaters or repulpers that morning. However, the investigators had already determined that no other African American men were working at 7:30 a.m. Therefore they quickly decided that Moore was being dishonest and he must be hiding his guilt. While Bowers has never been certain of the time of this event, he also has never wavered from his observation that the man he saw was a very dark, well-built, athletic, six-feet-tall, 190-pound black man without facial hair. He restated this observation to these authors.

The investigators, however, failed to recognize several extenuating factors: First, Bowers had also worked a full night shift the night before Monfils's disappearance. Two African American, male night-shift workers from the converting department had also worked that same night shift, until about 6:00 a.m. They were Charles Binns and James Johnson.

Binns fits Bowers's description of the man he saw almost perfectly.

He is a very dark-complexioned, six-feet-tall gentleman who is so athletic that—thirteen years after the trial, at age fifty—he was still playing basketball recreationally. While not exactly clean-shaven, Binns told these authors that he had a "Don Johnson look" in those days—a shadowing that might be difficult for the average person to identify at a distance. James Johnson and Moore are racially mixed and are both light-complexioned African American men. All three of them are tall. Moore and Binns are about six feet tall, and Johnson is six feet four inches. According to his ex-wife, in those days Johnson was sometimes clean shaven, sometimes not. Moore was known to be rarely clean shaven and he always had a substantial mustache.

Bowers insists that he has no firm idea as to the time of his observations, variously estimating that the time "could have been 6:30 or 7:30 or whatever." Bowers had worked a long and unusual graveyard shift from ten o'clock Friday evening until ten o'clock Saturday morning. He had no reason to note the time that someone may have wandered through his work area during any shift—the locker room containing employee showers and restrooms was located right next to Bowers's work area to the south. In fact, the route through Bowers's area made sense for many of the mill employees; it was a fairly direct and somewhat quieter route between their posts and the locker room. It also steered clear of the dust, heat, and humidity of the paper-machine area.

For seven and a half hours, Bowers, Johnson, and Binns were all working at the same time. In recalling the average night shift of those days Binns said, "We took a lot of walks in those days." Today Bowers acknowledges that his observation could very well have occurred during the time when Binns and Bowers were both punched in.

Bowers was a recent hire. Most people did not know him, and he did not know most people at the mill. He believed that Rey Moore was the only African American man who was working that day, because that is what the investigators told him.

Six months after Bowers's observation, the Monfils family filed a civil suit against Basten, Hirn, Johnson, Kutska, and Piaskowski, as well as union president Marlyn Charles and mill worker Randy Lepak. Eight grayish photos of the men—each the size of a postage stamp— were put into the local newspaper. In spite of the fact that Rey Moore was neither very dark nor clean shaven, his photo stood out from the others. And so Bowers identified Moore, the only African American in the photos, as the guy he had seen walking through his area six months earlier. From then on, he would stick to his assumption that it was Moore he had seen.

This identification of Moore—from a single photograph in the local newspaper—violated every standard of proper forensic procedure. Experts state that 60 to 80 percent of wrongful convictions involve mistaken eyewitness identifications. Moreover, cross-racial identifications are especially error-prone.

The best procedure for eyewitness identification requires a double-blind photo lineup that contains only one suspect and five others who reasonably resemble that suspect. To avoid intentional or unintentional hints, the person presenting the lineup to the eyewitness should not know which photo is that of the suspect. There is absolutely nothing in the record of the Monfils case that shows this or any other photo lineup was used to help Bowers identify the black man. It is not clear how vigorously Bowers was pushed to identify Moore, but it is clear that nearly every factor for making a mistaken identification was present.

Rey Moore is not a very dark African American man. He was not without facial hair. And he was not the African American man seen near the repulpers at any time that morning. While it is true that Moore was the only African American man working at 7:30 a.m., it was much more likely that Bowers had observed the very dark and athletic Binns at an earlier time.

Without question, Bowers lost track of time that day. In his statement to Officer VanRooy, Bowers said his day-shift coworker David Wiener arrived at work at 6:15 a.m. Under normal circumstances this would have been correct. Wiener's timecard, however, shows that he punched in at 5:15 a.m. It was the first day of deer-hunting season in Wisconsin, and Wiener had relieved his partner, Ron McLester, an hour earlier than normal so that McLester could get a head start on his hunting. Like most people who do not have a specific reason to recall a particular event, Bowers was simply remembering things as they usually happened.

> "He's [Rey Moore] the only black man working at James River that day."
>
> —John Zakowski's closing arguments to the jury, trial day 27

Jailhouse Testimony of a Con Man

James Gilliam is an experienced con man, a career criminal, and a convicted murderer. Gilliam was also a witness for the state on day 16 of the Monfils trial.

Prior to testifying, Gilliam—who is considered a habitual criminal by the Wisconsin court system—had been convicted on at least six different occasions. He had also served time in prison twice: once for robbery in Wauwatosa, Wisconsin, and another time for the nonfatal stabbing of two men at Lotharios Night Club near Green Bay. After the Monfils trial, in October 2000, Gilliam was arrested for the first-degree intentional homicide of his wife, Katrina. He is currently serving a life sentence without the possibility of parole.

On April 12, 1995—the same day the Monfils arrests were made—the Green Bay police had also taken Gilliam into custody. This time, he was accused of using a butcher knife to threaten Connie Manders, a woman who wanted to end her relationship with him. Gilliam ended up in the Brown County jail at the same time as the Monfils defendants. He claimed it was during this time that Rey Moore had talked to him about Monfils's death; that Moore had "confessed" to him. The idea that Moore would confide in Gilliam was likely accepted by the police because Gilliam is also African American.

In a signed statement to Detective Randy Winkler, Gilliam said, "Rey told me that he got involved about two days before the fight started when Keith Kutska got hold of him. Rey said Kutska told Rey that Monfils was going around and blabbing his mouth and he was going to get them all fired."

When asked about this, Moore said he "discussed not one word with anybody" at the jail—that he was depressed and kept to himself.

Moore further stated that he did not remember even seeing Gilliam at the jail, much less talking to him.

Gilliam's statements about Moore were unsupported hearsay. They contradicted the known facts. Two days before Monfils's death, Kutska had not yet acquired the tape from the police. Kutska had no definite idea who had called the cops. He did not contact Moore or anyone else that Thursday. On Friday night—when Kutska finally had the tape—he made calls to Brian Kellner and Jim Melville as well as to Marlyn Charles, Mike Piaskowski, and Randy Lepak. Kutska did not contact Moore on Friday. In fact, Kutska never contacted him.

So why would Gilliam say what he said? That is pretty easy to figure out. Gilliam understood firsthand the seedy "you scratch my back I'll scratch yours" world of the career criminal. For nearly two years, in 1993–94, he had been a paid informant for the police. He had used drugs, but he also informed the police on other people who had drugs in their possession. He would then get paid 10–20 percent of the street value of the confiscated drugs by the police. At the Monfils trial he testified, "The highest I really ever got was a payment of about $500. All the rest was 100, 150, 200, 300, you know."

To Gilliam, it did not really matter whether or not his fabrications about Moore jibed with the facts. He had been making deals with the police for years. It was business as usual for him. Individuals in his position know that they will typically be taken care of if they tell the police what they need to hear—the cops do not have to promise anything overtly. It's a wink and a nod.

On the day of his sentencing, Gilliam had his lawyer tell the district attorney that he had something to offer in the Monfils case. Instead of jail time or prison for threatening Connie Manders with a butcher knife—thanks to the powers-that-be—Gilliam received two years probation and was set free. Three years later, he stabbed his wife nine times and killed her in front of her fourteen-year-old son.

In the spring of 2006 these authors contacted Gilliam at the Waupun Correctional Institution, requesting a meeting to review his testimony concerning Rey Moore. In our introductory letter we told him of our belief that Moore was a truly innocent man and that the Innocence Project at the University of Wisconsin Law School was investigating Moore's case.

Gilliam replied with the following letter dated May 18, 2006:

> After receiving your letter as dated above, I have made a decision as to your request, and I think it would be a honor for me to assist you in the completion of your book concerning "The Monfils Conspiracy: Six Innocent Men," and would be very interested in helping Mr. Moore.
>
> So feel free to contact me either by phone or letter, so that we may set up time for you to come to Waupun. Also, I would like your assistance in getting a radio since I don't have any Electronics, if you can help please send me the following radio:
>
> WR-1 Cherry Wood Radio
>
> Item No. WR1c
>
> Color: Cherry wood
>
> Price: $100
>
> Ship to: James Gilliam Jr., #76762
>
> 396 South Drummond Street
>
> Waupun, Wisconsin 53963-0351
>
> Address to order Radio:
>
> C. Crane Company Inc.
>
> 1001 Main Street
>
> Fortuna, CA 95540-2008

When we finally met with Gilliam in the prison media room, he contradicted his trial testimony. He told us that Moore was completely innocent and that Moore had "tried to stop the other men." Apparently Gilliam had conveniently forgotten his testimony at the Monfils trial when he claimed that Moore had hit Monfils while participating in the alleged assault.

Early in the interview, Gilliam began fidgeting, then he looked away, seemingly indifferent. "You know you guys are costing me money. I have a job here," he complained. We assured him that we appreciated his time. We also told him that we were definitely not connecting the possibility of a radio with his help. Upon hearing mention of the radio, he "knowingly" agreed that there was no connection. Possibly thinking that we had gotten his silent message, he quickly got back on task.

From there, Gilliam was more than ready to tell us whatever he assumed we wanted to hear. But what we heard was nothing more than adlibbing on his part. We could easily tell that it was just his method of conning his audience—feeling his way through a story until he landed on something to which we might respond favorably. If nothing came of one piece of the story, he would cast his narrative in another direction and see where that got him.

In the end, Gilliam's ramblings made us realize just how unreliable any information from him would be. At one point, those ramblings included a bizarre tale about Monfils's wife having an affair with a Milwaukee drug kingpin and "insider information" that every paper mill up and down the Fox River Valley was a swinging door for a rampant drug trade.

To us, it seemed to be a wasted trip until we realized that we had just witnessed the man creating a story to please his listeners. We could not help but wonder how Gilliam ever became one of the state's key witnesses at the Monfils trial or how his testimony could continue to represent a major stumbling block for the remaining five men during the appeals process.

Hearsay Testimony—Moore Gets Dragged In

Brian Kellner's Fox Den role-play statement placed all five defendants who were with Keith Kutska around the time of Monfils's disappearance at the bubbler assaulting him. Specifically, Rey Moore was said to have shaken the cassette tape in Monfils's face, telling him he "couldn't deny that he made the phone call."

But if Kellner's information is not the truth and the role-play did not happen, where did Kellner come up with such a specific detail to plug into his story? Enter Detective Winkler. In a detail sheet, Winkler described how he had encouraged Dale Basten to speculate about what might have happened to Monfils. Although Winkler dated this detail sheet December 8, 1992, the police report formats collected by these authors (see appendix V) show that he actually created it almost two years later, in 1994.

During their actual interview in 1992, Winkler and Basten were at the tissue chest where Monfils's body had been found. When asked by Winkler to speculate as to what might have happened to Monfils, Basten freely told Winkler what he thought. It was not his wisest move. It was against common sense and all good legal advice, but he also knew he had not harmed Monfils. And really, Basten figured, helping the police was the right thing to do.

Basten suggested that maybe someone had pushed Monfils and Monfils then may have struck his head on the wall of the tissue chest, which would account for the head injury. Basten also pantomimed a suggestion that someone might have been shaking the tape at Monfils and saying, "We got the fucking tape. You can't deny it now."

Like everyone else at the mill, Basten was trying to guess at what may have happened. It was a mystery to everyone. This particular conjecture resulted from a brainstorming session that Basten had had a few days earlier with Ed Keehan, a retired James River engineer. Their discussions had produced several speculative scenarios describing what might and might not have happened to Monfils. This was just one of them. True to form, Detective Winkler boldly wrote in his detail sheet, "After Basten got done I felt he [Basten] had confessed to killing Tom Monfils."

Somehow Basten and Keehan's speculation about Monfils not being able to "deny making the phone call" and the "shaking of the tape in his face" became a part of Kellner's Fox Den scenario, and Rey Moore's name was attached to it.

Police Testimony—Winkler Strikes Again

Randy Winkler's flawed trial testimony against Rey Moore is exposed in chapter 12. As much as anything, Winkler's "unofficial" addendum to his original detail sheet—the account of Moore hearing Kutska's two phone calls—is a smoking gun that will never go away. In addition, Winkler volunteered at trial that he "felt Rey Moore was involved in Tom Monfils *homicide-* [authors's emphasis] as early as November 29, 1992," the day of his very first interview with Moore. This appears to be extremely prejudicial, since the autopsy report indicating homicide was not even produced until ten days later, on December 8.

That is the case the state presented against Moore: four elements of entirely circumstantial evidence fit to a theory—no solid facts and no solid evidence, just suspicion, inference, and innuendo. It is the same kind of indirect finger-pointing and speculation aimed at each of the other men. At the end of the five-week trial, all the prosecution had presented was a house of cards. Not one piece of evidence presented by the state stands on its own as irrefutable and untarnished—not one. Besides fabricating evidence against Moore, the prosecution applied its deceitful tactics to several other situations, all in an effort to create guilt where there was none. Here are just a few examples.

A Ladder Becomes a Body

Six months into the Monfils investigation, "beater-man" David Wiener and several other James River workers were celebrating the wedding of coworker Ty Bouzek. Sometime late that evening, Wiener called the Green Bay police from the reception hall to tell them he had just remembered something from the day Monfils died. He immediately went to the police station, where he made a statement to a detective.

Wiener explained that he worked at James River in the repulping area. He said that he was working the day Monfils disappeared—right next to the isolated storage area where the tissue chest was located in which Monfils was found. He told the detective that he heard someone at the wedding say the name "Rodell." Suddenly, he said, he remembered that at 6:30 on the morning Monfils disappeared, he saw Dale Basten and Mike Johnson "carrying something heavy like a ladder near the vat where Tom's body was found." He also said he could not tell what they were carrying.

By the time of the trial, Wiener's sudden recollection of Basten and Johnson "carrying something heavy like a ladder" at 6:30 a.m. had become Basten and Johnson carrying Monfils's body at 7:45

a.m.—an hour and fifteen minutes later. The changes in the details between Wiener's original statement and the facts produced in his trial testimony were essential to the state's theory.

Both Basten and Johnson adamantly deny being anywhere near the tissue chest the day of Monfils's disappearance. Johnson testified that he had no reason to be near the tissue chest and had not been back there "for over a year." The state's response was that Wiener had no reason to lie about his sudden recollection. Therefore Basten and Johnson must be lying, and both must be guilty.

Mike Johnson and the Popcorn Man

Mill worker Jim Boucher had once worked on paper machine 7 with Tom Monfils. Boucher was sometimes referred to as "the popcorn man" by coworkers because he would make up large bags of popcorn for everyone to enjoy as they passed through his area.

While leaving the mill one morning in the early stages of this case, Mike Johnson was interviewed by WFRV-TV, Channel 5, in Green Bay. When he was asked if he knew Monfils, Johnson mistakenly told the reporter that he knew him as the popcorn man.

At some point after his interview, Johnson realized that Monfils was not the popcorn man, that it was Boucher. At one point, Johnson had correctly told the police that he did not know Monfils. When the police stumbled across his TV interview, they accused Johnson of lying. And if he had lied to them, they figured, he must also have something to hide. Johnson and his attorney, Eric Stearn, tried to explain the mix-up to the authorities. The authorities would hear none of it.

After conviction but before sentencing, Johnson earnestly expressed his concerns that the prosecution would unfairly use the TV tape against him at the sentencing hearing. He knew that the truth about his mistake had already fallen on deaf ears. Stearn assured him that Zakowski's office had "promised" not to do that. A promise notwithstanding, Zakowski's office did use the tape against Johnson. Johnson and his family were devastated.

Closing Arguments to the Jury

Witnesses who are called to the stand are bound by oath to tell the truth. This stricture does not apply to the prosecutors, especially during closing arguments or rebuttal. In their efforts to vilify the six defendants, DA John Zakowski and assistants Larry Lasee and William Griesbach showed an obvious willingness to work around the edges of truth and justice.

In a summation to the jury, a district attorney will normally review the evidence that was presented at trial to support a guilty verdict. In this case, however, the state flooded the jurors with hypotheses, conjectures, speculation, blind guessing, and baseless inferences.

These authors first interviewed Zakowski and Lasee in March 2003. In a blatant mischaracterization of the facts during that interview, Zakowski stated that on the morning of November 21, 1992—when Mike Piaskowski called the foreman to report Monfils for not being on the job—Piaskowski demanded that Monfils be "replaced." Zakowski said that Piaskowski's use of the word "replaced" continues to convince him that Piaskowski is guilty. By using *that* word, Zakowski told these authors, Piaskowski indicated that he had prior knowledge of what happened to Monfils. It was an inference that Zakowski had also used in his closing arguments at trial.

"Absolutely nothing could be further from the truth," says Piaskowski. "A thorough search of the many interviews of other people addressing this issue is proof that I wanted them to 'find Tom' and that I never said, 'I want Tom replaced.' The only use of the word 'replace' is found in Pat Ferraro's summary of what I said to him."

If the prosecutors had done their homework—and citizens most certainly have the right to expect at least that much—they surely would have discovered that these claims were completely unsupported. Unfortunately for Piaskowski, that homework was never undertaken. Instead, the state dramatically emphasized this falsehood at least five times in closing arguments—Zakowski three times during his final words to the jury and Lasee twice in his rebuttal.

"My question to Zakowski and Lasee is simple," says Piaskowski. "Why?"

Again and again, the state's argument, conclusions, misquotes, and theories were presented as if they were evidence for the jury.

The absence of physical evidence was transformed into proof of guilt through illusionary testimony. The lack of corroboration for the state's suppositions was blamed on a "code of silence" by the plant workers. Denial of involvement by the defendants was called proof of conspiracy. Misquotes of the defendants's actual words were turned into incriminating phrases. The question to Zakowski and Lasee is also simple, and it echoes Piaskowski's: "Why?"

Guilty! Guilty! Guilty! Guilty! Guilty! Guilty!

For a very long time a trophy from the Monfils case hung on a wall in John Zakowski's office. It was a framed copy of the *Green Bay Press-Gazette* with the word "Guilty" splashed across its front page six times in huge, bold letters. It proclaimed the outcome of the Monfils trial.

Curiously, that trophy was missing the day these authors first sat down with Zakowski to get his perspective on this case. It was Ash Wednesday, and John's forehead still bore the ashes he had received earlier at Mass. The conversation in the room that day was extremely helpful.

We walked out of there wondering how an earnest guy like John Zakowski could have gotten it so wrong and how he could remain so blind to his error. Zakowski tried to explain away every dubious aspect of his case, including the good old-fashioned commonsense notion that told us no six guys on this planet would go to prison for each other for the rest of their lives.

In a way, it was a little sad—thinking of Zakowski alone with his trophy. No wonder he was miffed when Judge Terence Evans of the U.S. Court of Appeals for the Seventh Circuit critiqued Zakowski's greatest triumph as "conjecture camouflaged as evidence" and "inference stacking." That could not have felt very good.

Still, for all the pathos one might feel after Judge Evans and four other federal judges dulled the shine on Zakowski's trophy, one has to feel a lot more empathy for the five innocent men still awaiting justice today. Worse by far, Tom Monfils's family has yet to receive truth and justice for their fallen husband, father, son, and brother.

Better than DNA Statistics

Based on the statistical validity of DNA evidence, wrongfully convicted people are freed every week. The accuracy of DNA tests is in the range of a *billion to one*. By comparison, the odds of winning the Powerball lottery are *146 million to one*. The courts have accepted DNA statistics as proof beyond a reasonable doubt. However, there is statistical evidence of the innocence of these six men that far exceeds the DNA numbers relied on to identify rapists and establish paternity.

Consider this: What are the odds that you know anyone who would do what the six men in the Monfils case are accused of doing? Who do you know that would give up their children, their grandchildren, their parents, their jobs, their life savings, their retirement, their homes, a cottage, their reputations, and their freedom—all to protect someone they worked with but scarcely knew? Throw in the idea that such a person would not cut a deal with the police and would, instead, sit quietly in prison since 1995 to continue the cover-up.

You probably do not know anyone like that. For argument's sake, however, let us say that you could find one such person in every one hundred you meet—that makes the odds a hundred to one. Add to that the chances that you could find *six* people in a row who would do such a thing, and the odds—after multiplying a hundred six times—become *a trillion to one*. These are the odds against winning the Powerball jackpot not once, but twice!

The Green Bay authorities believe that they defied those incredible odds and lucked into finding six men who would turn their backs on everything they loved in order to play a part in the conspiratorial murder of a coworker. The obvious reasonable doubt here strikes a person in the face like a blow from a sledgehammer.

Such astronomical odds are far more powerful and far more meaningful than "conjecture camouflaged as evidence," The investigators failed to move beyond their original assumptions. They bucked the odds and just plain got it wrong!

15

Eyewitnesses to Innocence

The key was Piaskowski. If they found Piaskowski guilty, it would mean they believed Kellner and our theory of what happened that morning.

—District Attorney John Zakowski

The innocence of Dale Basten, Michael Johnson, Keith Kutska, and Rey Moore can be proven by two people: Connie Jones and Mike Piaskowski. The eyewitness accounts of Jones and Piaskowski also help underscore the innocence of Michael Hirn. These two facts put both Jones and Piaskowski directly in the line of fire of a police department and a district attorney dead set on getting Keith Kutska. Before this case could move forward, both Jones and Piaskowski would have to be dealt with in order for the authorities to get their man. In the end, Jones had her testimony twisted away from the truth; Piaskowski was dragged in as a coconspirator.

Jones was also a suspect when her earliest testimony did not fall in line with the police theory. It was only in the nick of time—by caving into the state's insistent version of what she had seen—that Jones escaped the conspiracy net that dropped on Basten, Hirn, Johnson, Moore, and Piaskowski.

Connie Jones's Morning

As a tester in the pulp lab at James River, Connie Jones had day-shift responsibilities that consisted of collecting pulp samples and recording data from various computers and other measuring devices around the paper machines. She normally needed about twenty minutes to complete this part of her duties and was usually finished by about 7:00 a.m.

On Saturday, November 21, 1992, however, she was running late. First, she had discovered a contaminant in the form of bleach-liquor residuals in the secondary-fiber pulp. This meant she had to take time to notify the paper-mill foreman and the stock-prep operators in order to prevent production problems from occurring. At nearly the same time, paper machine 9 had begun to experience a tensile-strength problem that may have been pulp related. This required her to immediately run a "freeness test" on the pulp samples brought in by that machine's crew. On the top of that, the river water-quality checks from the previous night shift were overdue and still had to be done. Jones had clocked in at 6:02 that morning, but it was well after 7:00 before she was finally able to begin her normal daily routine.

Shortly into her rounds, at about 7:20, Jones was collecting pulp samples at the 9 blend hopper. After exiting coop 7, Mike Piaskowski saw Jones there and told her about Monfils's anonymous call to police.

Jones continued her rounds and brought the pulp samples from the blend hopper back to the pulp lab. There, she made a test sheet from each sample. While the test sheets were drying, she left the lab to obtain the necessary data from various computers. Her first stop was at coop 7, where she again saw Piaskowski.

En route to her next stop at the coop of paper machine 9, Jones passed a man in the area of machine 7's weigh-sheet table. He looked, she said, as though he was "deep in thought, like something was bothering him." She told these authors that he appeared to be "processing." Somewhat concerned, she made a mental note of her sighting as she continued to coop 9. When Jones entered the coop, she saw Basten,

Johnson, and Kutska, along with others. Dave Daniels, paper machine 9's fourth hand, was one of those "others" and verifies that the other three men were present when Jones entered.

In coop 9, Jones listened to the tape of Monfils calling the police. When she asked who the person was that had made the call, Kutska pointed out the window, saying, "That's him over there in the blue hat." The man Kutska pointed to was outside coop 9. He was working alone near the south end of paper machine 9, just north of paper machine 7. To Jones's surprise, it was the same troubled man she had seen just a minute or so earlier.

After hearing the tape and logging the necessary data from the computer, Jones left coop 9. She thought she would get a closer look at the guy who had called the police, so she specifically looked for him on her way back to the pulp lab. Try as she might, she did not see Monfils around anywhere.

The only other person in the area was Piaskowski, who was still in coop 7. He verifies seeing Jones pass by and he also remembers wondering about Jones's reaction to hearing the tape. He left coop 7 and headed toward coop 9. As he passed through Monfils's work area, Piaskowski did not see Monfils either.

As Jones reached the pulp lab, she encountered the pulp-master operator, Rey Moore, in the aisle. She told him about the tape in coop 9 and suggested that he might want to take a walk over there to hear it. "Really!" said Moore, his wide-open eyes expressing dismay.

Just a minute or two after Piaskowski arrived at coop 9, Moore entered. Someone inside said, "News sure travels fast, look who's here already." It was a reference to Moore's union involvement as a shop steward and his reputation as a guy who could work things out between the workers and floor supervisors.

Moore listened to the tape and asked, "Who is this Monfils fellow?" Without looking, Kutska gestured toward machine 7, mentioning again that Monfils was "the guy in the blue hat." Piaskowski, Moore, and others looked out the window in that direction, but Monfils was nowhere to be seen. Nor was anyone else. As machine tender on machine 7, Piaskowski had to account for his work crew. So he left coop 9 and headed back to his job.

A few seconds later, Kutska and Moore decided to head toward machine 7, hoping to catch a glimpse of Monfils. Kutska would be happy to point out Monfils to a curious coworker.

Mike Pie's Search

When Piaskowski did not see any of his crew on the job, he proceeded to the south end of paper machine 7. He thought he might find Monfils there occupying himself with some busy work. Meanwhile, Kutska and Moore had gone only as far as coop 7 and went inside. The backtender, Dennis Servais, was there.

When he did not find Monfils at the south end of machine 7, Piaskowski headed back to coop 7. Once inside, he asked Servais if he had seen Monfils. Servais said he had not. Piaskowski then asked if Monfils had told Servais where he was going. Servais again said no.

At that point, Piaskowski asked Servais if he knew where the fourth hand, Pete Delvoe, was. Servais directed Piaskowski to the backside of machine 7. There, Piaskowski found Delvoe washing the floor. Piaskowski asked Delvoe the same series of questions about Monfils. Again getting negative responses, Piaskowski finished checking the backside of the machine for Monfils and headed back to coop 7.

Servais verifies this entire sequence of events, stating that Kutska and Moore came into coop 7 between 7:45 and 7:50 a.m. and Piaskowski a minute or two later. Servais also affirms Piaskowski's questions about Monfils's whereabouts and his return to coop 7 after his interaction with Delvoe.

Mike Hirn states that he was at the smoking table near coop 9 when he saw Piaskowski walking just ahead of Kutska and Moore as they made their way from coop 9 to coop 7. This is somewhat verified by Piaskowski, who recalls Hirn standing in the doorway between machines 7 and 9 as Piaskowski was returning to coop 7. Piaskowski does not recall the exact time he saw Hirn, but definitely recalls seeing him within this scenario.

After Hirn watched Kutska and Moore pass, he decided to follow them to coop 7 and saw them enter it. Once Hirn neared the coop, however, he could see that Monfils was not there. Hirn decided that he had been gone long enough and that he should return to his job in the shipping department.

On his way back, Hirn passed machine 9 and noted that its third and fourth hands, John Mineau and Dave Daniels, were about to start a turnover. Mineau verifies this, stating that he remembers Hirn heading north toward the shipping department at about this same time. Mineau, who typically recorded the time at the start of a turnover, logged this one at 7:47. Hirn has consistently put his time of return to shipping as "just prior to that turnover, about 7:45 a.m."

Piaskowski, Servais, Kutska, and Moore were inside coop 7 discussing Monfils's absence from his work area. Back in coop 9 Johnson left to put the cover back on the stock-flow valve in machine 9's basement. Basten, who was still in coop 9 monitoring the stock-flow meter, decided to head to the ice machine located in the main aisle, south of paper machine 7, in order to get some ice for a sore arm.

Wearing a blue hat, Basten passed coop 7. From inside the coop, Moore pointed to Basten as if to ask, "Is that him [Monfils]?" "Wrong blue hat," someone said.

With that, Basten stuck his head into the coop, only to learn that Monfils was yet to be found. Basten teased Piaskowski and Servais about expecting "shorthand pay" and then headed for the ice machine. There, Basten chatted with color-man Dan VandenLangenberg and supervisor Pat Ferraro. Ferraro was on his way to the secondary-fiber department to follow up on the bleach-liquor problem. They were noting the pulp readings at the main stock-prep panel near the ice machine. This was between 7:50 and 7:55. Basten returned to machine 9 and joined up with Johnson, and soon thereafter they both returned to the instrumentation shop.

It was near this time that Piaskowski paged Ferraro. By the time Piaskowski talked to him, Ferraro was already at the secondary-fiber plant. Piaskowski asked Ferraro if he knew where Monfils was. Ferraro did not. Piaskowski then told Ferraro to come to coop 7. There was some "heavy shit going down," he told Ferraro, emphasizing the bizarre events that seemed to be unfolding.

A few minutes after that call, Moore left coop 7 and returned to his work area. On the way, he briefly stopped at Connie Jones's pulp lab. He informed her that Monfils was off his job and that he still did not know who the guy was. Jones remembers the time was about 8:00 and that it was twenty minutes after she had first seen Moore and told him about the tape.

Ferraro finished his work in the secondary-fiber plant and came to coop 7 accompanied by VandenLangenberg. As they entered, VandenLangenberg noted the time. It was 8:15. After Ferraro talked to Piaskowski and then Kutska, he immediately began to look for Monfils.

Shake Jones Down, Drag Piaskowski In

Nowhere in this scenario—so plainly set out in the eyewitness testimony of Connie Jones and Mike Piaskowski and corroborated by others—is there any account of a group of fellow workers surrounding Monfils, as the authorities describe. And there is no amount of unaccounted time during which such a confrontation could have occurred.

The observations and testimony of Jones and Piaskowski cover that period of time during which Monfils disappeared from his work area and the time when the search for him began. Their descriptions account completely for the whereabouts of all of the men except Mike Hirn and almost completely account for his whereabouts as well.

So exactly how did the authorities manage to bag Kutska in spite of the eyewitness testimony of Jones and Piaskowski? To eliminate Piaskowski's testimony, they simply claimed he was a part of the conspiracy to harm Monfils and cover up his death. They turned him into one of the defendants.

As for Jones, the police and prosecution persuaded her that her memory was inaccurate about the details of the events she observed from coop 9. Convinced of their premature theory and despite clear evidence against it, the detectives presented her with a Hobson's choice—she saw Monfils either tending to a paper break or working on a turnover. They offered nothing else, ignoring all other possible activities that could have occurred in the nearly thirty minutes between turnovers. A week before trial and under the stress of police scrutiny, Jones conceded that the police must be right—that she saw a paper break and that her memory was wrong.

The police had failed to consider, or had completely ignored, a third and far more likely possibility—that Monfils was doing a spur-of-the-moment cleanup at the north end of paper machine 7 with an air hose. That was a common occurrence during any mill shift. It happened after paper breaks, after blade changes, after getting a cart of cores; oftentimes it was just busywork.

The fact that Jones most probably saw Monfils doing a cleanup is confirmed by the actions of the fourth hand, Pete Delvoe, and by his trial testimony. Both Piaskowski and Servais had observed Delvoe washing down the floor on the backside of paper machine 7 fifteen minutes after the 7:34 turnover. This is exactly what Delvoe would be expected to do *after* all the dust and paper shards were blown from the front side of the job site to the backside of the machine, an operation resulting from a spur-of-the-moment cleanup by the third hand—Monfils.

The prosecution needed to prevent Jones's original testimony from derailing their theory. Without ever considering the more likely possibility of a cleanup, the prosecution proceeded to convince Jones that she saw Monfils working on a paper break, not on a turnover. By doing this, the prosecution could apply her testimony to an earlier time frame that morning, preventing her from being the "eyewitness to innocence" that she is. Sadly, they succeeded.

In the process, the prosecution threatened her job and her family's security by implying that she could be charged as part of the conspiracy. She feared that she might land in prison simply for being in coop 9 when Monfils vanished.

Worse yet, without a court order authorizing it—certainly not one that can be produced by the Brown County district attorney or clerk of courts offices—the cops invaded Jones's bank account and intimidated her with the information they obtained.

Somehow they learned that there had been a recent sizeable deposit. With that information, Winkler accused Jones of taking a bribe from Rey Moore. It was an unfair and likely an illegal tactic but one that scared the hell out of Jones, as she told these authors. The truth of the matter was that Jones, a hard-working African American woman, had been ordered by a probate court to deposit her family's inheritance from a recently deceased relative into her bank account for distribution at a later date. The allegation of it being bribe money was all so seedy and, to be perfectly honest, seems to be borne out of some small-minded racism to boot. After all, Moore is also an African American.

In early 2005, twelve years after Monfils's death, these authors sat down with Jones for a four-hour discussion. By then, she had retired from the mill but not before she found herself bumped out of her pulp-lab position and jockeyed from one low-end job to the next all over the mill. She ended her career working as a fourth hand, ironically, on the now-infamous paper machine 7. Even more ironically, she now knows firsthand the difference between a paper break and a turnover, and she realizes that Monfils was almost certainly tending to neither when she saw him from inside coop 9 that morning.

One of the things Jones has consistently noted was the absence of any large paper rolls in the aisle when she made her way to coop 9 or when she was in coop 9. The state used that fact as pressure to convince her that she had not seen a turnover, which normally would have resulted in two giant paper rolls sitting there in the open. However, Jones arrived in the area several minutes after the machine 7 turnover was completed, after the rolls had been hauled away.

Tom Zdroik, the roll hauler, had already had ample time to pick up both rolls before Jones walked by. Removing the rolls takes less than a minute or two. Although Zdroik does not remember exactly when he picked up the rolls on that particular day, he does say that it is very likely that he could have been waiting there for the turnover to be completed and picked them up very quickly as a result.

Dale Basten recalled seeing Zdroik waiting for the rolls from a turnover that morning, suggesting that Zdroik was at the ready as rolls were coming off the machines. That was Zdroik's common practice, said many paper workers.

The fact that Jones did not see the paper rolls in the aisle did not matter one way or the other—except to the state in its efforts to push her to fall in line with its theory. Moreover, picking up paper rolls after a typical turnover requires that the roll hauler drive through the bubbler area four times. Zdroik testified that at no time did he see any confrontation or any aggregation of people in the bubbler area. He also testified that he never saw a wet and slippery floor, which would have indicated a recent effort to hose the area down and to get rid of evidence following a confrontation.

It seems obvious. Tom Monfils must have left the paper-machine area shortly after Jones and the others in coop 9 saw him working near the north end of machine 7. Then, according to all records, he was never seen again.

Jones, the state's own eyewitness, has stated consistently that Dale Basten, Michael Johnson, and Keith Kutska, as well as Jon Mineau and others were with her in coop 9. She reiterated this view in her interview with these authors. As she left coop 9 she saw Mike Piaskowski still in coop 7 and seconds later she saw Rey Moore at the entrance to the pulp lab. All of these sightings occurred during the few minutes in which the authorities say Monfils was confronted and beaten at the bubbler. These people are all accounted for during the time Monfils vanished.

By all verifiable accounts, Jones was the last person to see Monfils and the very first person to look for him. Because her testimony exonerates the six men convicted in this case, the state had no other choice but to try to move the time of Jones's testimony out of the way in order to breathe life into their bubbler-confrontation theory. Because Piaskowski could fill in all the gaps in Jones's eyewitness account, the police neatly threw him into the hopper that included all the members of their conspiracy theory. The bottom line? By discrediting Jones and Piaskowski, the police and district attorney betrayed two truths about their case. They were hell-bent to get Kutska at any cost and they were unwilling to let the facts lead them to the truth.

Eyewitness to Innocence Timeline

The following timeline covers those essential minutes when Tom Monfils disappeared from his workplace. It was assembled from the detail sheets of the GBPD—making it *their* timeline—or at least the one they could and should have developed. It represents the most plausible, realistic, and accurate account of what happened between 7:21 and 8:05 a.m. that morning. Most importantly, it underscores the fact that Connie Jones and Mike Piaskowski are eye witnesses to the innocence of five men who remain incarcerated today. (See appendix II for a more detailed timeline covering the events of November 21, 1992.)

TIME	WITNESS	EVENT
7:21 a.m.	Piaskowski	Told Jones about the audiotape near paper machine 9's blend hopper.
7:22	Jones	Took pulp samples from the blend hopper and returned to the pulp lab to process them for testing.
7:27	Piaskowski	Left paper machine 7, made a brief stop at coop 9, and returned to coop 7.
7:29	Computer	Recorded a turnover on paper machine 7 beginning at 7:29.
	Piaskowski	From coop 7 saw Monfils at control panel at the beginning of 7:29 turnover.
7:31	Mineau	Left coop 9 to get ice; saw Jones in the pulp lab, who said she knew about the tape.
7:34	Monfils	Marked the rolls from the 7:29 turnover; logged time in the production report as 7:34.
7:36	Jones	Left the pulp lab, went to paper machine 7 for computer data; saw only Piaskowski present in coop 7 when she was there.
7:38	Johnson	Saw Jones in coop 9 for 3–4 minutes.
	Jones	Left coop 7 and walked to coop 9; saw no paper rolls from paper machine 7 in aisle. Noticed Monfils near paper machine 7 scale. Also saw someone sitting at the 9 smoking table. Entered coop 9, noted Daniels, Boulanger, and possibly Mineau present.
7:40	Daniels	Remembers Johnson, Basten, and Jones in coop 9, with Moore entering after Jones left.

	Jones	Identified Johnson, Basten, Kutska and three others in coop 9 with her. Observed Monfils working near south end of paper machine 9.
	Kutska	Saw Monfils standing by core cart; saw no turnover or paper break going on.
	Piaskowski	± Heard the outside coop 7 air-lock door open; no one entered coop.
7:42	Delvoe	± Saw Monfils going toward coop 7's air-lock entrance.
	Basten	(7:42–7:51) Noted Daniels and Jones in coop 9; saw Jones leave and later Moore arrive.
	Jones	Looked for Monfils while returning to the pulp lab; saw nobody at bubbler or smoking tables.
	Jones	Noted Piaskowski still in coop 7; Monfils was nowhere to be seen.
	Piaskowski	Went back to coop 9 after seeing Jones pass coop 7.
7:43	Jones	Met Moore in the aisle while returning to the pulp lab, told him of tape in coop 9.
	Moore	Entered coop 9.
	Piaskowski	Entered coop 9 and recognized Kutska, Mineau, and others. Moore entered front door a moment or so later.
	Daniels	Saw Moore in coop 9 after Jones was gone.
7:46	Piaskowski	Left coop 9 and went back to paper machine 7; saw Hirn standing near doorway south of the 9 smoking table.

	Hirn	Followed behind Kutska and Moore to coop 7; Monfils not around. Headed back to shipping department; saw Mineau at dry end of paper machine 9.
	Mineau	Saw Hirn heading back to his workplace.
7:48	Kutska	(7:45–7:50) Walked to coop 7 with Moore and entered.
	Servais	Saw Moore and Kutska come into coop 7.
7:50	Servais	Piaskowski entered coop 7 and asked Servais if he had seen Monfils. Kutska and Moore present, with Kutska trying to describe Monfils to Moore.
	Piaskowski	Left coop 7 to find Delvoe to see if he knew where Monfils was; continued around machine looking for Monfils. Returned to coop 7.
7:54	Basten	± Left coop 9 to get ice; saw role hauler driver waiting to pick up next pair of rolls from paper machine 7. Saw Moore and Piaskowski in coop 7. Entered coop 7 air lock, opened coop door, made "shorthand pay" comment and heard the "wrong blue hat" response.
7:56	Ferraro	± With VandenLangenberg; saw Basten at stock-prep panel; they joked about "milking the system."
	Piaskowski	Paged Ferraro from coop 7; Moore and Kutska present.
	Servais	Performed and logged the 7:58 turnover on paper machine 7.
7:58	Moore	Stopped at the pulp lab on way back to pulp-mill department and mentioned to Jones that he had not seen Monfils.

8:00	Jones	About 20 minutes after she last saw him, Moore stopped at the pulp lab and said Monfils is missing.
8:05	Johnson	Decided to leave coop 9 and do the "chart run."
	Basten	Returned to instrumentation shop; went past coop 7; crew working; did not see Moore or Kutska.

A Few Words from Mike Pie

Five others and I were falsely accused and unfairly convicted. There is no getting away from that fact. There is also no way for me to get away from the unsolicited and unwelcome connections that I share with the other guys. I certainly identify with and have great empathy for them, yet I owe no allegiance to any of them—especially Keith Kutska.

Even though I know that he is innocent, I personally blame Kutska for everything. No, not for killing Monfils, or even wanting Tom hurt in any physical way, but I do hold him responsible for everything else that has happened, including the circumstances that led to Tom's death. Kutska is the person that put into motion the events—whatever they were, that ultimately resulted in Tom's death. His careless actions also ruined my life and the lives of countless others.

His self-centered arrogance destroyed my "everything." He took nine years out of my life and changed the rest of it forever. He turned the last years of my beloved father's and grandmother's lives into a hell on earth. He kept me from attending both of their funerals. He caused me to miss the marriage of my daughter, Jenny. He prevented me from repairing my own marriage. He cost me my livelihood, my home, my savings—and all of my personal possessions. He ruined my pension, my social security benefits, my plans for a decent retirement, and my daughter's inheritance—everything I had worked for. I owe him nothing! Trust me when I say I have no love for Keith Kutska.

But still he and I do have one very important thing in common—the same thing that we had in common in November of 1992. He is also innocent of this crime.

—Mike Piaskowski

The Framing of Mike Pie

Let us be clear about this: Mike Piaskowski's knowledgeable testimony would have blown this case apart had the investigators only been more open minded. Along with Connie Jones, he is a critical witness to the innocence of the other five men. He is also a powerful witness to the falsehood of that bubbler scenario.

Despite the presence of nearly 300 workers at the mill that day, Detective Randy Winkler was unable to produce one eyewitness to his fiction—not one. Furthermore, Brian Kellner has now completely disavowed his statement. Today, he emphatically declares that Keith Kutska speculated, and only speculated, about this case as the two of them aimlessly rambled through twelve long, beer-soaked hours that ended at the Fox Den tavern.

To grasp how desperate the prosecution was to destroy Piaskowski's observations, one need only read excerpts from the decision and order of U.S. District Judge Myron L. Gordon, when granting Piaskowski's petition for a writ of habeas corpus.

- Page 1: "No physical evidence tied Mr. Piaskowski to the crime, no testifying witness saw him participate in it, no one confessed, there was no testimony from the petitioner or any other witness that he took part in the murder or intended to."

- Page 2: "The evidence is insufficient to sustain the petitioner's conviction for party to the crime of first degree murder."

- Page 7: "The question for a court of review is not whether it would have convicted but whether any reasonable jury could have found guilt beyond a reasonable doubt."

- "In order for [Piaskowski] to succeed, I must conclude not only that no rational jury could have convicted him but also that the Wisconsin appellate court's determination to the contrary was objectively unreasonable. For the reasons that follow, I find that Mr. Piaskowski has carried that burden."

- Page 9: "Based on the evidence, no reasonable jury could have found Mr. Piaskowski guilty of each element of the crime under either of the theories offered by the prosecution ... "

- Page 10: "First, as the trial court observed, Mr. Kellner had little, if any credibility."

- Page 11: "I am unable to conclude that a rational application of the reasonable doubt standard could establish Mr. Piaskowski's presence at the bubbler."

- Page 12: "The record leaves the [jury] totally in the dark as to the critical question of whether the petitioner did anything that would make him guilty as a party to the murder."

- "Deciding what [Piaskowski] did requires blind guessing."

- Page 14: "Although the state's case is plausible, there are simply too many other possibilities to allow a rational jury to accept [Piaskowski's guilt] beyond a reasonable doubt."

- Page 15: "The ultimate finding of guilt in this case required the jury to pile speculation on top of inferences drawn from other inferences. Each step along the way required the jury to eliminate one or more of the alternatives, thus multiplying the risk of error. Such a verdict is not rational."

- Page 16: "To take away [Piaskowski's] liberty based on the weak circumstantial evidence present here would do violence to the standard of proof beyond a reasonable doubt."

- Page 18: "The trial court concluded that there was a 'great deal' of other evidence to establish the defendant's guilt. However, the court did not discuss that evidence in any detail."

- "[The trial court] did not mention any specific testimony, differentiate between any of the defendants, or describe why their testimony was important other than to note that the jury could have found that the defendants were not entirely truthful."

- "The trial court did not refer to the standards set forth in *Jackson* [case law being discussed], and there is nothing in the court's decisions that even remotely resembles the type of analysis called for in that decision. The court did not consider any of the elements of aiding and abetting for conspiracy under Wisconsin law, much less whether the state had proven them.

The court did not analyze how any of the evidence applied to Mr. Piaskowski specifically, but rather it treated all of the defendants as a unified group."

- Page 20: "This court's review of the trial transcripts, comprising thousands of pages, has uncovered no such evidence. Not a single witness testified that Mr. Piaskowski kicked or beat the victim, and there is a total absence of any other proof."

- Page 22: "Thus the appellate court's decision of the evidence left open the possibility that Mr. Piaskowski's conviction rests upon perjured testimony."

- Page 23: "This case involved a horrible crime and weak evidence of guilt."

- Page 24: "the Double Jeopardy Clause of the Fifth Amendment [of the United States Constitution] bars a retrial."

The state took one more whack at Mike Piaskowski and appealed Judge Gordon's decision to a three-judge panel from the U.S. Seventh Circuit Court of Appeals. The excerpts from their decision affirming Judge Gordon's ruling are equally damning. Writing for the appeals court is Judge Terence Evans:

- Page 7: "A strong suspicion that [Piaskowski] is involved in a criminal activity is no substitute for proof of guilt … "

- Page 8: "The jury's conclusion that Piaskowski participated … with … the others to kill Tom Monfils … is speculation."

- Page 9: "This, however, like so much else in this case, is *conjecture camouflaged as evidence* [authors's emphasis]."

- "In short, the two stage inference that [Piaskowski's words], 'shit going down' was murder … requires a leap of faith that no reasonable jury should be allowed to take."

- Page 10: "In this case the chain of inferences the state attempts to forge fails in multiple places."

- "Having determined that no rational jury could convict Piaskowski, little further analysis is required to confirm Judge Gordon's conclusion … "
- Page 12: "there is scant evidence … that supports Piaskowski's guilt."
- "Our decision today *is* the functional equivalent of an acquittal … the state may not retry Piaskowski."

It is really that simple: two eyewitnesses—Connie Jones and Mike Piaskowski—who together can document the innocence of five men who remain incarcerated at this very moment. Why was one of them coerced into changing her story to protect herself and the other convicted along with the other men because he would not change what he knew to be true? Why did their accounts not spare these five men and send the police and district attorney in the correct direction as they set about solving this case? These are questions that only the authorities can answer. However, both Jones and Piaskowski sit ready, willing, and able to testify on behalf of Dale Basten, Michael Hirn, Michael Johnson, Keith Kutska, and Rey Moore, should each man get his much-warranted day in court. They are simply waiting for the call.

16

No Rational Jury

*No reasonable jury could have found
Mr. Piaskowski guilty.*

—U.S. District Judge
Myron L. Gordon

The task confronting the Monfils jury was staggering. From the outset, this case had been no ordinary whodunit. It centered on a horrific workplace death under extremely mysterious circumstances. Tom Monfils was hardly your typical homicide victim; his accused murderers—normal working guys and family men—were far from your average alleged murderers. They could have been nearly any of Green Bay's 100,000-plus citizens. The fact that there were six alleged murderers muddied the waters even further.

And so the Monfils trial began—with a jury from a distant Wisconsin county sequestered a couple of hundred miles away from home. The jurors were told upfront that there was no physical evidence and no eyewitness to prove what the prosecution claimed had happened—no definitive proof of any kind. It would be a case built on circumstantial evidence, hearsay, and what is legally known as "inference stacking."

Some people, including some of the defense attorneys, told these authors that they believed the trial was the final move in a high-powered game of brinkmanship by the authorities—a last ditch effort to get someone to crack. None of them did. The fact that not one of the six men could provide what the authorities wanted to hear—especially facing the hard reality of a criminal trial and the possibility of prison—indicated one of two diametrically opposed things: Either the police and the DA had it right, and these men were part of a deadly union conspiracy of silence; or the authorities had it dead wrong and the guys were completely innocent.

The northeast Wisconsin community seemed split down those very same lines. It was now up to this imported jury to weigh the prosecution's case against that basic tenet of the U.S. Constitution: that every citizen is innocent until proven guilty beyond a reasonable doubt. Warts and all, the Monfils trial was underway.

This Was Not O. J.

Because of its many quirks, the Monfils trial would have normally caught the interest of the national media. Instead it was eclipsed by the O. J. Simpson double-murder trial, wrapping up in Los Angeles, just as the Monfils trial got underway. However, the connection between the two trials cannot go unexplored. Brown County DA John Zakowski and former Green Bay Police Chief Bob Langen each suggested that if it had not been for the Simpson trial, the Monfils trial would have received a lot more national attention.

From jury selection to closing arguments, the Simpson trial dominated the front pages of U.S. newspapers for well over a year. Without a murder weapon or an eyewitness, the prosecutors in the Simpson trial had also presented a case built on a web of circumstantial evidence.

On Tuesday, October 3, 1995, just twenty-five days before the Monfils jury reached its guilty verdicts, the Simpson jury acquitted the celebrity defendant. Once the questionable verdict was announced, much of the nation seemed to embrace the infamous "not in my back yard" mind-set. Georgi Hirn, Mike Hirn's stepmother, remembered her own dismay when she overheard one of the jurors say in a post-trial interview with Hazel Sanchez of Green Bay's Channel 2 news, "We were not going to let what happened in California happen in Green Bay." Hirn also recalled four other jurors nodding in agreement. Many people have told these authors that they believe—at least in part—that the Monfils defendants paid a heavy price for the perceived mistakes of a California jury.

The Verdict

At 6:21 p.m., on Saturday, October 28, 1995, the jurors in the Monfils case filed back into a jam-packed courtroom. They had reached their verdicts. Their every motion was studied by those present: families and friends, spectators and supporters, the media, the prosecution, the six defendants and their attorneys, and an overflow of police officers. Stone-faced, the imported jurors from Racine County took their seats, purposely avoiding eye contact with anyone in the room. For the briefest instant, the courtroom was dead silent as the community awaited their decision.

Outside, the late-autumn Wisconsin evening enveloped the Brown County courthouse in a shroud. Up and down Green Bay's streets, kids in Halloween costumes were trick-or-treating. The city's adults kept an open ear for "breaking news" in the Monfils case. A community sat on edge, awaiting the outcome of a case that had consumed it for much of the past thirty-five months.

The trial portion itself had ended the previous evening. Judge Bayorgeon had instructed the jurors on their critical, final task: to arrive at a verdict of either guilty or not guilty for each man, depending on their evaluation of the evidence against that particular person. Lesser charges, they were told, were not an option. Following these instructions, the sixteen original jurors were pared to twelve—eight women and four men—and sent off to decide the fate of the six defendants.

These dozen jurors were now back, having spent a total of ten hours—including breaks, a noon meal, and the selection of a foreperson—deliberating one of the most complex murder cases in Wisconsin history. The defendants stood at the edge of a precipice; the stakes were all or nothing.

After admonishing the spectators and media that he would "not tolerate any disruption or demonstration" or he would give the order to "clear the courtroom," Judge Bayorgeon began the proceedings. In a booming voice that echoed through the courtroom, he started reading the verdicts:

First it was Keith Kutska. "GUILTY!" he bellowed. The spectators stirred. The judge looked up.

Next it was Mike Piaskowski. "GUILTY!" he repeated. A muffled and agonizing shriek of astonishment was heard. Piaskowski's family began crying. The judge glared.

Rey Moore was next. "GUILTY!" he boomed for the third time. Disorder erupted.

"You're fuckin' nuts. You're fuckin' nuts," a spectator screamed out. It was Moore's daughter.

"Remove her please!" the judge yelled. Security moved quickly. She was led from the courtroom. Others followed her out. "If there is any further demonstration I will clear the courtroom before proceeding!" Judge Bayorgeon added.

He continued. "Michael Hirn. GUILTY!" Several spectators stood and willingly left the courtroom in disgust.

Judge Bayorgeon quickly went on. "Dale Basten. GUILTY! Michael Johnson. GUILTY!"

As quickly as that, it was over. The friends, families, and lawyers of the defendants were devastated. The Monfils family, their friends and supporters, and the prosecutors were elated. The media was scrambling. Order was not orderly.

"The clerk will poll the jury," the judge commanded.

"Diane Albright—are these your verdicts?" "Yes they are." "Terri Bealhen—are these your verdicts?" "Yes they are." "Gwen Edmund-Berry—are these your verdicts?" "Yes they are." The six men and their families were numb as the rest of the jurors were polled. One by one, Cynthia Burchyett, Paul Gilanyi, Sharon Hechimovich, Dennis Heusdens, Kathy Hoffman, Donald Kalous, April Sedaska, Mildred Redmond, and Morris Sims each answered that they had also reached guilty verdicts for all of the men.

With that, Judge Bayorgeon thanked and released the jury. For them, five grueling weeks were over. For the Monfils family, the jolting loss of their loved one had reached some level of bittersweet closure.

For the six men and their families, a three-year nightmare had taken a gut-wrenching new turn.

The case presented to the jury by the prosecution had been an intricate brew of circumstantial evidence and raw conjecture. Six guilty verdicts, however, indicated that this jury had discerned no crucial differences among the individual men in the state's theoretical mix presented during the trial. With "GUILTY" reverberating throughout the courtroom, the jury had sent the men—one and all—tumbling down that nightmarish precipice.

That night the jurors hurried back to their own lives and essentially disappeared from sight—at least in terms of this case. Ever since that night in 1995, they have shown a puzzling reluctance to reemerge and discuss their decision.

Twelve Silent Chairs

No matter how you slice it, the jury in the Monfils case convicted six innocent men, sending them to life in prison for a crime they did not commit. No matter how convincingly the evidence was presented to them and no matter how steadfast the jurors may want to cling to those guilty verdicts today, the evidence for finding the men not guilty far outweighed that for finding them guilty.

Strategically it was advantageous for the state to admit the weakness of its case at the very beginning of the trial, during the opening statements. Assistant DA Larry Lasee began the trial by stating to the jury, "If details are extremely important to you, you're going to be disappointed. There are gaps."

From there, the prosecution's strategy was clear: gloss over those gaps while pretending to build bridges of clarity with an exuberant line of conjecture. It was the jury's task to eyeball each one of those gaps and see them for what they were—red flags of reasonable doubt. Somehow they missed all of them.

In the summer of 2004, these authors attempted to contact the Monfils jurors to gather their thoughts for this book. A cover letter and questionnaire were mailed along with a self-addressed, stamped envelope. A nominal incentive was offered for each juror's help: "For your troubles, we'll donate $10 to a charity of your choice in your name." This was not about money, after all. It was about justice—

granting these authors the insights that only members of the jury could give. The cover letter was honest: The authors disagreed with the juror's findings but welcomed their input into this book.

**Tom Monfils Murder Trial
Juror Questionnaire**

Defendants: Dale Basten, Michael Hirn. M...
Keith Kutska. P...

Defense Attorneys: A...
St...
Ti...

Prosecutors: Bro...
Assi...
Assis...

Judge: James...

Please answer these questions ... needed. If you do so, please mark the answer(. ...responding question number.

We now know from one of them that members of this jury promised not to comment on the case after delivering their verdicts. But foreperson Gwendolyn Berry's response seemed to run deeper than that.

Not one juror answered the questionnaire. Only two responded at all, both declining to provide any information.

Jury foreperson Gwendolyn Berry returned her blank questionnaire with a Post-It note stating, "I am not interested in reliving this." Alternate juror Jackie Sillix responded by e-mail, skeptical of the "real identity" and the motivations of the people sending the questionnaire. She did not explain her suspicions. But once her concerns were addressed, she decided she "didn't want to get involved."

A telephone conversation with the mother of a third juror seemed like a step in the right direction: She would have her daughter, who was playing softball that evening, get in touch. Communication from the softball-playing juror never happened though, despite additional attempts to contact her.

That was it. No other juror was even that forthcoming. That was the full measure of the willingness of these sixteen people to reflect—for this book—on their time on a jury that sent six men to prison for life.

As a result, these authors must rely on a few scant statements made to reporters to determine why these jurors did not cut through the state's vigorous, yet anemic, case. However, even *Green Bay Press-Gazette* reporter Paul Srubas, who covered the trial and its aftermath, told these authors that he was also surprised by how few of these jurors have been willing to go on record over the years regarding the trial and their verdicts.

They Bought the State's Case and Hurried Home

In retrospect, it is difficult to understand how these jurors could not have found themselves beset by reasonable doubt. Were they actually fooled because, going in, the prosecution admitted that it had a weak case? Then, as the trial dragged on for five long weeks, did they somehow feel that the sheer volume of testimony was more compelling than its actual weight?

It was an important part of their job to meticulously dissect this case, to determine the exact role of each of the men in the state's theory, to weigh the credibility of the evidence against each man, and then to reach a consensus. Granted, it was no easy task—though it was *their* task.

If ever the devil was in the details, it was in this case. That is why the *Press-Gazette* reported on Thursday, September 28, 1995, that the prosecutors in the trial wanted the jurors "to see the big picture, while the defense lawyers want them to concentrate on the brush strokes." The article was titled "Forest or Trees?" It was clear that the defense attorneys wanted their clients to be seen as just that—individual "trees," with thoughts and emotions plainly distinguishable from those of one another. But just how could the defense do that in a *joint trial?*

No defense attorney pounded harder at that theme than Gerald Boyle, who told the jurors that his defendant, Mike Hirn, was not "like the rest of these guys." While Boyle was way off base—"the rest" of the men were not murderers either—one can understand his desire to separate his client from an alleged "mob of conspirators." In the end, Boyle's antagonistic defense strategy—to acknowledge and accept the prosecution's case but to blame the other defendants—created an unfair catch-22 for the other defendants. It was another one of the many pitfalls resulting from the men being forced into a joint trial: damned if you do and damned if you don't.

The state also paraded out a reluctant Brian Kellner. Through his Fox Den role-playing story—allowed under a special ruling by Judge Bayorgeon—Kellner introduced double-hearsay evidence into the courtroom. In the process, the door swung wide open for the prosecutors to attach blatant speculation at the point where Kellner's hearsay ended.

Without Kellner's testimony and a joint trial, nothing worthwhile could be brought against the men. The rest of the trial testimony was similarly pockmarked. The Fox Den incident that Kellner brought to trial was—on its face—rife with the smell of too much beer and too little reality. In his post-trial rulings, Judge Bayorgeon essentially said just that. A rational jury would have seen Kellner's barroom story as the biggest gap in the state's case, not the key DA John Zakowski still holds it up to be.

Mix Kellner's forced fairy tale with some good old jailhouse scuttlebutt, an exotic repressed memory, and a healthy dose of inexpert testimony, stir it briskly, and you have the state's case. That was it. That was the "evidence" that this jury took into its final deliberations, and that was exactly the "evidence" on which they found every one of these men guilty. And they did it in record time. Strip away the jury's breaks, their lunch hour, the time it took them to get set up and pick a foreperson, and in very short order—about half of the time a papermaker would spend at the mill on a single day—this jury returned with six supposedly independent guilty verdicts.

Who Were These Jurors?

What are the tangible facts that can be assembled about this jury, which sent six innocent men to prison and then hurriedly returned home? The quick answer is that the jurors came from a pool of more than a hundred people from Racine County in southeastern Wisconsin. It had been chosen because of the sensational pretrial publicity generated in northeast Wisconsin about the case.

The peculiar process of selecting a single jury to decide the fate of six individual defendants in a single trial was unusual enough. It began in a very crowded Racine County courtroom on Tuesday morning, September 26, 1995, with Judge Bayorgeon presiding. The six defendants and their attorneys were also present, as was the district attorney and his staff.

Judge Bayorgeon began by asking each prospective juror if he or she were related to or knew any of the men who were on trial. Just six hours and thirty-seven minutes later, twelve jurors and four alternates had been impaneled. Was this the best jury that could be culled from the pool? That is hard to say. "With six separate defense teams each trying to do what's best for their client," Piaskowski lamented, "jury selection was confusing at best. It really was quite unfair."

Piaskowski related that he and his attorney, Tim Pedretti, had liked a particular potential juror, a retired mill worker who had also been a union member. Piaskowski figured that a guy like that would have insight into the inner workings of a mill, and he would know the genuine impossibility of any kind of union conspiracy. However, when it came time to eliminate one of the potential jurors, Robert Parent, Rey Moore's attorney, struck the guy from the jury pool. Piaskowski was bewildered. During a short recess, Piaskowski asked Parent, "Why did you strike *him*? He was the perfect juror!" Parent replied, "I had to strike someone."

This was not the first problem Piaskowski and Pedretti would confront in a joint trial, and it would not be the last. Piaskowski described this as an "eye-opening" experience: "Unexpectedly, my top choice for a juror was stricken by Rey Moore's defense attorney. How fair is that? It was obvious to me right at that moment that I was not only pitted against the prosecution, but the other defendants as well. Wasn't I entitled to the same rights as any other American?"

Attorney Parent went on to do some great work at the trial—possibly the best work of any of the men's lawyers. However, it also became clear at that early moment that the six men's defense attorneys were working at serious cross-purposes, further dispelling the whole union-conspiracy myth. With seven parties—six defenses and the prosecution—striking potential jurors, Piaskowski felt it looked "a lot more like a matter of just crossing names off a list than an exacting quest for the very best jurors." The cross-purposes of the defenses would be a boon to the prosecution throughout the trial.

The final panel consisted of twelve women and four men. Only one juror had taken any classes beyond high school. Only one had any kind of connection to a labor union, and that was rather remote. Attorney Pedretti scribbled on several of the female jurors's questionnaires that they were "too protected." He was concerned about their real-world experience.

DA Zakowski said he was satisfied with the jury, adding, "You work with what you get. It's always a crap shoot with a jury." Mike Hirn's attorney said, "It's the biggest guessing game in the world trying to figure out what jurors will do. You're looking for a gut feeling that the people will be fair and impartial."

The next thing they knew, the sixteen members of the newly assembled jury were whisked northward up Interstate 43 to Green Bay. They were checked into the Downtowner Motel, just two blocks from the courthouse. There they would live under the watchful eye of bailiffs for the next five weeks. Their task would be a demanding one. The trial had no clear-cut end in sight, and they were far from home. For a month and a week, these jurors would spend all their time on a physical, mental, and emotional treadmill. It was six straight days in the courtroom and each night under court supervision at the motel. Sundays were a day to relax, engage in monitored conversations with family members, and brace for the resumption of the trial the next day.

The case itself was tough: extraneous information, gruesome particulars, multiple defendants, and lots and lots of testimony by witnesses—often with only vague pieces of the story to tell. The prosecution had warned the jury that it had no eyewitnesses, no physical evidence, and few details. It was up to the jurors to either disentangle an apparent Gordian knot or decide that the knot could not be undone.

It was an exhausting challenge, one that sometimes seemed to take its toll. Numerous individuals have told these authors of seeing various jurors catching a catnap while court was in session. One female juror in particular was reported to have been seen sleeping "often."

Guilty Verdicts All Around, Then Silence

On Saturday evening, October 28, the jury walked back into the courtroom and declared that it had found all six men guilty. The six guilty verdicts said that all twelve of these jurors had seen the forest and dismissed the individual trees. In less than ten hours, they had reviewed twenty-eight days of testimony, supposedly sifted through the state's entire case, evaluated the merits of each of the six defenses, and weighed the impact of all the evidence against each of the defendants. They were either a very efficient jury that cut through their task like a teenager mowing a lawn or a jury that did not much concern itself with the details—like a teenager mowing a lawn.

Basten, Hirn, Johnson, Kutska, Piaskowski, and Moore were all found guilty.

Local TV reporter Paul Adler reported that the jurors refused their 5:00 p.m. meal break once they had reached their verdicts—suggesting that the jury was in a bit of a rush to get the whole thing over with. Adler reported that the jury was "very anxious to get the verdict out" and "in a hurry to get home." By late Saturday evening, the jurors were all home. In their wake laid a community numbed by their decisions.

The following afternoon, Paul Srubas and fellow reporter Anne

Klemm set up camp at the *Press-Gazette* offices and made calls to every one of the jurors. "There was a Packer game," Srubas remembered, "and the offices were real quiet." Srubas was amazed that they could contact only two jurors. The others were "either not home or not answering their phones," he said.

Still, they had the two jurors, at least. "There was some involvement by everybody," said juror Morris Sims. "I know we did what was in our hearts. None of us had any reservations," stated fellow juror Sharon Hechimovich.

Sims said that he became convinced that the men were guilty "as soon as they started taking the witness stand." This was especially true of Keith Kutska, who, Sims said, "lied." Sims added, "I think they know who did it and just are not saying."

Hechimovich said that the statements by Kutska and Rey Moore on the stand did not match their earlier statements. She did not seem concerned that Detective Randy Winkler had tampered with Moore's earlier statement—something attorney Parent had exposed at trial. She said that the jury also had doubts about the sincerity of Dale Basten's breaking down and crying on the witness stand.

Sims suggested that the jury's deliberations "were a struggle for a while" because some jurors were undecided about some defendants. He stated that the jurors had to "fight off disbelief that people could commit such violence." Now there was a mouthful—an apparent leap of faith for the prosecution. Was it also a Freudian acknowledgement of a guilty-until-proven-innocent disposition? The jury solved its issues, said Sims, by going "back to the point, just putting the pieces together."

Hechimovich described the jury's apprehension about going back into the courtroom once they had reached their verdicts. She said that the jurors decided not to show any emotion as they returned to their seats. "I didn't want to look," she remembered.

Following the delivery of the verdicts, the jury returned to the deliberation room, and Hechimovich stated that several jurors "broke into tears out of sympathy for the defendants's and Monfils' families." Leaving the courthouse, Hechimovich said she and other jurors were emotionally shaken by a man who screamed at them that they would all go to hell.

Srubas was especially interested in Sims's take on the repressed-memory testimony of David Wiener, the testimony in which Wiener claimed to have seen Basten and Johnson "carrying something heavy" near the tissue chest where Monfils's body was found. It had been one of the key components in the state's case. Near the close of the interview, Srubas asked Sims about it. Sims's response was another question, "Which one was Wiener again?"

From there, all these jurors slipped back into their lives. The only other word from any of them came on January 19, 2001, when U.S. District Judge Myron Gordon ruled on a habeas corpus filing by defendant Mike Piaskowski, declaring in a twenty-five-page ruling that the evidence presented by the prosecution was insufficient to sustain Piaskowski's conviction.

This time, reporter Andy Nelesen found three jurors willing to talk. Kathy Hoffman said of Piaskowski's release, "We looked at all of the circumstances, and all six of those men put themselves in that particular time and moment."

What "*particular time and moment?*" would have been a great next question. Not one of the men, or anyone else for that matter, ever put any of the men in a *time and moment* when they harmed Monfils. The question was not asked.

Sims was again available. "I think he [Piaskowski] did have a part in it," he said. "There are a couple that played a lesser role, but I think he was in on it more."

Foreperson Gwendolyn Berry said, "This is a case I've tried to put out of my mind. What one judge saw as reasonable, another saw as unreasonable. That's our judicial system. We did what we thought was reasonable at the time."

Hoffman and Sims told Nelesen that there were discussions among the members of the jury about varying degrees of involvement by the men in what the jury believed happened to Monfils. However, both said that the jurors decided they were "all accountable." Sims said, "It wasn't like half the people said guilty and half said not. It was pretty clear-cut." Hoffman added, "I highly believe that Mike Piaskowski went and got that rope. He knew where that weight and rope [found around Monfils's neck] were. I believe he went and got them."

Hoffman's *belief* in this fiction proves how inattentive she really was.

Nowhere in the entire twenty-eight-day trial was there any evidence or testimony presented that Piaskowski got that weight or that rope. None! The reason for that is simple: He did not get the weight and rope! The only point in the trial where Hoffman ever heard any reference to Piaskowski getting the weight and rope was in John Zakowski's summation at the end of the trial. It was a statement Zakowski made based on pure speculation.

Hoffman seemed lost when it came to evaluating that bit of information. Yet she claimed to Nelesen, "I listened with wide-open ears and the evidence was quite interesting. It just all made sense." She had clearly failed to distinguish Zakowski's *interesting speculation* from the facts of the case.

Judge Gordon, a man infinitely more capable of separating fact from fiction, did not believe much of Zakowski's "interesting" case. He wrote:

> Based on the evidence, no reasonable jury could have found Mr. Piaskowski guilty of each element of the crime under either of the theories offered by the prosecution, for two reasons. First, the evidence does not permit a jury, acting rationally, to conclude beyond a reasonable doubt that Mr. Piaskowski was at the bubbler when the confrontation began. Second, even accepting that he was [there], all of the state's evidence and all of the reasonable inferences that can be drawn from it can establish nothing more than his presence during a part of the crime.

These jurors could not do much more than sit back and watch as Piaskowski walked out of prison a free man in April 2001. By July, Judge Gordon's ruling to set Piaskowski free had also been upheld by a second federal judge from the Eastern District of Wisconsin and a three-judge panel from the Seventh Circuit Court of Appeals in Chicago. A total of five federal judges had essentially graded this jury as "unreasonable" and "irrational" and charged it with failing its duty.

Perhaps this is why, today, the members of the Monfils jury sit in very silent chairs. After leading her peers to their guilty verdicts in 1995, foreperson Berry is working hard to put this all behind her.

She does not want to "relive" her decision. Other jurors just are not available to talk about their decisions. Sadly, five men in prison and a sixth—set free but with his life forever impaired—relive these decisions each and every day.

In contrast, a huge thank-you goes out to one juror who has recently apologized to Mike Piaskowski for having been a part of his wrongful incarceration. In essence, that juror exposed the inherent injustice in this joint trial, saying "It's too much to process and just too easy to just make the same decision for [all six] of the defendants." Hopefully, that juror will be available for further help in correcting some very serious wrongs that linger over the case.

Judge Gordon Sees the Light

When U.S. District Judge Myron Gordon reviewed the case against Mike Piaskowski in January 2001, he saw what every unbiased, clear-thinking, rational person would see: *There is no case!* Gordon's ruling was based on his thorough examination of the evidence presented against Piaskowski. In essence, he said that what looked like a Gordian knot was merely a series of loops and twists that the jury could and should have unraveled. Judge Gordon's ruling was upheld by the Seventh Circuit Court of Appeals.

In writing for the Seventh Circuit, Judge Terence Evans refers to a "beating" that never occurred. However, Evans was working without the benefit of the work of these authors in debunking the Fox Den role-play myth:

> The state's meager circumstantial evidence against Piaskowski is also innocuous. The fact that Piaskowski was present in coop 9 prior to the beating and entered coop 7 after the beating, 2 or 3 minutes after Kutska and Moore, proves little because Piaskowski spent much of his workday in those areas. The state also makes much of the fact that Piaskowski complied with Kutska's direction to report Monfils missing and added on his own accord that there was "some shit going down." According to the state, the fact that Piaskowski made the report without asking what had happened

and added his personal assessment of the situation proves that he was part of a conspiracy to commit the murder. It does no such thing. Monfils was, in fact, missing, and as Delvoe confirmed, Piaskowski had been looking for him prior to returning to coop 7. True, a quick-thinking Piaskowski could have been trying to make Delvoe into an alibi witness by asking if he had seen Monfils (when he really knew Monfils was in the vat). This, however, like so much else in this case, is conjecture camouflaged as evidence.

Some Juries Do Get It Right

In tragic contrast to the jury in the Monfils case, the jury in movie and TV actor Robert Blake's murder trial deliberated by considering the evidence presented to them. Whether Blake was guilty or innocent does not matter. On behalf of all U.S. citizens, the Blake jury rejected the circumstantial evidence and the inferences presented to them. They protected the rights of every citizen by declaring that the case against Blake just did not add up to the prosecution's theory.

Also—unlike the Monfils jury—several of the Blake jurors were immediately willing to share their thoughts, including insights into their deliberations, with their fellow citizens.

Foreman Thomas Nicholson said the jury "couldn't put the gun in his [Blake's] hand." "The primary thing, from what I saw," he said, "was that the circumstantial evidence was flimsy. I never felt comfortable at any time about the evidence in its total. It kind of had a lot of holes in it. There were lots of links missing out of the chain."

"As things progressed," said alternate juror Michael Pollack, "it just turned out there were a lot of gaps."

Juror Lori Moore said the evidence presented "didn't point to his guilt … We didn't have enough evidence to show that he was guilty."

Flimsy circumstantial evidence? Holes? Links missing? Gaps? Not enough evidence? Is it any wonder that—by contrast—the Monfils jurors remain tight-lipped about *their* decision?

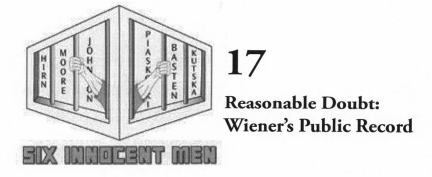

17

Reasonable Doubt: Wiener's Public Record

Wherever he steps, whatever he touched, whatever he leaves, even unconsciously, will serve as a silent witness against him.

—Edmond Locard

What exactly does reasonable doubt mean as a jury weighs the guilt or innocence of a person against the evidence presented in a court of law? To many, "reasonable doubt" is some vague phrase from some far-off court case. To the six defendants facing conviction in the Monfils case, however, reasonable doubt meant the razor's-edge difference between freedom and going to prison for potentially the rest of their lives. They prayed—as did their families—that a panel of impartial jurors would carefully consider the staggering lack of evidence against them.

Instead, the six men got a jury that bought every bit of prosecutorial slight-of-hand and hurriedly reached a verdict that ended their month-long absence from home. Had the jurors rolled up their sleeves and meticulously sorted out the validity of the evidence and how that evidence could be applied against each defendant, their task would have taken much longer than it did. Had they done that, they would have likely acquitted some or all of the defendants.

How the Monfils jury did not find itself overcome by serious doubt is anyone's guess—no juror has ever bothered to explain his or her reasoning in depth. However, a federal judge did not mince words when he called the jury unreasonable.

Reasonable doubt should have grabbed the jurors by their individual and collective throats as they considered the prosecution's case. They should have acquitted the men based on each and all of the following.

- The clumsy work of the Green Bay Police Department as it recovered Monfils's body, ignoring and likely destroying physical evidence
- The absence of any eyewitness testimony
- The absence of any physical evidence of a confrontation
- The absence of any physical evidence of a murder
- The absence of any physical evidence showing that the bubbler area was a crime scene
- The absence of any reliable evidence connecting any defendant to a crime
- The use of testimony based on drunken, double-hearsay, barroom speculation
- The use of a jailhouse informant who had been paid for his testimony in the past
- The incredible demeanor of the jailhouse informant
- The use of non-expert witnesses to support prosecution theories
- The admission by the lead detective that he had altered police reports
- The contradictory testimony of the lead detective
- The unanswered questions surrounding the autopsy results
- The absence of a rational motive for the defendants to take Monfils's life
- The commonsense and statistical improbability of the prosecution's union-conspiracy-of-silence theory
- The fact that none of the accused men tried to save himself by turning on the others
- The totality of the prosecution's case that—true to its

admission in opening statements—was built on suspicion, speculation, inference, conjecture, and hearsay
- The possibility—however slight—that Monfils may have committed suicide

Any one of these points was substantial enough to trigger doubt. En masse, they would have caused a reasonable jury to rush back into the courtroom with six acquittals.

These are eighteen specific reasonable-doubt issues that this jury should have spotted. However, there was at least one other piece of critical information that the prosecution kept from the jury—information concerning another of Monfils's coworkers, David Wiener.

A Public Record the Jury Should Have Seen

David Wiener's peculiar role in the Monfils case falls into two parts: his questionable trial testimony and the questions that surround him as a person of strong interest in this case. On the stand, Wiener painted a vague picture for the prosecution of Dale Basten and Mike Johnson carrying "something like a ladder" in the area of the tissue chest. This was the same David Wiener who worked closer to the tissue chest where Monfils's body was found than any of the six defendants—indeed anyone in the entire mill. He was working—nearly alone—the day Monfils disappeared.

These authors attempted to contact Wiener, without success. Finally, he replied in a sudden and fleeting telephone call. He said that he would not meet or discuss the case with us but would "stand on his public record" instead. That was it.

As a result, only Wiener's "public record" can be presented here. Without Wiener's explanation of it, that public record is pretty damning and certainly gives rise to reasonable doubt in the Monfils case. By presenting that public record, we are not pointing fingers at Wiener. However, the public record that he chooses to stand on is riddled with unanswered questions. Those questions—let alone their answers—would have raised a mountain of reasonable doubt for the Monfils jury had it been allowed to see Wiener's public record.

How intricately tied together are Wiener's role as a lead prosecution witness and as a person of interest in this case? That is anyone's guess. Again, only he can explain that relationship. It could be simple: Like every other mill worker, he was afraid of the police shining their light in his direction. Once it was cast on someone, it did not go away, and that person could be dragged into something he or she had no part in. Or it could be much more complicated: Was Wiener afraid of having the light shine in his direction because he knew far more than he had told the authorities? Whatever the case, he himself could shed much, much more light on this case than he has to date.

David Wiener Was Definitely Capable of Murder

David Wiener killed another human being. That is an undeniable fact. Wiener shot and killed his younger brother, Tim, thirteen months after Tom Monfils died. Two years later, at the Monfils trial, Wiener took the stand as a key witness for the prosecution.

In the state's rebuttal—the last words to the jury before deliberations—Assistant DA Larry Lasee said, "There is no evidence that he [David Wiener] is capable of that kind of vile act [murder]." Lasee was parsing a fine legal line, working hard to remove Wiener as an alternative suspect in Monfils's death.

In the grand scheme of things, however, Lasee's words constituted a bald-faced lie. At the very moment Lasee looked the jury in the eye and uttered those words, Wiener was sitting in a prison cell for taking his brother's life. Nonetheless, the knowledge of Wiener's capacity for killing another human being was successfully withheld from the jury by the prosecution—with the assent of Judge Bayorgeon.

The roadblock was successful. Lasee could embrace the legal technicalities: Evidence that Wiener had killed his brother had not been introduced into the Monfils trial. The jury would never know that Wiener, who worked closer to the crime scene than anyone in the mill and who had a shaky account of his whereabouts that morning, had actually been convicted of the "vile act" of murder. The prosecution kept all that hidden.

Wiener Fits the Profiles

John Douglas pioneered the art of criminal profiling for the FBI and has written extensively on the subject. In his books *Journey into Darkness* and *Mindhunter*, Douglas lists several common profiles of a killer—at least six of which match David Wiener's "public record." His behavior and activities during the Monfils investigation seem to eerily fit four of Douglas's profiles.

Profile 1: First-time killers usually feel compelled to confide in a relative or a friend.

According to several of Tim Wiener's friends, Tim and David Wiener had an ongoing love-hate relationship. Tim would sometimes bring David into his circle of friends for weekend card games and beer. Tim's friends were seldom comfortable with this, they said, because David would easily become angry and hostile when he lost—sometimes to the point of a physical encounter with Tim and the others.

Did the brothers share a dark secret? It was just over a year after the death of Tom Monfils when the brothers had an intense argument over a minor matter. David had refused Tim's request to help him park his car in a favorable spot near Lambeau Field before a Sunday football game.

After the game, Tim and his fiancée, Charlene Gawryleski, went home to change before going out for dinner. Tim called David, and a heated telephone conversation between the brothers ensued. Charlene heard Tim say, "Go ahead and call the cops!" David hung up the phone as Tim repeatedly demanded to know why his brother had refused to assist him with the car-parking plan. "There came a time [in the conversation]," Gawryleski said, "when Tim told David that he was going to 'narc' on him." Gawryleski told these authors that she plainly heard those exact words. A frustrated Tim Wiener decided to drive across town and have a serious talk with David. After making dinner arrangements with Gawryleski, he left.

At his house across town, David was sitting on the stairs facing the front door with two loaded handguns—a Smith & Wesson .357 Magnum and a Ruger .44 Magnum Super Blackhawk. His wife and son were in the basement family room. When Tim came through the front door and started up the stairs, David pumped four shots into him—one into his arm and three into his torso. Even though Tim was unarmed, David claimed that it was a matter of self-defense—that his brother "broke into the house."

During the fifteen minutes it took Tim to drive from his home on the west side of Green Bay to the town of Allouez where David lived,

David had called his mother to announce, "I'm locked and loaded." If Tim came into the house, he told her, he was ready to use his guns. According to Gawryleski, David also repeated this threat to another person, the fiancée of a third brother, Richard.

Instead of being charged with first-degree intentional homicide, David Wiener, John Zakowski's top witness in the Monfils case, was charged with mere reckless homicide. The morning after his arrest, he was released from custody on a simple signature bond. The next day, the *Green Bay Press-Gazette* ran a picture of Wiener in the courtroom—not in the familiar orange jumpsuit afforded most other inmates, but in his own civilian clothes.

In the past, Wiener had not been shy about getting in touch with the police about trivial matters. He called the police when his neighbor's stereo was too loud. He called the police when some neighbor kids "egged" his house. He contacted the police several times during the ongoing Monfils investigation. But when his life was in danger to the point that he felt compelled to lie in wait with loaded guns, he did not call the police or 911. Instead, he called his mother and another brother's girlfriend.

Profile 2: Killers often inject themselves into the police investigation in an effort to determine if they are suspects, to steer the investigation away from them, and to ascertain where the investigation is headed.
Detail sheets obtained from the Green Bay Police Department show that Wiener was interviewed several times. Wiener himself initiated every one of these contacts. Just three days after Monfils's body was discovered, Wiener called the police department and asked to talk to someone there. He showed up there with a story that covered the time when Monfils went missing. He also produced diagrams of his work area—which included the area where Monfils's body was discovered.

A month after Monfils's death, Wiener called the GBPD again. This time he complained that Dale Basten was asking a lot of questions about what Wiener had seen the day of Monfils's disappearance. Wiener implied that Basten must have been checking to see if he [Basten] had been spotted in the area that day. In fact, Basten had actually been asked by Detective Randy Winkler to snoop around and to find out what he could.

Three months after Monfils's death, Wiener—while he was on a personal leave—again called the police to complain that Basten had been questioning Dave Webster, a coworker, about Wiener's leave of absence.

Profile 3: First-time killers often exhibit emotional problems and take a leave of absence from work.

A few weeks after Monfils's death, Wiener took an extended four-month leave of absence from work to deal with mental and emotional problems brought on by what was termed "work-related stress" following the event. He was under continuing psychiatric care and complained of anxiety attacks.

Profile 4: First-time killers usually are males about 25 to 35 years of age.

Wiener was thirty-one years old when he killed his brother and thirty years old when Monfils met his death.

Profile 5: A first-time killer usually commits the crime close to home, in a familiar place for him, a comfort zone.

Monfils was found at the bottom of the tissue chest, an isolated area near Wiener's daily job responsibilities. This was Wiener's workplace home base. Only Wiener and a helper were assigned to be in this area at the time of Monfils's disappearance and death.

Wiener told the investigators at one point that "we are the black sheep back there." He went on to explain that the area is so isolated that he was the last one to know things because so few workers would bother to go back there.

Profile 6: When a suspect in a homicide case kills someone else, he goes to the top of the list of suspects in the first case.

Wiener killed his own brother fifty-three weeks after the death of Tom Monfils. John Douglas points out that this type of development is a red flag that police simply cannot ignore. Nonetheless, Wiener was never listed as a suspect in the Monfils case. Less than twenty-four hours after killing his brother, Wiener was released from jail on a signature bond of just $10,000, with the blessing of DA John Zakowski. In contrast, each defendant in the Monfils trial was strapped with a cash bond of $300,000.

In this case, Douglas's profile of a killer was ignored. On the heels of killing his brother, Wiener did not go to the top of the suspect list.

In fact, he was not on any of the eight suspect lists turned over to the defense in discovery. Instead, he remained at the top of another list—one labeled "Witnesses for the Prosecution."

Zakowski Backs Up Wiener

At the same time and with the benefit of only a cursory look at the facts, DA Zakowski declared that the Tim Wiener homicide had nothing to do with the Monfils case. He curiously told the *Press-Gazette*, "It seems that every time something is brought up, there's a reference to the Monfils case. The world doesn't revolve around the Monfils case."

Zakowski also denied that Wiener's rapid release from jail had any connection with his role in the Monfils case. "That's utterly ridiculous," Zakowski said. He continued to defend his treatment of both cases:

- "There were no deals cut or contemplated in the Tim Wiener case; that's a completely separate thing."
- "There's been a lot of sensationalism in the media regarding Monfils and this incident, and I want to put that to rest."
- "There is absolutely no tie-in that we see between this incident and Monfils. That speculation should end immediately."
- "This was an incident between two brothers, and the history between them, and certain incidents that happened that day!"

In regard to the Wiener case, Zakowski callously dismissed the killing of a human being as a simple "incident." For the prosecution, characterizing Tim Wiener's death as an isolated incident may have been a necessity. The reason? Because six months earlier, David Wiener had made himself into a valuable star witness for the prosecution in the Monfils case with a drunken story of a repressed memory.

"Rodell" and the Repressed-Memory Story

Six months after the death of Monfils and six months before he killed his brother—David Wiener became the state's only "eyewitness" in the Monfils case. On May 14, 1993, while celebrating at a wedding reception at the Swan Club in nearby De Pere, Wiener called the Green Bay police at 10:00 p.m. to speak to a detective "about the Monfils murder." He had an unusual story to tell. As requested by police, Wiener immediately drove to the police station.

While talking with friends at the wedding, he told police, the name "Rodell" came up. Unexpectedly, Wiener claimed, a long-suppressed memory then recurred to him. Suddenly, he remembered that six months earlier he had seen Mike Johnson and Dale Basten near the furnace room by the crime scene on the day Monfils disappeared. He now remembered, he said, that he was at the table in his break area facing east toward the cull cutter and the furnace-room door.

ON TRIAL: The Monfils 6

WIENER: DON'T LOOK AT ME

Brown County District Attorney questions David Wiener in court Monday.

David Wiener (seated) inserted himself into the Monfils investigation early and often. He became DA John Zakowski's (standing) lead witness against Dale Basten and Mike Johnson. For two years, he was the prosecution's key witness. *Green Bay News-Chronicle* front page and photo

All he could see, he said, were Basten's and Johnson's heads above and behind the cull cutter machine. They were both moving along, crouched down or stooped over, as if they were carrying something heavy like a ladder. It was just before "I pumped out the #1 or #2 beater around 7:15 a.m.," Wiener said. (It must be noted that Tom Monfils was very much alive at that time. He had logged a turnover at 7:34 a.m. and was observed by several people as late as 7:40.)

Ten days after his late-night interview, at the urging of the police,

Wiener changed the time of his observation. At first, he said his repressed-memory sighting had occurred between 6:45 and 7:15 a.m. The police told him that time frame did not fit and then asked him if it could have been later than that. They referred Wiener to his logbook. After looking at it, Wiener agreed it was possible that the time frame was between 7:30 and 8:00.

Eight weeks before his repressed-memory incident, on March 15, 1993, Wiener had testified before Judge Naze at a John Doe hearing. At that hearing, DA Zakowski had repeatedly pressed Wiener to recall what he must have seen that morning. The following exchange between the district attorney and Wiener is taken from the transcript of the hearing:

Page 670

    Q. It's an isolated area where you can see everything up and down that aisle way; isn't that right?

    A. Provided there, there isn't [sic] cores in the way.

Page 672

    Q. Why do you think Mr. Monfils was thrown in that beater or vat?

    A. I—at first, I thought it was suicide, but when I was approached by Basten, I think maybe things got out of hand with him. Maybe something, some—maybe he knocked him unconscious. I don't know.

    Q. Knocked him unconscious and then had to get rid of the body, went past that aisle where you could have seen this person or persons take the body and then gone and put that body in that vat; isn't that true?

    A. It would have been hard for me to see because the cores are in the way as you look through (to) No. 9.

    Q. But you could have seen them—you've been at that plant. Could you have seen through them?

    A. Yes, it's possible, yes.

Page 677

    Q. Is it because Basten knows you are in that isolated area where you'd have the opportunity to see what was going on (in) this aisle or that aisle where Tom Monfils might have been walking through to get back to the locker room when being followed by either Mr. Hirn or Mr. Moore? Isn't that true?

A. I suppose that's a possibility.

Page 684

Q. And who do you think could have done it?

A. Basten, Basten scares the hell out of me.

Q. But Basten wasn't anywhere around that day, was he?

A. Not that I seen. Like I say, you could, you could get through there, but it would be awfully hard for me to see unless it was a time that I wasn't there.

Eight weeks after this exchange—an exchange during which he received the information on what the authorities claimed he should have been able "to see" or "could have seen"—Wiener had his repressed-memory episode. Wiener never explained why the word "Rodell" triggered his repressed memory other than to say that it was the name of a part-time summer employee a year earlier.

Suicide and a False Alibi

Even though Wiener worked closer to the vat where Monfils's body was found than anyone else in the mill, his first contact with the GBPD was not until November 26, four days after Monfils's body was discovered. And it was Wiener who made the initial contact, not the other way around, as should have been the case. He phoned the police and asked to come down to the station to talk to them. Detective Sergeant Robert Haglund interviewed Wiener. Haglund took a five-page statement from Wiener and wrote a two-page detail sheet on the interview. The story Wiener gave that evening would be repeated and debunked at the John Doe hearing four months later.

In his report Haglund wrote, "When Wiener called and ask[ed] to come in to talk tonight he said he had to because he has been seeing a doctor for the past year about having anxiety attacks and this was really bothering him that the police wanted to talk to him." There were two things that Wiener apparently wanted to get on the record:

1. Suicide: Monfils must have put himself into the tissue chest.
2. Alibi: Wiener had been with Keith Kutska for forty minutes from 7:45 to 8:25 a.m., the day of Monfils's disappearance.

In his report, Haglund noted Wiener's push for the suicide theory: "He [Wiener] did want it to be known that for someone to end up in the closet [tissue chest] they would have to get in themselves [sic]. He said this is because if they were being dragged back there thru the hall he would have seen them. The only other way is up the latter [sic] from the first floor and only one person can get up it at a time so no one could have dragged him up."

In a second reference to suicide, Haglund wrote that Wiener "also said that if you didn't want to be found, the chest to use would be the one Monfils was in, because all machines draw from that closet so it is usually full." Wiener made a third reference to the idea of suicide in his signed statement to Haglund: "Around 11 a.m. I went out to check along the river."

About two weeks later, an apparent suicide note was found in the phone book of coop 7. Eventually, the state crime lab identified Wiener as the probable writer of that note.

As for the forty-minutes-with-Kutska story, Wiener's account completely falls on its face for two important reasons: First and foremost, although most everyone recalls seeing Kutska early that morning, none of the many workers in the area recalled seeing Wiener with Kutska. That includes Kutska himself, who explained, "I couldn't have had a forty minute anything with anybody. I had a paper machine to run and we were having stock-flow problems."

In addition, the foot traffic in and out of that area to hear the audiotape was continuous, and any workers at the 9 smoking table had a clear view of the working end of paper machine 7. In those forty minutes, at least one—if not two—turnovers would have occurred on machine 7.

After those turnovers, the roll hauler would have made four to eight passes right in front of that smoking table, picking up the paper rolls. Wiener would have seen all that activity and all those people. But he insists he saw no one other than Kutska for that entire time. And what about all those smokers in the area who usually congregated at the 9 smoking table to read a magazine or newspaper or to use the nearby bubbler? According to Wiener, however, not one worker showed up to enjoy these comforts for the entire forty minutes.

At the John Doe hearing, DA Zakowski promptly recognized the holes in Wiener's impossible story. However, rather than recognize Wiener's creation as an alibi for Wiener himself, Zakowski incredibly accused him of trying to create a false alibi in order to protect Kutska.

In that hearing, Zakowski tipped his hand to a premature conclusion that Kutska was responsible for Monfils's death. He showed that the authorities were not open to any other possibility. Having caught Wiener in a serious breach between his story and the facts, he completely let Wiener off the ropes—in effect, coaching him to change his story instead. The plain truth is that Wiener was not with Kutska for forty minutes at 7:45 or at any other time that morning. He certainly was not presenting a false alibi for Kutska.

Wiener's alibi actually starts at 7:30 on the morning that Monfils disappeared, when he pumped out beater number 3 and refilled it. After that was done, at 7:40, Wiener says he then decided to get the tape from Kutska so he could play it for coworkers Charles Bowers and Dan VandenLangenberg. He headed, he says, for the back door of coop 9.

This is within a minute or two of the last sighting of Monfils at the dry end of the 7 paper machine by Connie Jones and others. After the 7:34 turnover, Pete Delvoe saw Monfils heading for the air lock that led into coop 7. Mike Piaskowski was in coop 7 at the time and recalls hearing the front air-lock door open but no one coming into the coop. The air lock also exited to the 3-4 room, a large storage area between the paper machines and Wiener's work area.

Wiener's statement goes on to say that only one person—he thinks Jon Mineau—was in coop 9 when he first got there. Wiener then says he went out the front door of coop 9, headed south, and found Kutska at the smoking table. He says he smoked a cigarette with Kutska, went into the small coop 9 where he heard the tape twice, went back and had another cigarette with Kutska at the smoking table, and then went back to his work area with the tape and tape player in hand.

When Wiener repeated his story at the John Doe hearing, Zakowski suggested that this would have taken maybe thirty minutes. Wiener insisted it was longer, forty minutes. He put his return at 8:25.

By all accounts, only this last sentence of Wiener's story seems to be factual. VandenLangenberg had been in coop 7 with weekend mill supervisor Pat Ferraro in response to Piaskowski's page about Monfils's absence from his workstation. VandenLangenberg recalled that he looked at the clock in coop 7. It was 8:15. Shortly thereafter, he left the coop, went to the foreman's office, spent a few minutes there, and then went to the beater room, where he engaged Bowers and Wiener. Bowers verifies this, remembering that this was when VandenLangenberg told him about the tape and the fact that Monfils was off the job. Wiener then left VandenLangenberg and Bowers in the beater room to get the tape from coop 9 so they could hear it. VandenLangenberg says that Wiener "must have heard [the tape] before because he was only gone one or two minutes." It was about 8:25.

The facts show that Wiener must have heard the tape before then. Kutska, Jon Mineau, and David Webster all support VandenLangenberg's conclusion. Mineau has a clear recollection of a conversation with Wiener in coop 9 earlier that morning, around 7:00, concerning the identity of the caller on the tape. Mineau thought the voice was that of Dick Marto, a supervisor from a different shift. Wiener corrected him and pointed out that it was Monfils's voice. It is noteworthy that Mineau was also the person Wiener put in coop 9 in his forty-minute alibi.

In a civil deposition taken November 3, 1993, Kutska also recalled that Wiener was probably one of the people who had listened to the tape in coop 9 between 6:15 and 7:05.

By Mr. Berk [taking the deposition]:

Q. Regarding that last question, didn't David Wiener tell you that he had heard—first of all, didn't he tell you that he knew about the tape being in the mill before it was played for Tom Monfils?

A. Yes

Q. And didn't he tell you that the tape was played for him before the tape was played for Tom Monfils?

A. Yes

Q. Didn't he tell you that he, himself, David Wiener, took the tape player and the tape and played it for other employees in the mill?

A. Yes, he did.

Q. And, in fact, didn't he tell you that going to hear that tape was the first thing or one of the first things he did that morning?

A. Yes.

At the trial, Webster testified that Wiener told him he had heard the tape in coop 9 before it was played for Monfils at 7:15. Wiener has always denied that he heard the tape before Monfils disappeared. If so, Mineau, Kutska, VandenLangenberg, and Webster would all have to be wrong.

Connecting Only Some of the Dots

On the last day of the trial, in order to dissuade the jury from accepting the defense contention that Wiener warranted strong consideration in Monfils's death, Assistant DA Larry Lasee made the following false statement to the jury during the state's rebuttal: "The problem with the Wiener theory is there is absolutely no evidence in this record, save one piece, that David Wiener heard that tape before 8:30 in the morning. And that only piece of evidence is Keith Kutska saying probably David Wiener."

Once again, Lasee seems to have been playing a game of misleading notions. His words "in this record" are not only deceptive—the prosecution had all of Jon Mineau's statements in their possession—they could be downright dishonest. Kutska was not the only witness who testified at trial about Wiener hearing the tape before 8:30—at a time much earlier than the time to which Wiener himself testified. As noted above, VandenLangenberg, Webster, and Mineau all corroborate Kutska's testimony, a fact that the prosecution knew all too well.

But wait. Why does the time when Wiener heard the tape matter? If he had heard the tape before Monfils walked through Wiener's work area about 7:40–7:45, he would have known that Monfils had made the call to the police. Wiener had an avowed and well-known disdain for snitches.

Why then would the prosecution work so hard to shelter Wiener from scrutiny by the jury? To anyone willing to consider all of the information, that might be a fairly simple question to answer. Wiener was a lone wolf—someone who, if he had harmed Monfils, would have likely acted alone. If Wiener was guilty, then six men sitting in the courtroom with the words "union conspiracy" hanging over their heads were not guilty.

Lasee's rebuttal statement was another of the state's shell games. This time, the prosecution meant to hide the testimony of David Webster. But Webster's testimony was not the only evidence of Wiener hearing the tape much earlier that the state jettisoned to keep the Wiener theory off the jury's radar. Hidden under the state's second shell was Dan VandenLangenberg's testimony. "He [Wiener] must have heard it [the tape] before," VandenLangenberg has stated, "He was gone for only one or two minutes."

Under a third shell was Jon Mineau. In no fewer than three official documents in the files of the Green Bay police—all in the prosecution's possession—Mineau stated that he was present when Kutska played the tape for Wiener just after paper machine 9's 6:52 turnover. These include a Brown County Circuit Court sworn deposition, a signed GBPD statement, and a transcribed tape-recorded interview from the James River Corporation's own investigation.

For unknown reasons, Mineau, a very important and first-rate eyewitness, was never called by the state to testify on the stand. He had been working as the third hand on machine 9 that fateful day. He had been a large part of the police investigation. Oddly, Mineau—whose testimony would have been able to shed a great deal of light on the entire case—was not called to testify by the prosecution or by the defense.

The Fake Suicide Note

Before Monfils's death was publicly declared a homicide on December 9, 1992, workers discovered a possible suicide note from Monfils in a phone book in the small coop 7. Used only sporadically by paper machine crews, the coop was usually empty. On the front of the phone book was written, "Page 152." Circled on page 152 was Tom Monfils's telephone listing. In the margin next to Monfils's name was written

"I DO NOT FEAR DEATH, FOR IN DEATH WE SEEK LIFE ETERNAL."

Did Monfils actually write this note? Not according to the state's own forensic-handwriting expert, Jane Lewis of the Wisconsin State Crime Laboratory in Milwaukee. With over ten years of forensic-handwriting experience, including stints with the FBI and the Secret Service, Lewis determined that she was unable to associate Monfils's known handwriting with the note.

A total of nineteen handwriting samples were submitted to the crime lab for Lewis's examination. These included samples from all of the defendants, other possible suspects, coworkers who had access to the small coop, and a late submission from David Wiener. Lewis determined that none of these people could be associated with the note, with one notable exception—Wiener.

It is interesting to note that Wiener's sample was obtained not by a direct request from the authorities, but almost by accident. In the late fall of 1994, while Wiener was locked up for killing his brother, Detective Randy Winkler used the idea of taking a handwriting exemplar from Wiener as a reason to visit him in prison. After analysis, it turned out that Wiener's handwriting was close enough to that on the suicide note to warrant samples of Wiener's every day, standard handwriting.

Based on these, Lewis determined that Wiener—the prosecution's key witness to that point—was the probable writer of the suicide note. At trial Assistant DA William Griesbach pressed Lewis to say if it was possible that someone other than Wiener had written the note. She testified, "Possible—but unlikely."

Remember, the jury did not know that two years had passed since Monfils's death and that Wiener was already sitting in prison for killing his brother when the investigators finally bothered to obtain these incriminating handwriting samples from him. The jurors did not know that Wiener was a convicted killer when he testified before them. Had they been allowed to connect his fake suicide note with his killing of his brother and his messy accounts of his whereabouts the morning Monfils disappeared, reasonable doubt would have flooded the jury room. Instead the prosecution ignored the results of their own forensic analysis, spruced up their tattered witness, and forged ahead with their case.

In a completely bizarre closing argument, the district attorney put it this way: "One thing is absolutely certain, ladies and gentlemen, if David Wiener wrote that note, he certainly didn't kill Thomas Monfils."

Wiener's Jailhouse Statements

Shortly after David Wiener testified at trial, five different inmates at the Oshkosh Correctional Institution overheard statements made by him indicating that he had killed Tom Monfils. After the trial was over, several of the inmates contacted Judge Bayorgeon and the defense attorneys with this incriminating information. The sworn depositions of these five inmates were presented to the court during the appeals for each of the six defendants.

It is understood that all facts presented in the appeals process are interpreted in a light most favorable to the prosecution. Even so—without logic or reasonable explanation—the Wisconsin Court of Appeals District III waved off these statements with an obscure comment that the five inmates could have had a hidden agenda.

Convicted felons routinely offer testimony favorable to the state in order to bolster their chances for a deal. Prosecutors are often eager to cooperate with them. However, to a jailhouse or prison informant there is absolutely no advantage—and more likely a huge disadvantage—in offering testimony that challenges a successful prosecution. The appeals court failed to explain what these five individual prisoners could have possibly gained by reporting facts that were detrimental to the state's case for the conviction of the Monfils defendants.

Affidavit of Jodi Rosen Wine

The following deposition was submitted to Brown County Circuit Court Branch V in the appeal of Dale Basten before the trial judge, James Bayorgeon:

> Jodi Rosen Wine, being first duly sworn, deposes and states as follows:
>
> I am an attorney, duly licensed to practice in the courts of Illinois, and admitted pro hac vice by the Wisconsin

Court of Appeals to participate in State v. Basten, No. 95-CF-242.

On August 15, 1996, my colleague Robert Byman and I had separate meetings with Edward Wnek ("Wnek"), Roy Swanson ("Swanson") and Harrison Marcum ("Marcum") at the Oshkosh Correctional Center in Oshkosh, Wisconsin. During those meetings, Wnek, Swanson and Marcum revealed that:

- Swanson heard David Wiener say either "They can't go back on their deal if they found out I did it" or "they can't go back on their deal if they find out I was involved."
- David Wiener told Wnek that a pipe was used to kill Monfils.
- David Wiener told Wnek "those metal pipes can do a lot of damage."
- David Wiener told Wnek that the weight around Monfils's neck was tied with a heavy twine rope.
- David Wiener told Marcum and Wnek that Wiener wrote the suicide note.
- Wiener told Wnek that he was forced to write the note or get caught, and that the District Attorney cleared his name on the suicide note in exchange for Wiener's testimony.
- David Wiener told Wnek that "the two guys" never carried the body.
- David Wiener told Wnek, after Basten and the other defendants were convicted, that "I'm in the clear, those guys got nailed for what I might have done" and "I'm in the clear for taking the stand for the D.A."

FURTHER AFFIANT SAYETH NOT.

(Signed and notarized) *Jodi Rosen Wine*

Five More Affidavits

William F. Craig, a private investigator retained by Tim Pedretti, Mike Piaskowski's defense attorney, obtained notarized affidavits from prisoners Edward Wnek and Harrison Marcum. In addition, two more witnesses from the Oshkosh prison, Lawrence Hansford and Michael Grunkowski, came forward with signed affidavits that corroborate attorney Wine's story. These affidavits include the following statements.

Lawrence Hansford, June 19, 1996
- I remember when David Wiener came up to the table and said, "What would they do if they found out that I killed him?" or words to that effect.
- Wiener was angry with Monfils because he considered him a snitch.
- Wiener would say that the five white guys were innocent.
- He said that he wrote the suicide note and that he could get life for the Monfils death.
- He never said why Tom was killed but he did talk a lot about his dislike for snitches.

Michael Grunkowski, June 7, 1996
- David Wiener said, "What will they be able to do if they found out that I was the one that actually killed Tom Monfils" or words to that effect.
- David Wiener also said that he got some sort of deal to testify.

Edward Wnek, June 7, 1996
- Wiener would talk about how another man got nailed for his part in the crime.
- He talked about how Mike Hirn had nothing to do with the crime.
- Wiener said that Tom would turn anyone in, so he paid with his life.
- Another time, Wiener said that they would be surprised if they found out that he did kill Tom. (With a laugh) he said, "What if I did?"
- At one time, he talked about some kind of pipe being used to

kill Tom Monfils.

- Wiener said, "I'm clear of it. What if they found out I was the one that really did it?" or words to that effect.

Harrison Marcum quoting Wiener:
- "They charged me at first, but dropped the charges for my testimony."
- "What could happen now if they found out I killed him?"

Affidavit of Charlene Gawryleski

William Craig also obtained the following affidavit from Tim Wiener's fiancée, Charlene Gawryleski.

> Your affiant Charlene Gawryleski, being duly sworn upon oath, states as follows:
>
> My name is Charlene M. Gawryleski and my date of birth is February 8, 1969. At the time of Tim Wiener's death, I was living with him.
>
> I recall November 28, 1993 as the day that David Wiener killed Tim Wiener. I remember being in the presence of a phone call when Tim was talking to David. From what I could tell, Tim sounded annoyed but not in some intense anger. He was talking about some mix up with arrangements for a ride to a Packer Game. The details are well documented and I believe the public record to be correct.
>
> The conversation went on to Mr. Wiener giving Tim a ladder that David must have wanted. There came a time when Tim told David that he was going to *narc* [authors's emphasis] on him. In our crowd, "narc" means to tell the police on someone. I have always believed that Tim was referring to some involvement of David's in the Tom Monfils case. It is my opinion

that is the reason or part of the reason that David shot Tim.

Right after the conversation, Tim went out the door to go to David's house. He said, "I'll be back at six o'clock, so we can go eat dinner." I would like to say that Tim idolized David even though they would have disagreements from time to time. I also know that David was very paranoid after the death of Tom Monfils. I remember a time at Christmas that David stayed home in a locked house and armed because of the Monfils situation. The rest of his family came over to Mr. and Mrs. Wiener's home. I also would like to say David took a lot of pain pills. I recall an incident after I had some dental work done. David saw the pills and asked if he could have some. Before I could answer, he had taken the few that I had left in the bottle.

Dated this 20th day of April, 1996

Charlene Gawryleski

Trading Testimony for Freedom

Despite the fact that David Wiener made a phone call alerting his mother he was armed, that he waited for his brother with loaded weapons, and that he gunned him down, Wiener was merely charged with and prosecuted for reckless homicide. When he received a ten-year sentence for his crime, Wiener threw down the gauntlet to the prosecution. On May 14, 1994, in an article in the *Green Bay Press-Gazette*, reporter Thomas Content wrote:

> David Wiener said Friday he was surprised authorities didn't cut a deal with him on his sentence, given what he claims to know about the murder of Thomas Monfils, one of his co-workers at the James River Paper Mill.

Wiener was sentenced Thursday to 10 years in prison

for the Nov. 28 shooting death of his brother, Timothy. It was the maximum sentence allowed for a second-degree reckless homicide. In a telephone interview from the Brown County Jail on Friday afternoon, Wiener said that because of his sentence, he has no intention of cooperating with authorities investigating the Monfils murder. "I feel sorry for the Monfils family because if they think this [Wiener's 10-year sentence] is really going to make me talk now, when it eventually goes to court it's not going to be easy," he said. In fact, Wiener said he has no plans to testify in the Monfils case. I will not come forward at all," he said. "I have come forward to the police, but I will not testify, not in a kangaroo court like I was just in [Thursday]. That's a joke."

Exactly five months later, on October 14, 1994, Detective Randy Winkler responded to this challenge and visited Wiener at the Oshkosh Correctional Institution. During the visit, he apparently offered a deal for Wiener's testimony. This is proven by Wiener's attorney, Steven Miller, who documented the offer in a letter to Winkler dated October 17, 1994. It reads:

Dear Officer Winkler:

I am writing to inform you that I currently represent Mr. Wiener. I understand you met with my client in prison this past week concerning the Monfils investigation *and intimated his cooperation could affect his current status* [authors's emphasis]. Please be advised that neither you nor any other law enforcement officer or state's attorney are to have any further meetings or contact with Mr. Wiener without my expressed authorization. Any further contact will have to be arranged through my office.

If you have any questions or would like to discuss this further please do not hesitate to contact me.

Sincerely,

Steven L. Miller

In a two-and-a-half-page detail sheet on the visit, Winkler stated, "I told David that he was going to be brought back to Green Bay to testify and he said he would."

There are at least five very solid reasons to seriously challenge the veracity of Wiener's testimony in the Monfils case:

- The likelihood that Wiener was the probable author of the fake suicide note.
- The letter of Wiener's attorney to Winkler chastising Winkler for visiting his client and "intimating his cooperation could affect his current status."
- The signed and notarized affidavits of Edward Wnek, Harrison Marcum, Lawrence Hansford, and Michael Grunkowski quoting Wiener as stating that the prosecution dropped the suicide-note evidence in exchange for his testimony.
- The eventual reduction of Wiener's sentence for killing his brother by two years after his testimony at the Monfils trial. This reduction made him immediately eligible for parole.
- The fact that—without objection from the authorities in Green Bay or Brown County—Wiener was paroled after serving just a little over three years of his original ten-year sentence for the murder of his brother.

Timelines and Time-Lies

On many occasions, David Wiener changed either his story or his times—often, it seems, with the encouragement of the police and the prosecution. All together, Wiener gave five different versions of his whereabouts the morning Monfils disappeared: his original statement to the police, his John Doe hearing testimony, his civil-suit deposition testimony, his preliminary-hearing testimony, and his trial testimony.

There were two major problems that necessitated Wiener's continual manipulation of his timeline. The first problem, his forty-minutes-with-Kutska story, cannot be reasonably explained away. In an interview with these authors, prosecutors Zakowski and Lasee simply dismissed Wiener's contradictions by saying that he got his times wrong. It is not the times that are wrong, however. It is the private forty-minutes-with-Kutska part that simply does not fit. Moving times around cannot fix that.

The second major problem is that Charles Bowers, Wiener's helper and the only other person working on the beaters with him that morning, had left the area at Wiener's suggestion for forty-five minutes. In a pretrial interview with defense attorney Tim Pedretti dated May 27, 1994, Bowers said that he left on his forty-five-minute trip to the napkin-and-toweling department at 7:30 a.m. Ron Klumb, supervisor of napkin and toweling, reported to the police that he saw someone that he recognized as being from the paper machine area at around 8:00. Klumb said he felt that it might have been Tom Monfils. But it is far more likely that he saw Bowers while he was on his forty-five minute excursion. As many as five other third-floor napkin-and-toweling-department employees also reported seeing someone from the paper machines in their area around that time.

At trial four months later, Bowers agreed with Robert Parent, Rey Moore's defense attorney, that he had left his work area at 7:30. On cross-examination by Assistant DA Griesbach, Bowers agreed that the time of his trip could have been around 9:00. When these authors interviewed him, Bowers said that it could have been either 7:30 or 9:00—he is not sure. Bowers said that over his twelve-hour night shift, which had begun at 10 the night before, he had lost track of time that morning.

In a civil deposition taken February 3, 1994, Wiener stated that his forty-minutes-with-Kutska story was still true, but he now changed the time in which it took place. He claimed that everything he had said before was off by one hour: that he really had been with Kutska from 8:45 to 9:25 (not 7:45–8:25, as he previously contended) and that he had played the tape for Bowers and VandenLangenberg at 9:25. Not only does this version contradict previous testimony, it required Bowers and VandenLangenberg to wait a full forty minutes for Wiener's return with the audiotape. This is a length of time that both Bowers and VandenLangenberg completely dispute. It also conflicts with Bowers's forty-five-minute trip to the napkin-and-toweling department if his departure is revised from 7:30 to 9:00.

At trial, Wiener's story changed again. He testified that from 6:30 to 8:30 or 8:45 he was in the beater-room area with Bowers. After nearly three years of clinging to his forty-minutes-with-Kutska story, it was now shaved to twenty minutes. However, this version presents its own set of problems. Wiener testified he did not return the tape and tape player to Kutska until 10:00—meaning he had the tape for a full hour and a half. This completely contradicts the statements of Randy Lepak, Jim Wolford, Tom Zdroik, Paul Dahlgren, Diane Ferry, Ron Roskoski, and others, who all say they listened to that tape during that time.

Not one of David Wiener's five stories is consistent with the facts.

Closing Thoughts

As many as a half-dozen James River employees observed a paper machine worker in the third-floor napkin-and-toweling department, but there was never any follow-up to these sightings. Apparently the investigators felt it was not worth pursuing this significant but confusing fact. If they had fully investigated this lead, the questions about Wiener's ever-changing times and Bowers's uncertainties might well have been answered. And—if those questions were answered—perhaps there would be less mystery as to what happened to Tom Monfils.

Reasonable doubt enveloped this case. The jury should have had ability to cut through the prosecution's smoke and mirrors and distinguish the truth from deception and manipulation. The blinders donned by the investigators in the earliest hours of this case seem to have been passed on to the prosecutors and then on to the jury. The jury failed at the critical job entrusted to them.

However, when it comes to the reasonable doubt that surrounds David Wiener, the blame can be placed squarely on the table in the DA's conference room. The evidence against Wiener—although also circumstantial—was and is substantial. Gunning down his brother aside, Wiener's own words and actions create many questions in this case. Here is a summary.

- During the time in question, Wiener and a temporary coworker, Charles Bowers, were working closer than anyone else to the tissue chest where Monfils's body was found.
- Wiener told Bowers to leave the area and take an extended break during the time in question.
- Wiener fully understood the role of the tissue chest and had partial responsibility for its operation.
- Wiener worked with the tissue chest on a daily basis and was completely familiar with the surrounding work area.
- Wiener sought out the police to give them an account of his whereabouts during the time of Monfils's disappearance.
- Wiener's original statement to the police about being with Kutska for forty minutes during the time in question turned out to be false.
- Wiener changed the account of his whereabouts several times.
- Wiener tried to convince the investigators that Monfils's death was a suicide.
- Wiener was identified as the only probable author of a phony suicide note.
- Wiener took an extended leave of absence from work after Monfils's death was ruled a homicide.
- Six months after Monfils's death, Wiener sought out the police to report a sudden repressed memory.
- Wiener's convenient repressed memory created a nice alibi for him and pointed a finger at Basten and Johnson.
- Wiener was recognized by the police as being noticeably intoxicated when he made his repressed-memory statement to them.
- Wiener became the key prosecution witness after he told the investigators about his repressed memory.
- Wiener had an avowed disdain for snitches and considered Monfils a snitch.

It cannot be said that Wiener—or anyone else, for that matter—killed Tom Monfils. The following things, however, can be said with certainty and without reservation.

- The six men convicted of murdering Monfils did not do so.
- The Green Bay Police Department botched the crime scene.

- The authorities's fixation on Keith Kutska prevented them from investigating this case properly and arriving at the truth of what happened to Monfils.
- Wiener's public record deserved a much closer and unbiased look.

Is it possible that David Wiener somehow killed Tom Monfils? One cannot say with certainty. However, that possibility is a major issue of reasonable doubt that should have been thoroughly examined by the police and the DA—an issue the jury should have been allowed to hear about. Today, the reasonable-doubt issue requires a harder and longer examination—the circumstantial case against Wiener dwarfs the circumstantial case against the six convicted men. Finally, the public record on which Wiener chooses to stand underscores the issue of reasonable doubt, undermines his reliability as a prosecution witness, and puts him front and center as a person of strong interest in this case. None of that is going away without Wiener answering the questions of an unbiased party.

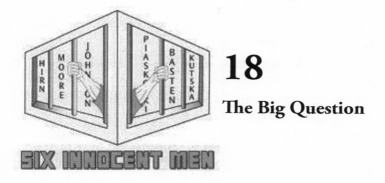

18

The Big Question

New opinions often appear first as jokes and fancies, then as blasphemies and treason, then as questions open to discussion, and finally as established truths.

—George Bernard Shaw

It is the question that is asked most often about the Monfils case: *"If these guys didn't do it, then what did happen?"* Without dodging that question, let us say this: Today, the answer remains a mystery, the nagging void in this case.

This book exposes a mountain of facts that point to the clear innocence of these six men. When it comes to speculating about the exact circumstances of Tom Monfils's death, however, these authors are reluctant to do so. Our objection to the case as presented by the authorities is that it is based on raw, unproven speculation. It is the same objection five federal judges expressed when ruling on Mike Piaskowski's writ of habeas corpus. We hesitate to complicate the mess by throwing further speculation into the mix.

Unless the real perpetrator—if there is one—steps up and accepts responsibility for his or her actions, we may never know exactly what happened to Monfils. That is a tragedy. The fact that much of the starting evidence in this case was tainted or destroyed is another tragedy. Not knowing the real answer, however, does not make these six men guilty. Nothing is accomplished by having a wrong answer. Only the real answer will produce truth and justice. Continuing to hang Monfils's death on innocent men does no one any good at all.

For those who insist on hearing other possibilities, this chapter presents four potential scenarios—each consistent with all of the known facts and inconsistent with none of them. In each of them, Monfils is described grabbing his own jump rope from the railing where it hung at the back of coop 7 and leaving the job without notifying anyone.

All of these scenarios have Monfils leaving his work area under tremendous stress. The police had released to Keith Kutska, his tormentor, a taped copy of his anonymous call after they had assured Monfils that they would not do so. Kutska had the tape on the mill floor, and he was playing it for anyone who wanted to listen—even for some who did not. In addition, Kutska was lying to his coworkers, telling them that he had not actually taken a piece of electrical cord.

Monfils had the scolding words of Mike Hirn ringing in his ears. He saw a coworker, Andy Lison, roll his eyes at him. He saw Connie Jones on her way to the 9 coop where, she too, would hear that damned tape and Kutska's self-serving sob story. Monfils's paper machine was running smoothly. He had at least twenty minutes to get out from under the microscope before the next turnover, plenty of time to take a walk to sort things out.

Each of these scenarios has Monfils traveling through the 3-4 storeroom to the west of paper machines 7 and 9 on his way to the locker room. He was known to take that route daily. It passes the tissue chest where his body was found.

Again, not one single shred of evidence produced in this case contradicts any of these scenarios.

Scenario 1—A Reckless Accident

What if Monfils's death was the result of the unintentional but irresponsible actions of a coworker?

334

Perhaps Monfils was sick of the nasty looks and caustic comments from his coworkers and decided to get away from them all. What if, for instance, a forklift driver was hauling a load of pulp through the area where he was walking? Say that driver knew that Monfils had made the anonymous call and—thanks to Kutska's lie—believed that Monfils had falsely accused Kutska of theft. What if that driver decided to charge at Monfils with his load of heavy pulp bales and stop short, just to give him a good scare and teach him a lesson? What if the tipsy load tumbled and fell on Monfils, causing terrible head injuries and more? What if that driver then panicked, making another bad decision to get rid of the body?

Scenario 2—Road Rage without a Car

What if Monfils died as a result of a verbal confrontation with a single coworker that got out of hand?

What if he decided to head for the locker room just to be alone for a while? What if, near the furnace room, he encountered a lone employee? It would have been obvious to Monfils that this guy already heard the tape and Kutska's sob story. Say this guy got in Monfils's face as soon as he saw him, swearing and calling him names. Say Monfils had had enough. What if he threw a punch or shoved the guy away from him, sending the coworker into a rage? Now it was "Katie bar the door!" What if the guy grabbed a nearby hard object and Monfils went down, dazed and half-conscious? What if, before he could recover, his attacker grabbed the jump rope and wrapped it tightly around Monfils's neck and he passed out? What if the guy then panicked and set out to cover his tracks?

Scenario 3—an Intentional Assault

What if Monfils was intentionally attacked by a lone mill-floor hothead who saw him as a snitch for making the anonymous call?

Perhaps, as he walked through the 3-4 room, Monfils was preoccupied with the stressful events that had just occurred. The mill was buzzing with talk about Kutska's tape and the anonymous phone call. What if somebody came from out of the shadows behind Monfils with a pipe in his hand? What if Monfils started walking a little faster and the guy started running? What if they barely made it through the furnace room and into the beater room when a blow to the back of the head caused Monfils to go down? What if he was out cold?

Scenario 4—the Possibility of Suicide

What if Monfils took his own life in the face of the intense pressure he was under the morning he disappeared?

The police had pulled the rug out from under him. They had assured him that the tape of his phone call was going nowhere. Now Kutska had it at work. It had been played a dozen or more times. What thoughts raced through Monfils's mind after finding out that the police had betrayed him and that an intimidator like Kutska had the tape? Correct or not, Monfils had already expressed concerns to the police about his own safety. What would his workdays be like from then on? What if the union pulled his card, and he lost his job? What did his future hold at that point? According to many who knew him, the mill was his life.

The Big Question in Perspective

Each of these four scenarios—accidental, emotional, intentional, and suicidal—is more feasible than one involving six near-strangers joining forces to harm Tom Monfils, hiding his body to cover their tracks and remaining completely silent about it for more than sixteen years despite facing the rest of their lives in prison.

Were these and other possible scenarios ever investigated? Not according to any source these authors have been able to find. In the absolute pursuit of truth and justice, all possibilities should have been considered and then ruled out or investigated more aggressively. Instead, "Way to go, Kutska!" set the course of this investigation even before Monfils's body had been removed from the tissue chest.

Could One Man Have Done It Alone?

A misconception often expressed by some individuals—including the police and prosecution—is that one person could not have lifted Monfils's body up and over the wall of the tissue chest.

Though the task would have been difficult for one person to

accomplish without assistance, it is definitely possible if the heavy metal weight was used to help in lifting the body. The rope could have been attached to the fifty-pound weight at one end and to the body at the other. By first putting the weight over the wall, at most only 130 pounds of additional lift would be required to boost or maneuver the 180-pound body over the four-foot wall. Lifting the entire load, all at once, would not have been necessary.

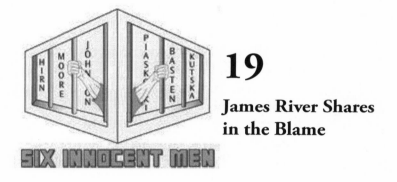

19

James River Shares in the Blame

The truth is rarely pure and never simple.

—Oscar Wilde

The transgressions of the Green Bay Police Department and the Brown County district attorney's office are presented throughout this book. The numerous missteps of the James River Corporation, however, have never been fully explored.

The cops may have stupidly handed the tape of Monfils's anonymous phone call over to Keith Kutska, but it was the company that sent Kutska on his quest for the tape in the first place. The cops and the company then joined forces with a common mission: Hang the responsibility for Monfils's death on Kutska.

Kutska was their straw man. This tactic served to take both the police and the mill off the hot seat in one fell swoop. However, if Kutska was not held directly responsible for Monfils's death, then the culpability of the cops and the company became much harder to explain away. In the process of heaping blame on Kutska though, other innocent workers would have to be painted as his shills.

Caught in the Middle

For the average James River paper-mill worker, being caught in the middle of this investigation was a lot like being stuck in a two-on-one tag-team wrestling match. There you were, alone in your corner, while across the ring loomed the scowling visages of the cops and the company. You had nothing to hide from the police, and you had no intention of endangering your livelihood with your employer. Nonetheless, you found yourself between a rock and a hard place.

According to every worker these authors interviewed, the experience was excruciating. A coworker had been found dead in the mill. And now the cops were pushing you to say things you could not truthfully tell them, and the company seemed to be nodding its encouragement. At first, the company seemed to be a detached bystander when it could have been in the workers's corner. Eventually, however, the company became an active partner in the investigation, even menacing its own employees when it felt it was needed.

The police theory of what had happened to Tom Monfils was unproven, but that was the one they were hammering home—with the mill's blessing. The mill's honest workers could not provide facts to support that erroneous theory. Yet their very job hung by a very thin thread—the company's perception of their cooperation. That dilemma caused sleepless nights for many workers and their loved ones.

Loose Lips

The company's first inexplicable faux pas came at Keith Kutska's disciplinary meeting on November 11, 1992. At the meeting, Kutska was suspended from work for five days without pay for not stopping and opening his laundry bag at the gatehouse. He had a good reason not to open it: It contained a pilfered fifteen-foot length of electrical cord. At the meeting, he denied he had the contraband in his bag.

The meeting had ended when, for no apparent reason, one of the mill managers, Paul Dolson, told Kutska the circumstances that led to the attempted search of his bag by the gatehouse guards. Someone inside the mill had phoned the Green Bay police about the possible theft, and the police in turn had alerted the guards.

Had that information not been passed to Kutska, the best he could have ever done was to spend the rest of his days wondering why the guards had tried to stop him. End of story. No tape. No quest for a tape. No confrontation of Tom Monfils with a tape.

The company had handed Kutska the key to Pandora's Box. A week later, the police would hand him the box. From that point forward, the cops and the company were bound inextricably together.

An Unexplained Phone Call

The mill's blunders hardly ended there. Just as bizarre as divulging to Kutska something he need not have known was a mysterious phone call placed from the private office of one of the mill managers the morning of Monfils's disappearance. The call seems to have found its way under the rug to this point, but it begs for a closer look. It was a call made to the police station from the office of the mill's human resources director, Jack Yusko, during the time Monfils was missing. On that call, a person claiming to be Monfils asked the police about the release of the anonymous tape to Kutska.

The person who made that call has never come forward nor has that person ever been clearly identified. The only things known for sure is that the call came from Yusko's office and that, a minute or two later, Yusko himself placed a call from the same phone and talked to union president Marlyn Charles.

Who made the deceptive call to the police, and why was that person never cited for interfering with a potential police investigation? The caller certainly was not Monfils, and it was not any of the union mill workers—they had no access to that office.

The Company and the Cops

Rather than focusing on needed counseling for their employees during a time of emotional stress, the mill hierarchy seemed to join the police and the DA in treating its workers as a group of union thugs. They provided an office inside the mill for Detective Randy Winkler from which he would pursue a premature theory of murder, conspiracy, and a union cover-up. Eventually, the mill bosses applied the iron hand of an internal investigation in an effort to force the issue.

Even if a worker had been a hundred miles away in a deer-hunting stand the morning of Monfils's disappearance, he or she was treated like a person with an inherent allegiance to some mythical union brotherhood with a willingness to mislead the authorities. If a worker was unfortunate enough to be working that morning, his or her honesty seemed to be the first thing called into question.

Early on, the mill imported Frank Pinto—the lead investigator for internal affairs at the corporate level. According to most workers, Pinto started off the company's independent investigation evenhandedly enough. But when he too drew blanks, he seemed to simply become an unofficial extension of the GBPD.

Anyone who listens to Pinto and Yusko's interrogation of Don Boulanger—just three weeks before the trial—can hear some basic assumptions on their part. These were assumptions they shared with the police by that time: Boulanger must be a part of the conspiracy, and he is withholding the truth and covering for the others.

The purpose of Pinto and Yusko's eleventh-hour grilling of Boulanger was to shore up the idea of a bubbler confrontation between Monfils and his coworkers. Pinto and Yusko did not have knowledge of any bubbler confrontation from their own investigation—no worker had told them of observing such an incident. They had learned of it from the police.

Pinto and Yusko then set about trying to prove such a confrontation had occurred—something at which the police themselves had failed—by picking on Boulanger, an older, more vulnerable worker. They pressured him without mercy, trying to get him to admit to seeing such a confrontation and to put coworker Jon Mineau into the mix. Boulanger did his best to cooperate while trying to tell the unpopular truth—that he had not seen the confrontation they wanted him to describe.

Eventually, Pinto and Yusko browbeat Boulanger into vaguely saying what they wanted to hear—that he *may* have seen such a confrontation. For the worn-down Boulanger, it was either that or spend hours more being grilled and having his job threatened.

A disconcerted Boulanger would eventually be put on the witness stand, where he would reiterate his anemic account of a bubbler confrontation, the threat of his job still hanging over his head like the the sword of Damocles.

However, without threats and intimidation and with truth as his only goal, the now-retired Boulanger has told these authors that he saw no such confrontation and no hint of such a confrontation. He was completely intimidated into saying that he had.

Cooperate or Else

Another damning aspect of the cop-company partnership came in a company directive to its workers regarding the police investigation. Like Boulanger, every mill worker interviewed for this book has said the same thing: They heard the company's directive loud and clear, and they felt its threatening specter in every contact they had with the police. The words may have been to foster "cooperation with the law enforcement authorities," but the message was obvious: Cooperate with the police investigation *or your job could well be in jeopardy*.

NOTICE

TO: ALL EMPLOYEES

SUBJECT: INVESTIGATION OF THE DEATH OF TOM MONFILS

The Green Bay Police Department has announced that Tom Monfils's death has been ruled a homicide. James River Corporation, United Paperworkers International Union (UPIU) Local #327 and UPIU Local #213 all strongly desire, support and encourage any person who may have any knowledge or information about the circumstances of the death of Tom Monfils, or any other information they may think relevant, to promptly report that information to the Green Bay Police Department. Locals #327 and #213 and James River all join in urging cooperation with the law enforcement authorities during their investigation of this case. The telephone number to call the police with information concerning the investigation is 448-3227 Inspector Keon or 448-3241 Detective Division.

Charles A. Warren   Marlyn W. Charles

Vice President   President, Local #327

Wayne J. LeCloux   Michael K. Grones

President, Local #213   UPIU International Representative

On the surface, the mill's directive seemed appropriate enough. Cooperating with the police was the way to get at the truth—in a normal investigation where *the police themselves were unsullied*. Such a directive might have produced an accurate result.

Workers who were with Keith Kutska the morning of Monfils's disappearance could tell the truth until they were blue in the face; they were never going to satisfy the police. Even worse, their conscientious efforts to be forthcoming by recalling additional or slightly different details of that morning were interpreted as showing a lack of cooperation.

Kutska had the strongest alibi of any worker at the mill that morning. He was the man performing in the center ring, playing the tape for everyone he could. He was the guy whose actions and whereabouts were the most substantiated and the most documented. If the cops were going to nail Kutska, they would have to take down every alibi witness in the process. With the help of James River, that is exactly what they did.

Keep in mind that the mill's directive had called for "cooperation with the law enforcement authorities." It had neither urged the workers to tell the truth nor reassured them they had nothing to fear. Rather it suggested that if they went along with the authorities, their jobs would be safe. The difference was as stark as night and day.

Pete Delvoe's experience with the mill's way of doing things is nearly identical to that of a lot of his coworkers. At about 8:41 a.m. on December 12, 1994, Delvoe was escorted into one of the mill offices by Yusko to be interviewed. Delvoe had given a statement in the earliest days of the investigation, but here he was again two years later. Randy Winkler—in sole command of the case since that January—was waiting for Delvoe in the office. So was Winkler's partner, Ken Brodhagen.

In the detectives's presence, Yusko reminded Delvoe that he was getting paid while he was being interviewed and that his "cooperation" was a "job expectation." With that, Yusko left the room. It was Delvoe alone with the two detectives—with no union or legal representation at his side.

Basically, Yusko had body slammed Delvoe to the mat, made the tag, and now the two cops were poised to grill him. Whatever emerged from that room would now be a matter of Delvoe's words against the words of Winkler and Brodhagen. Delvoe already knew of Winkler as a threat maker and an intimidator. Here he was, on the ropes completely alone, his job at stake.

Delvoe made it through the ordeal, though not without emotional and mental scars.

Surviving the Bullies

Other mill workers also negotiated their way through the investigative thumping. Steve Stein, Tom Hendricks, Jim Melville, and Al Kiley each took his lumps but managed to stay standing with his job intact. Others were not so lucky. Marlyn Charles and Randy Lepak lost their jobs. Jon Mineau was fired the day before the trial began—in the long run, for nothing more than the appearance of "not cooperating."

The police did not hesitate to bludgeon workers with the mill's directive either. Jim Melville's December 1994 interview—covered in detail in chapter 12—was a perfect example. Winkler told Melville that the cops had new information via some tape recordings and that the recordings suggested Kutska's guilt. It was a pumped-up allusion to the worthless VerStrate tapes.

Melville did not bite. In fact, he stood firmly on what he knew to be the truth. The cops were not at all happy with that. They did not like Melville's attitude, and they sure did not like that kind of brashness from any mill worker—not when the mill's directive demanded cooperation. It was the best weapon they had; they could beat any worker at any point with the club labeled "talk or else it's your job." Melville, however, narrowly escaped their clutches.

Mill worker Tom Hendricks was also able to push back with the facts and keep his job, although barely. At one point in Winkler's browbeating of him, Hendricks asked if he was calling him a liar. Winkler avoided the question, instead asking Hendricks why he had asked. "Because," said Hendricks, "then I can tell you to kiss my ass. I don't lie for anyone about anything." Like Melville, Hendricks kept his job because what he insisted on as the truth was the truth. The cops could not change the facts of what Hendricks—and Melville—told them.

Unlike most of the other mill workers, Hendricks was even willing to let his insistence on getting at the truth jeopardize his job security.

This, however, made him a rarity. In a later interview with Winkler at the mill, Hendricks challenged the detective's investigation of the statement made by David Wiener that he had seen Mike Johnson and Dale Basten carrying something heavy in the area around the tissue chest where Monfils's body was found.

Hendricks sensed that Winkler was manipulating the scene in order to substantiate Wiener's information. Hendricks could not stomach the idea that Winkler would willingly change things around, and he let his objections be known. Jack Yusko showed up at about that time and told Hendricks that one more word would cost him his job. Hendricks backed off, reluctantly.

Unfortunately, workers like Brian Kellner, Connie Jones, and even Don Boulanger, for that matter, were not so steadfast. They let the company's directive turn them into targets. As a result, each of them was bullied into the corner. Alone in the ring against the police and the mill, they were more than intimidated. Who could blame them?

Certainly those in charge of the James River Corporation were as stunned and saddened by the terrible events in this case as were its workers. But they had a larger responsibility to respect their employees rather than wash their hands in support of the police. James River's share of the blame began when it informed Kutska of the anonymous phone call that precipitated this entire calamity. It certainly did not atone for that error by throwing the rest of its workers to the wolves.

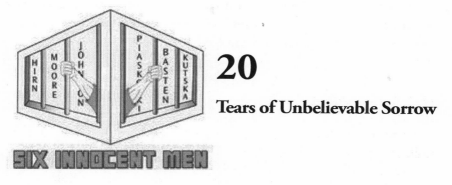

20

Tears of Unbelievable Sorrow

This is the first chapter of a book whose ending is yet to be written.

—Judge James T. Bayorgeon

In the wake of the travesty of justice that this book recounts in detail, there are hundreds of injured souls: the family of Tom Monfils, some of whom we know have questions in their hearts; the families of other workers, who watched their loved ones live through a nightmare, some beaten down mentally and emotionally by a police department and a district attorney who still think there are liars among them; the families of the six men convicted of murdering their coworker. Now it is time for the five wrongly imprisoned men to give voice to their long-withheld thoughts and emotions, and for their loved ones to speak on behalf of their incarcerated husbands and brothers and fathers and sons.

Giving Them a Voice

Forget the hype. Along with the completely exonerated Mike Piaskowski, the five men behind bars whose words appear on the following pages were never "The Monfils Six." They were never silent, never holding back any information from the authorities. They have been painted as members of a group of thugs and as part of a union conspiracy of silence. That is the way the cops, the DA, and the media have portrayed them. Do not believe it. The six have been talking all along, trying desperately to get someone to listen.

What follows are pure, unadulterated words from the heart—each of the five men speaking for himself, along with family and friends voicing their deeply felt emotions. (Mike Piaskowski's thoughts appear in print throughout this book, indeed they inform every page of it.) Please listen.

Dale Basten Speaks

> It's hard enough to read about what happened at the trial, but it's even harder to write about it. It's hard to think of the lawyers struggling with the biggest trials of their careers. You're removed from your home of thirty-some years, your cottage of seven years, your children, your friends, and all the things you've worked for and saved for in your life. You're forced into a prison where you don't want any of these people as your friend. They'll steal a stamp from you, like they'd steal a purse from an old grandma on a street corner while she is waiting for a bus. Even the guards who are fair will turn on you if their supervisors tell them to. I have been here a long time for something I did not do. I want my children and my life back.

Letter from Dale Basten's Daughter Emily

My name is Emily Basten, and when I was just ten years old, my father, Dale Basten, was charged for a crime he did not commit and taken away from me. I had to grow up with no father figure, no dad to come to my school events, cheerleading tournaments, or birthday parties. I didn't have a clue what was going on at that age. I learned later in life why he was forced to leave. To a little girl of ten all I knew was that he was taken away. I never thought for a minute that he left my eight year-old sister and me on purpose because he was the most wonderful father someone could ever ask for. Although I was only allowed ten years with him it seemed like longer because he did everything with us. He would take us to fairs, parks, stores, restaurants, and car races. Everywhere he went we would go.

My father always made time for us no matter how busy his life was. I remember my father to be the most talented and intelligent person; he was an extremely hard worker, a musician, a mechanic, and a very loving and dedicated father who always promoted education. I have always wanted to make him proud, and he is the reason I am the person that I am today. Because my father has always been my role model, I am a college student working toward a career in veterinary medicine. He taught me to be the humanitarian that I am; I never understood any of the allegations against him because they are so far from who he really is. My father would tell us that the spiders that snuck into the house were actually our "uncle" and not to kill them but to bring them outside.

Even though my father was in my life for only a short while, it seems as though it was longer because of all the time he spent with his kids; we were the most important things in his life and we will always be. Having him taken away from me was the hardest thing that I have and will ever have to go through in my life. The murder trial disrupted our childhood wildly, and we didn't have much money after my father was put into prison. My sister and I had to switch schools because of all the news coverage dealing with the case at the time. Our childhood and our father were taken from us; the entire ordeal has been extremely traumatizing. All we have ever wanted was to have a normal family life with our father again.

My father has missed out on so much in his children's lives. The last memory I have of my father before he was taken away to jail was that he brought my sister and I trick or treating around the neighborhood, he was a very friendly and outgoing man to all of our neighbors. My dad never got the chance to see me grow up, and he never had the chance to help me with my homework or see me graduate from high school. He has missed out on so many fundamental years in my life. All I want is my father back in my life. I have missed a lot of his years and he is much older than what he was when he went into prison. I hope and pray every day that he will get an appeal and be able to live in the same town as us and be in our lives again. My father has already had to miss seeing both of his parents, my grandparents, live out their lives in their golden years. He has also missed funerals and other important family events. The one thing that I ask for is just to have my dad at my wedding when I get married; he has missed so much in my life. All I have ever wanted was to have him walk me down the aisle, so I plead to all of the people that read this book to realize just what has happened and to help us fix this situation and make it right. Please help us get our father back into our lives; so many years have gone by already and life is so short.

—Emily Basten

Dale Basten with daughters Emily and Amber

Letter from Dale Basten's Daughter Amber

My name is Amber Basten. I am nineteen years old. I am the daughter of Dale Basten. When I was eight years old my father was heartlessly taken out of my life. I have never been the same since.

When I look back at my childhood I see the perfect life. I was part of a loving family living in a nice area. We had wonderful neighbors and friends and were grateful for each day. I had the normal expectations any normal eight-year-old would have. I went on like this until one dark and awful day. Suddenly my life had changed. My father was no longer there to be a part of my life. He could no longer pick me up from school. He wasn't there to play his guitar and sing to me anymore. He would never again be able to teach me math on his fingers or make me brush my teeth. We no longer had family vacations or rides in the country. I have never since heard him wish me "good night blonde bunny." I miss him so much.

After he was gone my life took several unusual twists and turns, things that landed me in a few strange, unfamiliar, and unwanted places. I had to grow up so quickly that I lost a large part of my childhood. Instead of enjoying the worry-free life-learning experiences of a young girl, I have had to cope with the unwarranted reason my father was gone and locked up. I had to endure many hardships both publicly and personally, including a loss of communication with family and conflicts at school. Had my dad been able to be there for me when I needed him, I know these things would have never happened.

I still experience days where it is difficult to even get out of bed. Days where I dwell on the long, hard battle and the toll it has taken on my family and me. If he was no longer absent in my life, I feel as though I could live again, free of the constant heartache that affects me both socially and academically at times.

I have held onto the first eight precious years of memories with my father so I can learn from him and better myself. I also hold them dear so I can continue to believe that we will be together again someday. My father is in a place he does not belong. I believe in my heart of hearts that he did not commit this crime.

My father meant the world to me as a little girl and he always will. He deserves to have his life back and I the rest of mine. He is intelligent, kind, admirable, and innocent. I desperately need him in my life so that I can be the same person that he has always been to me.

I love you Dad.

—Amber Basten

Keith Kutska Speaks

The death of Tom Monfils was a terrible tragedy. However, from the beginning of the investigation of his death, the authorities had no intention of holding the person responsible for his murder accountable. Their intentions were solely self-serving.

It's true. I stole a 15-foot piece of electrical wire from a dumpster at James River. It's also true that I denied stealing it, and it's also true that I later took responsibility and owned up to stealing it.

It's well understood that Tom Monfils made a call to the police that I was going to steal that electrical wire, and that I acquired a tape-recorded copy of that call from the police. I found out about it from the management people at James River. I discussed and got approval from the union's representatives to request the police to give me a copy of that call to the police. The purpose was to file union charges and let the other employees at James River know who called the police. I had no reason to know that someone would take his life. To this day I don't believe anyone on this planet would have known.

As for me and the men I was convicted with, we are innocent men convicted by a state-sponsored perjury. The police, after two years of investigation, found a weak, insecure person who was vulnerable and forced him to tell a lie that they fabricated and spoon-fed into his mouth with threats and intimidation to have him fired, to have his children taken away and to have him thrown in jail. The lie was to blame me for Tom's death because I made them look foolish for giving me that tape. The men convicted with me were collateral damage because they would not falsely incriminate me and lie for the police. The witness who was forced to commit perjury had admitted his trial testimony was false and forced upon him by the police. But he isn't the only one who lied during our trial. The person I believe murdered Tom Monfils also committed perjury. The prosecutor defended it; indeed, even the prosecutor himself stood in open court during his closing argument and lied to the jury. Even more shocking is that when the perjury was brought to the trial judge's attention after the trial, he condoned it by ruling it was not misconduct.

If anyone thinks this is difficult to believe, all they have to do is a thorough examination of the case record. The people in this nation are under the assumption that we have the best judicial system in the world. I also thought that. But the truth is that's just a myth the authorities want the people to believe, like the "white hat" goodness of baseball, hot dogs and apple pie.

The saddest fact of all is the authorities's top priority was to satisfy their self-serving need for personal vengeance at the expense of the justice Tom Monfils's family deserves. They were the ones cheated most of all.

Letter from Keith Kutska's Wife, Ardie

Keith and I met when we were 19 years old. Within a year we were married. Our son followed in 1972. Both of us felt that we grew up together. It's so very hard to even think about how turned around our lives have become because of Keith's wrongful conviction and his fourteen years of being locked up. We were just a normal family. Keith liked to fish, our son liked dirt bikes, and I had my horses. We always went camping, as far into the woods as we could. Now, those things are just memories.

When we moved to Abrams it was my dream home. It was the place you didn't want to leave. We were all happy to live there. It seemed like everything we'd worked for was coming together. Our son fell in love with a beautiful girl and got married. Things were good for us in all ways.

When the sky fell down, it fell hard. Our granddaughters (twins) were born a month before they took Keith away. Keith was in prison in a far-off state when our grandson was born. He didn't get to see him until he was three.

There is no way for me to describe to others what the people in my life have been through. Nothing can prepare a person for the living hell that our lives have become. This injustice has cost us in every way imaginable. Keith never got the chance to do "grandpa things" with his grandkids. He would love the chance to show his granddaughters the stars and take his grandson trout fishing. But all they know of their grandpa is that he can't be with them.

I feel like I live two lives at the same time. There is the work face that I put on every day. I need that one a lot. It helps at home too. The other face is the face I hide. Too much pain inside. It never goes away. It can't and it won't, until my husband is home where he belongs.

There is nothing to do but go on, just like the nightmare goes on. I guess you just get used to things. At first, there were mean phone calls and hang-up calls and then all the letters that came. I had to do a lot of things that I had not planned on doing. All the little things a person takes for granted in life are changed forever for me. I try to be as positive

Keith Kutska with his wife. Ardie.

as possible in my life, but that's not so easy. I think that there are a lot of people who have been very kind to me. And that helps so much to know that.

My life is way different than the way I had planned. Keith and I were supposed to grow old together. All this time has been wasted; it is lost and we will never get it back. I want the world to know that what has happened to our family and to me should never have happened. Keith would never have been part of murdering another human being. Yes, Keith did want Tom Monfils to face the union for making his phone call, but he never harmed Tom in any way. Please help us get our husband, dad, and grandpa back.

—Ardie Kutska

Letter from Keith Kutska's Son Clayton

What can I say? My father and I were just getting to a wonderful point in our relationship, whereas we were becoming friends besides being father and son. I had been recently married to a wonderful woman, had two beautiful daughters, a mortgage, and for once I wanted all the fatherly advice I could get.

Suddenly the source of that advice was yanked away, and at an exciting but scary time. I no longer had him there to turn to. I dealt with depression, anger, despair, and frustration at a time in my life which should have been nothing but joyous. These things affected my ability to be a father myself, and a husband. I might have failed miserably were it not for my loving wife; she was the pillar I could cling to, and she helped me pull myself up and get back on my feet.

Now I have come to terms with what has happened, out of necessity. I feel a great loss, for me, my wife and children, my mother, for the time that we can never get back. I am baffled that this travesty of justice has been allowed to go on for so long, and that it happened at all.

Still, there are people who know that my father is innocent, just as we do, and I appreciate their efforts to free him while we can still have time with him. I look forward to the day he rejoins our family and we can catch up on all the things we've missed out on.

—Clayton Kutska

Mike Johnson Speaks

As a Christian man, I recognize the trials and tribulations I must face and endure in this world (2 Tim. 3:12). I realize that as I continue to profess my innocence, I will never be allowed to leave prison. Already this prison system has sought to withdraw my medium security classification and send me to a maximum-security institution because I continue to claim I am falsely accused and unjustly convicted of a crime I did not commit or have any knowledge about. I wait patiently for my Lord to rescue me (Luke 18:7 and Rom. 8:28).

I know I didn't harm Tom Monfils. God knows I didn't harm Tom Monfils. I can't understand why David Wiener pointed a finger at me like that!

Letter from the Family of Mike Johnson by Stepdaughter Joan Van Houten

Dearest Mike,

I've been told they are done with the book now and have invited us to submit a plea to the readers about this case and for you. I don't know that I have ever done anything so difficult. Where do I begin? How do I find the words powerful enough to transport them from their world, a world we thought we knew so well, into the nightmare that has become our life? What words could possibly begin to express how it feels to watch an innocent man, a decent and loving man, lose his life one slow day at a time?

When you came into our lives, not even we realized just how much we needed you. There was mom, a young widow trying to raise two young daughters on her own, there was my younger sister, quiet and lost in the aftermath of our father's death, and then there was me. I was so afraid all of the time. I had watched my father drift away from us as cancer took him, watched my mother cry night after night and watched my little sister trying to make silent sense of all this pain and suffering around her. It seemed all I could do was watch, powerless to stop any of it.

Then there came you; this man who came to us self-assured, unafraid of the challenges and wanting to show us how wonderful and awe inspiring the world around us truly was. You invited all of us into your life and gave us gifts beyond all measure. In time, my mother learned the virtue of patience, my sister the skill to observe the world around her and understand, and me, I was given the gift of strength to not only endure but to overcome. With you was your daughter and eventually our brother came; with you was security that only family can bring.

Who were you to me? You were the man who showed me that integrity says everything about a person's character. You were the man who continuously insisted that my mother marry you so your life together would not be a sin. You were the man that taught me the importance of understanding that I made an impact every day in the world around me and that I would be impacted by that world as well. Because of you, I've learned to see beyond myself.

Who are you now? When this nightmare began and the very foundation you built your life upon came crumbling down, you

Mike Johnson with son Mike, Jr.

were a man in belief; you believed in God, in His existence, His mercy. Today, you are a man who built a new foundation by being a man of Faith. It is this Faith that gives you what none of us can … HOPE. You have Faith that God is beside you, Faith in His will for the truth to be known, Faith that He knows your face and will not forsake you. And in your darkest hours, you've found the courage to face each new day with renewed hope. I hold to your Faith, Mike. I have to because I don't have the forgiveness you've shown in the people who have knowingly ripped our lives apart. And so again, it's because of you that strength finds me.

Mike, I can make no plea worthy of who you are and what you mean to us. I can only tell you how much we love you, need you, and believe in the man you are. And as I have been writing this letter to you, worried about doing right by you, I have come to believe that a plea to the reader isn't necessary after all because in your Faith I find Faith in the intelligence of the people around us. I have Faith, Mike, that they will demand justice and not mere justifications. They will demand answers and not tainted theories. The people, Mike, will see the truth, and this truth will set you free.

Please know that you are always cherished, never forgotten. We love you and miss you every moment of every day.

In Love, Hope, Faith.

On Behalf of Your Loving Wife Kim, Son Michael, Daughters Michelle, Joan and Dawn, Son-in-laws Kyle, Karl and Carl, Your Nine Grandchildren, and Your Great-Grandson.

—Joan Van Houten

Mike Hirn Speaks

I am proof that innocent people go to prison. I did not commit nor do I have any knowledge of this crime. My family and friends are also victims of this crime because I was taken away from them. The public and the community have a right to know the truth and have justice in this case. My son has grown up without really knowing his father. He has lost out on my companionship.

I have a lot of support from family and friends who really know me and not what I was unfairly portrayed to be. I would like them to know how much I appreciate their love and support.

I would like people to know that even though the justice system failed in this case, I believe the truth will set me free. I'd like the public to know I took four polygraph tests [and passed them all] but they aren't admissible in court. The public needs to know that this black spot on the community won't go away until justice prevails and the real culprit for this crime is behind bars. I was naïve to the prison system and thought anyone who was in prison deserved to be here. That is the furthest thing from the truth. The public needs to be more educated about the prison system because it's becoming a business for the State of Wisconsin.

And finally, what the judge said to me at sentencing was "This is the first chapter of a book whose ending is yet to be written." How apropos!

I've lost years of my life, but if someone out there can help this innocent man come home to his family and friends, I'd appreciate the help. I've never given up and I remain positive that any day could be my last day here. I understand that the Green Bay Police and the D. A. don't want the truth to come out because it would show how inept they were in the prosecution of this case. What happened to the old adage "It's better to let ten guilty men free than to put one innocent man in jail?" Let's right the wrong that has gone on since 1995.

Letter from Mike Hirn's Mother and Stepfather, Trudy and Mike Dalebroux

I really do not know how to start this letter because everything involved in this travesty has been so devastating on our family. Just where does a person begin with a story this unbelievable? I guess I'll start by saying that I am Michael's stepfather. I came into his life when he was only seven years old. Since I've known Michael I've learned of his deep love of life, for all creatures and mankind. I know deep in my heart he would never injure, much less, murder anyone for any reason. He is not a violent person.

During Michael's youth we were an active outdoors family, traveling to Grandma and Grandpa's cottage on Boulder Lake both summer and winter weekends and vacations. Water skiing, swimming and snowmobiling were the highlights of the seasons spent there. As Michael grew older he bought his own ski boat, an ATV, and a couple of snowmobiles, which he was very proud of and he lived to enjoy. He took great pleasure in sharing those experiences with others.

All of his loves he planned to share with his son, who was born in 1991. Michael doted over his son and looked forward to a life full of teaching him all about life and the out of doors. This dream was taken away from Michael when he was falsely accused and found guilty of a crime he was not a part of. His son is fifteen and in high school, a young man now. They have already lost more than fourteen years having been three years old when his father was taken from him. Due to the distance from home to the places his dad has been incarcerated, he only gets to see his dad six or eight times a year, and for only three hours a visit. This is a total injustice in itself to deprive a son from the father he loves so much.

Mike Hirn, right, with his brother Jeff

Michael's mom's health has become very delicate over the years of his incarceration. She has lost most of her eyesight and needs a wheelchair to get around any distance. His grandmother, who is like a second mom to Michael, is ninety-two years old with failing health. Our income is limited, so not only are the long trips to visit Michael hard on his mom and grandmother physically but financially devastating to the family budget as well. To get a three-hour visit, which is only available on weekdays, means I need to take a full day away from work. These hardships may not sound like much to an outsider, but believe me, the whole experience to date has been devastating, to say the least, on our family.

We have lost our only other son, Jeff, to a motorcycle accident six years ago. Michael not being able to be with the family during our period of extreme grief made the emotional effect of this much worse. Within the last three years he has also lost his grandfather and grandmother on my side of the family, and Diane Koltz, a very close friend. Michael's absence from us is something that should never have happened and those years can never be replaced.

Faith is our only hope. We have faith in our son because we know that he is completely innocent. We have hope that when the information in this book is published there will be an outcry for justice. We also have faith and hope in our Lord that he is looking over our Michael and protecting him. We pray for the day he comes home to us; hopefully that day will be very soon.

The trial was an example of how an innocent person can be in the wrong place at the wrong time and end up in prison. Something like this could happen to you or me, and it is not right that our justice system can let this happen. We need to do something to prevent this from ever happening again. There should be hard facts incriminating someone, not false stories, statements, and theories. But first we need to correct the wrongs that have already been made.

We are a family just like you. We are good citizens with strong faith in God. We always believed that the system worked, and we pray it still can. Please help us get our Michael out of prison. Michael's mom and grandma need to see him regain his freedom before it is too late. Michael's son needs to have his father beside him as he grows to be a man. We pray for the day when we can be together again as a family.

—Mike and Trudy Dalebroux

Letter from Mike Hirn's Father, Stepmother, and Half-Brother: Garth, Georgi, and Zak Hirn

We have been asked to write about how our lives and our family have been affected by the arrest, trial, and wrongful conviction of our son and brother, Michael Hirn. How does the average family do that in a way that will reach out to readers and make them realize that there is something terribly wrong? That an innocent man is behind bars in prison?

We can talk about these things in concrete terms: how much time has passed; the changes in our family like the death of Michael's older brother, Jeff. And we are no longer able to see Michael's son, our grandson. We can describe the uncertainty that we live with, never knowing if Michael will be moved to another prison, where that prison might be, and whether he will be safe. We can talk about changes in our family's health, like Georgi's cancer or Garth's heart trouble. We can talk about how our relationships in our community have changed because of our relationship to Michael—a relationship we are proud of by the way.

Looking at it in concrete terms pins some things down so that they are easier to look at and analyze and come to terms with; at the same time it is like writing your own obituary. How do you pin down the essence of your life? What do you want people to remember about you and your family? What about you and your family really matters, and what tangible mark have you left on the world that is of any real significance?

What can we say about what our family—especially our son—has gone through that will capture the essence, the real impact of its effects upon each one of us?

The answer is simple. It's just one word. Grief. We live with the same stages dying people and the people close to them go through. For us, these stages are present every day: denial, anger, bargaining, and depression. Some days or some moments, one is stronger than at other times, and the pain subsides. Then another eruption of anguish takes you to your knees, and all the stages come rushing through you at once until the only help is falling to the ground in a throbbing numbness.

There is a fifth stage to grief—a stage that is still far out of our family's reach: acceptance. Let's face it! Mike's ill-founded conviction and his tragic incarceration are very real, yet we have gone on with something resembling normal life. We have had no choice. But we still have not reached the point where we have surrendered to the idea that this is normal or right. Nor have we written off the loss and moved on. That is impossible because we know that Mike is innocent.

After fourteen years of this indescribable pain, our prayers remain the same. We pray that The Lord will open eyes and that the truth will be found. We pray that Mike is soon released.

—Garth, Georgi, and Zak Hirn

Rey Moore Speaks

The thing that amazes me about this case is how quickly people put aside common sense to buy all of this. They never stop to think that the police might have made a mistake. They accept that six people who did not really know each other could do all this in a short time without leaving any physical evidence; as the state's witnesses have said, nothing was out of place!

Given all of this, the hardest part has been what this has done to my children. I had four wonderful, bright, trusting children, with three at home. The ones at home were still in school and they were A and B students. After this happened, their lives have been turned upside down. No longer are they the beautiful free spirits they once were. They are only a shell of their former selves. Depression has set in, and I don't know if they will ever overcome it. To see what this injustice has done to my children is just ripping my heart out.

I know one day God will vindicate my children, and that is what I hang my hope on.

I would like people to read the trial transcripts and not make up their minds on bits and pieces.

Letter from Rey Moore's Daughter Ivy Summers

Write a letter telling a person how my father's wrongful conviction affected me and my family—yeah, like that is even possible. The effects of that conviction burn today, as if he were convicted yesterday. The pain, the heartache, the humiliation, the shame, the loneliness and despair are feelings that cannot be put on paper.

Rey Moore with his family and Mike Piaskowski's sister, Christine (background).

I could tell you all about the caring things my father did for his children, what a wonderful father he was. How he would take us to get ice cream at Cathy's Custard in the summer, how he scared us when he told us ghost stories about Robert Greenbush, and how he took my brother fishing every chance he could. I hold these personal memories in my heart.

However, I cannot tell you stories of how my Dad looked when I brought home an A on the paper he had just helped me research.

I cannot tell you the joy I saw in his eyes when he saw me graduate from high school. I cannot tell you what he wore on my wedding day. I cannot tell you how I felt when he came to the hospital when his first grandchild was born. Those memories were taken from me. Those memories do not exist. My father has missed so much of our lives, and that is something that can never be given back to us.

Our entire family has gone through this nightmare, and I am still bitter about it. My mother was forced to be a single parent. I thank God everyday for her. If it weren't for her hard work and strong love, my father's incarceration could have been so much harder. She is the glue that holds us together. Thank you Mom.

We have received so much help and support from our friends, and I could not have gotten through this without them. Thank you to all.

My family looks to the future, as the past is just too painful. My family is waiting the day my Father can come home, so we can start our lives with him again and start making new memories.

—Ivy Summers

Letter from Rey Moore's Friend Sami Lee Phillips

I have known Rey Moore for over 25 years, longer than I have known anyone outside of a relative. During this time Rey has shown himself to be a wise and caring father, thoughtful and loving husband, and an active and generous member of his church and community. Rey has given freely of himself to his professional and political organizations and remains a steadfast and true friend to me now, and I expect will forever. Rey is a good man and a quality person, a far cry from the murderous conspirator he is convicted of being.

Rey's earliest years, as were mine, were spent growing up on a farm in a rural southern community. We often share stories of these experiences, of growing up, of working hard and overcoming the hardships of doing without, but also of the joy and sense of pride that comes from that as well as from the love of a caring family. After the tragic loss of his parents, Rey and his siblings came to Milwaukee to live with his grandmother. This wonderful woman provided a loving

Christian home and helped to develop the faith that to this day provides the strength Rey needs to bear this miserable blow he has been dealt.

Rey enjoyed the outdoors and shared this joy with his children. They went fishing and took camping trips together. Rey installed an aboveground pool in the backyard for his kids and even built the deck and fence with his own hands. He did all his own landscaping and even set aside a part of his lot for fruit trees and growing food. While it was by no means a new house in which they lived, Rey took great pride in homeownership and the little Shangri La they created for themselves in their own little yard. And so, in light of all this, of the loving family and friends, the rewards of his work and sense of fulfillment and contentment, one may be drawn to ask, "Why would Rey throw all of this away?" Well, I have the answer: He didn't. He didn't relinquish; it was taken from him.

I won't go into the details of the injustice that was done. You have read the book for yourself, and now you know. Rey was wrongly convicted by use of a contrived and circumstantial timeline and hearsay testimony, the use of which severely bent and very nearly broke the intent of the law.

From the beginning of the investigation, Rey was more than cooperative with the authorities. I once asked him if he didn't think he should have an attorney present and, in his sweetly naive way, he answered that he didn't think that was necessary since he had nothing to hide, as if the truth shall set him free. Oh, if only that were true. If right conquers might ... if Justice always prevails ... But it is not a sweetly naive world in which we live. For some time now, slowly, almost painlessly and unnoticed, rights and freedoms in this country have been disappearing, including, and especially, the right to justice and a fair trial.

However, all hope is not lost, for there are things that you, Dear Reader, can do. You can fight ignorance and complacency. Now that you have read this book, pass it on, and in that way share the knowledge with others. Stand up for your rights, demand them and exert them. Become an informed voter. Participate in politics. Seek and share knowledge at every turn, for therein lies the hope of freedom and justice for you, for Rey, and for the future. And finally, you can make your voice be heard, even if it is only in a simple letter, as this is. But call for it loudly as if your life depended on it, as it just might one day—for if this can happen to Rey it can happen to any of us. There is a new battle cry in this battle for rights and freedom. Never forget it: "Justice for Rey—Free Rey Moore." Only then can there be satisfaction that Justice has been served.

Having said all of this, I find myself thinking of the Tom Monfils family and their suffering for the loss of their loved one. I at least have a hope, however small it may be, that I will see Rey again and moreover, have him return into my life at some point in the future, by exoneration, parole, or even pardon. But they can have no such hope for their future. Their loved one is gone, never to return into their lives. How can there be a future without hope? How can there be hope without a future? Let us then hope for, and strive for, a future that includes justice—justice for Rey and justice for Tom.

—Sami Lee Phillips

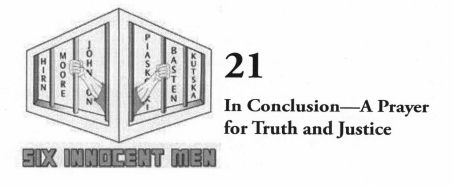

21

In Conclusion—A Prayer for Truth and Justice

All great truths began as blasphemies!
—George Bernard Shaw

George Bernard Shaw wrote the epigraph above following World War I. *Our* blasphemy does not end with this book; it is now merely documented.

Five men, wrongfully convicted of murder and still behind bars, must be exonerated—fully. At the very least, they must be retried—separately. Along with the already-absolved Mike Piaskowski, they are innocent. This is the truth—however blasphemous the Green Bay Police Department, the Brown County district attorney, and others may want to shade it.

This book has been a long time coming—far too long for Tom Monfils, the first victim, and for these six innocent men. With its publication, these authors rededicate themselves to securing final justice for all of them.

In these pages, we have related the pivotal role played by the GBPD at the very beginning of this injustice. We have closely examined the role of lead detective Randy Winkler in steering the investigation toward the police theory. We have shown that Brown County District Attorney John Zakowski zealously picked up the torch without conducting his own investigation. We have exposed the many areas of reasonable doubt and the shell games played by the prosecution at trial. We have explained how the so-called evidence in this case is a sham.

Sixteen years after Tom Monfils's tragic death, we present some concluding items in this chapter that are meant to give readers a final pause. Here also are some looks at the case as it stands today. These are our closing thoughts on a case that continues to gnaw at Green Bay's gut and to be a thorn in the side of the police and the district attorney.

The Jailhouse Feud

For those who have wondered why none of these men implicated any of the others just to save his own skin or why they would cover up for each other, there is more evidence that puts that kind of silliness to rest.

Their six-week trial ended on Saturday, October 28, 1995, with guilty verdicts all around. The six men were whisked away to cells in the Brown County jail—all of them staring straight into the harsh reality of spending the rest of their lives in prison.

That very same night, according to Lieutenant Steve Henry of the GBPD, some of the men asked to be moved to cell blocks completely separate from the others. In fact, jail worker Jim Kowalkowski told *Green Bay Press-Gazette* reporter Don Langenkamp that "Keith Kutska asked me to get Dale Basten away from him. Nobody wants to be with Dale Basten … and Mike Hirn told me he doesn't want to be near any of those guys."

Based on his interviews with the jail staff, Langenkamp tagged this episode as a "jailhouse feud." The upshot of the feud was that Hirn and Basten were moved to separate cell blocks from the others and each other, while Piaskowski and Moore were placed in one cell block and Kutska and Johnson in another.

Even if one believed in the union-conspiracy claptrap, the following seems clear: That night—with the men confronting the reality of their guilty verdicts, facing the certainty of years in prison, and angry with their so-called fellow conspirators—this alleged conspiracy disintegrated into six very solitary pieces.

These men were not mobsters, hardened to the system and beholden to a code of silence. They were your typical sons, brothers, and fathers—blue-collar guys—and now they had lost everything of importance in their lives. Here they were, convicted and incarcerated—demanding to be separated from one another. If they had ever been hiding the truth, it would have come out that night. If they were angry, guilty men, someone would have sung like a canary. The guy with the least involvement in the crime—had a crime been committed—would have been pointing fingers at the others like a drowning man grabbing onto the nearest life raft. With the opportunity to lash out at the others and say anything to possibly save his neck, any one of them could have invented a story. Instead, each man kept his honor and maintained his innocence.

> "I was scared to death of what one of the other guys might make up just to save his skin."
>
> —Mike Piaskowski

Why did none of this occur? The answer is ridiculously simple: These men had nothing more to give the authorities. They had each told the police and DA everything they knew numerous times. Each had struggled again and again to give the authorities the truth. No one had stooped to lying. At the cajoling of the police, however, they had even speculated about the possible involvement of one another—at least twenty-six times!

Here was a jailhouse feud among the so-called conspirators, but no one decided he had had enough of the alleged conspiracy to go one step further and finally rat out his comrades. Amazing—unless, of course, there was never any conspiracy in the first place!

After All These Years, Why Have They Not Talked?

If you still believe that these six men were part of a union conspiracy, you have to admit to wondering how this alleged conspiracy has lasted this long. After all, these guys have been separated from one another since 1995. Their lives have been ruined in nearly every imaginable way. Yet—if you hang onto that union-conspiracy nonsense—you have to somehow believe that their motivation to stay quiet still outweighs the desire of *any* and *every* one of these men to enjoy a beautiful summer day with his family.

District Attorney Zakowski, an ardent supporter of the union-conspiracy myth, was asked why these so-called conspirators have kept quiet, even after so many years. After this long, you would think one of these allegedly selfish men would have decided to cut himself a break by saying something—anything—to someone. Zakowski said, "I think they are so invested in this lie at this point that they can't come forward. They would embarrass themselves in front of their friends and family."

Wow! Zakowski's line of reasoning is astonishing. Their families have already suffered in every conceivable way: financially, socially, mentally, emotionally. There is not much room for further embarrassment there! As though that was not enough—more than sixteen years after Monfils's death—not one of them will do the right thing because they are all worried about their reputations and how an admission of guilt would look to their families. Again, amazing—but not very logical!

In 2004, Mike Johnson put it this way: "Do you think I haven't thought about the fact that I could call John Zakowski and say, 'John, I want to talk'? I could do that. I could invent a story." When asked why he did not, Johnson pointed toward heaven and said, "Because that would be a lie, and I'd have to square that lie with Him."

Why have they not talked? They have. But the real question is, why have they not said what the police and DA wanted to hear? The answer is, because that was not the truth. When the truth did not jibe with the official theory, the six were doomed. Even today, their truthful innocence remains their ticket to freedom or the shackles that will bind them forever.

A Very Real Catch-22

Your date for parole eligibility has finally arrived. You have served your time, knowing all the while that you were locked up for a crime you did not commit.

The days and hours and months and years have finally ticked away.

They have not been easy. You have had the ups and downs of filing appeals only to have them denied at every level. You have endured your assigned time. You have had to learn everything the hard way. You have poured all your energy into serving your time with the most dignity you could muster. You have sent prayer upon prayer heavenward, having to believe in your heart that all of this was somehow a part of God's plan for you.

You have kept your nose clean. You have done the best you could to utilize the opportunities available in prison and to show an appropriate measure of respect to prison employees and fellow inmates. In essence, you have had to resign yourself to biding your time, honoring yourself in the process, and waiting for this day when you would finally be set free.

Then you are brought in front of the parole board. The members of the board review your case and your time in prison. They remark that your behavior has been exemplary. At last, it would seem that your chance is at hand to rejoin your loved ones outside of these concrete walls and bars of steel. You are asked by one of the board members if you are now willing to assume responsibility for your crime and express sincere remorse.

No! This cannot be happening! You have done everything right in preparing for this moment. Now you are being asked the impossible: You must either admit to something you absolutely never did and express earnest regret for having done it, or you will be returned to the cell you have called home for way too long already.

It is right there in the palm of your hand. Mouth the right words, and you are quite possibly a free man. You are wracked with anguish—conflicting feelings racing through you like electricity.

"I can't do that," you finally utter in a voice that does not even seem like your own. "I didn't do this, and saying I did would be a lie. I can't do that to myself or to my family. I can't do that to the victim's family, either."

As you make your way back to your cell block completely overcome with emotion, you are shaking, in tears. You now realize that you will very likely wither away in prison alone—a victim of your own innocence and a system that will have none of it. "What's the difference now?" you say to yourself, "The real 'me' died a long, long time ago anyway."

Dale Basten, Mike Hirn, Mike Johnson, Keith Kutska, and Rey Moore all know that they will never be released from prison under their present circumstances. To a man, they have told these authors that they will never admit to having anything to do with harming Tom Monfils—because they did not.

Guilty men would have admitted their guilt and taken a deal long ago. Guilty men would have admitted their guilt at their very first parole hearing, knowing it was their only ticket out. These men have said repeatedly that they cannot and will not do that—that each of them would rather die an old man in prison than be unfaithful to the truth of their innocence.

<u>DOIN' TIME</u>

PRISON LIFE—DEADLY STRIFE

Den of evil fare

ATMOSPHERE—BURNS SO CLEAR

Toxin in the air

ERODED WILLS—WASTED SKILLS

Souls lay vacant bare

ENDLESS DAYS—ETERNAL STAYS

Abysmal deep despair

SORDID NEEDS—TWISTED DEEDS

Bitter sad affair

CAUSTIC BLAME—UGLY SHAME

Guilt for all to share

BROKEN DREAMS—NIGHTMARE SCREAMS

Tainted empty prayer

FAMILY TIES—SIBLING CRIES

Slain in mode unfair

JUSTICE BLIND—TRUTH UNKIND

Bias far from rare

FATAL PART—FUTURE DARK

Enough not seem to care

—Mike Piaskowski
Dodge Correctional Institution, 1999

A Letter Says It All

Almost six years after the trial, in a letter to the *Green Bay News-Chronicle,* Mike Piaskowski's appellate attorney, T. Christopher Kelly, addressed DA Zakowski's media comments about Piaskowski's then-recent exoneration:

Zakowski Still Doesn't Understand Piaskowski Is Innocent

As Mike Piaskowski's lawyer, I was shocked to read prosecutor Zakowski's false claim that "Mike Piaskowski is the only one who could have known the rope and weight" found around Tom Monfils's body "were there."

The evidence at trial clearly established that the rope was accessible to anyone in the plant. The existence of the rope was no secret, and there was no reason to believe that Piaskowski had more knowledge of it than anyone else who worked in the same area.

The evidence also established that weights were located all around the plant. It is not surprising that the attorney general's office chose not to make the argument that Zakowski now makes, because that argument is based on a misrepresentation of the evidence.

Zakowski apparently is unwilling to concede that he prosecuted an innocent man. Nonetheless, five federal judges have now concluded that Zakowski presented no evidence that would prove Piaskowski's guilt.

His attempt to blame the attorney general's office for the reversal of Piaskowski's conviction and his misrepresentation of the evidence reflects sour grapes, not the truth.

The truth is that the federal courts have reviewed every bit of evidence presented at the trial and concluded that no rational jury could have found Piaskowski guilty.

It is unfortunate that Mike Piaskowski lost over five years of his life due to an ill-considered prosecution before the truth of his innocence finally came to light.

Chris Kelly—Kelly, Habermehl and Mays, S.C.

All the Earmarks of a Wrongful Conviction

Attorney Kelly called Piaskowski's conviction the result of an "ill-considered prosecution." Before that, the faulty prosecution was spawned by an ill-conceived investigation. The police and district attorney got this one wrong—plain and simple. However, it is not *entirely* their fault. They cannot be blamed for their lack of experience. There are few mysterious deaths to solve in northeastern Wisconsin. In most Green Bay-area murder cases, there are eyewitnesses, clear-cut scenarios, and confessions of guilt to help solve the crime. True mysteries remain few and far between. The prosecution's normal challenge is to secure a palatable plea bargain.

The police and district attorney could be taken to task for not realizing they were in over their heads. Perhaps they should have acknowledged their own lack of experience and called for assistance from parties more practiced in such matters. Hubris and the conflict of interest caused by the police department's release of the audiotape to Kutska likely prevented that. The minimal involvement of FBI and Justice Department agents in the case in 1994 only led to some head-scratching and the advice these agencies gave to Mike Hirn and Mike Piaskowski to "get a good lawyer."

However, the GBPD and Brown County DA must be held accountable for their inability to let go of their initial "way-to-go-Kutska" theory when development after development proved it to be incorrect.

According to wrongful-conviction experts, the police and the district attorney made just about every common mistake in this case.

It was not unreasonable for them to entertain the idea that Kutska had harmed Monfils—that was a logical and good place to start. After all, Kutska himself said that he had "put Tom on Front Street" by securing the tape of Monfils's phone call and making it public. The mistake of the authorities was in hanging on—like addicts—to that theory. They refused to allow themselves to be led by the evidence. They let tunnel vision dominate their investigation, and they apparently turned a blind eye to any alternative. David Wiener, for example, was never a suspect—even after he proved his capacity for murder by shooting his brother.

Cross-racial identifications are another common cause of mistakes in wrongful convictions. Rey Moore, an African American, was identified by Charles Bowers as being in the tissue-chest area early on the morning of Monfils's death. Bowers was a recent hire who did not know Moore. Based on what the police told Bowers, he believed that Moore was the only African-American man working during his twelve-hour shift. With no further thought and without the benefit of a photo lineup, Bowers identified Moore as the African-American man that he saw stroll through his area. When Moore contradicted Bowers's observation, he was regarded as a liar who had something to hide. Among the facts ignored by the police were that two other African-American men were working in the mill during the first seven-plus hours of Bowers's shift.

The use or misuse of jailhouse informants shows up repeatedly when wrongful convictions are scrutinized. Murderers, rapists, wife-beaters, and others facing jail time are seldom restrained by the thought of mere perjury. Criminals who have no moral compass are more than willing to do whatever it takes to escape a stretch in prison. In this case three incarcerated witnesses were used to provide spurious testimony for the prosecution. One of them was David Wiener, who was in prison for killing his brother. Another, James Gilliam, was in jail for threatening a girl friend with a knife.

A third jailhouse snitch, James Charleston, was sitting in the Brown County jail for felony burglary when the Monfils arrests were made. At trial, Charleston would testify that he and Basten had been watching TV in jail when a news story aired identifying Wiener as a witness against Basten in the Monfils case. At that point, Charleston would testify, Basten referred to Wiener as a "fuckin' squealer."

Basten had not said that. He wanted to explain to the jury that he had actually called Wiener a "fuckin' killer"—not a squealer. However, the judge had previously ruled that information about Wiener killing his brother was to be kept from the jury. The most Basten could say before the jury was that he had "said something else" in reference to Wiener. As a result, Charleston looked like a reliable witness, and Basten looked like he was trying to twist words and shade the facts.

In prolonged and difficult cases that end up with a wrongful conviction, it is not unusual to find the media continually demanding results. For more than two years between the time of Monfils's death and the arrests of the six men, the *Green Bay Press-Gazette* and four local television stations continued their demands for a resolution of the case.

Upon analysis, wrongful convictions are all too often the result of false or mistaken testimony by prosecution witnesses. In the Monfils case, we have the continual efforts of police and prosecution to convince Connie Jones that she must have seen a 7:18 a.m. paper break, even though it had never occurred. Eventually, she as well as others succumbed to their pressure and reluctantly agreed to testify as the prosecution wished.

After twenty-four months of failure, the lone detective still working the case interrogated Brian Kellner for eight grueling hours and produced an uncorroborated hearsay statement, which the prosecution would characterize as a confession by Keith Kutska.

Today, most wrongful convictions are discovered as a result of DNA analyses, which provide a statistical certainty in the vicinity of a billion to one. There is no DNA evidence in this case. However, there is this statistical certainty: If one person in a hundred is foolish enough to spend his life in prison to protect a casual acquaintance or stranger in the workplace whom he knows to be guilty of a crime, the probability of six people doing so is an overwhelming trillion to one.

That is why everyone familiar with this case—police and layman alike—have said, "I just can't believe that none of these guys came forward to save himself." This book shows that they did. They just could not escape the ever-evolving string of theories concocted by the police and the DA—a clear recipe for wrongful conviction.

John Zakowski's Phony Key

Ask DA John Zakowski what the key to his victory in the Monfils case was, and he will most certainly tell you: It was the Fox Den role-playing incident. He said it in April 1995 when Basten, Hirn, Johnson, Kutska, Moore, and Piaskowski were arrested. He said it to the jury at the trial. He said it following the men's convictions. He said it to these authors in a 2003 interview. He has said it to the media often.

There is, however, something seriously wrong: Zakowski's key does not fit the door it is supposed to unlock. On its face, the 1994 Fourth-of-July-weekend role-play never occurred. It could not have. Even the logic of the situation is flawed—based on the GBPD's own investigation.

There are, however, many other problems with Zakowski's key. For one, there is no basis for the idea that the Fox Den's owners, Ron and Charlotte Salnik, played a part in or covered up such a role-play. The Salniks had no allegiance to Kutska, let alone to a paper-mill union to which they had no ties whatsoever. Then there is the idea that two of the alleged major role-players, Brian Kellner and his then-wife, Verna, sat on such crucial information until Randy Winkler coaxed it out of them. This scenario suggests that they were both were unwilling to do the right thing earlier, and that neither their individual honesty nor the substantial reward money was reason enough for them to come forward with the story. These are all red flags that Zakowski should have seen when Winkler first brought him news of the role-play.

Zakowski's key is at best a skeleton key—one designed by its very vagueness to unlock most any door. In the state's closing arguments, Zakowski made eleven individual endorsements of Kellner's testimony. It was certainly a case of "thou doth protest too much." Why would Zakowski need to hammer home Kellner's value nearly a dozen times if the strength of his testimony was as solid as Zakowski said it was?

Here are Zakowski's emphatic attempts, in his closing argument taken verbatim from the trial transcript, to polish his key.

Page 64, line 17

We turn to the testimony of the other significant state witness, Brian Kellner. And, ladies and gentlemen, I submit to you, if not the, one of the most credible witnesses in four-and-a-half week jury [trial] that we've had.

Page 69, line 13

This is extremely important information. This is extremely important evidence, because this tells us how Tom Monfils eventually died. What led to his death? It comes from Mr. Kutska himself. And it's recounted through his friend, Mr. Kellner.

Page 69, line 21

And in effect, ladies and gentlemen, if you believe Brian Kellner, then every one of these defendants is guilty because they've all lied about it. They're all lying about what they did.

Page 70, line 4

Now, Kellner is crucial. But he's also; I believe, one of the most, again if not the most credible witness in this trial.

Page 70, line 15

Well, I think Brian Kellner understands the importance of telling the truth. And that's exactly what he did from this witness stand.

Page 70, line 21

He's [Kellner] telling the truth. No motive to lie.

Page 71, line 24

> See, if Kellner was just fabricating a story for glory or fame or to get somebody in trouble, why would he stop here? Why wouldn't he take it to its logical conclusion?

Page 71, line 16

> Something else in terms of generating or evaluating Mr. Kellner's credibility, there is no Winkler [deception] factor here.

Page 73, line 3

> Kellner was simply telling what Kutska said. He's telling the truth. He received nothing. He's gaining nothing.

Page 73, line 20

> And probably the most important, the most important reason why you know Brian Kellner is telling the truth is because Keith Kutska says he isn't.

Page 74, line 8

> And then, you know, there's another factor you can look at in evaluating somebody's credibility—their demeanor on the witness stand. And I just want to say I was very impressed with Mr. Kellner. He was up there a long time. He answered a lot of difficult questions from the defense council. But he always answered, yes, ma'am; no, ma'am; yes, sir; no, sir. I think if you look back and think about Brian Kellner—that is one witness that you can trust. He's telling you the truth.

If Zakowski had such an outstanding product, he would not have felt compelled to oversell it like that. Not everyone, however, bought Zakowski's pitch like the jury did. In fact, trial judge James Bayorgeon had a strikingly different view of Kellner's value than did Zakowski. In his Decision and Order from the February 12, 1997, postconviction hearings for Dale Basten and Mike Johnson, Judge Bayorgeon did not seem to cherish Zakowski's key much at all:

Page 3, line 5

> In the Court's view, when Mr. Kellner's testimony was presented at trial, it was barely credible. He recounted an instance, which occurred after an all-day drinking bout. Mr. Kutska was intoxicated when the events occurred. Mr. Kellner was very close behind him in his level of intoxication. Mr. Kellner's ex-wife testified that she was so drunk she had little recollection of anything that happened.

Page 3, line 24

> To say his testimony was critical to the conviction vastly and greatly over estimates its importance.

Essentially, Judge Bayorgeon chucked Zakowski's key out the window. One might then ask how—in the name of truth and justice—Bayorgeon's and Zakowski's two very disparate views of the same testimony can reconcile themselves.

There is even more evidence that Zakowski's key is not the bright, shiny, effective device that he has made it out to be—this from Kellner himself. At the 1997 postconviction hearings, Kellner told the court that he had lied and made untrue statements while testifying at the trial. Far more damning, he also told the court that he had informed Zakowski and others before the trial about the discrepancies in his police statements and that they had done little to nothing about it. Remember, Kellner was *not* an eyewitness of any kind to the alleged goings-on at the bubbler or tissue chest the day Monfils disappeared; in fact, he was not even working that day. He was deer hunting in Oconto County—more than 75 miles away.

Here are excerpts from those postconviction hearings in which Kellner tells the world, point blank, that his testimony about the Fox Den role-play was pure hogwash. Attorney Christopher VanWagner, appearing on behalf of Mike Johnson, is questioning Kellner.

Page 53, Lines 19–25

> Q. When you testified that he [Kutska] said that at trial, was that truthful or   untruthful …?

> A. Untruthful.

Page 48, Line 23

> Q. Was it true that Keith Kutska told you that?

> A. No.

Page 53, Line 4

> Q. So when you testified at trial that Kutska told you the names of others, the defendants in this case, besides the ones you've named, you were being untruthful?

> A. Yes, sir.

Page 47, Line 13

> Q. Was that answer, or those series of answers, at any point given truthfully when you gave them at trial?

> A. No.

Page 49, Line 7

> Q. Was it truthful sir?

> A. No, sir.

Page 52, Line 7

> Q. So, when you testified at trial that Keith Kutska specifically named individuals and described their role in the confrontation that followed, you were being untruthful?

> A. Yes, sir.

Page 126, Line 16

> Q. And are you telling us today that was untruthful at the time?

> A. Yes, sir.

> Q. And you knew it was untruthful at the time?

> A. Yes, sir.

Kellner admitted that he had lied at trial. He also said that he had tried to set the record straight with Zakowski and others but had gotten nowhere in his efforts.

So Zakowski had to be painfully aware that his skeleton key—Kellner's Fox Den role-play malarkey—was completely unreliable. He also had to know that Kellner was far more likely to be a target for a perjury probe than he was for a citizenship award for honesty. Then how is it that, many years later, Zakowski still calls the role-play and Kellner's testimony of it the key to his case? Is it because—without that key—there is no door, no room behind that door, and absolutely no case?

Postconviction —Zakowski's Case Is Crumbling

Shortly after the Monfils trial ended, DA Zakowski expressed his relief to the media:

> *The key was Piaskowski. If they [the jury] found Piaskowski guilty, it would mean they believed Kellner and our theory of what happened that morning.*

It was yet another instance of Zakowski holding up his phony key. Kellner's perjured testimony has been clearly debunked elsewhere in these pages. By affidavit, Kellner has also stated that the role-play never occurred. The fact that Zakowski has always clutched Kellner's story so tightly suggests the ultimate frailty of his case. In fact, if one reads Zakowski's statement regarding the conviction of Piaskowski closely, one can discern his own admission of just how fragile his case was—and is.

Each of the four primary elements in Zakowski's post-trial statement has been sternly contradicted by the judges in this case—the trial judge, James T. Bayorgeon; U.S. District Judge Myron L. Gordon; and Justice Terence T. Evans, Seventh Circuit Court of Appeals:

- Judge Bayorgeon on *Kellner*: "In the Court's view, when Mr. Kellner's testimony was presented at trial, it was barely credible. He recounted an instance, which occurred after an all-day drinking bout. Mr. Kutska was intoxicated when the events occurred. Mr. Kellner was very close behind him in his level of intoxication. Mr. Kellner's ex-wife testified that she was so drunk she had little recollection of anything that happened."

- Judge Gordon on *Piaskowski's* guilty verdict: "No physical evidence tied Mr. Piaskowski to the crime, no testifying witness saw him participate in it, no one confessed, there was no testimony from the petitioner or any other witness that he took part in the murder or intended to."
- Judge Gordon on the *jury*: "Based on the evidence, no reasonable jury could have found Mr. Piaskowski guilty of each element of the crime under either of the theories offered by the prosecution."
- Justice Evans on the *state's theory*: "This, however, like so much else in this case is conjecture camouflaged as evidence."

Zakowski sold the idea of Piaskowski's guilt, Kellner's testimony, and the state's theory to the jury. The judges's careful scrutiny of these and other elements in the case, however, has exposed the weaknesses that were there for all to see. As a result, Zakowski no longer has Piaskowski's conviction. He no longer has Kellner's testimony. He never had a reasonable jury. And his unsupported theory does not have the respect of the courts. In truth, Zakowski can only cling to the other five unreasonable verdicts and hope that no one notices at this point.

"Innocent until proven guilty"—such a basic component of the U.S. justice system—is often nothing more than lip service. In most cases, particularly those ending in wrongful convictions, the presumption of innocence is ignored by the jury. Sadly, it is common for many citizens to presume that a person arrested by the police and brought to court is there for a good reason. The prevailing thought is, "If they didn't do anything, they wouldn't be there." This puts every accused person—especially an innocent person—at an immediate disadvantage. Keith Kutska's attorney, Royce Finne, put it this way: "The first thing I tell a client is, 'You will have to prove you are innocent.'" When federal judge Terence Evans characterized the case against Piaskowski as "conjecture camouflaged as evidence," he described just how powerfully this presumption of guilt can lead a jury astray.

The Continued Skepticism of Judge Bayorgeon

At the postconviction hearings, Judge Bayorgeon characterized Kellner's testimony as "barely credible." Indeed, in the wake of this trial, Judge Bayorgeon has often seemed to express a healthy skepticism. Underlying many of his words is an incredulous tone that seems to speak volumes. That sentiment could first be heard at the Thursday, December 21, 1995, sentencing hearing—about two months after the Racine County jury had rendered their guilty verdicts and he had signed off on them:

> *It's frightening that if these gentlemen can commit this crime, what about the other person on the bus? Look at yourselves. Look in the mirror.*

Judge Bayorgeon expanded on his observations, suggesting that the men had little or no criminal record and that there was no indication that they were capable of committing such a heinous crime. He was right: These men are no different than the rest of us. A good look in the mirror—warts and all—reflects their innocence, not their guilt.

Then, at Michael Hirn's postconviction sentencing hearing, Judge Bayorgeon ominously declared,

> *This is the first chapter of a book whose ending is yet to be written.*

Finally, when Judge Bayorgeon retired in 2004, his concerns for these men prompted him to write a highly unusual and sympathetic letter to the Wisconsin Parole Commission. Referring to the five remaining incarcerated men, it read in part:

> Each of the above named individuals is presently serving a term in the Wisconsin State Prison as a result of a sentence which I imposed. I customarily receive notices of parole hearings. I am now retiring and will not be on the bench when these individuals will be up for parole. Therefore I would like to place on the record, at this time, my thoughts with respect to their parole …

> The most unique aspect of this case was the fact that these individuals, other than the unique offense, were hard working stable members of the community. They

were not criminals but got caught up in a situation which quickly got out of control.

I cannot speak for their conduct during their term of incarceration. However, from my point of view of all that has transpired in this case, it would seem to me that favorable consideration for early parole would be appropriate. I set parole eligibility dates which I felt would provide adequate punishment for the offense and absent other facts, of which I am unaware, have seen nothing that would be gained by further confinement.

I would appreciate it if you would make notation in the respective records of these individuals with respect to this correspondence.

(Signed) Judge James T. Bayorgeon

A Final Appeal for Truth and Justice

It is not the intention of these authors to humiliate John Zakowski. To be sure, we invite him to become the champion of truth and justice by righting this wrong. It is within his ability. We understand that he only acted with what was presented to him, but justice did not prevail. Yes, the men were convicted. However, not one of them has had *his* day in court. Thanks to a joint trial, they were presented to the jury as an inanimate object—a mythical mob of six barely identifiable persons.

Lurking like a menacing dark cloud over the case was the fact that one of the codefendants, Keith Kutska, *was* guilty. Not guilty of homicide—but guilty of stealing five dollars worth of electrical wire. Not guilty of orchestrating a physical confrontation with Tom Monfils—but guilty of putting a spotlight on Monfils in the workplace to humiliate him. It was that kind of "guilty" Keith Kutska who was portrayed as the ringleader of this mythical mob and likely produced a guilty verdict for all the men.

With four hard consonants in the short space of eleven letters, even Keith Kutska's name clunks off the tongue as though it belongs to a guilty man. Very few people with even a passing awareness of the case forget Kutska's name. He, however, is innocent of murder. So are the others. Being tied to Kutska in a joint trial effectively prevented the other five men from making a clear case for their innocence. And without being tied to Kutska, each of them would have been found innocent by any reasonable jury.

The state rationalized that it would be "too expensive for the taxpayers" for each man to have his own separate trial. These men and their families were devastated. They also were taxpayers. Truth, justice, and a fair trial certainly did not seem too expensive to them. They were no different than a hundred thousand other hard-working Green Bay citizens who paid their taxes, went to church, supported their families, and cheered for the Packers. Today the price of this injustice has far outstripped the original cost of separate trials.

The U.S. Constitution says unequivocally that each citizen deserves his or her day in court—to be judged on his or her own. The whole idea of a jury of one's peers in our country is to ensure a fair trial. That did not happen in this case. Without a trial of his own, each man was forced to endure all the smears heaped upon the other defendants.

In a separate trial, such hearsay testimony that this book has exposed and examined would have been inadmissible, and the jury would have heard none of it.

With that we appeal to the entire judicial system—the courts, the Wisconsin attorney general, and District Attorney Zakowski. We appeal to Judge Bayorgeon. These six innocent men must be exonerated. Short of that, the five remaining defendants—Dale Basten, Michael Hirn, Michael Johnson, Keith Kutska, and Reynold Moore—must be granted new trials. In this way, each of these citizens will finally have his own day in court. Then they will undoubtedly join Mike Piaskowski in the ranks of all exonerated victims of wrongful convictions. It is the only way that truth and justice can prevail in this case. It is time for the tears of unbelievable sorrow to end.

Finally

For nearly eight years, we have toiled with the heavy weight of five innocent men in prison on our shoulders. Their wrongful incarcerations have haunted us as we pressed forward to complete this project with due speed *and* due diligence. However, we did not set out to just publish a book. Our first goal always was to thoroughly reexamine this case, put the facts out there, and let the citizens of northeastern Wisconsin and the rest of the United States judge for themselves. Our quest does not end here. Now we turn our sights to getting the wheels of truth and justice to turn in the direction of these innocent men.

If you are as moved as we are, please support our future efforts to obtain justice for Michael Hirn, Keith Kutska, Rey Moore, Michael Johnson, and Dale Basten.

Political cartoonist Lyle Lahey has the final "word" on the Monfils case. Sir William Blackstone's original idea—a basic building block of the U.S. justice system—said it was better to err on the side of caution than to round up a bunch of innocent citizens based on a hunch or a self-serving bias. Thank you, Lyle.

Epilogue

In 2004, these authors sent a questionnaire to each of the Monfils jurors about the case. Only two bothered to respond at all; both said they did not want to get involved. In late 2007, however, a juror surprisingly contacted Mike Piaskowski to apologize for her role in wrongfully sending him to prison.

In further communication, the juror stated that—for at least the first two weeks of the trial—she found it impossible to distinguish the six defendants from one another. She ended by stating that it is too easy for a jury to assign the same verdict in a joint trial to all the defendants rather than keep separate the facts about each. In fact, she questioned the efficacy of the U.S. justice system altogether, relying as it does on "untrained" and "unsophisticated" jurors.

We are grateful that she has come forward.

Appendix I: Researching the Timeline

We have constructed a minute-by-minute timeline of the events of the morning of November 21, 1992. It appears in Appendix II. Ninety percent of this effort is the result of examining and carefully analyzing all of the documents produced by the Green Bay Police Department. We also reinterviewed various witnesses to clarify their statements and to resolve conflicts. In addition, we contacted and interviewed several potential witnesses whom the investigators ignored or failed to contact. These documents and other sources include:

- Signed statements by mill workers and other witnesses
- Detail sheets or reports produced by the GBPD investigators
- Crime scene photos, other photos, and videotapes
- Mill diagrams and documents
- Audiocassette recordings
- Transcripts of the John Doe hearings in March 1993 and April 1995
- Transcripts of the depositions from the civil lawsuit filed by the Monfils family (November 1993–June 1994)
- Transcripts of the preliminary hearing in April 1995
- Transcripts of interviews conducted by James River corporate security personnel from January through March 1993 and in August 1995
- Transcripts from Wisconsin unemployment compensation hearings (April 1993)
- Transcripts from union arbitration hearings (August–September 1993)
- Trial transcripts (September–October of 1995)
- Transcripts from all subsequent state and federal postconviction hearings and rulings (1997–2001)
- Articles from the *Green Bay Press-Gazette* and the *Green Bay News-Chronicle* (1992–2001)
- Television news records
- Phone records from the James River Corporation and local telephone companies

Of course, the raw data in the timeline contains some conflicts in terms of estimated times. Because no mill worker was permitted to wear a watch on the job, the timeline's approximate times are based on various wall clocks at the mill, several computers, and telephone-company logs (the most accurate source). While the various clocks were not synchronized, our analysis of them produced no gross discrepancies.

Our timeline is also based on the descriptions each witness provided about what he or she saw and did the morning of November 21. We also noted how long each event lasted. The sequence of events, the description of each event, and the duration of an event, punctuated by reliable time data allowed us to confidently identify an accurate timeline. Very often, people could recall the duration of an event much more accurately than exactly *when* that event took place.

It was crucial to assume that every witness was telling the truth to the best of his or her ability. For these men and women at the mill, November 21 was just another routine day at work. They had no reason to create a mental note or written diary of the events of the day as they unfolded. When interviewed by the investigators, they did their level best to be helpful. Unlike the investigators, we did not assume certain witnesses were lying. We made sure that conflicting statements were resolved by common sense, comparison to the statements of all available witnesses, and the knowledge of experienced mill personnel. Often witnesses made assumptions based on what *usually happened on a typical day* rather than on what *actually happened that day*. When two or more people agreed on the same observation, most apparent contradictions were resolved.

We examined the telephone company's record of the times of outgoing calls from the mill. We also used computer data showing the start time of each turnover and other events involving the paper machines. Based upon what work a person was engaged in at the mill that morning, we could closely determine the time of any relevant observation that person made. When witnesses described events in terms of the start, middle, or end of a particular turnover, we knew almost exactly when those events happened.

One example of our efforts to utilize all available resources to nail down accurate times and durations of particular events involves the 2.6-minute paper break that took place during the 7:03 a.m. turnover on paper machine 7. Randy Lepak, Mike Piaskowski, and Dennis Servais all agree that the paper break occurred at 7:03. The 2.6-minute *duration* was noted on a computer printout; but according to Rob Miller, who wrote the program that generated this printout, the actual *time* of the paper break can only be placed somewhere between 6:49 and 7:16. The computer printed this report at 7:18. The police cherry-picked that time, 7:18, to create a false scenario to fit their theory. That is exactly what they should not have done! 7:03 is within the known span of time for that break, and three eyewitnesses support it.

In another time-related matter, our analysis resolved the problem of Mike Hirn's informing the police that he had arrived in the area at 7:15 and had observed a paper break on paper machine 7 at that time. We interviewed Hirn and learned that he had not actually *seen* a paper break—that he had made one of those assumptions based on what *usually happened* as opposed to what *actually happened* that day. "All I know," Hirn told these authors, "is that I saw a whole lot of paper dust blowing in the air." He assumed there had been a paper break because—based on his experience of what was typical—paper breaks create a great deal of dust that has to be cleaned up with an air hose *after* the break. Problem resolved.

Our timeline had to be consistent with all the facts and inconsistent with none. We could not and did not ignore or change times to fit a premature theory.

Another example of our analysis shows how we were able to get things right. Rey Moore said he arrived at coop 9 at about 7:20, but he said that he could be off by 15 minutes *or more*. He then spent his time there trying to identify Monfils, whom he did not know. Monfils had been conspicuously active in the area of paper machine 7, busy with a turnover from 7:29 to at least 7:34. Moore, however, never did see Monfils. Clearly Moore had not arrived until after that turnover and after Monfils had disappeared. That, along with the observations of other witnesses, puts Moore's arrival in coop 9 near 7:43 or 7:44. Connie Jones notes that Moore stopped at her pulp lab just after 8:00 to inform her that Monfils was off the job. She said it was about twenty minutes after she had sent Moore to coop 9, a fact consistent with our timeline.

All of this data has been recorded on a spreadsheet. It has been organized into a "master" timeline, which appears in Appendix II, and into separate timelines for each of the witnesses in Appendix III. We have included both forms so that the reader can follow the movements of each person as well as the overall course of events on that tragic morning.

Finally, it should be noted that the timeline we have developed is in sharp contrast to the one developed by the Green Bay police. In reality, there should be no difference. The information generated by the GBPD—their detail sheets and statements—was the starting point for our timeline. Our timeline then is really their timeline—the one they could have, and should have, developed.

Appendix II: The Timeline

Abbreviations: estimated time (±); statement to James River corporate investigator Frank Pinto (Pinto); statement (stmt); detail sheet (dtsht); civil deposition (CD); paper machine (PM); turnover (TO); John Doe hearing (Doe); Dan VandenLangenberg (DVL).

TIME	WITNESS	EVENT	CITATION
4:45 a.m.	Graves	Keith Kutska arrived at work; relieved Jerry Puyleart; walked to coop 8.	01/20/94 dtsht; 01/21/93 Pinto, p. 24
5:00 a.m.	Graves	Randy Koffler, S. Gajeski, Jim Frisque, Marlyn Charles arrived.	01/20/94 dtsht
	Graves	Saw Kutska in coop 9, who played tape for Graves, DeBauche, and Olson.	01/20/94 dtsht
5:08	Wiener	Punched in.	Time card
5:15	Charles	(± 15 minutes) Made copy of tape.	01/21/93 Pinto, p. 25
5:22	Binns	Punched out.	Time card

395

5:55	Wiener	Went to work station; relieved partner.	Doe, p. 616
6:00 a.m.	Daniels	Is sure he heard tape in coop 9; Randy Lepak was present.	Trial, day 6, p. 8
6:15	Bowers	Said Wiener started working.	CD 06/13/94, p. 6
6:20	Wiener	Saw Monfils by the cull cutter.	Doe, p. 621
6:30	Bowers	Saw athletic, dark, black man (six feet, 190 pounds), with no facial hair.	Stmt to attorneys Apple and Pedretti
6:30	Lison	Told by Kutska of tape in coop 9 at PM 1.	12/05/92 stmt
6:30	Servais	Heard tape in coop 9.	01/19/93 Pinto, p. 6
6:31	Delvoe	TO (logged as 6:32 by computer).	Doe, p. 379
6:35	Kutska	Told Dave Daniels to call instrumentation.	01/21/93 Pinto, p. 29
6:35	Lison	(± 5 minutes) Heard tape in coop 9; Servais already in coop 9.	12/05/92 stmt
6:40	Basten	Notified of problem on PM 9.	12/04/92 stmt; 12/01/92 dtsht
6:40	Lison	Left coop 9; saw Monfils and Delvoe do TO at p.m. 7.	12/05/92 stmt
6:42	Lison	(± 3 minutes) Returned to PM 1; told Andrews and Swiecichowski about audiotape.	12/05/92 stmt
6:45	Mineau	(±) Took sample to Connie Jones in pulp lab.	11/30/92 stmt

6:49	Computer	Recorded activation of sheet scanner after a paper break (1.4 minute).	Printout
6:50	Basten	Sent Mike Johnson to PM 9.	12/01/92 dtsht
6:52	Mineau	Logged TO (6:52).	Computer
6:58	Piaskowski	TO indicator lights turned on.	Piaskowski
7:00 a.m.	Basten	Received call from Daniels; sent Johnson to coop 9.	12/04/92 stmt
	Johnson	Basten sent Johnson to coop 9 to check stock-flow problem.	Trial, day 25, p. 81
	Kutska	Johnson came to coop 9; basis-weight problem.	01/21/93 Pinto, pp. 32, 29
	Kutska	Played tape for Wiener (probably) before 7:05.	Trial, day 19, p.109; CD 11/3/92, p. 106
	Mineau	Entered coop 9; Wiener, Kutska present; "Dick Marto discussion" took place.	11/30/92 stmt
	Webster	Said Wiener told him he heard tape before Monfils did.	Trial, day13, p. 6
	Computer	TO (logged as 7:03).	Log
7:01	Miller, R	Paper break occurred between 6:49 and 7:15.	Intercepted documents
	Servais	Paper break occurred at 7:03 TO.	12/03/92 dtsht
	Piaskowski	Paper break occurred at 7:03 TO.	Piaskowski
7:03	Servais	Paper break was before 7:16, before "Tom talk."	Doe, pp. 549, 550

	Servais	Paper break occurred at 7:03 TO.	CD 11/21/93, p. 23
	Piaskowski	Crew got sheet on reel.	Piaskowski
	Servais	Crew got sheet on reel.	12/03/92 dtsht
7:05	Piaskowski	Returned to coop 7.	Doe, pp. 246, 247, 249
7:06	Johnson	Left coop 9; went to basement; checked basis-weight valve and flow meter.	Trial, day 25, p. 82
	Lepak	Received call from Kutska to go to coop 9.	Doe, pp. 455, 56
	Lepak	Noted TO and paper break at PM 7; saw Piaskowski and Monfils.	Trial, day 10, p. 276
7:08	Johnson	Returned to instrumentation shop to get Basten; returned to basement	Trial, day 25, p. 87
7:09	Lepak	In coop 9 for 5–10 minutes.	Doe, pp. 459, 460
	Lepak	**(±) Put Basten (likely Johnson) in coop 9 "before" "Tom talk."	Doe, p. 502; trial, day 10, p. 276
7:10	Delvoe	With Monfils, finished 7:03 TO.	Doe, p. 388
7:11	Delvoe	Saw Monfils enter coop 7 after TO and paper break	Piaskowski; Doe, p. 388
7:12	Boulanger	(±) Signaled Kutska that Monfils was going back to coop 7.	Trial, day 6, p. 201
	Lepak	Entered coop 7.	Piaskowski
	Kutska	Entered coop 7 just after Lepak.	Piaskowski; CD 11/03/93, p. 113

7:13	Johnson	Saw Mineau at basis-weight valve with metal stock-sample cup.	Trial, day 25, p. 87
	Piaskowski	Tom talk began.	Doe, p. 187
7:15	Basten	Summoned by Johnson to PM 9.	12/01/92 dtsht
	Hirn	Left shipping.	12/17/92 stmt
	Hirn	Saw Delvoe blowing dust from 7:03 paper break.	Common practice
	Kutska	Left Tom-talk in coop 7.	Doe, p. 539
	Mineau	Saw Johnson and Basten in basement at basis-weight valve.	12/01/94 dtsht
	Servais	Scanner rail reset after 7:03 TO/paper break.	Computer
	Johnson	Returned to coop 9 with Basten; no one there.	Trial, day 25, p. 88
	Servais	Meeting in coop 7 with Monfils occurred after paper break.	CD 11/21/93, p. 143
	Servais	Entered coop 7 and witnessed Tom-talk; Kutska had left already.	Doe, p. 539
7:17	Johnson	Kutska entered coop 9 with tape player.	Trial, day 25, p. 89
	Lepak	Left Tom-talk in coop 7; went to coop 9 and then to PM 8.	Doe, pp. 200, 456, 466
	Piaskowski	Left Tom-talk in coop 7.	Doe, p. 545
7:18	Computer	Recorded activation of sheet scanner.	Printout
	Johnson	Returned to coop 9 with Basten.	Trial, day 25, p. 88

	Hirn	Saw activity at PM 7; assumed paper break.	12/17/92 stmt
	Hirn	Actually saw large amount of paper dust in air.	Interview at Racine Correctional Inst.
	Servais	Left Tom-talk in coop 7 with Lepak.	Doe, pp. 546, 547
		Left 9 smoking table; went to east side of PM 7.	12/15/94 stmt*
	Kutska	Saw Piaskowski and Lepak; entered coop 9.	CD 11/03/92, p. 120
7:19	Hirn	Entered coop 9 right after Tom-talk; Lepak left shortly thereafter.	12/17/92 stmt
	Piaskowski	Started rounds; saw Connie Jones at PM 7 and 9 blend hopper; mentioned tape.	Doe, p. 200
	Delvoe	Heard tape in coop 9.	12/15/94 dtsht
7:19 *		At 9 smoking table; saw Monfils at production log table; saw someone (from corner of his eye) start TO; saw nobody at bubbler; went to east side of PM 7.	12/15/94 stmt*
7:20	Delvoe	Heard tape; Kutska, Lepak, and two "instrument guys" there.	Doe, p. 419
	Delvoe	Noted Hirn's presence in earlier stmt but not at John Doe hearing.	Doe, pp. 431, 432
	Jones	Left pulp lab; went to blend hopper (her rounds usually took about 20 minutes).	12/02/92 stmt

	Jones	Started rounds; told by Piaskowski about the tape (approximately 7:15).	Doe, p. 315
	Mineau	Logged TO on PM 9.	Log
	Servais	Continued report at PM 7 control panel.	Doe, p. 550
7:21	Basten	Arrived at PM 9; Mineau had been in the basement.	12/01/92 dtsht
	Basten	Arrived at coop 9 with Johnson; Jones and Moore definitely not there.	12/02/92 dtsht
	Basten	Came to coop 9; Kutska on the phone with Marlyn Charles; then Kutska called his wife.	12/04/92 stmt; trial, day 15, p. 105
	Hirn	Heard Kutska call Marlyn Charles.	12/17/92 stmt
	Piaskowski	Talked to Connie Jones at 9 blend hopper.	Doe, pp. 201, 203
	Kutska	Called Marlyn Charles (1.5 minutes).	Phone log
7:22	Jones	Took stock samples from the 7, 9 blend hopper at PM 7 wet end.	Doe, pp. 201, 203
7:24	Hirn	Heard Kutska call his wife.	12/17/92 stmt
	Kutska	Called his wife at home (24 seconds).	Phone log
7:25	Jones	Returned to lab to process stock samples.	Doe, p. 320
	Servais	"Estimated" that Piaskowski left coop 7 (actually close to 7:18).	Doe, p. 557
7:26	Kutska	Piaskowski made brief (1 minute) visit to coop 9.	CD 11/18/93, p. 99

7:27	Daniels	Noted Mike Hirn in coop 9.	12/07/94 stmt
	Daniels	Noted Kutska, Lepak, and Piaskowski in coop 9.	04/19/94 dtsht
	Kutska	Went to 9 smoking table with union manual.	1/21/93 Pinto, p. 55; CD11/03/93, pp. 127, 128
	Piaskowski	Made brief (1 minute) stop at coop 9.	Piaskowski
7:28	Mineau	In coop 9; Kutska was playing tape and Hirn was listening.	11/30/92 stmt
	Piaskowski	Went back to coop 7 from coop 9; stayed 10–15 minutes.	Doe, p. 216
	Servais	Estimated that Monfils left coop 7; TO lights come on.	Doe, p. 555
7:29	Computer	TO (logged as occurring at 7:34).	Doe, p. 401
	Delvoe	Left coop 9 for TO on PM 7; Mineau in coop 9.	12/15/94 dtsht
	Piaskowski	In coop 7; saw Monfils at control panel starting the TO.	Doe, p. 214
7:30	Bowers	**Saw athletic, dark, black man (six feet, 190 pounds) without facial hair. (Most likely was seen before 5:30.)	12/11/92 stmt 11/30/92 dtsht
	Bowers	Went to napkin-and-towel-department (third floor)—gone 45 minutes!	05/27/94 stmt by attorney Pedretti; trial, day 14, p. 262
	Stein	Wiener told Bowers to "get lost."	Bowers and Stein interviews
	Wiener	Pumped out beater 3.	Trial, day 12, p. 96

	Wiener	**First heard of the tape from DVL.	Doe, p. 626
7:31	Hirn	Joined Kutska at 9 smoking table.	12/08/94 dtsht; 12/22/94 dtsht
	Kutska	Was joined by Hirn at 9 smoking table.	CD 11/18/93, p. 123
	Mineau	Got ice; saw Jones in pulp lab; she said she had heard (about) tape.	11/30/92 stmt
7:32	Kutska	Sent Hirn to say something to Monfils.	CD 11/18/93, p. 107
	Delvoe	Saw Monfils take off roll; Hirn borrowed a cigarette.	Doe, pp. 407, 408
	Hirn	Borrowed cigarette from Delvoe.	Doe, p. 401
	Hirn	Spoke to Monfils as he walked to 9 smoking table.	Doe, p. 401; CD 11/18/93
	Hirn	Returned to 9 smoking table; smoked cigarette and left pack for Delvoe.	Doe, pp. 407, 408
7:33	Kutska	Saw Monfils weighing rolls; saw Delvoe put new cores on shaft.	CD 11/18/93, p. 107
	Mineau	Returned to coop 9; Monfils was working on 7:34 TO; saw Hirn talk to Monfils; new cores were on the shaft; saw Kutska at 9 smoking table (about 7:40).	11/30/92 stmt
	Kutska	Returned to coop 9.	CD 11/18/93, p. 107
7:34	Log	Monfils marked rolls at 7:34 TO.	Log

	Servais	From 7 smoking table, saw Monfils mark roll.	Doe, p. 560
7:35	Basten	At 9 smoking table with Kutska and Johnson; saw Monfils (his hat and hair) behind roll.	12/04/92 stmt; trial, day 5, p. 6
	Hirn	Saw Monfils helping Delvoe tape cores.	11/25/92 stmt
	Johnson	At smoking table with Kutska; saw top of Monfils's head (cap and hair).	Trial, day 25, pp. 94, 98
	Servais	Left 7 smoking table.	1/19/93 Pinto p. 21; 12/23/92 dtsht
7:36	Jones	Entered coop 7 and took data from computer.	Piaskowski; Doe, p. 322
7:37	Jones	Noted only Piaskowski was in coop 7, not Servais.	Piaskowski; Doe, p. 322
	Delvoe	At 9 smoking table after TO; Hirn gone; cigarettes still there.	01/20/93 Pinto
7:38	Johnson	Jones in coop 9 (3–4 minutes); heard tape.	Trial, day 25, p. 95
	Hirn	Did NOT see Jones at any time at coop 9.	01/14/93 dtsht
	Jones	Saw no rolls in aisle (said roll hauler probably took them).	01/06/93 dtsht
	Jones	Saw Monfils sitting on "stool" (probably weight-sheet table); walked to PM 9 control panel; no paper rolls in aisle; saw someone (probably Hirn) sitting at 9 smoking table.	Doe, pp. 326, 327

7:39	Jones	Saw Daniels (and possibly Boulanger, Mineau) in coop 9.	01/11/93 dtsht
7:40	Daniels	Saw Johnson, Basten, Jones, and then Moore in coop 9.	12/07/94 stmt
	Jones	Saw Johnson, Basten, Kutska and three others in coop 9.	01/06/93 dtsht
	Wiener	Filled beater 3.	Trial, day 12, p. 96
7:41	Jones	Noted she was running late.	01/06/93 stmt
	Jones	Saw activity (Monfils cleaning) from inside coop 9.	Doe, p. 335
	Jones	Saw men working around the TO area.	Doe, p. 347
	Kutska	Saw Monfils standing by core cart; no indication of a TO or paper break.	Trial, day 19, p. 54
	Piaskowski	± Heard air-lock door open.	Piaskowski
7:42	Basten	(7:42 to 7:51) Saw Daniels and Jones; saw Jones leave and Moore arrive a minute later.	12/01/92 dtsht 12/02/92 dtsht
7:43	Jones	Returned to lab; saw nobody at bubbler or smoking tables; saw Piaskowski in coop 7; neither Hirn nor Monfils in aisle.	Doe, p. 338
	Piaskowski	Saw Jones head back to pulp lab; went to coop 9.	Doe, pp. 191, 211
	Jones	Met Moore in aisle as she returned to lab (± 7:40).	Doe, pp. 343, 355
	Servais	Entered coop 7 (shortly before Hirn).	Doe, p. 559

	Johnson	Johnson, Basten, Kutska at smoking table (Jones had just left).	Trial, day 25, p. 96
	Servais	Hirn stopped in coop 7 and said he had talked to Monfils.	Doe, pp, 559, 565
	Piaskowski	Saw Moore enter coop 9; also saw Mineau.	Doe, p. 225
	Daniels	Entered coop 9.	Doe, pp. 191, 211
	Daniels	Saw Rey Moore in coop 9 after Jones left.	04/19/94 dtsht
	Daniels	Saw Mineau in coop 9.	11/29/92 dtsht
	Daniels	Entered coop 9.	Doe, pp. 220, 232; 11/25/92 stmt
7:44	Delvoe	(± 7 minutes) Saw Monfils going toward coop 7.	Doe, p. 412
	Moore	Entered coop 9.	Doe, pp. 191, 211, 220, 232; Hirn (11/25/92 stmt)
	Wiener	**Went through coop 9; saw Mineau there.	Doe, p. 630
7:45	Servais	Says Hirn left coop 7; stayed 2–3 minutes.	Doe, pp. 559, 565
	Wiener	**"First" saw Kutska that day at the 9 smoking table.	Doe, pp. 624, 629
	Wiener	** Stayed at the table with Kutska 20 minutes.	Doe, p. 632
7:46	Hirn	Walked behind Kutska and Moore to coop 7 and returned to his work area in shipping.	FBI 12/28/94

	Piaskowski	Walked back to PM 7; saw Hirn standing near the 9 smoking table.	Doe, pp. 225, 557
	Hirn	Returned to the job site; shook Mineau's hand at the dry end of PM 9.	12/11/92 stmt
	Mineau	Does not remember seeing Moore in coop 9 before 9 a.m.	08/17/93 dtsht; 11/30/92 stmt
	Mineau	Saw Hirn heading back to shipping.	12/01/94 dtsht
7:47	Winkler	**Monfils was seen alive at bubbler; Boulanger exhorted Mineau to do 7:47 TO.	Kellner-Winkler "myth"
7:48	Kutska	Entered coop 7 with Moore (7:45–7:50).	CD 11/03/93, p. 136
	Mineau	At dry end of PM 9 (7:47 TO).	11/30/92 stmt
	Mineau	Executed TO.	Interview
7:49	Kutska	Walked to PM 7 with Moore.	Doe, p. 225
	Servais	Moore and Kutska entered coop 7 (2–4 minutes after Hirn left).	CD 11/21/92, p. 51
7:50	Servais	Piaskowski entered coop 7 (4–5 minutes after Hirn left).	CD 11/21/92, p. 52
	Servais	(±) Piaskowski returned to coop 7; asked if Servais had seen Monfils; Kutska described Monfils to Moore.	Doe, pp. 574, 557, 578
	Piaskowski	Walked to wet end of PM 7 looking for Monfils.	Doe, pp. 228, 248

7:51	Piaskowski	Walked around PM 7; talked to Delvoe.	Doe, p. 416
7:54	Basten	(±) Went for walk to get ice for his sore arm; saw Moore and Piaskowski in coop 7; no Monfils	12/01/92 dtsht
	Basten	Saw tow motor waiting at PM 7 to pick up rolls from next TO.	12/04/92 stmt
7:55	Basten	Saw Piaskowski and Moore in coop 7; made "short-hand pay" comment; heard "wrong blue hat" comment.	12/08/92 dtsht
	Basten	Passed coop 7; commented about short-hand pay.	Doe, p. 255
	Mineau	Returned to coop 9 from TO (first one back).	11/30/92 stmt
	DVL	(±) Along with Ferraro, bumped into Basten at stock-prep panel.	03/19/93 dtsht
	Piaskowski	Called, paged Ferraro; Moore and Kutska in coop 7.	Doe, pp. 250, 255
7:56	Basten	(±) Walked to stock-prep panel; Ferraro and DVL there; heard "wrong blue hat" comment; saw Lepak at bulletin board.	12/01/92 dtsht; 12/01/92 stmt
	Basten	At stock-prep panel; heard "milking the system" comment.	DVL 03/19/93 stmt
	Servais	Did TO in place of Monfils (logged as 7:58).	Doe, p. 251

7:58	Moore	Headed back to work; stopped at pulp lab; had not seen Monfils.	Doe, p. 345
8:00 a.m.	Basten	Said Ron Klumb had seen "Tom" on third floor.	12/02/92 dtsht
	Hirn	Took break with Dave Rienow; they played cribbage.	01/04/93 dtsht
	Jones	Moore stopped at pulp lab; said Monfils is missing.	Doe, p. 344
	Johnson	Replaced basis-weight valve cover (downstairs); decided to leave coop 9 and do the "chart run."	Trial, day 25, pp. 96, 100
8:01	Basten	Returned past coop 7; saw crew working; did not see Moore or Kutska.	12/01/92 dtsht
8:03	Kutska	Called his son Clayton from coop 7 (no answer).	Doe, p. 258; phone log
	Mineau	Kutska came into coop 9; he said Monfils was missing.	11/30/92 stmt
8:04	Basten	Smoked his pipe; talked to Mineau (5 minutes).	Trial, day 25 p. 99; day 23, p. 100
	Delvoe	Finished TO; saw Moore in aisle at south end of PM 7.	Doe, p. 419
	Kutska	Left coop 7; went to coop 9; said Monfils was missing; returned to the 9 smoking table.	CD 11/18/93, p. 57
	Wiener	**Kutska got tape and tape player from tool locker.	Doe, p. 632
	Wiener	**Went with Kutska to small coop 9 to hear tape.	Doe, p. 634

8:06	Wiener	**Was alone with Kutska for another 10 minutes (until 8:25).	Doe, pp. 636, 637
	Basten	(±) Left PM 9 with Johnson; went back to the instrumentation shop.	12/04/92 stmt
8:09	DVL	(±) Heard Piaskowski's call to Ferraro on pager.	03/19/93 dtsht
	Basten	(±) Left PM 9 with Johnson; went back to the shop.	12/04/92 stmt
8:10	DVL	Piaskowski said, "Monfils took off or whatever. Get somebody over here or find Tom."	CD 06/13/94, p. 24
	Wiener	**Lit another cigarette at the 9 smoking table.	Doe, p. 639
	DVL	Ferraro showed up at coop 7 with DVL	CD 11/18/93, ~ p. 56
8:12	DVL	In coop 7; noted time; Piaskowski said Monfils was missing.	11/25/92 stmt
8:15	Lepak	(± 15 minutes) In lobby with Wolford; heard Monfils was missing; went to coop 9.	Doe, p. 472
	Wiener	**Walked back to the 9 smoking table with Kutska.	Doe, p. 637
	Wiener	**Saw no one else during this 30–40 minute period.	Doe, pp. 638, 648
	Ferraro	Went to the 9 smoking table; Kutska there alone.	CD 11/18/93, p. 56; 11/25/92 stmt
8:16	Kutska	Back at coop 9; put tape in soundproof small coop 9.	CD 11/18/93, pp. 58, 59

8:20	DVL	Looked at tissue chest; said, "A lot of areas to hide … there."	11/25/92 stmt; 03/19/93 dtsht
8:22	Bowers	(± 8 a.m.) DVL said Monfils was on the tape and that he was missing.	11/30/92 stmt
	DVL	Went to Wiener and Bowers's break table.	11/25/92 stmt; 03/19/93 dtsht
	Bowers	Wiener got tape from Kutska; Wiener "gone 10 minutes."	CD 06/13/94, p. 33
8:23	DVL	Wiener got tape from Kutska; Wiener "gone 1.5–2 minutes"	03/19/93 dtsht
	Bowers	He and DVL heard Wiener play tape.	11/30/92 stmt
8:25	DVL	Wiener played tape for DVL and Bowers.	03/19/93 dtsht
	Wiener	Played tape for Bowers and DVL.	Doe, p. 642
	Wiener	**To this point, no one had said that Monfils was missing.	Doe, p. 640
	Wiener	**Left the 9 smoking table with tape and tape player.	Doe, pp. 641, 647
	Bowers	Wiener got tape from Kutska.	11/30/92 stmt
8:30	Bowers	Wiener took tape to coop 1.	11/30/92 stmt
	Kutska	Wiener got tape from Kutska.	Trial, day 19, p. 109
	Wiener	Took tape to coop 1.	Doe, p. 643
	Servais	TO (logged as 8:32).	Computer

	Wiener	Played tape for Richie De France and Andy Lison.	Doe, p. 644
8:35	Bowers	Wiener returned from coop 1.	11/30/92 stmt
8:45	Lepak	(± 15 minutes) In coop 9 for 5–10 minutes; said Monfils probably went home for a gun.	CD 11/18/93, p. 68
	Lepak	(± 15 minutes) Wiener brought tape to coop 8; Wolford heard it.	Doe, p. 472
	Lepak	Kutska not upset; thought it was a big joke.	Doe, p. 474
	Wiener	**Claimed he got tape from Kutska.	4/24/95 prelim. hearing, ~ p. 429
	Lepak	Kutska left tape in coop 8.	Doe, p. 477
8:46	De France	Heard Wiener play tape in coop 1 (about 9:00).	11/29/92 dtsht
8:48	Bowers	Wiener returned tape to Kutska.	11/30/92 stmt
8:50	Wiener	Left coop 1; saw Kutska at dry end of PM 9; returned tape and player.	Doe, p. 645
8:51	Wiener	**Walked to Kutska's tool locker; Kutska put the tape in it (see 9:00 a.m.).	Doe, p. 646
8:53	Wiener	**Still heard nothing about Monfils being missing.	Doe, p. 646
	Wiener	Back at workstation.	Doe, p. 647
9:00 a.m.	Bowers	**Went to napkin-and-towel department (third floor). Gone 45 minutes!	Trial, day 14, p. 262
	Bowers	Got drink at bubbler.	CD 06/13/94, p. 79

	Kutska	Put tape into tool locker.	CD 11/18/93, pp. 64, 65
	Lepak	Brought tape back to Kutska at coop 9; Zdroik listened to it.	Doe, p. 477
	Mineau	Saw Moore and Kutska outside coop 9 (5 minutes).	11/30/92 stmt
	Kutska	Called his wife at Canterbury Farms.	Phone log
9:30	DVL	(± 15 minutes) Started to look for Monfils.	11/25/92 stmt
9:45	DVL	Sent Wolford and Lepak to look for Monfils.	11/25/92 stmt
10:00 a.m.	DVL	Checked tissue chest from "short fiber side."	03/19/93 dtsht
10:05	Wiener	**Brought tape back to Kutska.	Trial, day 12, p. 108
10:15	Wiener	**(±) First heard that Monfils was missing on DVL's pager.	Doe, p. 648
10:30	Wiener	Told Ferraro he would check river for possible suicide.	Doe, p. 649
1:00 p.m.	Wiener	(±) Went to shipping; asked Hirn what he saw. (Must have observed Hirn at 7:15–7:45.)	02/19/93 dtsht
6:45	Piaskowski	Punched out.	Time card
6:50	Piaskowski	Met with Charles, Kutska, Lepak and others in coop 8.	Doe, p. 278
7:00	Piaskowski	Left mill with Kutska and Lepak.	Piaskowski

*Two years later, on December 15, 1994, Delvoe indicated that these events occurred just before the 7:47 a.m. turnover on paper machine 9. However, he was also at the 9 smoking table at 7:18—just before the 7:20 turnover on the same machine. This observation is much more consistent with that turnover. He does not disagree.

**Statement is not consistent with other known facts.

Appendix III: The Witnesses

Abbreviations: estimated time (±); statement to James River corporate investigator Frank Pinto (Pinto); statement (stmt); detail sheet (dtsht); civil deposition (CD); paper machine (PM); turnover (TO); John Doe hearing (Doe); Dan VandenLangenberg (DVL).

WITNESS	TIME	EVENT	CITATION
Basten	6:40 a.m.	Notified of problem on PM 9.	12/04/92 stmt; 12/01/92 dtsht
	6:50	Looked for Johnson; sent him to PM 9.	12/01/92 dtsht
	7:00	Received call from Daniels; sent Johnson to coop 9.	12/04/92 stmt
	7:15	Summoned by Johnson to PM 9.	12/01/92 dtsht
	7:21	Arrived at PM 9; Mineau had been in basement.	12/01/92 dtsht
	7:21	Arrived at coop 9 with Johnson; Jones and Moore not there.	12/02/92 dtsht
	7:21	Arrived at coop 9; Kutska on the phone with Marlyn Charles and then with Ardie Kutska.	12/04/92 stmt; trial, day 15, p. 105
	7:35	At smoking table with Kutska and Johnson; saw Monfils's hat and hair behind the roll.	12/04/92 stmt; trial, day 15, p. 106
	7:42	(7:42 to 7:51) Saw Daniels and Jones; saw Jones leave and Moore arrive a minute later.	12/01/92 dtsht 12/02/92 dtsht
	7:54	(±) Went for a walk to get ice for his sore arm.	12/01/92 dtsht

		Saw tow motor waiting at PM 7 for next TO to pick up rolls.	12/04/92 stmt
	7:55	Saw Moore and Piaskowski in coop 7; no Monfils	12/01/92 dtsht
	7:55	Saw Piaskowski and Moore in coop 7; made "short-hand pay" comment; heard "wrong blue hat" comment.	12/08/92 dtsht
	7:55	Passed coop 7; commented about short-hand pay.	Doe, p. 255
	7:56	(±) Walked to the stock-prep panel; Ferraro and DVL were there; saw Lepak at bulletin board.	12/01/92 dtsht; 12/01/92 stmt
	7:56	At stock-prep panel; heard "milking the system" comment.	DVL 03/19/93 stmt
	8:00	Said Ron Klumb had seen Monfils on the third floor.	12/02/92 dtsht
	8:01	Returned past coop 7; crew was working; no Moore or Kutska.	12/01/92 dtsht
	8:04	Smoked pipe; talked to Mineau (5 minutes).	Trial, day 25, p. 99; day 23, p. 100
	8:09	(±) Left PM 9 with Johnson; went back to the shop.	12/04/92 stmt
Binns	5:22 a.m.	Punched out.	Time card
Boulanger	7:12 a.m.	(±) Signaled Kutska that Monfils was going back to coop 7.	Trial, day 6, p. 201

Bowers	6:15 a.m.	Said Wiener started working.	CD 06/13/94, p. 6
	6:30	Saw athletic, dark, black guy (six feet 190 pounds) with no facial hair.	Stmt to attorneys Apple and Pedretti
	7:30	Saw athletic, dark, black man (six feet, 190 pounds) with no facial hair. (Most likely was seen before 5:30.)	12/11/92 stmt; 11/30/92
	7:30	Went to napkin-and-towel-department (third floor)—gone 45 minutes!	05/27/94 stmt by attorney Pedretti; trial, day 14, p. 262
	8:22	(± 8 a.m.) DVL said Monfils was on the tape and that he was missing.	11/30/92 stmt
	8:22	Wiener got tape from Kutska; "gone 10 minutes!"	CD 6/13/94, p. 33
		He and DVL heard Wiener play tape.	11/30/92 stmt
	8:30	Wiener took tape to coop 1.	11/30/92 stmt
	8:45	Wiener returned from coop 1.	11/30/92 stmt
	8:50	Wiener returned tape to Kutska.	11/30/92 stmt
	9:00	** Went to napkin-and-towel department (third floor); gone 45 minutes!	Trial, day 14, p. 262
	9:00	Got drink at bubbler.	CD 06/13/94, p. 79
Charles	5:15 a.m.	(±15 minutes) Made copy of tape.	01/21/93 Pinto, pp. 25, 27

Computer	7:00 a.m.	TO on PM 7 (logged as 7:03).	Log
	7:29	TO on PM 7 (logged as 7:34).	Doe, p. 401
	6:49	Recorded activation of sheet scanner after a paper break (1.4 minute).	Printout
	7:18	Recorded activation of sheet scanner after a paper break (2.6 minutes).	Printout; Doe, p 549
Daniels	6:00 a.m.	Is pretty sure he heard tape in coop 9; Lepak was present.	Trial, day 6, p. 8
	7:27	Saw Hirn in coop 9.	12/07/94 stmt
		Saw Kutska, Lepak, and Piaskowski in coop 9.	04/19/94 dtsht
	7:40	Saw Johnson, Basten, and Jones in coop 9; then saw Moore after Jones left.	12/07/94 stmt
	7:43	Saw Moore in coop 9 after Jones left.	04/19/94 dtsht
De France	8:46 a.m.	Heard Wiener play tape in coop 1 (about 9:00 a.m.).	11/29/92 dtsht
Delvoe	6:31 a.m.	TO (logged as 6:32 by computer).	Doe, p. 379
	7:10	With Monfils, finished 7:03 TO.	Doe, p. 388
	7:11	Saw Monfils enter coop 7 after paper break and TO.	Piaskowski; Doe, p. 388
	7:19 *	At 9 smoking table; saw Monfils at production log table; saw someone (from corner of his eye) start TO; saw nobody at bubbler; went to east side of PM 7.	12/15/94 stmt*

	7:20	Heard tape; Kutska, Lepak, and two "instrument guys" in coop 9.	Doe, p. 419
	7:20	Noted Hirn's presence in earlier stmt but not at John Doe hearing.	Doe, pp. 431, 432
	7:29	Left coop 9 for TO on PM 7; Mineau in coop 9.	12/15/94 dtsht
	7:32	Monfils took off roll; Hirn borrowed cigarette.	Doe, pp. 407, 408
	7:37	At 9 smoking table after TO; Hirn gone; cigarettes still there.	01/20/93 Pinto
	7:42	(± 7 minutes) Saw Monfils going toward coop 7.	Doe, p. 412
	8:04	Finished TO; saw Moore in aisle at south end of PM 7.	Doe, p. 419
DVL	7:55 a.m.	(±) With Ferraro, bumped into Basten at stock-prep panel.	03/19/93 dtsht
	8:10	(±) Heard Piaskowski's call to Ferraro on pager.	03/19/93 dtsht
	8:10	Piaskowski said, "Monfils took off or whatever. Get somebody over here or find Tom."	CD 06/13/94, p. 24
	8:12	Ferraro showed up at coop 7 with DVL.	CD 11/18/93, p. 6
	8:15	In coop 7; noted time; Piaskowski said Monfils was missing.	11/25/92 stmt
	8:20	Looked at tissue chest; said "a lot of areas to hide … there."	11/25/92 stmt; 03/19/93 dtsht
	8:22	Went to Wiener and Bowers's break table.	11/25/92 stmt; 03/19/93 dtsht

	8:23	Wiener got tape from Kutska; "Gone 1.5-2 minutes!"	03/19/93 dtsht
	8:25	Wiener played tape for DVL and Bowers.	03/19/93 dtsht
	9:45	(± 15 minutes) Started to look for Monfils.	11/252/92 stmt
	10:00	Sent Wolford and Lepak to look for Monfils.	11/25/92 stmt
	10:00	Checked tissue chest from "short fiber side."	03/19/93 dtsht
Ferraro	8:16 a.m.	Went to 9 smoking table— Kutska is alone.	CD11/18/93, p. 56; 11/25/92 stmt
Graves	4:45 a.m.	Kutska arrived at work; relieved Jerry Puyleart; went to coop 8.	01/20/94 dtsht; 01/21/93 Pinto, p. 24
	5:00	Randy Koffler, S Gajeski, Jim Frisque and Marlyn Charles arrived.	01/20/94 dtsht
		Kutska in coop 9; played tape for Graves, DeBauche, and Olson.	01/20/94 dtsht
Hirn	7:15 a.m.	Left shipping.	12/17/92 stmt
	7:18	Saw activity at PM 7; assumed paper break.	12/17/92 stmt
		Actually saw large amount of paper dust in air.	Interview at Racine Correctional Inst.
		Saw Delvoe blowing dust from 7:03 paper break.	Common practice

	7:19	Entered coop 9 right after Tom-talk; Lepak left shortly thereafter.	12/17/92 stmt
	7:21	Heard Kutska call Marlyn Charles.	12/17/92 stmt
	7:24	Heard Kutska call his wife.	12/17/92 stmt
	7:31	Joined Kutska at 9 smoking table.	12/08/94 dtsht; 12/22/94 dtsht
	7:32	Borrowed cigarette from Pete Delvoe.	Doe, p. 401
		Spoke to Monfils as he walked back to 9 smoking table.	CD 11/18/93; Doe, p. 401
		Returned to smoking table; smoked cigarette; left pack for Delvoe.	Doe, pp. 407, 408
	7:35	Saw Monfils helping Delvoe tape cores.	11/25/92 stmt
	7:38	Did not see Connie Jones at any time in coop 9.	01/14/93 dtsht
	7:46	Walked behind Kutska and Moore to coop 7 and returned to his job site.	FBI 12/28/94
	7:46	Back to job site; shakes Mineau's hand at PM 9 dry end.	12/11/92 stmt
	8:00	Took break with Dave Rienow; they played cribbage.	01/04/93 dtsht
Johnson	7:00 a.m.	Was sent by Basten to coop 9 to check stock-flow problem.	Trial, day 25, p. 81
	7:06	Left coop 9 for basement; checked basis-weight valve and flow meter.	Trial, day 25, p. 82

	7:08	Returned to instrumentation shop to get Basten; went back to basement.	Trial, day 25, p. 87
	7:13	Saw Mineau at basis-weight valve with metal stock-sample cup.	Trial, day 25, p. 87
	7:16	Returned to coop 9 with Basten; no one there.	Trial, day 25, p. 88
	7:17	Kutska entered coop 9 with tape player.	Trial, day 25, p. 89
	7:35	At smoking table with Kutska; saw top of Monfils's head (cap and hair).	Trial, day 25, pp. 94, 98
	7:38	Jones in coop 9 (3–4 minutes); heard tape.	Trial, day 25, p. 95
	8:00	Replaced basis-weight valve cover (downstairs).	Trial, day 25, p. 96
	8:05	Decided to leave coop 9 and do the "chart run"	Trial, day 25, p. 100
Jones	7:20 a.m.	Left pulp lab; went to blend hopper (her rounds usually took about 20 minutes).	12/02/92 stmt
		Started rounds; told by Piaskowski about the tape (approximately 7:15).	Doe, p. 315
	7:22	Took stock samples (from 7, 9 blend hopper at PM 7 wet end).	Doe, pp. 201, 203
	7:25	Returned to lab to process stock samples.	Doe, p. 320
	7:36	Entered coop 7 and took data from computer.	Piaskowski; Doe, p.322

	7:37	Noted only Piaskowski was in coop 7, not Servais.	Piaskowski; Doe, p. 322
	7:38	Saw no rolls in aisle; said roll hauler probably took them.	01/06/93 dtsht
	7:38	Saw Monfils sitting on "stool" (probably weight-sheet table).	Doe, p. 326
	7:38	Walked to PM 9 control panel; no paper rolls in aisle; someone (probably Hirn) sitting at 9 smoking table.	Doe, p. 327
	7:39	Saw Daniels (and possibly Boulanger and Mineau) in coop 9.	01/11/93 dtsht
	7:40	Saw Johnson, Basten, Kutska, and three others in coop 9.	01/06/93 dtsht
	7:41	Noted she was running late.	01/06/93 stmt
	7:41	Saw activity (Monfils cleaning) from inside coop 9.	Doe, p. 335
	7:41	Saw men working around the TO area.	Doe, p. 347
	7:43	Returned to lab; saw nobody at bubbler or smoking tables; saw Piaskowski in coop 7; saw neither Hirn nor Monfils in aisle.	Doe, p. 338
	7:43	Met Moore in aisle as she returned to lab (± 7:40).	Doe, pp. 343, 355
	8:00	Moore stopped at pulp lab and said Monfils was missing.	Doe, p. 344
Kutska	6:35 a.m.	Told Dave Daniels to call instrumentation.	01/21/93 Pinto, p. 29
	7:00	Johnson came to coop 9; there was a "basis-weight problem."	01/21/93 Pinto, pp. 32, 29

7:00	Played tape for Wiener "probably before 7:05."	CD 11/03/92, p. 106; trial, day 19, p. 109
7:12	Entered coop 7.	Piaskowski; CD 11/03/93, p. 113
7:16	Left Tom-talk in coop 7.	Doe, p. 539
7:18	Saw Piaskowski and Lepak; entered coop 9.	CD 11/03/92, p. 120
7:21	Called Marlyn Charles (1.5 minute).	Phone log
7:24	Called his wife at home (24 seconds).	Phone log
7:26	Piaskowski made brief (1 minute) visit to coop 9.	CD 11/18/93, p. 99
7:27	Went to 9 smoking table with union manual.	01/21/93 Pinto, p. 55; CD 11/3/93, p. 127
7:31	Was joined by Hirn at 9 smoking table.	CD 11/18/93, p. 123
7:32	Sent Hirn to say something to Monfils.	CD 11/18/93, p. 107
7:33	Saw Monfils weighing rolls and saw Delvoe put new cores on shaft; returned to coop 9.	CD 11/18/93, p. 107
7:41	Saw Monfils standing by core cart; no indication of a TO or paper break.	Trial, day19, p. 54
7:48	Entered coop 7 with Moore (7:45–7:50).	CD 11/3/93, p. 136
7:49	Walked to PM 7 with Moore.	Doe, p. 225
8:03	Called his son Clayton from coop 7 (no answer).	Doe, p. 258; phone log

	8:04	Left coop 7; went to coop 9; said Monfils was missing.	CD 11/18/93, p. 57
	8:04	Returned to 9 smoking table.	CD 11/18/93, p. 57
	8:16	Back at coop 9; put tape into soundproof small coop 9.	CD 11/18/93, pp. 58, 59
	8:30	Gave Wiener the tape.	Trial, day 19, p. 109
	9:00	Put tape into tool locker.	CD 11/18/93, pp. 64, 65
	9:30	Called his wife at Canterbury Farms.	Phone log
Lepak	7:06 a.m.	Got call from Kutska to go to coop 9.	Doe, pp. 455–56
		Noted TO and paper break at PM 7; saw Piaskowski and Monfils.	Trial, day 10, p. 276
	7:09	Stayed in coop 9 (5–10 minutes).	Doe, pp. 459, 460
	7:09	**(±) Put Basten (likely Johnson) in coop 9 "before" Tom-talk.	Doe, p. 502; trial, day 1, p. 276
	7:12	Entered coop 7.	Piaskowski
	7:17	Left Tom-talk in coop 7; briefly stopped at coop 9; then went back to PM 8.	Doe, pp. 200, 456, 466
	8:15	(± 15 minutes) In lobby with Wolford, heard Monfils was missing; went to coop 9.	Doe, p. 472
	8:45	(± 15 minutes) in coop 9 for 5–10 minutes.	CD 11/18/93, p. 68
	8:45	Said Monfils probably went home to get a gun.	CD 11/18/93, p. 68

	8:45	(± 15 minutes) Wiener brought tape to coop 8; Wolford listened to it.	Doe, p. 472
	8:45	Kutska not upset; thought it was a big joke.	Doe, p. 474
	8:46	Kutska left tape in coop 8.	Doe, p. 477
	9:00	Took tape back to Kutska in coop 9; Tom Zdroik listened to it.	Doe, p. 477
Lison	6:30 a.m.	Told by Kutska at PM 1 about tape in coop 9.	12/05/92 stmt
	6:35	(± 5 minutes) Heard tape in coop 9; Servais was in coop 9.	12/05/92 stmt
	6:40	Left coop 9; saw Monfils and Delvoe do TO at PM 7.	12/05/92 stmt
	6:42	(± 3 minutes) Back to PM 1; told Andrews and Swiecichowski about the tape.	12/05/92 stmt
Log	7:34 a.m.	Monfils marked rolls at 7:34 TO.	Log
Miller, R.	7:01 a.m.	Paper break occurred between 6:49 and 7:15.	Intercepted documents
Mineau	6:45 a.m.	(±) Took sample to Connie Jones in pulp lab.	11/30/92 stmt
	6:52	Logged TO (6:52).	Computer
	7:00	Entered coop 9; Wiener and Kutska present; "Dick Marto discussion" took place.	11/30/92 stmt
	7:16	Met Johnson and Basten in basement at basis-weight valve.	12/01/94 dtsht
	7:20	Logged TO on PM 9.	Log
	7:28	In coop 9; Kutska was playing tape, and Hirn was listening.	11/30/92 stmt

	7:31	Got ice; saw Jones in pulp lab; Jones knew about the tape.	11/30/92 stmt
	7:33	Returned to coop 9; Monfils was working on 7:34 TO.	11/30/92 stmt
	7:33	Saw Hirn talk to Monfils; new cores were put on the shafts.	11/30/92 stmt
	7:33	Saw Kutska at 9 smoking table (about 7:40).	11/30/92 stmt
	7:46	Does not remember seeing Moore in coop 9 before 9 a.m.	08/17/93 dtsht; 11/30/92 stmt
		Saw Hirn heading back to shipping.	12/01/94 dtsht
	7:48	At dry end of PM 9 (7:47 TO).	11/30/92 stmt
		Executed TO.	Interview
	7:55	Returned to coop 9 from TO (first one back).	11/30/92 stmt
	8:03	Kutska came into coop 9; he said Monfils was missing.	11/30/92 stmt
	9:00	Saw Moore and Kutska outside coop 9 (5 minutes).	11/30/92 stmt
	7:34	Monfils marked rolls at 7:34 TO.	Log
Moore	7:44	Noted Mineau in coop 9.	11/29/92 dtsht
	7:44	Entered coop 9.	Doe, pp. 191, 211,220, 232; Hirn (11/25/92 stmt)
	8:00	Headed back to work; stopped at pulp lab; had not seen Monfils.	Doe, p. 345
Piaskowski	6:58 a.m.	TO indicator lights began their sequence.	Piaskowski

7:01	Paper break occurred at 7:03 TO.	Piaskowski
7:03	Crew got sheet back on reel.	Piaskowski
7:05	Returns to coop 7.	Doe, pp. 246, 247, 249
7:13	Tom-talk began.	Doe, p. 187
7:17	Left Tom-talk in coop 7.	Doe, p. 545
7:19	Starts rounds; saw Jones at PM 7, 9 blend hopper; mentioned tape.	Doe, p. 200
7:21	Talked to Jones at PM 9 blend hopper.	Doe, pp. 201, 203
7:27	Made 1-minute stop at coop 9.	Piaskowski
7:28	Went back to coop 7 from coop 9 (stayed 10–15 minutes).	Doe, p. 216
7:29	In coop 7; saw Monfils at control panel starting TO.	Doe, p. 214
7:41	(±) Heard air-lock door open.	Piaskowski
7:42	Saw Jones; went back to coop 9.	Doe, pp. 191, 211
7:43	Saw Moore enter coop 9; also saw Mineau in coop 9.	Doe, p. 225
7:46	Walked back to PM 7; saw Hirn standing near 9 smoking table.	Doe, pp. 225, 557
7:50	Walked to wet end of PM 7 looking for Monfils.	Doe, pp. 228, 248
7:51	Walked around PM 7; talked to Delvoe.	Doe, p. 416
7:55	Called Ferraro; Moore and Kutska in coop 7.	Doe, pp. 250, 255

	6:45 p.m.	Punched out.	Time card
	6:50	Met with Marlyn Charles, Kutska, Lepak, and others in coop 8.	Doe, p. 278
	7:00	Left mill with Kutska and Lepak.	Piaskowski
Servais	6:30 a.m.	Heard tape in coop 9.	1/19/93 Pinto, p. 6
	7:01	Paper break occurred at 7:03 TO.	12/03/92 dtsht
	7:03	Paper break occurred before he came back at 7:16, before Tom-talk.	Doe, pp. 549, 550
	7:03	Paper break occurred at 7:03 TO.	CD 11/21/93, p. 23
	7:03	Crew got sheet back on reel.	12/03/92 dtsht
	7:16	Scanner rail was reset from 7:03 TO and paper break.	Computer
	7:16	Tom-talk with Monfils occurred after the paper break.	CD 11/21/93, p. 143
	7:16	Entered coop 7 and witnessed Tom-talk; Kutska had left already.	Doe, p. 539
	7:18	Left Tom-talk in coop 7 with Lepak.	Doe, pp. 546, 547
	7:20	Continued rounds at PM 7 control panel.	Doe, p. 550
	7:25	"Estimated" that Piaskowski left coop 7 (actually close to 7:18).	Doe, p. 557
	7:28	Monfils had left coop 7; TO lights were on.	Doe, p. 555

	7:34	From 7 smoking table, saw Monfils mark rolls.	Doe, p. 560
	7:35	Left 7 smoking table.	1/19/93 Pinto, p. 21; 12/23/92 dtsht
	7:42	Entered coop 7 (shortly before Hirn).	Doe, p. 559
	7:42	Hirn stopped in coop 7, said he had talked to Monfils, and left after 2–3 minutes.	Doe, pp. 559, 565
	7:49	Moore and Kutska entered coop 7 (2–4 minutes after Hirn left).	CD 11/21/92, p. 51
	7:50	Piaskowski entered coop 7 (4–5 minutes after Hirn left).	CD 11/21/92, p. 52
	7:50	Piaskowski back to coop 7; looked for Monfils.	Doe, pp. 557, 578
	7:50	(±) Piaskowski back to coop 7; asked if Servais had seen Monfils.	Doe, p. 574
	7:50	(±) Kutska tried to describe Monfils to Moore.	Doe, p. 578
	7:56	TO (logged as 7:58).	Doe, p. 251
	8:30	TO (logged as 8:32).	Computer
Stein	7:30 a.m.	Wiener told Bowers to "get lost."	Bowers and Stein interviews
Webster	7:00 a.m.	Wiener said he heard tape before Monfils did.	Trial, day 13, p. 6
Wiener	5:08 a.m.	Punched in.	Time card
	5:55	Went to workstation; relieved partner.	Doe, p. 616

6:20	Saw Monfils walk by the cull cutter.	Doe, p. 621
7:30	Pumped out beater 3.	Trial, day12, p. 96
7:30	**First heard of the tape from DVL.	Doe, p. 626
7:30	Filled beater 3.	Trial, day12, p. 96
7:44	**Went through coop 9; saw Mineau there.	Doe, p. 630
7:45	**"First" saw Kutska at 9 smoking table.	Doe, pp. 624, 629
7:45	**Stayed at the table with Kutska for 20 minutes.	Doe, p. 632
8:05	**Kutska got tape and tape player from tool locker.	Doe, p. 632
8:06	**Went with Kutska to small coop 9 to hear tape.	Doe, p. 634
8:06	**Was alone with Kutska for another 10 minutes (until 8:25).	Doe, pp. 636, 637
8:15	**Lit another cigarette at 9 smoking table.	Doe, p. 639
8:15	**Walked back to 9 smoking table with Kutska.	Doe, p. 637
8:15	**Saw no one else during this 30–40-minute period.	Doe, pp. 638, 648
8:25	Played tape for Bowers and DVL.	Doe, p. 642
8:25	**To this point, no one had said that Monfils was missing.	Doe, p. 640
8:25	**Left 9 smoking table with tape and player.	Doe, pp. 641, 647

	8:30	Took tape to coop 1.	Doe, p. 643
	8:35	Played tape for Richie De France and Andy Lison.	Doe, p. 644
	8:45	**Claimed he got tape from Kutska.	04/24/95 prelim hearing, p. 429
	8:50	Left coop 1.	Doe, p. 645
	8:51	Saw Kutska at dry end of PM 9; returned tape and player.	Doe, p. 645
	8:53	Kutska put tape into his tool locker.	Doe, p. 646
	8:53	**Still heard nothing about Monfils being missing.	Doe, p. 646
	8:55	Went back to the beaters.	Doe, p. 647
	10:05	**Brought tape back to Kutska.	Trial, day 12, p. 108
	10:15	**(±) First heard on DVL's pager that Monfils was missing.	Doe, p. 648
	10:30	Told Ferraro he would check river; for possible suicide.	Doe, p. 648
	1:00 p.m.	(±) Went to shipping; asked Hirn what he saw. (Must have observed Hirn at 7:15–7:45.)	02/19/93 dtsht
Winkler	7:47 a.m.	**Monfils was alive at the bubbler. Boulanger exhorted Mineau to do 7:47 TO.	Kellner-Winkler "myth"

*Two years later, on December 15, 1994, Delvoe indicated that these events occurred just before the 7:47 a.m. turnover on paper machine 9. However, he was also at the 9 smoking table at 7:18—just before the 7:20 turnover on the same machine. This observation is much more consistent with that turnover. He does not disagree.

**Statement is not consistent with other known facts.

Appendix IV: The Important Dates

DATE	EVENT

1992

11-10	Tom Monfils calls the Green Bay Police Department and reports a pending theft by Keith Kutska of electrical cord.
11-11	Kutska is suspended for not opening his duffle bag at the guardhouse.
11-20	Kutska obtains audiotape of Monfils's phone call to the GBPD.
11-21	Kutska plays audiotape for Monfils. Mike Piaskowski and Randy Lepak are witnesses. Monfils disappears. The police are called.
11-22	Monfils's body is found in the tissue chest.
11-27	James River mill authorities suspend Kutska, Piaskowski, and Lepak.
12-10	A "suicide note" is found in a phone book in small coop 7.

1993

3-2	Piaskowski and Lepak return to work; Kutska is fired.
3-15	Two-day secret John Doe hearing is held. David Wiener gives a forty-minute false alibi.
5-15	Wiener gives police his repressed-memory "Rodell" story.
5-26	Susan Monfils files a civil suit against the GBPD suspects for the death of her husband.
5-27	Names and addresses of the civil-suit defendants are published in local and state newspapers.
7-28	Police initiate surveillance of their six suspects.
8-6	Kutska is cited for theft of the electrical cord.

8-29	*Inside Edition* airs a story on the case.
11-3	Depositions for the civil suit begin.
11-28	Wiener shoots and kills his brother Tim.
11-29	Wiener is released from the Brown County Jail on a signature bond.
12-9	Wiener is charged with reckless homicide.

1994

1-4	Randy Winkler becomes the lead (and only) detective on the case.
4-1	Winkler starts to take handwriting samples (seventeen months after discovering the "suicide note" in December 1992).
3-24	Wiener is convicted of reckless homicide for killing his brother.
5-12	Wiener is sentenced to ten years in prison.
7-4	Kutska and Brian Kellner have a twelve-hour beer-drinking session at the Fox Den bar.
11-29	Kellner is interrogated for eight hours over two days by Winkler.
11-30	Kellner signs a twelve-page statement written by Winkler.

1995

4-12	The six suspects are arrested. Another John Doe hearing takes place.
4-14	Piaskowski posts a $300,000 bail.
4-20	Dale Basten posts a $300,000 bail.
8-31	Frank Pinto angrily interrogates Don Boulanger.
9-26	Jon Mineau is fired by James River.
9-27	The trial begins.
10-9	Wiener testifies and incriminates Basten and Mike Johnson.

10-28	Guilty verdicts are returned for the six defendants.
12-15	Life sentences handed down for all six.

1996

5-29	Wiener's sentence cut to eight years, thus becoming eligible for immediate parole. Judge Naze cites his help in the Monfils case as a factor.

1997

6-18	Susan Monfils files a civil suit against the GBPD for releasing the audiotape.
6-27	Susan Monfils is awarded $2.1 million.
9-9	8:53 Wiener is paroled after serving three and a half years.

2001

1-9	Piaskowski is exonerated under a writ of habeas corpus granted by Federal District Judge Myron L. Gordon.
4-3	Piaskowski is released from prison.

Appendix V: Doctored Detail Sheets

Format 1

- This is the Green Bay Police Department's *official* detail sheet used by *all its detectives* in 1992, 1993, and part of 1994.
- "GBPD D–11 (90)" at the bottom identifies this particular form.
- "COMPLAINANT/VICTIM" at the top always appears on this form.
- *Randy Winkler stopped using this preprinted form* after he acquired his computer in April or May 1993.

GREEN BAY POLICE DEPARTMENT

DETAIL SHEET

DISPATCH #

FILE #   92-16653   DATE 03-07-93

COMPLAINANT/VICTIM   Thomas J. Monfils   TIME 1:00 p.m.

(if known)

On 02-28-93, at approximately 1:00 p.m. myself and Sgt. Brodhagen went to James River Paper Mill to correct some errors on a blue print drawing we have. I also collected an approximate 24"x60" sheet of Plexiglas that had been against the wall near the vat. The sheet was against the west wall and was in the same spot as it had been on the night the body had been found. Pictures taken on 11-22-92, show the same piece of Plexiglas in the same spot I removed it from.

On 02-25-92, I had been out to that area and we collected two steel bars that had been attached to steel poles that had also been against the west wall. Exhibit # RGW 1 was directly above where the sheet of Plexiglas was found. When I brought the sheet of Plexiglas into the station I checked it with a black light for body fluids. I located several spots and I drew a circle around them with a magic marker. I numbered the spots with a letter, A to L. Letter J was a red stain that was on the Plexiglas, and that appeared to match the red stain that was found on half of the safety glasses turned over to me on 12-01-92. These were found in the area of the vat after it was drained, and they were cleaning up the pulp. This peice of evidence had been marked 1 JY.

All these items were transported to The Wisconsin Crime Lab in Madison, by Sgt. Winkler and Sgt. Van Haute.

Page   1   of   1   page(s).   OFFICER' SIGNATURE

GBPD D-11 (90)   RANK

Format 2

- This is the *official* format for a GBPD detail sheet that supplanted format 1 in 1994. It was computer generated.
- "COMP/VICTIM" is always at the top of the form.
- Note that the lines of typed material are justified.
- *All other GBPD detectives* used it.
- Contrary to his testimony at trial, *Winkler never used this form.*

GREEN BAY POLICE DEPARTMENT
DETAIL SHEET

FILE # _____92-16653_____ DATE __04-08-94__

COMP/VICTIM _____THOMAS J. MONFILS_____ TIME __11:30 A.M.__

    The reporting officer approached Mr. MOORE's wife, and asked her what had happened. Ms. MOORE told the reporting officer that RAY MOORE had taken an overdose of Xanex. Then Ms. MOORE asked me who I was. When I identified myself and said that I was a partner of DET. SGT. R. WINKLER, Ms. MOORE became hostile towards me, and she wanted to know why I was up at the hospital. Ms. MOORE said that it was the Green Bay Police Department's fault that her husband had overdosed, because we had followed and harassed her husband about the MONFILS case, for the last year. Ms. MOORE stated that her husband hadn't done anything. She said that he had told us everything, but that we had our "theory" and we weren't about to change that theory now, because it would make us look bad. Ms. MOORE stated that everybody knows that the Green Bay Police Department can't solve murders. Ms. MOORE said that fact has been reported on national television. Then Ms. MOORE told me that she wanted me to leave the hospital. I told her that officers were dispatched, and I was going to stay and monitor the situation. Ms. MOORE then appealed to the Emergency Room Physician to have me ordered out of the Emergency Room. The Emergency Room Physician told Ms. MOORE that he saw Mr. MOORE try and strike her, when he was coming conscious, so he wanted the officers present. Ms. MOORE asked the Emergency Room Physician if she could at least close the door to the Examining Room that Mr. MOORE was in. The Emergency Room Physician told her that it would be alright.

    When Ms. MOORE was told that officers of the Green Bay Police Department would not be ordered to leave, Ms. MOORE said that she was going to report this to their lawyer, BILL APPEL. Ms. MOORE then left the area. Once Ms. MOORE left the area, the Emergency Room Physician told us that Mr. MOORE was restrained, it would be a while before he could be transported, and he had some patients

PAGE _2_ OF _3_ PAGE(S).

K. Brodhagen
KENNETH G. BRODHAGEN JR.
DET. SGT. - G.B.P.D.

Format 3
- This is an early attempt by Winkler to duplicate the official GBPD detail sheet.
- Only "VICTIM" is in the header.
- There is no signature line or signature.
- Winkler's name and rank are not aligned.
- The lines of typed material are not justified.
- No other detective used this form.

FILE # _____92-16653_____ DATE 05-28-93

VICTIM _____Thomas J. Monfils_____ TIME 3:50 P.M.

paper machine. Dale said he saw Rey Moore and Mike Piaskowski talking in the # 7 coop and he stopped in and said something about getting short hand pay because of Monfils being gone. Dale said after that he left the coop and walked over to the proportionate panel and saw Pat Farrow, and Dave VandenLagenburg. Dale said they made a few comments, and he remembered thinking to himself that Farrow didn't know Monfils was off the job yet. Dale said he saw Randy LePak by a bulletin board close to the # 1 Paper machine by the Paper Mill office, when he was talking with Farrow.

Dale said he walked back to the # 9 Coop and went in and sat down, and it was about 7:55 a.m.. Jon Mineau was also in the # 9 Coop, playing video games. Dale stated while he was in the # 9 Coop, he saw Rey Moore come in the back door, looked around and then left, and was only there for a few seconds. Dale stated when Rey came in, he looked as if he was looking for someone, and then left through the back door without saying a word. Dale stated Keith was not in the # 9 Coop at the time that Rey came in # 9 Coop and when he left the # 9 Coop a very short time later, Keith was not at the smoking table either, and he did not know where Keith was.

Page 4 of 7 Pages

Randy G. Winkler
Detective Sergeant

441

Format 4
- This is another of Winkler's attempts to duplicate the official GBPD version, circa mid-1993.
- Only "VICTIM" is in the header.
- There is no signature line or signature.
- The lines of typed material are not justified.
- No other detective used this form.

GREEN BAY POLICE DEPARTMENT
DETAIL SHEET

FILE #   92-16653   DATE   08-12-93

VICTIM   Thomas J. Monfils   TIME   9:00 P.M.

On 08-12-93, at approximately 8:30 p.m., Sgt. Brodhagen and made contact with <u>Jon R. Mineau</u> (06-26-56). We had requested Jon to tell us about the morning Tom Monfils was killed, asked him to take us on the walk that he took to get a cup of ice for his water.

Jon explained where he went and the things that he did and who he saw and where. Jon said when he walked to get the ice he saw that Tom was weighing the paper rolls. Jon said he walked through the 3-4 warehouse, and went to the ice machine in the main isle. Jon said when he came back he walked down the isle in front of the Pulp Lab, and saw that Connie Jones was in the Lab about? as he walked past. <u>Jon said Connie</u> had already heard the taped phone call of Tom Monfils.

Jon said he walked down the isle in front of # 7 and # 9 paper machine to get back to his working area, and saw Tom writing the information on the back side of the rolls of paper. Jon said he walked around the corner and filled his glass with water at the bubbler. Jon said after filling his cup with water he walked back toward the front of # 9 paper machine, and he saw

PAGE _1_ OF _3_ PAGES

Randy G. Winkler
Detective Sergeant

ORIGINAL

443

Format 5
- Winkler created this format in late 1993/early 1994. It is identical to the one used to produce a ten-page detail sheet smearing Dale Basten that was backdated to December 4, 1992.
- Only "VICTIM" is in the header.
- The lines of typed material are not justified.
- No other detective used this form.

GREEN BAY POLICE DEPARTMENT
DETAIL SHEET

FILE # _____ 92-16653 _____ DATE _11-02-93_

VICTIM _____ Thomas J. Monfils _____ TIME _2:30 P.M._

On 11-02-93, at approximately 2:00 P.M. I was handed a
yellowed lined piece of paper that had typing on it. It stated
that Avram Berk was representing Dale Basten and Dale was
requesting that we turn over copies of his statement to Dale's
Attorney. The paper was dropped off by a man and then the man
left. I did not see this man and do not know who it was.

I made a copy of the statement made by Dale and I put it in
an envelope and took it to James River. I went to Dale's work
area and gave told him I got a letter requesting it and didn't
know if it was legitimate request. Dale stated he didn't know
anything about it. I asked if his attorney wanted the statement
and Dale said he didn't know. I gave Dale the statement and told
him to call his attorney and let him know he had it. Dale stated
he was going to mail the statement to him, because every time he
calls his attorney it costs him money.

Dale went on to say that he was happy this thing is all over
and he thanked me for the times I had talked with him. Dale
stated it was a rough relationship, but glad it was over with the
civil trial starting he wouldn't have to do anything else. I
told Dale we were far from being done, and that he would still be
seeing us around. I told Dale that some day we would be
arresting him for the murder of Tom Monfils, and until then he
could see us around the mill.

I asked Dale about the tools he carried the day that Monfils
was killed and Dale said he carried them in the front of his
cart. Dale said he doesn't keep them there anymore, but that was
were they were. Dale asked me why I asked about the tools and I

PAGE 1 OF 2 PAGES

Randy G. Winkler
Randy G. Winkler
Det. Sgt. - G.B.P.D.

Format 6
- This shows *Winkler's* 1994 format which is identical to the one used to produce the detail sheet in which Rey Moore describes two phone calls that he did not hear. It was backdated to December 16, 1992.
- Only "VICTIM" is in the header.
- The lines of typed material are not justified.
- No other detective used this form.

GREEN BAY POLICE DEPARTMENT
DETAIL SHEET

FILE # _____92-16653_____ DATE _10-15-94_

VICTIM _____Thomas J. Monfils_____ TIME _5:15 P.M._

On 10-14-94, at approximately 9:55 a.m., I met with David L. Wiener (01-20-62) at the Oshkosh Correctional Facility. I met with David to get a sample of his hand writing to compare to the note in the phone book, Exhibit 1 VR.

I served Wiener with the Court Order and he said he didn't need that, he would have freely given a sample if requested.

I read Wiener his rights and he said he understood them and was willing to talk to me. Wiener said he knew about the note, but didn't see it or write it. Wiener said he remembered some guy saying he saw it and didn't do anything with it, and then another told another guy about it and that person told him to turn it over to the Police after talking to one of the guys that was involved.

I gave Wiener the **HANDWRITING EXEMPLAR** book and asked him to fill out the back of the front cover. After he was done with that I had him fill out the pages that were in the book as it was instructions told him. On the page where all the names are listed I asked him to print those names in all capital letters. On the last section of the book I asked Wiener to print the words "I DO NOT FEAR DEATH FOR IN DEATH WE SEEK LIFE ETERNAL".

When the book was completed I gave Wiener several sheets a sheet of paper and asked him to write with his left hand. I then asked him to use his right hand to write he printed the above with his left hand.

PAGE 1 OF 3 PAGE(S)

Randy G. Winkler
Det. Sgt. - G.B.P.D.

Format 7

- This shows another format *Winkler* created in 1994. It is identical to the one used to produce a doctored detail sheet used against Dale Basten that was backdated to December 2, 1992.
- The backdated and revised detail sheet had two more pages than the original.
- The original detail sheet was typed on the standard "GBPD D–11 (90)" form (format 1).
- "Complainant/Victim" is in the header; but only the initial C and V are capitalized, whereas *all* the letters in the names of the other categories are capitalized.
- The text lines of typed material are not justified.
- No other detective used this form.

GREEN BAY POLICE DEPARTMENT
DETAIL SHEET

FILE # _____92-16653_____ DATE _07-21-94_

Complainant/Victim _____Thomas J. Monfils_____ TIME _3:15 P.M._

On 07-21-94, at approximately 3:15 p.m. Dale M. Basten
(05-11-41), came into the station with Attorney Berg, for the
appointment to give a handwriting sample. I brought Dale up to
the conference room on the second floor, and the sample was taken
there. I used a form to tell Dale what to write and gave him
directions of where to write what I told him. See attached.

At one point when the sample was being taken, Dale got upset
and said he wasn't going to do this anymore. I told Dale that
there was a court order for him to give the sample. Dale pushed
the paper away from him, and set his pen down. After a few
seconds, Dale began to write again.

When the writing sample was completed, I took Dale to Photo-
Ident and rolled a set of his finger prints for comparison
purposes. Dale then left the station.

I marked the hand writing sample as **Exhibit 9 DMB** and the
comparison finger print cards as **Exhibit 10 DMB**, and placed them
into evidence.

PAGE _1_ OF _1_ PAGE(S)

Randy G. Winkler
Det. Sgt. - G.B.P.D.

Format 8
- This is *Winkler's* 1995 format.
- The date in the header does not match the date in the first line!
- "Complainant/Victim" is in the header, but it is in a smaller font.
- This change has caused the "Date" and "Time" lines to be misaligned.
- The lines of typed material are not justified.
- Other detail sheets with this 1995 format are dated December 1, 1992; January 19, 1993; January 28, 1993; and August 8, 1993.
- No other detective used this form.

GREEN BAY POLICE DEPARTMENT
DETAIL SHEET

FILE # _____ 92-16653 _____ DATE __04-19-94__

COMPLAINANT/VICTIM ___ Thomas J. Monfils ___ TIME __4:00 P.M.__

On 04-19-95, at approximately 4:00 p.m., David F. Daniels (06-20-41) came into the station for an interview about the homicide of Thomas Monfils. David wanted a copy of the statement he made because he was being deposed in civil court.

I gave Daniels a copy of his statement and he was talking about what happened the day Monfils was killed. Daniels stated that he should have seen it coming before it happened. Daniels stated he got to work around 6:05 a.m., and heard about the tape. Daniels said he should have told Monfils about it but didn't. Daniels stated he wished he had gone over to Monfils and tried to befriend him after the tape was played to him, but he didn't do that either.

I asked Daniels what he meant when he said he should have seen it coming, and he said he should have seen the murder coming. Daniels stated the way the guys were getting worked up about the tape and everyone coming around to hear the tape. Daniels stated the stage was set for something to happen.

I asked Daniels if he seen Monfils that morning and he said he did not. Daniels stated he was the fourth hand and they were having problems with the machine when he first got there and he was busy. Daniels said one of the first things he does in the morning is to go down and check the oliver and he did that, and after he came back he called Dale Basten to come up and fix the problem they were having with the paper machine. Daniels said that he didn't remember calling Basten but he was told by Mineau that he was the one that called Basten, and Basten sent Mike

PAGE _1_ OF _3_ PAGE(S)

Randy H. Winkler
Randy G. Winkler
Det. Sgt. - G.B.P.D.

451

Appendix VI: Floor Plan—Paper Machine Area

North

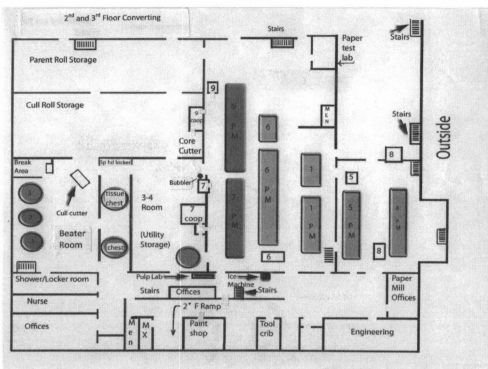

Appendix VII: List of Prominent People in the Case

Adelman, Lynn	U.S. District Court Judge
Basten, Dale	defendant
Bayorgeon, James	trial court judge
Berk, Avram	trial attorney for Dale Basten
Boucher, Jim	James River employee
Boulanger, Don	James River employee
Bowers, Charles	James River employee
Boyle, Gerald	trial attorney for Michael Hirn
Brodhagen, Ken	GBPD detective
Charles, Marlyn	James River employee and union president
Daniels, Dave	James River employee
Delvoe, Pete	James River employee
Easterbrook, Frank	U.S. Appellate Court Judge
Edmond-Berry, Gwen	juror
Evans, Terence	U.S Appellate Court Judge
Ferraro, Patrick	James River supervisor
Finne, Royce	trial attorney for Keith Kutska
Gilliam, James	jailhouse informant
Gordon, Myron	U.S. District Court Judge
Greenwood, Richard	Monfils civil-suit court judge
Griesbach, William	Brown County Assistant DA
Hamilton, Bruce	GBPD detective
Hechimovich, Sharon	juror
Heller, Joe	*Press-Gazette* political cartoonist
Hendricks, Tom	James River employee
Hirn, Michael	defendant
Hoffman, Kathy	juror
Johnson, Michael	defendant

Jones, Connie	James River employee
Kellner, Brian	James River employee
Kellner, Verna	Brian Kellner's wife
Kelly, T. Christopher	appellate attorney for Mike Piaskowski
Kutska, Ardis	Keith Kutska's wife
Kutska, Keith	defendant
Langen, Robert	Green Bay police chief (retiring)
Langenkamp, Don	*Press-Gazette* reporter
Lasee, Larry	Brown County Assistant DA
Lepak, Randy	James River employee
Lewis, James	Green Bay police chief (new)
Lewis, Jane	state Forensic Crime Lab examiner
Manion, Daniel	U.S. Appellate Court Judge
Mason, Mike	GBPD lieutenant
Melville, Jim	James River employee
Miller, Rob	computer consultant to James River
Mineau, Jon	James River employee
Monfils, Cal	Thomas Monfils's brother
Monfils, Joan and Ed	Thomas Monfils's mother and father
Monfils, Susan	Thomas Monfils's wife
Monfils, Thomas	victim
Moore, Reynold	defendant
Nusbaum, Bill	*Press-Gazette* publisher
Parent, Robert	trial attorney for Reynold Moore
Pedretti, Timothy	trial attorney for Mike Piaskowski
Piaskowski, Michael	defendant (exonerated January 2001)
Pinto, Frank	James River company investigator
Robinson, Nila	trial attorney for Dale Basten
Salnik, Charlotte	Fox Den bar owner
Salnik, Ron	Fox Den bar owner

Seidl, Jim	James River employee
Servais, Denise	GBPD detective
Servais, Dennis	James River employee
Sillix, Jackie	juror
Sims, Morris	juror
Srubas, Paul	*Press-Gazette* reporter
Stearn, Eric	trial attorney for Michael Johnson
Stein, Steve	James River employee
Stephens, Gregg	James River supervisor
Taylor, James	GBPD deputy chief
VandenLangenberg, Dan	James River employee
Van Haute, Al	GBPD detective
Verheyen, Ralph	James River employee
VerStrate, Dodie	confidential informant
VerStrate, Scott	confidential informant
Waggoner, Vance	trial attorney for Michael Johnson
Webster, David	James River employee
Wiener, David	James River employee
Wiener, Tim	David Wiener's deceased brother
Williams, Genie	Brown County coroner
Winkler, Randy	GBPD detective and lead investigator
Yusko, Jack	James River mill human resources director
Zakowski, John	Brown County district attorney

Acknowledgments

It would be impossible to list all the individuals who have made this book a reality. But let us start with all the former James River paper mill workers and their families. We asked for input from them and, nearly to a person, they came forward to help because they know that six innocent friends and coworkers went to prison: Steve Stein, Pete Delvoe, Don Boulanger, Greg Stephens, Chuck Bowers, Tom Hendricks, Roger Kane, Al Kiley, Jim Boucher, Richie DeFrance, Connie Jones, Brian Kellner, Verna Hayden, Mark and Todd Massey, Jim Melville, Randy Lepak, Scott Micolichek, Marlyn Charles, Jon Mineau, Dick Ozarowicz, Bruce and Julie Prue, and Carl Stencil. We also want to thank the families and many friends of the men: Francis and Pat Piaskowski, Emily and Amber Basten, Mike and Trudy Dalebroux, Garth and Georgi Hirn, Ardis Kutska, Clay Kutska, Joan Van Houten, Kim and Michael Johnson, Francine and Terry Enright, Chris and Mark Plopper, Jenny and Art Hruska, Marion, and Shelly and Helen Kraning, Ken and Lisa Piaskowski, Tracy and Lavara Pierner, Melissa and John Corlis, and Todd Charles. Thank you to the various defense attorneys and the other professionals and individuals who assisted us. They include Royce Finne, Robert Parent, Tim Pedretti, Avram Berk and Nila Robinson as well as Attorney Jim Sickle, Bill Craig, James LeQuia, Robin Williams, Paul Srubas, Cami Rapson, Marti Barribeau, Paul Harring, and Bob Platten, Sami Phillips. Thanks also to Ron and Charlotte Salnik. The list goes on. It was a pleasure getting to know you, getting your take on things, and benefiting from your insights and information.

A very special thank-you must go to Cal Monfils, who graciously agreed to meet with us on several occasions. Cal, it is hard to put into words our appreciation and our deep sympathy for what you and your family have been through. You are a fine representative of the Monfils family, and your open-mindedness and profound sense of fairness are to be commended. Thank you.

Also, thank you to Brian Kellner who, though reluctant at first, eventually became convinced that this book would also serve as his best way to set the record straight regarding his damaging testimony at trial.

A tip of the hat must also go to Brown County District Attorney John Zakowski and his staff, including office manager Susan Tilot. While we could not disagree more, John, we thank you for your time and for sharing with us your perspective. Also thank you to Assistant District Attorney Larry Lasee, who met with us early on. Like John, you could not be more wrong, but we respect your right to hold onto your error.

Also, thank you to retired Green Bay Police Chief Craig VanSchyndle.

Thank you to the many citizens of Green Bay and the surrounding area that encouraged us throughout this project with their openness and honesty. By sharing your serious doubts about the outcome of this case, you kept us going.

However, it's a "no thank-you" to the jurors who did not respond to our requests for information and to the officials who threw up roadblocks or sent us running around in search of information they could have easily provided themselves. The jurors showed us just why they got this case wrong. The authorities showed us that there is still an element of duplicity surrounding this case.

Finally, thank you Mike Piaskowski and the five men who remain incarcerated today—Dale Basten, Mike Hirn, Mike Johnson, Keith Kutska, and Rey Moore. You believed in us, and you trusted us with some of your darkest personal pain over being wrongfully imprisoned. We still wince when we consider your greatest fears—the impact of all of this on your loved ones. We will not let your faith in us end with the publication of a book. Getting each and all of you released is our fervent hope and goal, and this is merely one step in that direction.

We are sorry it has taken so long.

About the Authors

Denis Gullickson and John Gaie, with the collaboration of Mike Piaskowski, have combined their unique talents, abilities, and knowledge to create what unquestionably is the most definitive, accurate, and well-researched account of the astonishing miscarriage of justice that occurred in the Tom Monfils case.

Denis is the author of two books and many articles on the Green Bay Packers. With his wife, Kathy, and daughter, Rachel, he owns and operates Sugar Moon Farm, where they raise horses. Denis is also an educator. He teaches journalism and serves as the family coordinator at Oneida Nation High School. Denis is knowledgeable on the history of the Packers and of football in general, speaking to many groups on the subjects. He recently appeared in the Wisconsin Public Television special *Wisconsin Hometown Stories: Green Bay.*

John earned his M.S. in chemistry at the University of Notre Dame and went on to teach biochemistry, physics, and mathematics at Northeast Wisconsin Technical College for twenty-five years. Previously, he polished his writing skills teaching high school English.

Now retired after a forty-year career in education, he enjoys alpine skiing, golfing, and traveling. He has also been blessed with a cherished family of six children, three stepchildren, and eighteen grandchildren.

Mike Piaskowski was one of the six codefendants found guilty in the Monfils case. After nearly five and a half years in prison, he was exonerated of all guilt and released in April 2001 on a writ of habeas corpus. Mike has been an invaluable resource for this book as well as an experienced writer and researcher in his own right. Without his twenty years of expertise operating paper machines at the James River mill and

459

his eyewitness knowledge of the events surrounding the Monfils case, this book would not have been possible.

Denis, John, and Mike crossed paths many times, as can only happen in a small town like Green Bay. Denis was a student at Premontre High School in the late 1960s when John taught chemistry there. John married Mike's sister, Francine, in the mid-1970s. Around the same time, Denis worked at Sears with Mike's beloved father, Fran Piaskowski. In the mid-1990s, after retirement from NWTC, John was asked to teach chemistry at Oneida Nation High School and was reunited with Denis.

When John described Mike's arrest and conviction in the Monfils case, Denis adamantly asserted, "No son of Fran Piaskowski has ever killed anyone." John agreed wholeheartedly and stated, "Mike Pie is one of the finest men I've ever known. He would be the first to step in and stop a fight." Fascinated by these contradictions and by the facts of the case as related by John, Denis declared, "There's a book in this!"

Indeed there is.

Let Us Know What You Think—Get Involved

As authors, we invite your response to this proof of the innocence of the so-called "Monfils Six." The best way to get further information about the case, to register your thoughts on our work, or to offer assistance is to visit our Web site at www.monfilsconspiracy.org or www.sixinnocentmen.com.

We do not expect to convince everyone of the innocence of these men. There will remain those who support the official theory no matter what. However, here is an invitation to all open-minded individuals: Review the entire case as documented by the police paperwork and you, too, will conclude that there is no case. There never was.

Index

Manufactured By: RR Donnelley
                     Momence, IL USA
                     July, 2010